DOROTHY S. YOUNG

BONSAI

The Art and Technique

PRENTICE-HALL, INC.
Englewood Cliffs, New Jersey 07632

Library of Congress Cataloging in Publication Data

Young, Dorothy S.
Bonsai, the art and technique.

Includes bibliographies and index.
1. Bonsai. I. Title.
SB433.5.Y675 1985 635.9'772 84-3428
ISBN 0-13-079740-5

Printed in the United States of America

10 9 8 7 6 5 4 3 2

Editorial/production supervision and interior design: Paul Spencer
Cover design: Diane Saxe
Page layout: Meg Van Arsdale
Manufacturing buyer: John Hall

Cover photo: Full-moon maple, *Acer japonicum,* courtesy of *International BONSAI*. Photo by Dean N. Valavanis.

ISBN 0-13-079740-5 01

Prentice-Hall International, Inc., *London*
Prentice-Hall of Australia Pty. Limited, *Sydney*
Editora Prentice-Hall do Brasil, Ltda., *Rio de Janeiro*
Prentice-Hall Canada, Inc., *Toronto*
Prentice-Hall of India, Private Limited, *New Delhi*
Prentice-Hall of Japan, Inc., *Tokyo*
Prentice-Hall of Southeast Asia Pte. Ltd., *Singapore*
Whitehall Books Limited, *Wellington, New Zealand*

Contents

Preface

Bonsai is an ancient art. Along with other arts, bonsai has changed through the centuries and continues to change today. This book is an introduction to the old and the new in bonsai design, composition, and techniques. It describes Japanese, Chinese, and American methods, selection of plant material, tools, pruning and wiring, growing mediums, bonsai containers, potting techniques, and care and culture for indoor and outdoor bonsai.

Chapters 2 through 12 in Part One provide step-by-step instruction and practice in new and traditional techniques. The skills gained can be applied to bonsai in Chapters 13 through 18 and all of Part Two.

Part Two details bonsai forms and culture for nearly 200 species of trees, shrubs, and vines popular for bonsai in temperate and subtropical climates.

The book has been prepared for the novice with no previous bonsai experience. It is suitable for classroom use and for self-instruction. Because of its comprehensive approach, it is also a review and reference for the experienced grower.

Specialized terminology is kept to a minimum. A glossary of technical or unfamiliar words appears at the back of the book, as well as lists of species and styles of Japanese and Chinese bonsai and major organizations and their publications.

This book could not have been written were it not for my good fortune to have studied with knowledgeable bonsai teachers in America and the Orient and to have had many inquiring students whose questions aided my understanding of bonsai. Also, a large supportive group of colleagues and friends rendered assistance in ways that cannot readily be enumerated. To these and other individuals too numerous to mention, I wish to express my sincere and lasting appreciation. I am also most grateful to the following for special assistance:

My husband, Luther, who took and processed all the photographs not otherwise credited and provided constant help and encouragement.

My sons, especially Stephen, and Robert and his wife Wendy, for invaluable editorial assistance.

Wu Yee-sun, Hong Kong, for generously sharing his extensive knowledge of Chinese bonsai and rare photographs, including some from his book *Man Lung Artistic Pot Plants*.

Dr. William M. Klein, director of Morris Arboretum, University of Pennsylvania, for his interest and help, and staff members Ann F. Rhoads, Ph.D., plant pathologist, for valuable advice on the manuscript, and Paul W. Meyer, curator, for outstanding photographs.

Lynn Perry Alstadt, William N. Valavanis, David W. Fukomoto, the American Bonsai Society, and many other cooperative persons and bonsai societies that provided photographs or allowed their bonsai to be photographed.

Carol V. Lindemann for typing and editorial assistance in the preparation of the manuscript, the plant scientists who kindly answered my questions, and the reviewers who critically read the manuscript: Ann F. Rhoads, Morris Arboretum, University of Pennsylvania; William Smedley, President, American Bonsai Society; and Carl Solana Weeks.

Dudley R. Kay, agricultural editor, for continuing advice and guidance, and Paul Spencer, production editor, for transforming this bonsai material into its attractive, readable format.

Dorothy S. Young

Part One
Design and Techniques

I

Introduction

BONSAI DEFINED

Bonsai are living trees miniaturized in small containers and shaped into beautiful treelike forms. A bonsai can evoke the image of a stately pine, a lovely old maple, or an exotic banyan fig. It may be an ancient juniper with a twisted, weathered trunk, as shown in Fig. 1–1, or a stylized, imaginary tree, as seen in Fig. 1–2.

Bonsai are called living sculpture because they have three dimensions—height, width, and depth. However, unlike traditional sculpture, bonsai have an added dimension: life. They are alive, growing and changing with the seasons and through the years. Although a bonsai may attain a great age, it has mortality; sooner or later, its life will end. When the famous "Fudo," an unusually old and beautiful juniper bonsai from Japan at the Brooklyn Botanic Garden, reached the end of its life span and died, its trunk and branch structure were retained and are now displayed in a glass case where all may see a vestige of its former beauty.

As with sculpture, bonsai may be both a process and an object. The bonsai process involves horticultural and aesthetic techniques; as an object, the bonsai is a miniaturized tree in a small container. The process is the dwarfing (or making) of the bonsai, and the object is the present and ever-changing bonsai.

Bonsai is a Japanese word derived from the Chinese word *punsai* about one hundred years ago and is translated "shallow pot and tree." *Bonsai* is used as a noun in both the singular and plural; it never takes an *-s* in the plural. In speech, both syllables are spoken with equal emphasis. The first syllable, *bon*,

Figure 1-1 A Japanese bonsai, Sargent juniper (shimpaku), *Juniperus chinensis* var. *Sargentii,* in the National Collection at the U.S. National Arboretum. Photo courtesy of USDA.

Figure 1-2 A Chinese bonsai by Wu Yee-sun depicting the author of a famous novel, *The Dream of the Red Chamber,* beneath an orange jasmine, *Murraya paniculata.* Courtesy of Wu Yee-sun.

is pronounced with a long ō sound as in *bone* or with a short ŏ sound as in *bonfire*. The second syllable, *sai*, is pronounced ''sigh.''

The Appeal of Bonsai

The main appeal of bonsai stems from their miniature size, beauty, and tree identity, the creativity involved, and their close affinity with nature.

Miniaturization. Since time immemorial, civilizations and cultures have been fascinated by miniatures. Model making, for instance, is one of the oldest crafts, practiced from ancient times to the present. Among the artifacts of early civilizations are small clay models of people, animals, and everyday objects. Interest in miniatures is seen throughout history in exquisite jade or ivory carvings, tiny silver or gold statues, and children's toys and dollhouses. Twentieth-century miniatures appear in scale models of trains and spaceships. Plant specialists have responded to the lure of miniaturization and sought out or developed miniature roses, daffodils, irises, lilacs, conifers, and many other plants. One of the great attractions of bonsai is its minute size, a living tree only a fraction of a tree's usual dimensions.

The Decorative and the Unusual. As an art form, bonsai are admired for their beauty. A live, miniaturized tree is a prized ornament in the home or garden. To many people in Western countries, the Oriental origins of bonsai add an uncommon exotic connotation.

The Appeal of the Tree. People the world over share a special feeling for trees, perhaps because the two have existed together since the dawn of civilization. A bonsai grower is able to experience the wonder of a living tree in the palm of the hand.

Creativity. The joy of creating a work of art draws many people to bonsai. The development of a beautiful bonsai may extend over a long period of time. The process is heightened by the unique character of the art material—a living tree.

Peace of Mind. Bonsai may become an inner experience that brings peace of mind to the grower and viewer alike. This may be brought about by an awareness of the continual, and at times nearly imperceptible, growth of the bonsai, the result of a force within the tree that extends beyond the training and care provided by the bonsai grower. Bonsai is a partnership with nature.

Bonsai Techniques

Bonsai are made with the use of several age-old horticultural techniques that change the shape and size of a plant.

The Container. Bonsai are dwarfed by limiting their nutrients and growing space to a small container. The preferred container is a shallow, high-fired ceramic pot; but stone, metal, or plastic containers are equally serviceable. Every bonsai container has holes in the bottom or other provisions for water drainage. Containers for bonsai are far smaller than the tubs and deep pots used to plant trees and shrubs for conservatories, terraces, or wide walkways and streets. The restricted area for root growth in a small container is the chief means of keeping a bonsai small. Removed from its container and planted in the ground, a bonsai will revert to its normal size.

Pruning. Dwarfing is implemented by another age-old gardening practice, pruning, both light and severe. Light pruning of new growth each year keeps the bonsai small. Pruning the trunk and major branches produces the desired bonsai shape. Such pruning may be drastic when the shape of the plant material is changed extensively.

Mechanical Restraints. Bonsai are also shaped by old techniques such as tying a portion of a branch or trunk to a rigid pole. This Oriental practice is used today to support or reposition a bonsai or a tree growing in the ground. Hanging a weight on a branch to lower it is another old technique occasionally seen in bonsai. But today, wrapping wire around the trunk or a branch is the method commonly used to change the shape of a bonsai.

Bonsai Skills. Bonsai techniques are applicable to many private and commercial horticultural activities, particularly with container-grown plants and the artistic uses of plant material. Topiaries, for instance, are trees and shrubs shaped to resemble decorative objects such as geometric configurations, animals, and other figures. Their shape is controlled in much the same manner as bonsai by repeated pruning, shearing, and, at times, mechanical supports. Likewise, the growth of trees, shrubs, or vines trained as espaliers is directed by pruning and the use of mechanical restraints or fasteners to establish a linear pattern on a flat plane, such as a fence or wall.

Acquired bonsai skills are readily transferable to the pruning of trees and shrubs in gardens, parks, or orchards for whatever desired purpose. The knowledge of plants derived from bonsai is valuable in the selection of garden and landscape plant material. Working with bonsai also brings an increased awareness of form and texture in plants and a familiarity with Oriental design principles and motifs used in gardens and landscaping.

ORIGINS

China

Bonsai is a horticultural enhancement, not a necessity. It appeared in ancient times among civilizations that had acquired the wealth and skills to build cities and to produce architecture, art, and pleasure gardens such as the Han Dynasty more than two thousand years ago. Extensive imperial gardens built by the Han emperor, Wu, contained lakes and rocky islands with precipitous cliffs and high peaks duplicating the legendary Mystic Islands of the Immortals. The earliest bonsai may have been small replicas or tray plantings of beautiful garden scenes.

In his book *Man Lung Artistic Pot Plants*, Wu Yee-sun, the noted Chinese bonsai expert, scholar, and financier in Hong Kong, mentions a legendary East Han Dynasty magician, Fei Jiang-feng, who may have been among the first bonsai artists. Fei "had the power of shrinking and collecting in an urn, mountains and streams, birds and animals, people, pavilions, terraces and buildings, boats and carriages, trees and rivers."[1] A contemporary Chinese bonsai rock planting, reminiscent of Fei's sleight of hand, is seen in Fig. 1-3.

Historical evidence of Chinese bonsai more than a thousand years ago was discovered in the tomb of the Tang Dynasty prince Zhang Huai, who was buried in Shaanxi in A.D. 705. Murals portraying court life were found during excavations in 1971. Paintings depict two attendants, one holding in her hands a miniature rockery with dwarfed trees and the other a lotus-shaped pot containing a dwarfed tree with green leaves and red fruit. Throughout its history, Chinese

[1]Wu Yee-sun, *Man Lung Artistic Pot Plants,* 2nd enlarged ed. (Hong Kong: Wing Lung Bank Ltd. Art Publications, 1974), p. 62.

Figure 1-3 A Chinese rockery from the collection of Wu Yee-sun consisting of Ying Tak stone, Fukien tea, *Ehretia microphylla* and miniature buildings and boats. Courtesy of Wu Yee-sun.

bonsai has included both miniature tray plantings and specimen dwarfed trees.

Plants commonly used before 1300 included pine, cypress, plum, chrysanthemums, and bamboo. At that time, the plantings were more decorative than treelike. Bonsai with a treelike appearance became popular during the Ching Dynasty, which began about 1650. In China today, dwarfed trees are called *penjing*. This category is further divided into *she zhuang penjing*, referring to a dwarfed tree, and *shan shui penjing*, meaning a miniature landscape of trees or rocks. Contemporary forms of dwarfed trees and age-old rockeries are among the beautiful bonsai found in Hong Kong and the People's Republic of China.

Japan

While China influenced Japan's culture in numerous ways, it is not clear exactly when or how bonsai reached Japan. After the sixth century A.D., the Japanese adopted many attributes of civilization from China, including its written language, painting, architecture, and Buddhism. According to Wu, Japanese visitors to China may have observed bonsai during these early times, but bonsai did not become well known in Japan until the thirteenth century.

> As regards dwarf tree culture, its introduction to Japan was during the Yuan Dynasty (1280–1368) when Japanese ministers, merchants and students who had visited China brought back dwarfed tree culture to Japan . . . Toward the end of the Ming Dynasty, a government official called Chu Shun-sui, unwilling to serve under the Manchu rulers of the Ching Dynasty, fled to Japan, taking with him Chinese literature and culture as well as the art of pot plants. This marked the beginning of bonsai culture in Japan.[2]

After bonsai reached Japan, its Chinese characteristics were retained for many centuries as seen in Fig. 1–4.1. Rocks remained a vital element in the planting (Fig. 1–4.2), and specimen trees had a dramatic, exotic appearance (Fig. 1–4.3).

[2]Ibid., p. 64.

Figure 1-4.1 Rockery from *Senkeiban,* an illustrated guide for bonsai growers in Kyoto during the Edo period, compiled in 1822 by the son of a famous painter and bonsai artist to commemorate the work of his father, Buzen Sumiye. Courtesy of Kyuzo Murata.

Figure 1-4.2 A tall pine and rocks towering above a small building, illustrated in *Senkeiban.* Courtesy of Kyuzo Murata.

Figure 1-4.3 An old gnarled pine in a square container in *Senkeiban.* Courtesy of Kyuzo Murata.

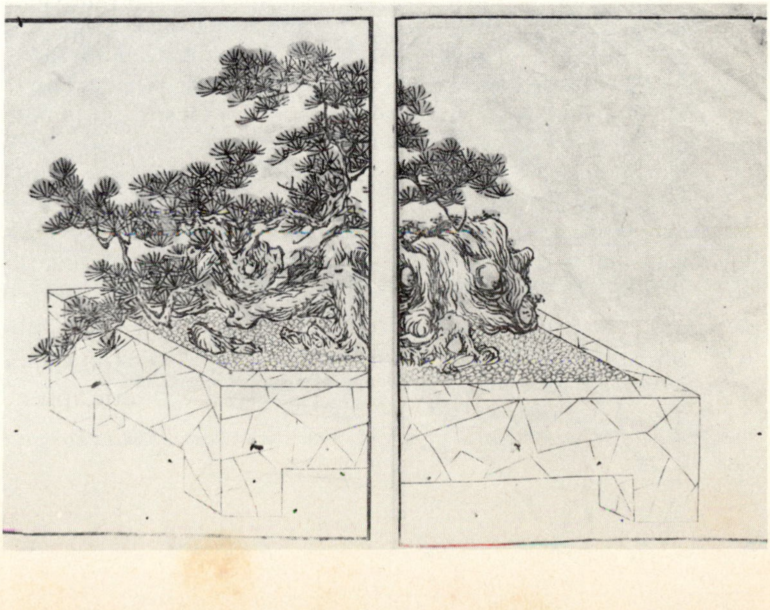

Gradually, bonsai in Japan became an expression of the national culture of its people and was developed to a high degree of perfection. Nonkey T. Ishiyama, a horticulturist trained in Japan, describes the influence of Chinese culture on Japanese gardens and how bonsai may have evolved in his native country.

> About 1400 years ago, when the Buddhist religion was imported from China, many civilizations were imported at the same time, and we learned many things from them. One of these was the drawing of pictures in the Sumi-e style, a style which is still seen in Japanese drawings. Such pictures showed rough, rocky places at the top of a mountain where there were few trees on steep rocky canyons. They were done with only one color, usually charcoal, Chinese ink or juice; the feeling was expressed only by dark or light.
>
> Copying these pictures and making them come to life was the secret of the Japanese garden. Rocks of suitable sizes and shapes were collected from mountains, fields and canyons. Suitable trees were also collected which had been growing between, under, or on top of rocks. These trees were carried great distances from the country to the city when transportation in Japan was very poor. Much time and muscle was needed to move them (human energy, not horse power, was used until the Meiji period); and because of the time involved, extra care had to be taken to insure the tree's survival after transplanting. For this reason they were often planted in wooden boxes at first, so they could have been the start of bonsai culture.
>
> The first Japanese bonsai were quite large, planted in wooden boxes and kept out-of-doors in the garden. A famous poem, *Hachi-no-Ki*, tells how a penniless ex-Samurai, named Sano-No-Genzaemon, enjoyed growing bonsai and how he burned them all one night in order to keep a guest warm. The container was made of wood, for how could a poor man afford a china pot of that size? Most of the people who grew bonsai in those days used wooden boxes for the same reason. The boxes were less expensive and could be made at home. . . . When bonsai was first started its shape was not controlled. However, year after year people admired the shapes of a few of the most attractive trees, so growers copied these few superior trees and changed the shape of their own trees. Little by little, the bonsai that we know today came into being. . . .
>
> Bonsai is not the original name of these trees. I am sure that after the Meiji period . . . the name bonsai began. Before that, what did we call these trees? The only name I have heard is *hachi-no-ki* which means tree in pot. *Hachi* (pot) *no* (of) *ki* (tree).[3]

The Meiji period (1867–1912) was a time of profound changes in Japanese language, industry, and government. Japanese bonsai-saikei master Toshio Kawamoto cites the year 1869 as the time when the Japanese word *bonsai* was formed.[4] The change in name marked a new appearance in the dwarfed trees of Japan. The former decorative trees in deep pots were replaced with trees of

[3]Nonkey T. Ishiyama, "Historical Notes on Japanese Bonsai," *Journal of the American Bonsai Society*, 5, no. 3 (Fall 1971), 43–45.

[4]Toshio Kawamoto and Joseph K. Kurihara, *Bonsai-Saikei* (Tokyo: Nippon Saikei Co., 1963), p. 23.

a more natural appearance in shallow containers. These plantings were the beginning of the distinctive dwarfed trees now known throughout the world as Japanese bonsai.

Japanese Styles. Japanese bonsai have been categorized into many styles reflecting tree shapes caused by varied environmental conditions. Japanese and Chinese styles are described in Appendix B. Further information on styles may be found in nearly every book on Japanese or Chinese bonsai; a selection is listed at the end of the chapter.

The Meaning of Japanese Bonsai. In Japan, bonsai may evoke a deep feeling far beyond the bonsai's beauty that is often difficult for Westerners to understand. The internationally famous Japanese bonsai master Kyuzo Murata provides a glimpse of the meaning of bonsai in Japan.

> The art of bonsai was developed in Japan when there were four seasons, clear water, and clean air all over the country, a 1500-year-old history, and many old but unchanging traditions or customs. Among all these things, the art of bonsai has grown to what it is today.
>
> We must not forget that the unique concept of what we call beauty in Japan is a little different from the western conception of beauty. . . .
>
> In Japan, we have the traditional *Noh* play or classic Japanese dance, which is the product of three-dimensional music and story. In your country, you have ballet. If ballet can be defined as a fusion or union of human sensibility and art, then bonsai can be defined as a union of nature and art. The *Noh* play or ballet expresses its movement in a relatively short period of time; nature expresses eternity in a very, very slow movement. The object of bonsai is to simulate nature, for you can hardly notice the slow growth of bonsai.
>
> When your concept of bonsai comes this far, you cannot avoid going into the world of *Wabi* or *Sabi*. It is an almost impossible task to try to establish the meaning of *Wabi* or *Sabi*, because they are concepts of feeling which were created and actually felt only by Japanese people over many, many generations and were unknown to Westerners until recently.
>
> *Wabi* is a state of mind, or a place, or an environment in the tea ceremony or in *Haiku*. It is a feeling of great simplicity, quiet and dignified. *Sabi* is a feeling of simplicity and quietness which comes from something old, used over and over again. . . .
>
> Picture yourself standing at a corner of Ryoanji's Stone Garden in Kyoto in the evening, in late autumn, in a misty rain. You are viewing the garden; the next moment you close your eyes and are deep in thought. Actually, there is nothing in your mind. It is empty, and yet your mind or heart is filled with certain contentment. That feeling is *Wabi*.
>
> I firmly believe that the final goal in creating bonsai is to create this feeling of *Wabi* or *Sabi*. This is the ultimate goal of the art of bonsai. . . . I cannot help thinking that the essence of philosophy is to seek truth, virtue, and beauty. And it so happens that this is the essense of bonsai.[5]

[5]Kyuzo Murata, "The Spirit of Bonsai," *Journal of the American Bonsai Society*, 9, no. 4 (Winter 1976), 82–83.

In summary, the recurring theme in Japanese bonsai is the beauty of a natural tree and an affinity with nature. As an art that idealizes trees and nature, Japanese bonsai may evoke transcendental feelings akin to those found in meditation or religion.

BONSAI TODAY

Introduction to America

The first Americans in large numbers to see and appreciate bonsai were the military and civilian personnel stationed in Japan following World War II. They returned home with reports, and sometimes examples, of beautiful dwarfed trees that delighted all who saw them. Because Japanese bonsai are unmistakably miniaturized trees, their beauty may be recognized and enjoyed immediately the world over. They speak for themselves without requiring the viewer to be skilled in the Japanese language or familiar with Japanese culture. Even a child can recognize a tree. Hence, the bonsai of Japan have a strong appeal and a universal identity.

Bonsai interest spread rapidly in the United States during the 1950s and 1960s. Americans learned bonsai from Japanese masters. During this same period, spanning a full generation, the United States and China did not have diplomatic relations or a free exchange of information. Thus, for several decades after bonsai was introduced in the United States, Japan was not only the prime source but the exclusive source of bonsai knowledge. As a result, American's introduction to bonsai came solely from Japan.

Bonsai moratorium in China. Following World War II, bonsai activity was practically nonexistent in China. The new government of the People's Republic of China embarked on an extensive program of reconstruction to restore the country after decades of war and foreign occupation. In the late 1970s, bonsai again was seen in China. Today, communes and work brigades in areas of Guangzhou (Canton), Hangzhou (Hangchow), and Shanghai are engaged in commercial bonsai production. Among other centers where bonsai are produced or displayed are the garden city of Suzhou (Soochow), which contains the Humble Administrator's Garden (Zhuozhengyuan) and the Linger Longer Garden (Liuyuan), and the botanical gardens of several major cities including Beijing (Peking). In addition, bonsai manuals and photographic albums of national bonsai exhibits are published.

Bonsai in Japan

Japan is the world leader in all aspects of bonsai production—bonsai trees, containers, tools, and publications. In Japan, bonsai is big business. Throughout the country, large and small farms grow and train seedlings and cuttings to various degrees of completion as marketable bonsai. Across the Inland Sea on the island of Shikoku, mile after mile of farms and nurseries specialize in pines for bonsai. There, thousands of bonsai and potential bonsai—from seedlings to large old specimen pines—are produced for Japanese and foreign markets.

Bonsai and bonsai materials are often marketed through regional auctions. Buyers from retail nurseries, department stores (many have a bonsai shop, sometimes located on the roof), souvenir shops, and other retail outlets are present along with commercial bonsai growers and sellers. The finest bonsai, however, are bought and sold through the Japan Bonsai Association, a professional organization of bonsai masters, nursery owners, and their apprentices. Each February the association stages, with the Japan Bonsai Society, the Kokufu Bonsai Show, the world's premier bonsai exhibit, in the Ueno Museum of Tokyo.

Bonsai masters in Japan are professionally trained horticulturists who, after years of apprenticeship, attain a high degree of skill and artistry in bonsai. They operate bonsai nurseries of excellent quality and provide all the plants, tools, containers, supplies, instructions, and services that their clients may require. Many of Japan's finest bonsai nurseries are concentrated in Bonsai Village, located in Omiya City, outside Tokyo. The Village, founded in 1925, is a "bonsai utopia" and the home of a number of Japan's most renowned bonsai masters and their retail bonsai nurseries.

Advanced horticultural techniques are employed in Japanese bonsai production. Japanese bonsai masters are able to rejuvenate trees consisting of only an old trunk and possibly one or two branches by grafting, or "implanting," new roots, shoots, and buds beneath and on the original trunk. In a relatively short time, perhaps less than ten years, the old trunk and newly grafted branches and shoots are shaped into a bonsai with beautiful foliage and an ancient appearance. However, only the core, consisting of the original trunk and possibly a few branches, is old. The top growth "implanted" on the core is new. Such skillful grafting techniques are not generally used for bonsai outside Japan.

Bonsai in Other Countries

In the United States and other Western countries, bonsai is on a smaller and less technically advanced scale. But despite its recent introduction, bonsai is well established in these countries.

In the United States, for example, a number of large wholesale nurseries grow and distribute bonsai and partially started bonsai plants. Japanese containers and tools are imported and distributed in large quantities. An increasing number of specialized retail bonsai nurseries (Fig. 1-5) offer bonsai as well as tools, containers, and plant material. Many general nurseries, garden centers, and mail order firms also sell bonsai and related materials. As with any art, when purchasing a valuable bonsai it is advisable to deal with a known, reliable source where the specimens may be viewed and inspected prior to sale. Individual and commercial interest in bonsai is also found in Canada, the Caribbean, Great Britain, Europe, Central and South America, Hawaii, South Africa, and Australia.

Figure 1-5 A portion of an American bonsai nursery. Courtesy of Rosade Bonsai Studio.

Bonsai Organizations

Bonsai organizations, from local clubs to international associations, exist throughout the world. Such clubs provide bonsai information, instruction, and opportunities for members to exchange ideas and meet fellow bonsai enthusiasts. Bonsai society publications contain news of activities and advertisements of bonsai sources. Membership is highly recommended. The names and addresses of major bonsai organizations are listed in Appendix A.

Where to See Bonsai

Bonsai displays and exhibits are among the best learning resources for beginner and experienced grower alike. An exhibit of living bonsai is like a laboratory, displaying the variety of species used, their many forms and shapes, and the diversity of containers. Seeing specimen bonsai in three dimensions is essential to understanding the art of bonsai.

Excellent bonsai may be seen at flower shows and exhibits of national, regional, and local bonsai societies. Horticultural organizations often stage bonsai shows or are sources of information on such shows in their area. Permanent bonsai collections located in various climatic regions of the United States are open to the public. Each one displays a sampling of species that may be grown for bonsai in its region. For those traveling a long distance to visit the collections, it is advisable to telephone or write beforehand to confirm the hours that the displays are open to the public.

Permanent Bonsai Collections

Arnold Arboretum of Harvard University
The Arborway
Jamaica Plain, Massachusetts 02130

This is the only extant collection outside of the Japanese Imperial Household that contains rare examples of bonsai of the Japanese pre-Meiji and the early Meiji periods. Nineteen specimens remain of the bonsai brought home from Japan by U.S. Ambassador Larz Anderson in 1913. The bonsai are displayed in a special lath house near the Dana Greenhouse and open to the public daily from May 1 to November 1.

Birmingham Botanical Gardens
2612 Lane Park Road
Birmingham, Alabama 35223

A permanent display of seventy-two bonsai and viewing stones is maintained jointly by the Birmingham Botanical Gardens and the Alabama Bonsai Society. The Bonsai Complex, located in the Japanese garden, is open every day of the year from sunrise to sunset.

Brooklyn Botanic Garden
1000 Washington Avenue
Brooklyn, New York 11225

This outstanding bonsai collection, the largest in the country, includes many specimen bonsai from Japan and warm-climate species suitable for indoor bonsai. A large selection of bonsai are rotated for viewing in a room of the main conservatory, which is open daily except Mondays from 10 A.M. to 4 P.M.

Huntington Botanical Gardens
1151 Oxford Road
San Marino, California 91108

Bonsai are displayed in a garden setting on the grounds of the botanical garden, open daily from 1 to 4:30 P.M. except Mondays and the month of October.

Longwood Gardens
Kennett Square, Pennsylvania 19348

Longwood Gardens, located 30 miles southwest of Philadelphia, displays Oriental and American bonsai in a special room of the conservatory, which is open daily from 10 A.M. to 5 P.M.

Morikami Park
4000 Morikami Park Road
Delray Beach, Florida 33446

A collection of subtropical and warm-climate bonsai, established by the Bonsai Societies of Florida, is part of Morikami Park and Museum of Japanese Culture, Palm Beach County Department of Parks and Recreation. The bonsai collection, displayed in a garden setting, is open daily except Mondays from 10 A.M. to 5 P.M.

Strybing Arboretum
Golden Gate Park
San Francisco, California 94122

Bonsai are on display near the administration building of the arboretum located in Golden Gate Park and open daily.

United States National Arboretum
24th and R Streets N.E.
Washington, D.C. 20002

This distinguished collection, a Bicentennial gift from the Japanese government and people, contains approximately fifty specimen Japanese bonsai and six viewing stones. The bonsai are displayed in a special setting near the administration building at the entrance of the arboretum. The exhibit is open daily from 10 A.M. to 2:30 P.M.

ADDITIONAL READING

BROOKLYN BOTANIC GARDEN STAFF, Kan Yashiroda, guest ed., *Handbook on Dwarfed Potted Trees, the Bonsai of Japan*, Plant and Garden Handbook 9, no. 3. Brooklyn, N.Y.: Brooklyn Botanic Garden, 1953. A compilation of bonsai articles by Japanese experts, this handbook, frequently reprinted, remains an excellent introduction to Japanese bonsai and bonsai techniques.

HU, YUNHUA, AND THE SHANGHAI BOTANIC GARDEN STAFF, *Penjing: The Chinese Art of Miniature Trees*. Beaverton, Ore.: Timber Press, 1982. The first book on Chinese bonsai in English from the People's Republic of China describes Chinese techniques for miniaturizing plants and contains detailed information on creating bonsai and rockeries of trees and rocks. Illustrated with color plates and black-and-white brush paintings.

ISHIMAYA, NONKEY T., "Historical Notes on Japanese Bonsai," *Journal of the American Bonsai Society*, 5, no. 3 (Fall 1971), 43–45. The author, born and educated in Japan, operated a landscape nursery near Washington, D.C. He was knowledgeable about bonsai and generously shared his expertise with others.

KAWAMOTO, TOSHIO, AND JOSEPH K. KURIHARA, *Bonsai-Saikei*. Tokyo: Nippon Saikei Co., 1963. A comprehensive book on bonsai and saikei techniques co-authored by Kawamoto, the innovator of saikei, miniature living landscapes of trees and rocks.

MURATA, KYUZO, *Bonsai: Miniature Potted Trees*. Tokyo: Shufunotomo Co., Ltd., 1964. The venerable dean of Japanese bonsai masters describes bonsai styles and his growing techniques. Reliable, readable, and informative.

NAKA, JOHN YOSHIO, *Bonsai Techniques*. Los Angeles: Bonsai Institute of California, 1973. Precise and detailed description of bonsai techniques and styles, with author illustrations. An advanced text on Japanese methods by a well-known Japanese-American bonsai master.

———, *Bonsai Techniques II*. Los Angeles: Bonsai Institute of California, 1982. This book, with photographs and many drawings by the author, is an expanded sequel to *Bonsai Techniques*.

PERRY, LYNN R., *Bonsai: Trees and Shrubs, A Guide to the Methods of Kyuzo Murata.* New York: The Roland Press Company, 1964, reprinted 1975. An excellent, firsthand report of the methods of the world-famous Kyuzo Murata. The author was his first American student and studied at his nursery in Bonsai Village for several years.

WU YEE-SUN, *Man Lung Artistic Pot Plants,* 2nd enlarged ed. Hong Kong: Wing Lung Bank Ltd. Art Publications, 1974. A comprehensive book on Chinese bonsai, profusely illustrated with color and black-and-white photographs from the outstanding bonsai collection of the author, a financier, scholar, and expert bonsai grower. Text in English and Chinese.

YOSHIMURA, YUJI, AND GIOVANNA M. HALFORD, *The Japanese Art of Miniature Trees and Landscapes: Their Creation, Care, and Enjoyment.* Rutland, Vt.: C. E. Tuttle, 1957. Reprinted in paperback. Yuji Yoshimura's teaching at the Brooklyn Botanic Garden in the 1950s and his subsequent residence in the United States as a Japanese bonsai master accelerated the development of bonsai in America. An outstanding book on Japanese techniques and styles.

2

Plant Material for Bonsai

Bonsai came as a shock to civilian and military personnel stationed in Japan following World War II. They were unprepared for the astonishing small size and incredible beauty of such trees. Many Americans and other Occidentals believed at that time that bonsai were made from special Japanese trees. This, of course, is not true. Bonsai may be grown throughout the world with ordinary trees native to a wide range of climates. It is not a tree's geographical origin but specific characteristics of its growth and appearance that make it suitable for bonsai.

CRITERIA FOR SPECIES USED AS BONSAI

Bonsai specifications may be divided into two categories. The first relates to the tree's ability to retain its distinctive treelike features, such as a bark-covered trunk and twiggy branching, when miniaturized, as shown in Fig. 2-1. The second category concerns the tree's growth habits and its tolerance to bonsai training methods. Each category is equally important. Theoretically, all trees can be made into bonsai. However, wide variation exists in their design potential and horticultural response. Growth characteristics wanted for bonsai are described here as a guide in assessing the bonsai potential of untried or native species and as an aid in the selection of suitable material.

Figure 2-1 A Japanese maple tree, *Acer palmatum,* as seen in winter; grown as bonsai in Japan. Photo courtesy of Lynn R. Perry.

Tolerance to Pruning

Every species undergoing bonsai training may be subjected initially to drastic pruning followed by repeated trimming of the new growth each year. A bonsai must be tolerant of pruning to survive. Species differ in this respect, especially under the stress of confinement to a container. For instance, after they are pruned, most species of maples, *Acer*, and junipers, *Juniperus*, easily produce new replacement growth. Trees that do not respond favorably to pruning require different handling. Species of beech, *Fagus*, for example, are weakened by frequent pruning. For most bonsai, however, pruning is not detrimental. Species popular for bonsai have proven their ability to withstand bonsai training methods, including pruning.

Adjustment of Roots to Container Growth

Bonsai are grown in small containers, but only species that are able to produce healthy growth in a highly restricted root space can survive. Trees that develop masses of fine roots in the ground adjust readily to container growth. Many species of holly, *Ilex*, boxwood, *Buxus*, and *Rhododendron* naturally form numerous thin surface roots at the base of their trunk. Roots of this type enable a plant to grow well in a small container. On the other hand, species with large tap roots must modify their root growth when moved to a small container. Frequently, in nature, when a tree's roots are trapped in a narrow stone crevice with little soil, large roots cease to expand, and a mass of small, new roots emerge to feed the tree. Likewise, most species used for bonsai are able to produce small roots when confined to a limited growing area.

Transplanting

Tolerance to transplanting, essential for bonsai, is closely related to the strength and vigor of the roots and their prompt resumption of growth after transplanting. This growth habit is not indicated by leaf size or other visible features.

Species frequently used for bonsai tolerate transplanting. When considering an untried species, try to obtain information beforehand concerning its response to transplanting. Knowledgeable sources include commercial landscape nurseries, arboretums, and horticultural institutions. Trees that are difficult to transplant in the ground and react unfavorably when their roots are disturbed generally show poor response to bonsai training.

Reducing the Rate of Growth

In a container, a tree grows at a far slower rate than in the ground. Slow growth generally produces the compact branching and foliage desired for bonsai. Most trees are able to modify their growth rate without adverse effects. However, a number of rapid growers appear unable to adjust their growth to the limitations of a small container. These trees send out strong new shoots at variance with the desired bonsai configuration. Unwanted shoots may be removed by pruning. If such shoots persist, however, the bonsai will become scarred by excessive pruning cuts or the tree will lose its vigor and decline.

Length of Internodes

A node is the location on a stem where a bud has formed, and an internode is the distance between two nodes, as shown in Fig. 2-2. All new shoots or leaves emerge from a bud (or node). Short internodes are favored for bonsai. Avoid plants with long internodes, characterized by open or rank growth.

The length of the internode reflects the tree's rate of growth. Fast-growing trees produce long internodes; short internodes are found on trees that grow more slowly. A tree will reduce the length of its internodes when its growth is

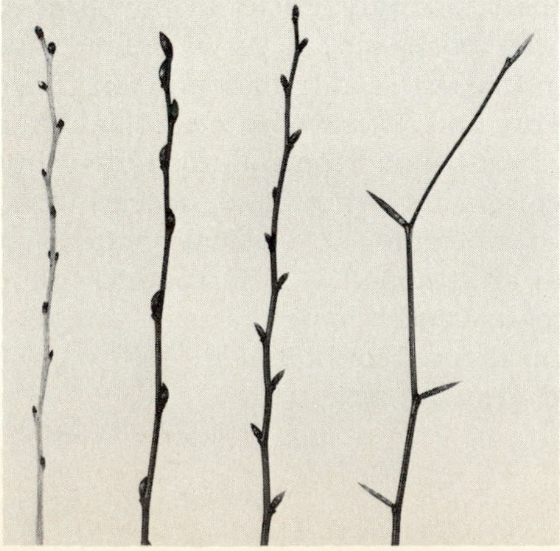

Figure 2-2 Variation in the length of internodes among species: left to right, a flowering cherry, two species of hornbeam, and an American beech.

slowed in a small container. The extent of the reduction, however, is limited. Hence, species with widely spaced nodes are difficult to transform into small, compact bonsai, while those with normally short internodes have a built-in advantage for bonsai.

Leaf Size

If leaf size is within reason, it is the last factor to consider in evaluating material for bonsai. Small leaves are desirable, and generally on bonsai they are no longer than about 4 inches. However, growth characteristics, such as the presence of many fibrous roots and the tree's adjustment to a small container, are far more important than the initial size of the leaves. The leaves will reduce in size as a result of bonsai techniques. Smaller leaves appear on a bonsai within a short time. The process is continuous and cumulative; the leaves become progressively smaller for many years.

Sometimes trees with unusually large leaves are used as bonsai, but they are selected for other reasons and are rarely displayed in full leaf. For instance, magnolias with large leaves are enjoyed as bonsai in the spring when their swollen flower buds with furlike covering are beginning to open before the leaves appear. Similarly, bonsai enthusiasts favor Japanese persimmons when they are heavy with fruit after their large leaves have dropped in the fall.

Bonsai growers who are willing to stretch their imagination may circumvent the taboo against large leaves by following the Japanese approach of letting each oversized leaf on the bonsai suggest a branch covered with foliage. This allows a place in the bonsai collection for an exceptional species that otherwise would be absent.

Flowers and fruit. Unlike leaves, which reduce in size easily, it is difficult to change the size of flowers and fruit. Species with both small flowers and fruit, such as crab apple trees (Fig. 2–3), are preferred. On bonsai with large flowers, such as tree peonies, or large-size fruit, such as oranges and apples, only a few flowers or fruit are retained to preserve the strength of the tree.

Figure 2-3 The small crab apples on this tree, *Malus* sp., are in scale with the size of the bonsai.

Types of Material

Bonsai growers select plant material from regular species of trees, which in the ground reach heights of 20 to 100 feet or more. Young specimens are horticulturally dwarfed and shaped to bonsai forms. Or, for a head start, many bonsai growers look for older trees, stunted by nature in the wild or by neglect and adverse growing conditions in yards and other areas, and reshape such trees to bonsai.

Trees and woody plants are superior to nonwoody (herbaceous) species for a number of compelling reasons. Among the most important is the tree's long life span. For purposes of bonsai, a tree's longevity is counted in decades and sometimes in centuries. Among the herbaceous species, annual plants and flowers live only one year; most perennials experience a relatively short life span. For this reason, experienced bonsai growers prefer trees known for their long life. While the bonsai expectations for short-lived trees, such as Siberian elm, *Ulmus pumila*, are limited, they, too, may be included in a bonsai collection or used as learning material.

Trees are excellent bonsai material for another reason: The material that constitutes a tree—essentially hard wood with a thin outer covering of living cells—is remarkably suited to bonsai training. The solid interior core, or xylem, which forms the heartwood of the trunk and branches, is no longer alive and is not harmed by the application of wire and other bonsai restraints applied to change its shape. Wire would quickly cut into and damage the trunk and branches of plants consisting of soft tissue.

A tree's growth pattern is adaptable to bonsai purposes. Each year a tree adds a new layer of cells that harden into wood under the covering of bark on the trunk, branches, twigs, and roots. By this process, all parts of a tree, from top to bottom, thicken year after year. Knowing this, the bonsai grower is able to develop a twig into a branch. A tree also grows in a linear way by sending out new shoots from the multitude of buds on the twigs and branches, thereby increasing its height and mass each year. For bonsai, these new shoots are selectively shortened to shape and dwarf the tree.

Dwarf Forms. At first glance, small dwarf forms of woody plants, especially dwarf conifers, appear to be ready-made material for bonsai. Their tiny needles and leaves are appealing. However, beneath the foliage often lies a jumble of crowded branches without a discernible trunk or a potential tree form. This is characteristic of most witches' brooms, which are crowded, small abnormal growths on the trunk or branches of larger trees, produced by genetic mutations or infection. In considering dwarf forms for bonsai, do not rely exclusively on the small size of the foliage. The major determinant is how well the interior structure can be shaped into a treelike form. In each instance a close examination is required.

Nonwoody Bonsai Material. At times, bonsai methods are applied to herbaceous and semiwoody plants. For instance, succulents and herbs may be shaped

Figure 2-4 Herbaceous plants on a stone, such as blue-eyed grass, *Sisyrinchium montanum,* left, and grassy-leaved sweet flag, *Acorus gramineus* cv. Pusillus, are often grown as accessory plantings with bonsai. Courtesy of David L. Andrews.

to suggest a little tree. Because the tissue of such plants is relatively soft, bonsai growers do not always apply wire but create a bonsai effect essentially by pruning and confinement to a small container. Grasses, rushes, sedges, wild flowers, dandelions, and other weeds are also dwarfed in this manner. When miniaturized, herbaceous plants retain their normal shapes and make interesting arrangements to be displayed with bonsai. An example is shown in Fig. 2-4.

Chrysanthemum Bonsai. Chrysanthemums are an exception to the nearly exclusive use of trees and woody plants for bonsai. Japan is famous for displays of beautiful chrysanthemum bonsai. These plants are difficult to grow as bonsai. Their training requires bonsai skill coupled with a knowledge of chrysanthemum culture and precise timing in pruning. The methods developed in Japan are detailed in *The Art of the Chrysanthemum* by T. Nakajima and H. C. Young (see ''Additional Reading''). Chrysanthemums are especially effective as bonsai in mild climates where the same plant may be used year after year. In climates where cold kills them, it is necessary to start over each year with a new cutting and train it into a bonsai for one growing season.

In summary, the horticultural criteria for bonsai training are interrelated, and together they determine a species' response to dwarfing techniques. It is not necessary that all favorable aspects be present in every species. Adjustments can be made. An experienced grower may circumvent a known handicap by modifying the training techniques. For the novice, best results are obtained by choosing plants that respond favorably to bonsai training.

Developing Desirable Species

In countries such as China and Japan with a long, continuous history of gardening, the most desirable plants for cultivation have become available by a process of selection. Over the centuries, unusually attractive specimens of trees and shrubs that respond favorably to pruning and transplanting are singled out for propagation and repeated use. During a long period of time, superior species are culled for cultivation. Many Oriental trees and shrubs used for bonsai are derived from this source.

In China and Japan, attractive plants found growing in the wild and in rough mountain terrain were brought back and introduced to cultivation. There is no record of the many wild "collected" trees, as they are called, that died as a result. One mountain species that survived to become magnificent bonsai material is the shimpaku juniper in Fig. 1-1. A similar selective process is now at work in other countries as bonsai enthusiasts join plant experts and botanists in the search for superior plants among native trees and shrubs.

Botanical Nomenclature

Botanical nomenclature is the universal language in horticulture. The following brief explanation of its use is essential reading for those who are not familiar with botanical plant names.

Botanical names are used to identify a plant precisely. With vernacular names, the same name may be used for different plants. For instance, *haw* may refer to a hawthorn or a holly. Possum haw is a holly *(Ilex)*, and Pensacola haw is a hawthorn *(Crataegus)*. In various regions of America, the same tree may be called a sycamore, a buttonball, a plane tree, or a buttonwood. To compound confusion, buttonwood is also the name commonly used for *Conocarpus erectus*, an outstanding bonsai from the Florida Keys. In botanical nomenclature, there is no such duplication of names. *Acer palmatum* (Fig. 2-1) always refers to a particular kind of maple, whether it is in Japan, Venezuela, or elsewhere. In addition, because botanical names are standard and always in Latin, their usage is worldwide and is not affected by national languages.

Making a plant into a bonsai does not change its bontanical name; this makes it possible to identify a bonsai easily and exactly when viewing bonsai exhibits, exchanging information, or purchasing a bonsai. Botanical nomenclature is used in plant reference works, bonsai publications, and nursery and plant catalogs.

The latinized nomenclature now in use was developed several centuries ago. The word *nomenclature* is derived from the Latin *nomenclatura*, "a calling by names" (*nomen*, name, and *clara*, calling). It is based on a binominal system (from *binary*, meaning "twofold") consisting of two connected terms, a noun and an adjective. The noun, which is always written first and capitalized, indicates the name of the genus and is called the generic name. A genus is a group of plants with significantly similar botanical characteristics. Examples of a genus are *Acer*, maple, and *Pinus*, pine. The second term indicates the name of the species. This is the specific name and is written second, as an adjective, and is not capitalized, as in *Acer palmatum*, Japanese maple, and *Pinus ponderosa*, ponderosa pine. In a few instances, however, the specific name is capitalized.

This occurs with species names derived from proper nouns such as the name of a person (*Malus Halliana*, Hall's crab apple), a name taken from a foreign language (*Cedrus Deodara,* cedar of Deodar), or the name of another genus (*Picea Abies,* Norway spruce, from *Picea,* spruce, and *Abies,* fir, meaning a spruce that resembles a fir).

In references and in technical usage, the botanical name includes the name of the person who named and first published the description of the plant. The name of the authority, as the person is called, may be abbreviated, especially if it is long. This practice is followed today as new plants are discovered and named. For example, a species of pyracantha, the Chinese fire thorn, was first described and named by Dr. Hui-Lin Li of the University of Pennsylvania. It is written *Pyracantha Fortuneana* H. L. Li.

Botanical names of plants are governed by the International Code of Botanical Nomenclature and may be changed from time to time. In the text, when the botanical name is followed by a second botanical name in parentheses, the second name is an earlier name that is no longer in use.

Abbreviations. In botanical usage, the name of the genus and the species is spelled in full, such as *Juniperus chinensis*, the first time it occurs in each chapter. If the generic name appears again in the chapter, it is shortened to its first letter, as in *J. chinensis*. Other abbreviations may follow the botanical name:

sp. (plural, **spp.**) = species
Follows the generic name when no species is indicated. Example: *Pinus* sp., a species of pine.

var. = variety
Follows the specific name and indicates a subspecies. Example: *Juniperus chinensis* var. *Sargentii*, a subspecies of Chinese juniper. Varieties are capitalized when they are derived from the name of a person.

cv. (plural, **cvs.**) = cultivar
Follows the specific name and indicates a cultivar, a term formed from *culti*vation and *var*iety, referring to a cultivated plant with a distinguishing feature that is retained in propagation. Example: *Pinus Strobus* cv. Nana, a dwarf eastern white pine. Cultivars are always capitalized, and to distinguish them from varieties, they are either enclosed in single quotation marks or preceded by the "cv." designation.

While it is not necessary to memorize botanical names, plan to use them to identify bonsai. The genera for bonsai are relatively few, and with use the nomenclature soon becomes familiar. Usage both in Part One and Part Two follows the 1976 edition of *Hortus Third*,[1] which lists, identifies, and describes plants found in cultivation in North America. *Hortus Third* is also the botanical reference for many of the species described in the text and should be consulted for additional information. Most plants used for bonsai are included in *Hortus*

[1]Liberty Hyde Bailey Hortorium Staff, *Hortus Third* (New York: Macmillan, 1976).

except wild plants and plants outside the Northern Hemisphere. *Yatsubusa*, a Japanese word that occurs in the text, literally means "eight buds"[2] and refers to dwarf forms of Japanese species that have dense foliage and small leaves yet retain a treelike trunk and branch structure.

SELECTED SPECIES USED FOR BONSAI

Chinese and Japanese species popular as bonsai in the Orient are listed in Appendix B. A large number of these trees and shrubs are now grown extensively in other countries throughout the Temperate Zone and are available at nurseries and plant markets.

In addition to Oriental species, native trees and shrubs the world over are sources of bonsai material. Native species found and used by bonsai growers in the United States and Canada are listed here by five geographical regions. Species with a wide geographic distribution will be found in more than one region, while others are limited to a small section within a region. Consult the listings for suggested bonsai material in your area.

1. California and the Southwest

Japanese-Americans in California were the first to make extensive use of native American trees for bonsai. In the Sierra Madre, the Tehachapis, and the Sierra Nevada ranges they found superb species of aged and weathered California junipers, *Juniperus californica*. From large windswept specimens with heavy trunks, they fashioned bonsai whose beautiful forms rival the century-old bonsai of Japan. One such specimen, found in the mountains and transformed into a bonsai by internationally known bonsai expert John Y. Naka, is shown in Fig. 2-5.

In contrast to the dramatic juniper from the mountains, another tree—this one small, with tiny leaves—was discovered in a California nursery and found to be excellent for bonsai. The tree is called Catlin elm, believed to be a dwarf form of the Chinese elm, *Ulmus parvifolia*, native to eastern Asia. Only the dwarf Catlin form is American.

California and the Southwest:
Native and Indigenous Species Used for Bonsai

Cupressus macrocarpa Hartweg Monterey cypress
Juniperus californica Carrière California juniper
J. occidentalis Hook. *(J. prostrata)* Sierra juniper
Olea europea L. European olive (naturalized)
Pinus cembroides var. **edulis** Voss Mexican stone pine

[2]William N. Valavanis, *The Japanese Five-Needle Pine* (Atlanta, Ga.: Symmes Systems, 1975), p. 50.

Figure 2-5 A California juniper, *Juniperus californica,* collected from the mountains in 1962 and trained as a bonsai for twenty years by John Y. Naka. Courtesy of John Y. Naka.

P. edulis Engelm. Pinyon pine
P. flexilis James Limber pine
P. ponderosa Dougl. ex P. Laws. & C. Laws. Ponderosa pine
P. radiata D. Don Monterey pine
Pithecellobium flexicaule J. Coult. Texas ebony
Quercus agrifolia Nee California live oak
Q. chrysolepis Liebm. Canyon oak
Q. dumosa Nutt. California scrub oak
Sequoia sempervirens Endl. Coast redwood
Taxodium mucronatum Ten. Montezuma cypress
Ulmus parvifolia Jacq. Chinese elm cv. Catlin, a dwarf form

2. *Coastal South and Southeast Region*

American bald cypress, *Taxodium distichum*, found throughout the South and Southeast, makes a striking bonsai. On a mature tree, the tall, dominant trunk, straight or slightly curved, is highly visible and crowned with a mass of light, graceful foliage. Many other native trees of Florida and the Caribbean are excellent for bonsai. Among the most distinctive are old specimens of buttonwood, *Conocarpus erectus*, collected in coastal waters and the Florida Keys. They are trained into stunning bonsai with thick, sinewy trunks and small leaves.

Ulmus crassifolia, the cedar elm of Mississippi, Arkansas, Louisiana, and Texas, adapts readily to bonsai culture and training and has proved to be one of the finest American elms for bonsai.

Coastal South and Southeast Region: Native and Indigenous Species Used for Bonsai

Acer barbatum Michx. Southern sugar maple
A. rubrum L. and var. **trilobum** C. Koch Red maple, swamp maple
A. saccharum subsp. **leucoderme** Desmarais *(A. leucoderme)* Chalk maple
Bucida buceras L. Black olive
Carpinus caroliniana T. Walt. American hornbeam, blue beech
Casuarina equisetifolia J. R. Forst. & G. Forst. Horsetail tree, ironwood
Celtis laevigata Willd. Mississippi hackberry, sugarberry
Chamaecyparis thyoides L. Swamp white cedar and cv. Ericoides
Coccoloba Uvifera L. Sea grape
Conocarpus erectus L. Buttonwood
Crataegus floridana Sarg. Florida haw, Jacksonville haw
C. larcimata Small Sandhill haw, Pensacola haw
C. mollis Scheele Downy hawthorn
Ficus aurea Nutt. Strangler fig, golden fig
F. citrifolia Mill. Shortleaf fig
Ilex vomitoria Ait. Yaupon, cassina, and cvs. incl. Schellings Dwarf
Juniperus silicicola L. H. Bailey Southern red cedar
Lantana Camara L. Lantana
Ligustrum vulgare L. Privet
Malpighia coccigera L. Miniature holly
M. glabra L. Barbados cherry
Nyssa sylvatica Marsh. and var. **biflora** Sarg. Swamp tupelo, sour gum
Pinus clausa Vasey Sand pine
P. Elliottii Engelm. Slash pine
P. virginiana Mill. Scrub pine
Pithecellobium flexicaule J. Coult. Texas ebony
Planera aquatica J. F. Gmel. Water elm
Taxodium distichum L. Bald cypress
T. d. var. **nutans** Ait. *(T. ascendens)* Pond cypress
Ulmus alata Michx. Wahoo elm, winged elm
U. crassifolia Nutt. Cedar elm
Zamia floridana A. DC. Sago palm, coontie

3. Northeast and North Central Region

Geographically, this Northeast and North Central region contains the northeastern section of the United States and southeastern Canada. Many of the following species, such as red maple, *Acer rubrum*, and white spruce, *Picea glauca* (Fig. 2-6), are found in both countries.

Figure 2-6 Bonsai of five Alberta spruces, *Picea glauca* var. *albertiana* (a form of dwarf white spruce), planted on a rock. Courtesy of Ralph R. Walker.

Northeast and North Central Region: Native and Indigenous Species Used for Bonsai

Acer rubrum L. and var. **trilobum** C. Koch Red or swamp maple
Carpinus caroliniana var. **virginiana** Fern. Northeastern hornbeam, blue beech
Chamaecyparis thyoides BSP. Swamp white cedar and cv. Ericoides
Crataegus L. spp. Hawthorn
Ilex decidua Walt. Deciduous holly, possum haw
I. verticillata A. Gray Winterberry
Juniperus communis L. Oldfield juniper, common juniper
J. horizontalis Moench Creeping juniper and cvs. including Bar Harbor and Wiltoni
J. virginiana L. Eastern red cedar and cv. Canaertii
Kalmia latifolia L. Mountain laurel
Larix laricina C. Koch American larch
Malus Mill. spp. Apple and crab apple
Picea glauca Voss *(Picea alba)* White spruce
Pinus Banksiana Lamb. Jack pine
P. rigida Mill. Pitch pine
P. Strobus L. Eastern white pine and cv. Nana, a dwarf form
P. virginiana Mill. Scrub pine
Thuja occidentalis L. Arborvitae and many cvs. including Little Gem

4. Northwest and Pacific Northwest Region

This wide area from the Rocky Mountains to the Pacific Ocean spans a range of climatic conditions. The coastal climate of the Pacific Northwest is a region

Figure 2-7 The dwarf form Iron Springs, a mutation of western hemlock, *Tsuga heterophylla,* discovered and trained as a bonsai by J. Blogg. Courtesy of Puget Sound Bonsai Association. Photo by Charles M. Gordon, Photojournalist.

with favorable growing conditions for bonsai. Although both eastern hemlocks, *Tsuga canadensis* and *T. caroliniana*, are difficult to maintain as bonsai in the eastern states, in the Pacific Northwest the native hemlocks, *T. heterophylla* and *T. Mertensiana*, grow well as bonsai. Iron Springs, a dwarf form of western hemlock (Fig. 2–7), has small needles, compact branches, and a true hemlocklike shape. Another native species, kinnikinick, or bearberry (Fig. 2–8), which does not thrive in warmer or drier regions, is grown as bonsai in Oregon and Washington.

A number of outstanding native trees are also used for bonsai in the Rocky Mountain states where climatic conditions are marked by cold, harsh winters and sudden sharp changes in temperatures. These include the Rocky Mountain juniper, *Juniperus scopulorum* (Fig. 17–13), Alpine fir, *Abies lasiocarpa*, and Colorado blue spruce, *Picea pungens*.

Figure 2-8 Bonsai of bearberry or kinnikinick, *Arctostaphylos media,* native to the Pacific Northwest. Courtesy of Dan Robinson.

Northwest and Pacific Northwest Region: Native and Indigenous Species Used for Bonsai

Abies lasiocarpa Nutt. Alpine fir
Arctostaphylos media Greene Bearberry, kinnikinick
Crataegus L. spp. Hawthorn
Juniperus scopulorum Sarg. Rocky Mountain juniper
Larix occidentalis Nutt. Western larch
Malus Mill. spp. Apple and crab apple
Picea glauca Voss *(P. alba)* White spruce
P. g. var. **albertiana** Sarg. Alberta spruce
Pinus contorta Dougl. ex Loud. Shore pine
P. c. var. **latifolia** Engelm. ex S. Wats. lodgepole pine
P. flexilis James Limber pine
P. ponderosa Dougl. ex P. Laws. & C. Laws. Ponderosa pine
Tsuga heterophylla Sarg. Western hemlock and cv. Iron Springs, a dwarf form
T. Mertensiana Carrière Mountain hemlock

5. *Hawaii*

The Hawaiian Islands have many residents of Oriental descent, and bonsai were grown there long before the islands became a state. It is difficult to separate native flora from the unknown number of plants that were washed ashore on Hawaiian beaches, took root, and became naturalized over a period of time. For example, *Casuarina* spp., known as ironwood, horsetail tree, and Australian pine, is native to Australia and the South Pacific islands. It is now naturalized over wide areas of the Hawaiian Islands and is popular for bonsai as a substitute for *Pinus* spp., most of which cannot survive Hawaii's warm climate. Perhaps the most distinctive Hawaiian species for bonsai is the beautiful ohio-lehua, *Metrosideros collinus*. An example is shown in Fig. 2-9.

Figure 2-9 Ohio-lehua trained as a bonsai by David Fukumoto. Photo courtesy of Fuku-Bonsai.

The brevity of the list of native plants popular for bonsai in Hawaii does not imply a shortage of bonsai material on the islands. On the contrary, an abundance of trees and shrubs from warm regions of the South Pacific, Asia, Australia, and the Americas are used for bonsai in Hawaii.

The Hawaiian Islands: Native and Indigenous Species Used for Bonsai

Brassaia actinophylla Endl. *(Schefflera actinophylla)* Schefflera
Casuarina Cunninghamiana Miq. Ironwood, Australian pine
C. equisetifolia J. R. Forst. & G. Forst. Ironwood, horsetail tree
Ficus microcarpa L.f. (*F. retusa*) Chinese banyan and cv. Retusa
Lantana Camara L. Lantana
Metrosideros collinus A. Gray Ohio-lehua
Schinus terebinthifolius Raddi Christmas berry

In selecting material for bonsai, both native and foreign (or exotic) species can be used. Each has certain advantages. While Oriental species have proved their adaptability to bonsai over a long period of time, it is not always possible to be aware of and duplicate their environmental needs in different parts of the world. On the other hand, species native to the region where they are used for bonsai are naturally suited to the existing environment.

PRACTICE AND REVIEW

1. After reviewing the criteria for selecting suitable plant material for bonsai, trim 6- to 12-inch shoots from a number of different species of trees growing in the ground. Choose assorted samples from trees of dissimilar appearances. On each shoot, locate the bud or leaf that forms the node and note the distance between the nodes. Arrange the shoots according to the average length of their internodes. How much variation is found among the different species? Based on their internodal length, which shoots are preferred for bonsai? Take other samplings to examine, and evaluate their growth as either spindly or compact in appearance; also observe the variation found in leaf size among plant material for bonsai. Last, try to find one or more species that, in your opinion, displays the highest number of visible characteristics desired for bonsai, and give reasons for your choice.

2. Prepare a list of species of trees in your area that are promising material for bonsai. If possible, try to observe species used as bonsai, or ask members of local bonsai clubs for their suggestions. Include trees popular for gardens and landscaping as well as trees in fields and forests. Use both botanical and common names in preparing your list. Regional guides to tree identification contain helpful information. When observing a tree, examine it closely for its bonsai potential. This practice will be helpful later in selecting material for bonsai.

ADDITIONAL READING

BAILEY, LIBERTY HYDE, AND ETHEL ZOE BAILEY, comps., *Hortus Third*, rev. and expanded by the staff of the Liberty Hyde Hortorium, Cornell University. New York: Macmillan, and London: Collier Macmillan, 1976. A definitive descriptive listing of plants in cultivation and an authoritive reference on preferred usage in botanical nomenclature. Includes cold-hardiness of each species by zone.

BERRY, JAMES BERTHOLD, *Western Forest Trees*. New York: Dover Publications, 1966. A corrected republication of the work originally published by the World Book Company in 1924. A nontechnical, illustrated guide to the identification of trees and their uses in eleven western states, written originally for students, teachers, farmers, and woodsmen. A handy reference for western trees.

BUSH, CHARLES A., AND JULIA F. MORTON, *Native Trees and Plants for Florida Landscaping*, Bulletin no. 193. Tallahassee: Florida Department of Agriculture and Consumer Services, n.d. An excellent soft-cover book with 144 well-illustrated pages describing about a hundred selected trees, shrubs, and vines native to Florida.

DEN OUDEN, R., AND B. K. BOOM, collabs., *Manual of Cultivated Conifers Hardy in the Cold and Warm-Temperate Zone*. The Hague: Martinus Nijhoff, 1965. An unmatched reference on all conifers in cultivation, such as species of *Pinus, Picea, Chamaecyparis, Juniperus*, and many other coniferous trees used as bonsai.

HARRAR, ELLSWOOD S., AND J. GEORGE HARRAR, *Guide to Southern Trees*, 2nd ed. New York: Dover, 1962. The Dover edition is an unabridged republication of the work first published by McGraw-Hill in 1946. Describes more than 350 species of southern trees and shrubs from the mangrove swamps of Florida Keys to the alpine forests of the Appalachian highlands. Comprehensive and clearly illustrated.

KURZ, HERMAN, AND ROBERT K. GODFREY, *Trees of Northern Florida*. Sarasota, Fla.: Omni Press. Soft-cover reprint of the 1962 ed. Describes trees at the southern limit of the Temperate Zone that are more closely related to northern species than subtropical trees of southern Florida. A well-written and well-illustrated reference for this region.

LI, HUI-LIN, *Trees of Pennsylvania, The Atlantic States, and the Lakes States*. Philadelphia: University of Pennsylvania Press, 1972. An excellent reference on native trees of Pennsylvania and the Northeast, with botanical descriptions and notes on their cultivation.

LITTLE, ELBERT L., *Atlas of United States Trees,* vol. 1: *Conifers and Important Hardwoods*. Misc. Publ. 1146, USDA Forest Service. Washington, D.C.: Superintendent of Documents, 1971. Large-format maps of the United States (and a few of North America) show the distribution of two hundred native species of American trees, including species widely distributed, such as *Acer rubrum*, as well as those with a very limited range, such as *Juniperus californica*.

NAKAJIMA, TAMEJI, AND H. CARL YOUNG, *The Art of the Chrysanthemum*. New York: Harper & Row, A Weathermark Edition, 1965. The only source of detailed information in English on growing chrysanthemums as bonsai. Profusely illustrated. It is out of print but may be available at libraries.

REHDER, ALFRED, *Manual of Cultivated Trees and Shrubs Hardy in North America*, rev. and enlarged ed. New York: Macmillan, 1962. A technical overview of North American trees exclusive of the subtropical and warmer temperate regions.

SUDSWORTH, GEORGE B., *Forest Trees of the Pacific Slope*. New York: Dover, 1967. An unabridged republication of the work first published by the Forest Service of the U.S. Department of Agriculture in 1908. A timeless volume unmatched for its clear descriptions and illustrations. Contains a table updating changes in nomenclature since the original publication date.

3

Bonsai Design

BONSAI AS AN ART FORM

In bonsai, art and horticulture are equally important and inseparable. Bonsai offers the potential for aesthetic satisfaction to everyone. As artist and philosopher Frederick Franck so aptly writes in his book on drawing and creative expression, *The Zen of Seeing*, everyone has an "artist within" because being creative is part of being human.[1]

Bonsai, in addition to its miniaturization, is distinguished from other art forms by being a living, three-dimensional entity. Within this context, a bonsai can be many things. It can be a disadvantaged tree that has survived adversity; it can be a poetic tree expressive of an imaginary world; it can be a tree endowed with literary, legendary, or symbolic meaning; it can be a single tree or a dense forest of many trunks and entwining branches. The many ramifications of a tree invite bonsai growers to be inventive by creating bonsai in forms that are personally significant or appealing. Today's bonsai can be expressive of contemporary as well as ancient cultures.

Simplification

Bonsai design utilizes components of a tree that are easily recognized. These components—whenever they are present—are incorporated into a bonsai. They are primarily a tapered trunk, visible surface roots, branches, coverings on the

[1]Frederick Franck, *The Zen of Seeing: Seeing/Drawing as Meditation* (New York: Vintage Books, A Division of Random House, Inc., and Alfred A. Knopf, Inc. ©1973).

trunk and branches, and the resulting tree form. The components may be combined in a multitude of ways. When planning a bonsai, it is important to keep in mind that it is not expected to be, nor can it be, a true-to-scale model of a tree. For example, the branches of a bonsai are few, while those of a tree are many. Needles or leaves on a bonsai are rarely small enough to be true to scale. For example, 1-inch-long needles on an 18-inch-high bonsai would be equivalent to 40-inch-long needles on a 60-foot pine. The skill of the bonsai grower creates the illusion of a beautiful tree.

This is done by simplification. The tree components are simplified as though they were viewed from a distance or through the wrong end of a telescope. Only the basic shape of the trunk is shown, not the many irregularities and protrusions that occur in nature. A relatively few well-placed branches give validity to the bonsai as a tree. These few branches can suggest a network of branches beneath the foliage. Last, the bonsai's overall form is simplified into a conical, oval, triangular, or other basic tree silhouette.

Other artists utilize a process of simplification when depicting trees in paintings. In painting trees, Rex Vicat Cole, a British artist and art instructor, described how an artist does not necessarily paint a literal copy of a tree but seeks to portray the essence of its form and texture.[2] In some paintings, a tree may appear realistic at first glance, but a close examination will reveal that the foliage on the canvas does not consist of leaves but of well-chosen dabs of paint that have no resemblance to the details of a leaf. Because of its small size, a bonsai, however, must be convincing at close range. For this reason, details are artfully added to reveal a tree's surface and texture, such as fissured bark on the trunk, a canopy of small leaves, or a fine network of twigs along the tip of the branches. These essential "trimmings" are the covering on the trunk and branches so essential to bonsai.

Styles

The tree components are not fully developed on all bonsai, and all components are not always present. As mentioned earlier, the components may be arranged in many ways. As bonsai evolved, the most effective and pleasing arrangements were used over and over and became patterns, or styles. A style is defined as a predetermined pattern for the arrangement of a bonsai's trunk, surface roots, branches, and overall form. Numerous arrangements and styles are possible. Figure 3–1 shows a vertical, upright trunk (also known as the formal upright style); Fig. 3–2 depicts a downward-hanging trunk in a cascade style. Many other bonsai styles are found between the upright and the cascading trunk. The precisely defined styles of Japanese bonsai and the more general Chinese styles are described in Appendix B. Learning the trunk and branch arrangement of

[2]Rex Vicat Cole, *The Artistic Anatomy of Trees: Their Structure and Treatment in Painting,* 2nd ed. (New York: Dover, 1965).

Figure 3-1 Engelmann spruce, *Picea Engelmannii,* trained in the formal upright style. Courtesy of C. Raphael.

Figure 3-2 Black pine, *Pinus Thunbergiana* cv. Corticosa, with a corky bark, in a cascade style. Courtesy of Wu Yee-sun.

the styles is one way of learning bonsai. Instruction on the major styles is provided in subsequent chapters. It is often difficult to find plant material that will match the requirements of a particular style. Instead of learning only the patterns, it is far better also to become a pattern maker. A bonsai pattern maker learns to recognize and evaluate the bonsai potential of the tree components in the plant material and then arranges the components into bonsai with pleasing treelike forms that may not necessarily conform to an existing style.

COMPONENTS

When working on a bonsai, start by taking an inventory of the structural components that are present. All components are seldom found in any one bonsai, nor are they seen on all trees. Only a few components are needed to transform plant material into a convincing and attractive bonsai.

Trunk

For bonsai, the ideal trunk has a wide, flared base, surface roots, and a taper that becomes progressively smaller as the trunk continues upward. The lower portion is clearly visible. To avoid the appearance of a monotonous, uninterrupted trunk line, let the upper section of the trunk be only intermittently visible through the foliage.

Use in Design. These characteristics of the trunk strongly reinforce the bonsai's identity. Such a trunk equates a bonsai with a tree. With a taper that emerges from a wide base, the trunk clearly belongs to a tree, as in the beautiful Japanese bonsai in Fig. 3-3. It cannot be mistaken for a fence post, cornstalk, or any other upright structure in the landscape. The wide base and surface roots provide visual support for the top structure of the bonsai. They are the focal point in the composition and connect the container and the tree. The presence of intricate surface roots around the trunk adds a beautiful detail that may mirror delicate branch formations on the tree. While strong surface roots are desirable on all bonsai, they are not always present. Visible roots are most needed when the plant material is not a true tree but a shrub, such as an azalea, shaped to resemble a tree.

Trunk taper, characteristic of mature trees, is not only an identity feature but a strong element in bonsai design. A pleasing pattern evolves as the outline of the trunk, widest at the base, gradually becomes smaller. Finally, the lines defining the trunk on either side come together and merge at the apex, thus ending the trunk. This is especially pronounced on excurrent trees. These are trees with a single undivided trunk and lateral branches as shown in Fig. 3-4. Lines coverging at the top of the trunk have the effect of halting the upward movement of the eye and redirecting it to the bonsai.

Figure 3-3 Japanese witch hazel, *Hamamelis japonica,* in the National Collection, U.S. National Arboretum. Photo courtesy of USDA.

Figure 3-4 Dawn redwood, *Metasequoia glyptostroboides,* at the Morris Arboretum of the University of Pennsylvania. Photo by Paul Sell.

Visibility. On a bonsai, the base and lower trunk are kept open to view. The lower trunk is the portion between the surface of the container and the bottom branches on the bonsai. Its length is proportionate to the final height of the bonsai. For a pleasing proportion, make the height of the lower trunk more than one-fourth and less than one-half the ultimate height of the bonsai.

Branches

The branches on a bonsai emerge at various elevations on the trunk and at different points around the circumference. The thickest branches are at the lowest location on the trunk. Branches become progressively smaller in circumference as they ascend the trunk. As a branch grows longer, it divides into two or more smaller branches, which, in turn, subdivide into further branches. These smaller branches form shoots that subdivide into twigs. The process of branch growth by division, repeated year after year, is called arborization or ramification.

Use in Design. The diverse location of branches on and around the trunk duplicates the natural growth pattern of trees and gives a bonsai three dimensions. (Bonsai with abnormal branch distribution are used in special styles.) As branches on a bonsai arborize, their resemblance to a tree increases. Branches are a powerful identity feature that adds grace and beauty to a bonsai.

To establish a pleasing, harmonious trunk-branch pattern, select the location of a branch in relation to the width of the trunk. Ideally, every visible branch on a bonsai is smaller in circumference than the trunk when they are both at the same elevation. This means that where a branch emerges on the trunk, the trunk is the larger of the two. As the trunk and branches grow upward, the trunk remains larger in diameter. When the trunk becomes thinner, the branches are thinner. The largest branches are located near the base of the trunk and smaller ones toward the top and along the periphery, mirroring the tree's normal growth. This strengthens the balance as well as the harmony in the design and avoids a top-heavy effect caused by large branches high on the trunk.

Coverings on the Trunk and Branches

Bark is a conspicuous covering on old trunks and branches, as in Fig. 3–5. Other coverings on branches and shoots include buds, leaves, needles, small twigs, flowers, fruits, and seeds.

Use in Design. Coverings on a tree are nature's greatest gift to bonsai. Each covering, from bark to buds, leaves to seeds, is a signal that the bonsai is a tree—and not any tree, but a specific living tree. Trees are known by their coverings. There is no question as to the identity of a bonsai wisteria in flower, a pine tree with needles, or a crab apple with fruit.

Figure 3-5 Bark covering on the trunk of an aged European hornbeam, *Carpinus Betulus,* at the Morris Arboretum. Photo by Paul W. Meyer.

Coverings are also a tremendous aesthetic asset. A maple bonsai, for instance, will display beautiful fall coloring, a cherry bonsai will be covered with profuse flowers, and a bonsai zelkova in winter, when its leaves have fallen, will be enclosed beneath an exquisite layer of delicate twigs. The covering on a bonsai can transform an ordinary specimen into one of great beauty. The covering plays another role: It covers. A covering of foliage, especially among evergreen trees, conceals awkward branch or trunk structures or other interior arrangements that, if seen, would mar a bonsai. Concealing faults in the plant material is an acceptable ploy in the art of bonsai.

The Tree Silhouette or Shape

Whenever possible, shape a bonsai to duplicate the counterpart of its species in nature. For example, a maple has a crowned or dome shape to its foliage, a conical outline appears on a mature fir, and the oval form complements many deciduous trees.

Use in Design. Copying the shape of a tree is yet another way to reinforce its identity. Each species of trees has a distinctive shape that is advantageous to mimic in bonsai. The overall form of a bonsai is the first image the viewer sees. The Japanese are masters in refining the treelike shape of each bonsai and far surpass others in this respect. The smooth contour of a well-defined tree shape is aesthetically pleasing; it is an invaluable asset in a bonsai.

COMBINING THE COMPONENTS

Arranging the tree-identity features of a potential bonsai into a unified whole involves the organization of its essential parts—the trunk, branches, roots, and so on. This will be the plan, or composition, of the bonsai. There are no rules that determine whether a composition is "good." The composition is pleasing when a bonsai is shaped as well as possible within its physical limitations. Pruning and wiring techniques for manipulating the tree components for this purpose are described in Chapters 4 and 5. To combine the component parts, select the best view of the components.

Trunk

The most desirable characteristics for bonsai include a thick trunk with its greatest circumference at ground level, as in the illustration (Fig. 3-6) of a Chinese quince, *Cydonia sinensis*. Surface roots, if present, are distributed around the trunk. Generally, no large root points directly at the viewer. The lower portion of the trunk is highly visible, while foliage partially conceals the upper sections.

The lower trunk is positioned so as not to extend outward directly toward the front of the container. Taper starts at the bottom of the trunk and becomes progressively smaller as the trunk extends toward the apex. At no place does the trunk shrink and become less in diameter than the sections above.

Figure 3-6 This Chinese quince, *Cydonia sinensis,* has many characteristics of the trunk and branches most wanted in bonsai. Photo courtesy of Lynn R. Perry.

Harmony. From bottom to top, harmony is an important element in the trunk. Ideally, the pronounced line of the trunk, whether it is straight, curved, or angular, reappears wherever the trunk is exposed to view. A straight trunk remains straight, a curved trunk continually curves (the length and degree of the curve may vary), and a noticeable angle at the bottom of the trunk is seen in other angles as the trunk continues upward. A trunk that is a mixture of straight lines, curves, and angles lacks harmony and fragments the design.

Branches

For purposes of bonsai design, branches are offspring of the trunk and share many features in common with their parent. They look alike and have the same covering. Treat branches as smaller versions of the trunk. Use them as a repeat motif by repeating the line of the trunk in the major branches.

Let the caliber of a branch be greatest at its point of emergence on the trunk, and obtain a pleasing taper through the subdivision of branchlets and twigs.

Proportion. Keep the branch length on a bonsai in the same proportions to the trunk as on trees growing naturally in the ground. On upright excurrent trees (trees with a single trunk and lateral branches), the length of most branches is well under one-half the height of the tree, as in Fig. 3-4.

Harmony. In the manner that all sections of the trunk are made harmonious with one another, develop the branches to harmonize with the trunk. Branches on a straight trunk are predominantly straight, on a curved trunk they are curved, and so on. Do not, however, extend the trunk-branch similarity to every branch. To do so would give the bonsai a contrived, mechanical appearance. An exception to this harmonious pattern is a bonsai that evokes an ancient tree. Here, branches that were once straight on a straight trunk are bent and twisted as though with age. This is seen especially on bonsai with large old massive trunks.

Figure 3-7 A harmonious pattern is seen in this old European beech, *Fagus sylvatica,* at the Morris Arboretum as its many branches appear as small young editions of the trunks. Photo by Paul W. Meyer.

Sometimes the overall shape of the branch is made to harmonize with the trunk. On excurrent conifers, for example, the branch has a tapered triangular shape, broad at its juncture with the trunk and tapering to a point at its outermost tip to duplicate the shape of the tree. In deliquescent trees, branches grow upward without a dominant trunk, as seen in the large old beech in Fig. 3–7. Many of the branches duplicate the shape of the tree by dividing and subdividing and in the process become each a small replica of the parent tree.

Branches on a Curved Trunk. When a major branch appears on the curve of a trunk, its most desirable position is on the outside of the curve. When it occurs on the inside of the curve, it tends to bisect the curvature and break the continuity of the trunk line. A branch on the inside of a curve, however, will not be distracting if its juncture with the trunk can be concealed by foliage. Such branches can be used to fill gaps in the shape of the tree.

Territory. To obtain the maximum effect of the relatively few branches in a bonsai composition, allow each major branch to occupy its own space without intrusion from other branches. Let branchlets and twigs overlap where dense growth is wanted along the periphery or to conceal an awkward arrangement in the interior of the bonsai.

To establish territory for the major branches, eliminate the following, called unwanted, or nonconforming, branches:

1. Branches that haphazardly cross one another in the viewer's line of vision (Fig. 3-8.1). When two strong branches cross, each branch loses the continuity of its line, and the unity of the design is weakened.
2. Strong branches growing perpendicular upward or downward on another branch (Fig. 3-8.2). These branches, growing parallel to the trunk, compete with the trunk line and sooner or later intrude into the territory of other branches.

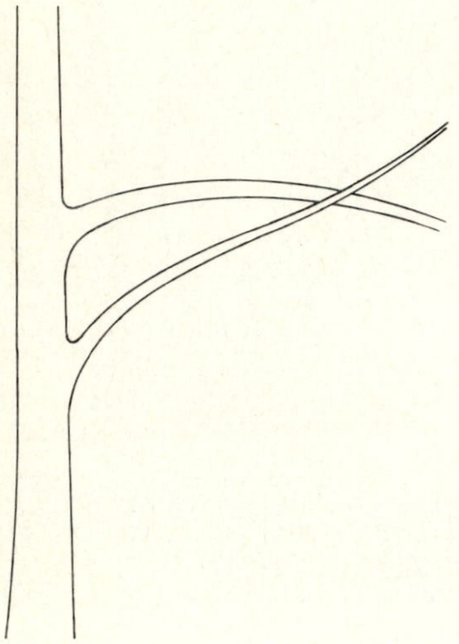

Figure 3-8.1 Reposition crossing branches.

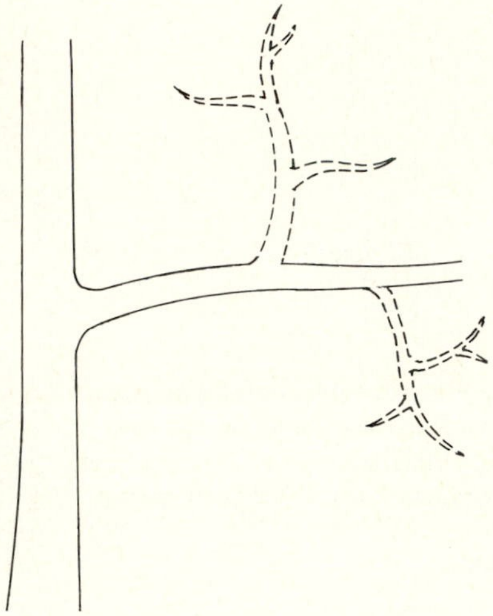

Figure 3-8.2 Remove branches up or down on another branch.

Figure 3-8.3 Eliminate inward-growing branches.

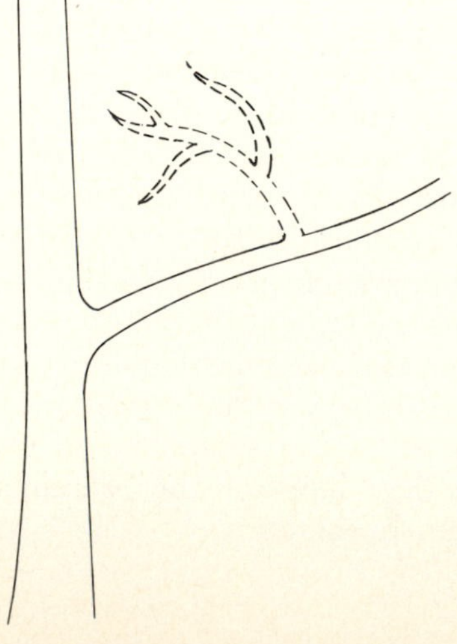

Figure 3-8.4 Rearrange branches growing against one another.

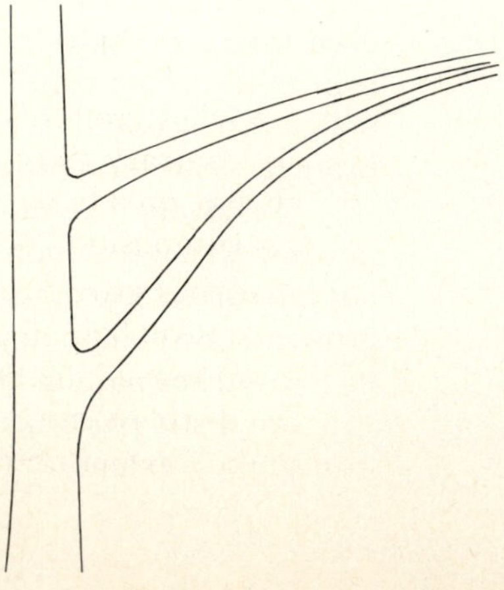

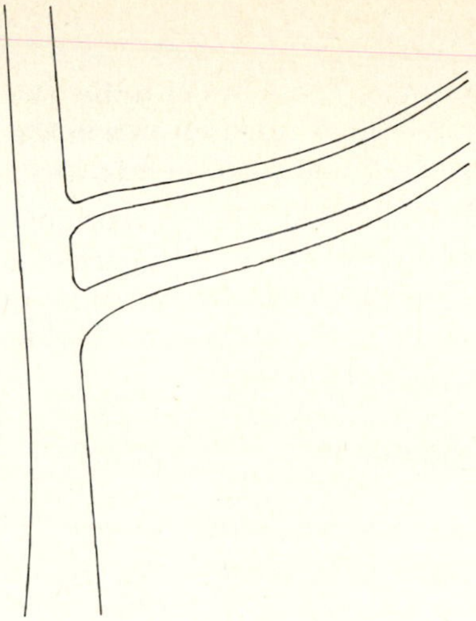

Figure 3-8.5 Avoid parallels.

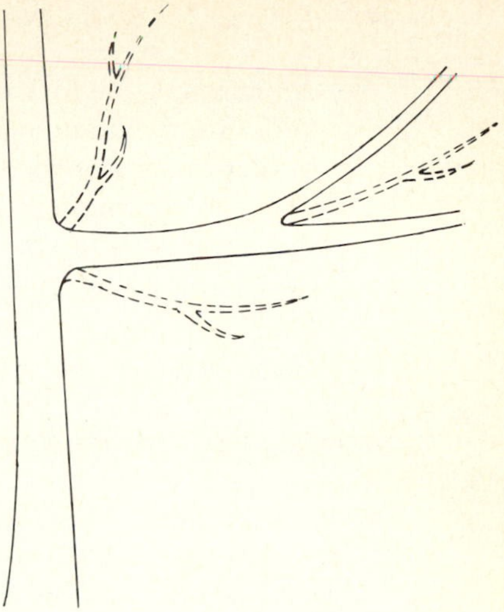

Figure 3-8.6 Cut dotted branches.

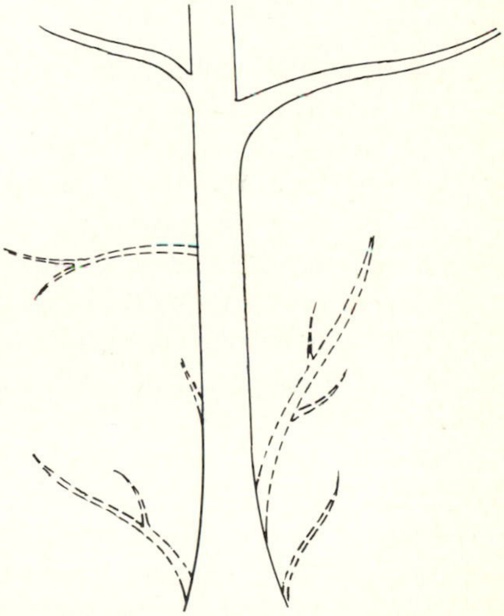

Figure 3-8.7 Cut shoots on the lower trunk.

3. Branches growing inward toward the trunk (Fig. 3–8.3). These branches are contrary to the tree's natural pattern of outward-growing branches. Hence, on a bonsai, an inward-growing branch is a confusing element in the composition.
4. Branches growing against one another (Fig. 3–8.4). These branches are disruptive; both branches lose their identity as they crowd against each other.
5. Branches parallel to one another (Fig. 3–8.5). Such branches form a stiff, simplistic pattern. Gradually widen the space between the two branches as they extend from the trunk.

6. A branch in the fork of two other branches or in the juncture of the trunk and another branch (Fig. 3–8.6). A third branch in the fork of two other branches (or between the trunk and another branch) competes with the others for attention. As it becomes larger, it will crowd the others and destroy the clear lines of the fork or juncture.
7. Small branches or shoots on the trunk below the major branches (Fig. 3–8.7). These are a distraction on the lower trunk and are removed to give clear visibility and emphasis to the trunk.

Coverings on the Trunk and Branches

Coverings on the trunk and branches, which add texture, color, and dramatic interest, are not a structural component of the bonsai design. However, for species with long flowers and hanging fruits, such as wisteria and crab apples, plan to arrange their trunk and branches to provide unobstructed space beneath for hanging objects.

The Tree Silhouette

Determine the future shape of the bonsai at the outset, and position the branches and trunk in accordance with the projected shape.

The lower half of a bonsai, including the bottom trunk and major branches, is fixed. The location of a branch at its point of emergence on the trunk is permanent. It may become longer or thicker, but it does not move up the trunk as the tree becomes taller. For this reason, when considering the proportional height of the lower trunk to the height of the tree, do not use the temporary height of the started bonsai; rather, base the proportions on the anticipated height the bonsai is designed to attain.

Space

Space, as used in design, is empty or unfilled space and is distinguished from mass, which occupies space. Empty space is referred to as "negative" space, opposed to the positive space occupied by mass. The skillful use of negative space adds great beauty to bonsai.

Seeing Negative Space. Negative space is found in the interior and along the exterior of a bonsai. It occurs wherever space is partially or completely enclosed by a line or mass. In Fig. 3–9, negative space is shown in black. In the composition, the distance between branches, the indentations on the silhouette, openings in the foliage, and the shape of the container all contribute negative space. Notice the harmony introduced in this bonsai as the negative space between the branches on the right side of the trunk becomes progressively smaller toward the top of the tree.

The effect of negative space is clearly seen where the two bottom branches

Figure 3-9 Patterns of negative space formed by the trunk line and the position of the branches are shown in black.

Figure 3-10 The largest area of negative space in a bonsai are often found on either side of the trunk between the two lowest branches and the top surface of the container.

of the bonsai in Fig. 3–10 are located at distinct distances from the top of the container. The dissimilar, or asymmetrical, space these two branches create is far more interesting than the identical space formed by two branches directly opposite each other.

Negative space becomes most effective in the design when it reappears in various sizes and locations throughout a composition. When the shape is repeated, it may be upside down, sideways, or in other unexpected positions. It is a playful element in the creative process because artists know that the negative space that results from their composition may be felt and experienced by the viewer without being consciously noticed.

Sources of Negative Space in Bonsai:

1. Openings in the foliage are highly visible forms of negative space.
2. A variation in branch length, deviating here and there from the established pattern, creates indentations along the periphery.
3. The angle formed at the juncture of the trunk and a branch or the fork of two branches may be repeated or modified elsewhere.
4. The space between branches may be varied by placing the branches at unequal distances apart.

Look for other areas of negative space, and incorporate them in the bonsai design at every opportunity.

Selecting the View

The essentials of bonsai composition involve the arrangement of the tree components for their best effect with consideration for harmony, balance, proportion, and negative space.

When the novice begins to examine bonsai material to evaluate the components, a new factor appears that affects all bonsai design: The components of a bonsai change as they are viewed from various directions. It is easy to see these changes by walking in a circle around a tree or a bonsai. With each change in the viewer's location, the appearance of the bonsai changes. This phenomenon is not confined to bonsai but is found among all three-dimensional asymmetrical objects, large and small.

To stabilize the components of a bonsai in one position, it is necessary to impose a deliberate restriction at the very start. First, carefully examine the potential material from all sides for the purpose of selecting the best view. Then, choose the view that provides the most pleasing trunk line and branch arrangement. This is called the "front" of the bonsai. It remains a permanent designation unless the bonsai is redesigned at a later date. All work in creating the bonsai is done to affect the front view, and, of course, when displayed, the front of the bonsai is always placed toward the viewer.

PRACTICE AND REVIEW

Design

Bonsai growers consider the design components as a storehouse to draw on and apply wherever possible. The composition of every bonsai is limited by the trunk-branch structure of the material. With this in mind, study the bonsai photographs in the text. Select a few and analyze in each instance which of the following design components were utilized:

1. A tapered trunk.
2. Surface roots.
3. A harmonious trunk line.
4. Well-distributed branches.
5. Branch length in proportion to trunk height.
6. Territorial space for major branches.
7. Bark texture, fruit, flowers, leaf size.
8. Overall tree form.

In addition, look for harmony, balance, and negative space in the bonsai.

Figure 3-11 An arrangement of three rocks with a planting of Fukien tea, *Ehretia microphylla.* Courtesy of Wu Yee-sun.

Negative Space

1. Observe in Fig. 3–11 how the juxtaposition of the two larger rocks creates a beautiful, intricate area of negative space between them. Where is other negative space repeated in this composition?

2. Trace the outline of two or three bonsai from photographs in the text and make a white-on-black image as in Fig. 3–9. Analyze the negative shape that you find. Are there places where you can modify the composition to form other areas of negative space? Can any area of the existing negative space be made more interesting?

ADDITIONAL READING

The following books describe methods used by artists to depict natural objects such as trees. For further information on bonsai styles, consult the Additional Reading section in Chapter 1 and the description of Oriental styles in Appendix B.

COLE, REX VICAT, *The Artistic Anatomy of Trees: Their Structure and Treatment in Painting*, 2nd ed. New York: Dover, 1965. First published by Seely, Service & Co. Ltd., London, in 1915. A guide for painters in developing artistic "shorthand" in depicting the structure of trees and their foliage in painting. Valuable to bonsai artists for its conceptual treatment of creating the illusion of a tree.

FRANCK, FREDERICK, *The Zen of Seeing: Seeing/Drawing as Meditation*. New York: Vintage Books, A Division of Random House, Inc., and Alfred A. Knopf, Inc., 1973. Drawn and handwritten by the author, the book is a human, positive approach to creative expression, particularly drawing. Provides methods of finding the "artist within," especially for persons not previously active in art.

SZE, MAI-MAI, *The Tao of Painting: A Study of the Ritual Disposition of Chinese Painting*, 2nd ed., Bollingen Series XLIX. Princeton, N.J.: Princeton University Press, 1963. A translation and commentary on a seventeenth-century Chinese painting manual, profusely illustrated. Bonsai enthusiasts will find many prototypes for bonsai in the section on trees.

4

Pruning

Pruning is one of the most important bonsai techniques. The practice exercises at the end of the chapter are essential for everyone, especially the novice, in developing manual dexterity in pruning.

A bonsai is pruned repeatedly during its entire life. Whereas the container dwarfs and the wiring shapes, pruning both dwarfs and shapes a bonsai. Alternatives may be found for wiring, but there is no substitute for the small container or for pruning.

Because pruning is closely timed to the tree's growth cycle, it is important to understand how a tree grows. The anatomy of a tree is shown in Fig. 4–1. As long as it lives, a tree grows by adding a new layer of growth each year to its roots, trunk, branches, and shoots. Without new growth, a tree dies. Fibrous roots in the ground and twigs on branches grow by extension as new roots and shoots sprout from the existing ones. The woody parts of a tree, including taproots, trunks, and branches, expand by surrounding their woody core with a layer of new growth. On a trunk, for example, new cells produced each year beneath the bark harden into wood. They form the rings that are visible in cross sections of old trunks. Old trees, including old bonsai, are mostly dead wood. The living tree is confined to the current growth.

Alex L. Shigo, a noted plant scientist, describes a tree as a "multiple perennial" plant. "Every growth ring can be thought of as an individual tree. Every new 'tree' envelops all the other trees."[1] Bonsai growers dwarf the perennial

[1]Alex L. Shigo, *Tree Decay: An Expanded Concept* (Washington, D.C.: USDA Forest Service, 1979), p. 14.

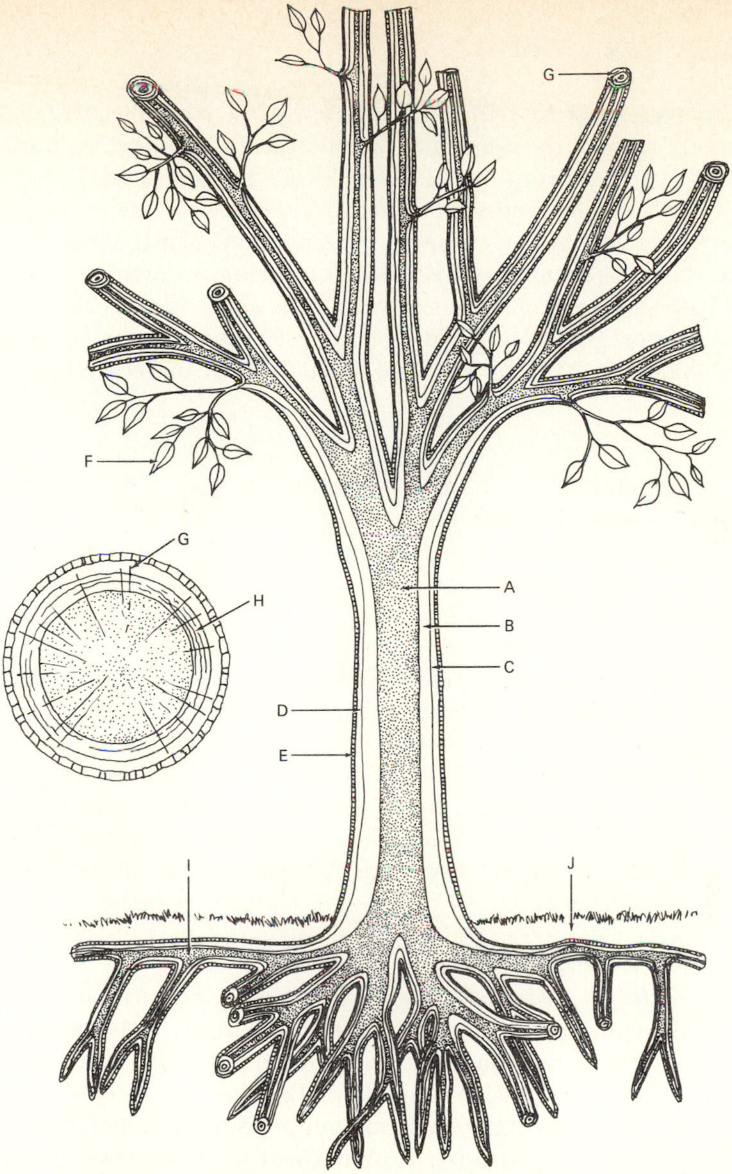

Figure 4-1 Anatomy of a tree. (*A*) *Heartwood.* Inactive cells provide structural support. (*B*) *Sapwood (xylem).* Ducts transport food materials and water upward from the roots. (*C*) *Cambium.* A living, growing layer of cells divide to form both bark and wood and compartmentalize wounds. (*D*) *Inner bark.* Phloem tissue carries food from leaves downward to the cambium and storage cells. (*E*) *Outer bark.* Layers of inactive cells protect and insulate the inner bark. (*F*) *Leaves.* Food production through photosynthesis takes place here. (*G*) *Medullary rays.* These radical ducts conduct food and water and serve in food storage. (*H*) *Annual rings.* In a cross section of tree growth, one ring normally indicates one year's growth. (*I*) *Roots.* Large roots provide anchorage, and tiny root hairs (not shown) absorb moisture and food material. (*J*) *Soil.* Bacteria and fungi make most soil nutrients available; mineral aggregates give support, drainage, and a growing area for roots. Drawing by Lillian Nicholson Meyer, adapted from "How a Tree Grows," *Horticulture,* Summer 1970, p. 102, reproduced courtesy of the American Horticultural Society; the original drawing, "How a Tree Grows," courtesy of The F. A. Bartlett Tree Expert Co., Stamford, Connecticut (Research Laboratories and Experimental Grounds, Charlotte, North Carolina).

tree every year by trimming the new growth on the twigs and branches. The woody roots of the perennial tree also produce a new layer of growth annually. This requires pruning only once every several years.

Bonsai pruning techniques are identical to those used on other trees and shrubs to change their growth or appearance. In the process of forming a bonsai, large plant material is pruned to bring it down to bonsai size. To keep a bonsai small and shape its growth, new shoots are trimmed each year. Reduction of new growth by pruning also decelerates a bonsai's metabolism and brings its foliage in balance with the limitations of the curtailed root system.

TOOLS

A large selection of Japanese bonsai tools, designed for every conceivable bonsai operation, facilitate the work of skilled, experienced bonsai growers. However, at the start, only a few basic tools, available from a variety of sources, are needed. These include small and medium-sized pruners, also called shears, a special tool with concave cutting blades which is convenient for pruning branches, and occasionally a small saw and a wood chisel. Good results depend, in part, on using high-quality tools and having the right tool for the job. A well-made tool, with proper care, will hold its cutting edge for a long time and will last for years. One or two tools of excellent quality and multiple use are a better choice than a larger number of poorly made tools. Many garden pruners made by American, Japanese, Swiss, and other manufacturers are excellent for bonsai. To choose pruners and other tools that are comfortable and easy to use, it is helpful to handle and examine different models, when possible, before making a selection.

Shears and Nippers

Pruners. Among general-purpose hand pruners, the blade-and-hook pruner, with one sharp and one blunt blade (Fig. 4–2), is used extensively for bonsai. The sharp blade passes through the material to be cut and continues beneath the smooth side of the hooklike blade. This type of pruner can be used to make clean, flush cuts without compressing the wood of the branch (or trunk) that remains. The garden pruner constructed on the principle of the anvil is not suitable for bonsai. As the anvil pruner cuts, one sharp blade strikes against the blunt anvil blade. The resulting compression is damaging to the tissue of the bonsai. In addition, many growers find the large-size blades unwieldy for intricate pruning.

The Japanese make a medium-weight bonsai pruner (or shears) with long tapered blades (Fig. 4–3). Both blades have a thin, sharp edge. They are capable of cutting a branch from either side simultaneously with a minimum of compression and damage to the wood and bark. Both the blade-and-hook pruner and the Japanese shears are recommended for bonsai use. The blade-and-hook pruner, with its heavier construction, can make a larger cut than the Japanese shears.

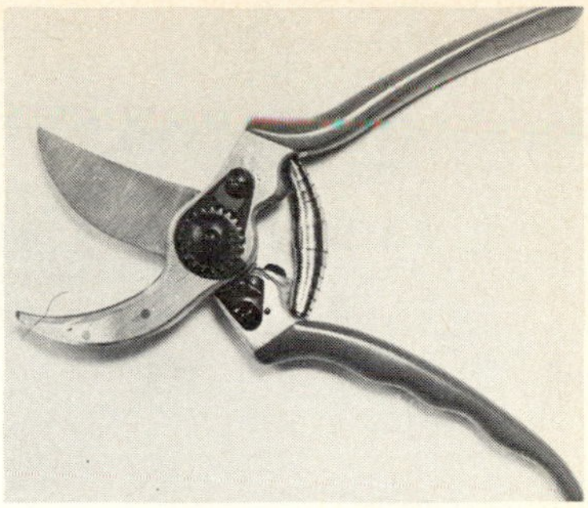

Figure 4-2 Blade-and-hook pruner.

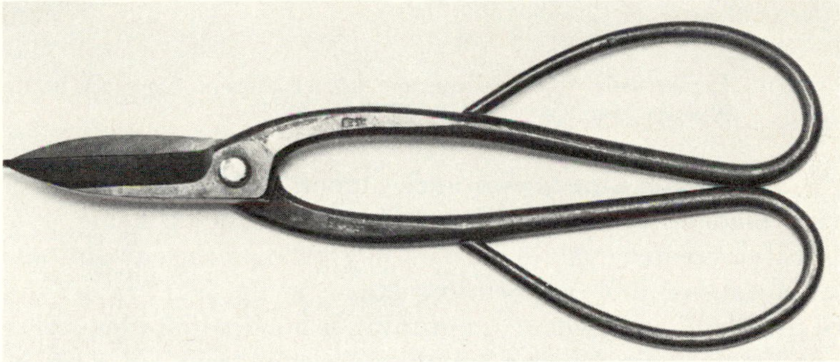

Figure 4-3 Japanese bonsai shears. Courtesy of Keith Valley Nursery, Inc.

Trimming shears. The most convenient tool for pruning leaves, soft shoots, and thin twigs is a pair of the small, lightweight shears shown in Fig. 4–4. It is a smaller version of the Japanese pruning shears with two sharp cutting blades. Bonsai growers sometimes use small household scissors for cutting leaves and soft shoots, but these are not strong enough for twigs or woody tissues. When lightweight trimming shears are not available, use the blade-and-hook pruner or the medium-weight Japanese shears.

Figure 4-4 Japanese bonsai scissors or light shears. Courtesy of Keith Valley Nursery, Inc.

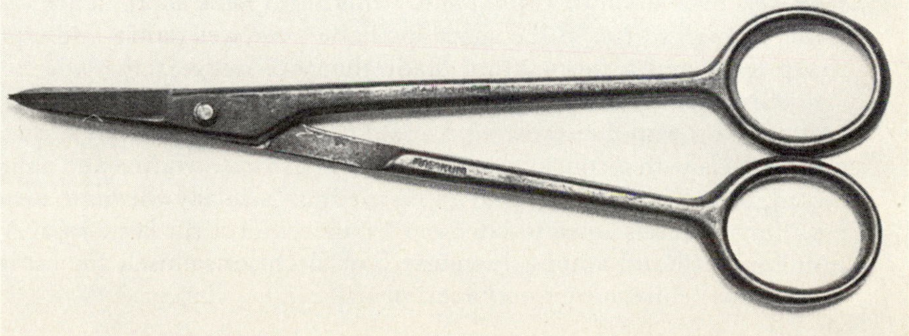

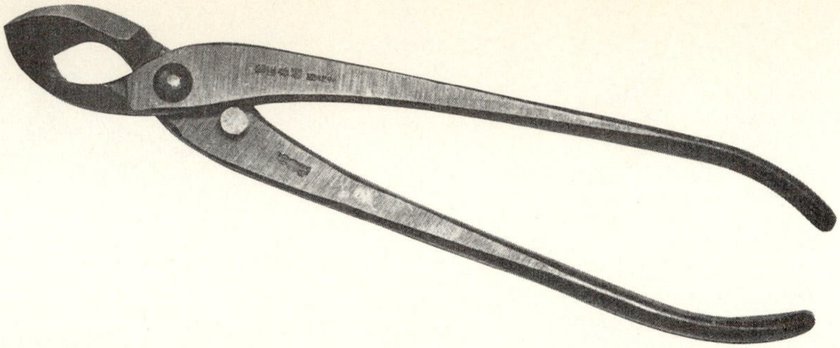

Figure 4-5 Japanese concave branch cutters. Courtesy of Keith Valley Nursery, Inc.

Branch Nippers. A branch nipper is a bonsai tool with two curved, concave blades that carve a slight depression as they cut (Fig. 4–5). The small hollow thus created enables the bark to grow over the cut without forming a bulge. This unusual tool, with cutting blades at the front rather than along the side of the blade, is also used for pruning branches that are hard to reach with conventional cutters. When the nippers are closed, the two sharp blades do not quite meet (which would create an anvil effect) but cross one another slightly. They are manufactured in a variety of sizes with various curves to the blades.

Lopping Shears. When a trunk or branch is too wide to cut with hand pruners, use long-handled loppers with blades similar to the blade-and-hook pruner. The long handles provide leverage that enables the loppers to make a larger cut. Loppers are available where garden and nursery tools are sold. They are particularly useful on large nursery stock or old trees dug from the wild.

Saws and Chisels

Saws. When a lopper or hand pruner is unable to reach the area to be cut, a saw is often serviceable. Many types are available. Folding saws with a blade that fits into the handle are sold for bonsai purposes. A carpenter's keyhole saw or a scroll or coping saw would also be a good choice. Select a saw small enough to use in the space available, yet well made and equipped with sharp teeth and a thin cutting blade that will not tear the wood.

Chisels. Wood chisels are helpful in smoothing the rough surface on cuts made by a saw and in creating a slight depression on the flat surface of a large cut. Chisels with a concave cutting edge in assorted widths and shapes are preferred, as in Fig. 4–6. A small and a medium size are adequate for most growers. Larger chisels and a wooden mallet are required for large jobs. A wide selection can be found among Japanese bonsai chisels, chisels for cabinetmaking, and artists' chisels for woodblock prints.

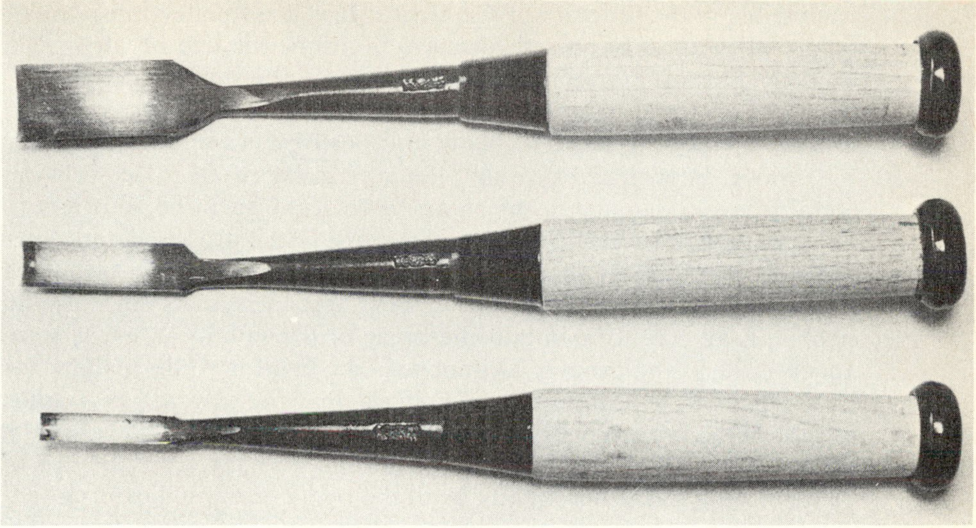

Figure 4-6 Wood chisels, small, medium, and large. Courtesy of Keith Valley Nursery, Inc.

Breaking in Shears and Nippers. Give newly purchased pruning shears and nippers a brief breaking-in period before using them to cut hard wood. If the handles move stiffly, flex them back and forth until they open easily. Sometimes a drop of household oil is needed to lubricate the surface of the crossing blades or the junction where the blades are joined together. When the blades open and close smoothly, try them on soft shoots first and gradually on larger cuts. The preliminary workout also gives the user a chance to become acquainted with the tool and get the knack of handling it.

Use of Tools

Shears and Nippers. Japanese pruning shears are designed to make their cuts with easy, comfortable hand pressure and are not intended to be forced. As a rule of thumb, they are used on branches and trunks with diameters up to about one-fourth the length of the blade. Garden hand pruners are generally able to cut up to about one-third the length of their blade. (Saws or loppers should be used for larger cuts.) When making a pruning cut, maintain an even pressure during the entire cut. The force required will vary according to the hardness of the wood. Maple wood, for instance, is hard and not as easily pruned as the soft wood of pine. On a difficult cut, do not force, twist, or wrench the blades, as this may cause permanent damage to the tool. Gently withdraw a jammed blade and make the cut with a larger or different tool.

Slender twigs and shoots may be cut with the tip of the blades, but for heavier or harder wood, keep the blades fully open and make the cut as far back as possible in the juncture of the blades. It is good policy to examine a bonsai before pruning to be sure the area to be pruned is free of wire. Take care at all times to avoid bringing the cutting edge of the shears in contact with wire. Never use pruning shears or nippers to cut wire, screening, or other metallic materials that may nick the blade and destroy its usefulness.

Saws. First, make sure that the area to be sawed is free of wire or other metal to avoid damage to the sharp teeth of the saw. To start a cut, pull the blade backward several times along the line of the proposed cut. After a slight groove appears, make the cut with a regular back-and-forth (or push-and-pull) stroke with American or European saws. Japanese saws cut only on the pull stroke. Take care to maintain the blade of the saw in an even, straight line, and keep it in the groove. Do not twist or bend it while making the cut.

On small bonsai cuts, it is unlikely that the saw will be trapped by the weight of the branch or trunk pressing on the blade and preventing its movement. Should this happen on a large bonsai, do not release the saw by pulling or wrenching it. Rather, gently bend the trunk or branch causing the pressure away from the cut to free the saw, or insert a small wood wedge in the opening of the cut to allow the sawing to continue. Take care not to tear the bark at the completion of the cut.

Wood Chisels. Wood chisels are intended for use on wood. The cutting edge is easily nicked when it strikes metal or other hard surfaces. In using the chisel, keep the cutting edge directed away from the hands and body. Do not force or deeply gouge the tool into the wood; apply it slowly, using even pressure and short, shallow strokes.

To hollow a flat surface, start in the center area and work outward toward the edge. As the chisel approaches the edge, reverse the direction to make a clean, sharp cut through the bark along the rim of the hollowed area. Keep hands and fingers away from the cutting edge of the tool and the direction of the cut.

Care of Tools

Simple care and maintenance will preserve the sharp cutting blade on a new tool for a long time. After using the tools, wipe the blade with a slightly damp cloth to remove sap, soil, and moisture. Persistent stains or resin may require turpentine. Scrape off encrusted deposits with a wooden, not a metal, spatula. Very fine steel wool and oil will remove rust. Occasionally, rub a small amount of household oil over each tool to protect the surface. When not in use, store the tools in a dry, damp-free location. A tool case is convenient and protects the tools from damage. They range from a simple canvas roll-up satchel to fitted metal carrying cases. A leather case with Japanese tools is shown in Fig. 4-7. A plain box will also serve for storing the tools when they are not in use.

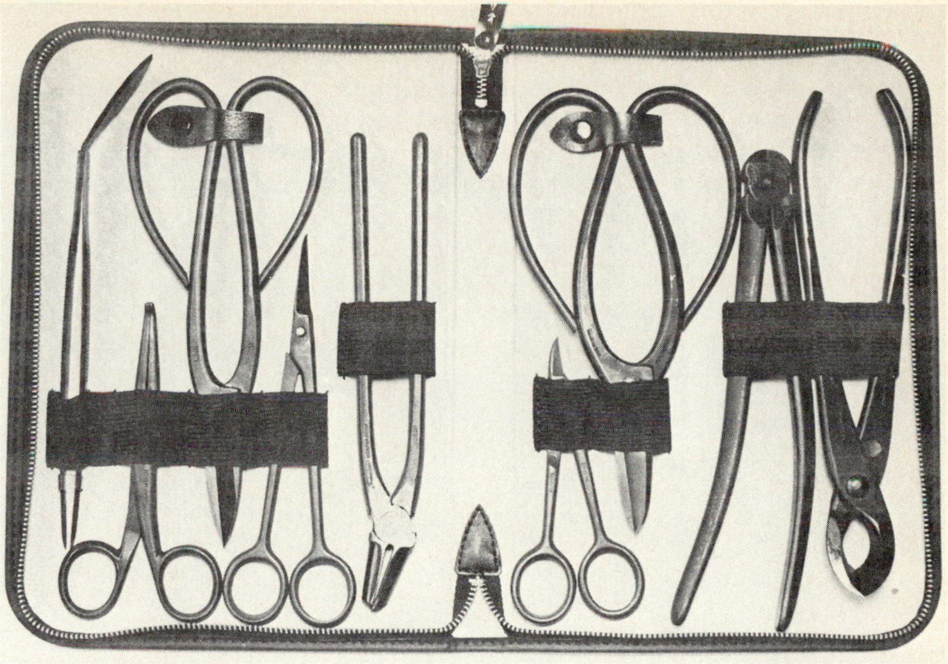

Figure 4-7 Japanese tool kit with concave branch cutter, wire cutter, shears, small wire cutter, bark stripper, scissors, medium-weight shears, wire remover, and tweezers. Courtesy of Keith Valley Nursery, Inc.

HOW TO PRUNE

The tool must be clean and sharp to make a cut that does not tear the wood or bark. When working with a bonsai or plant material where a front view has been selected, do all pruning with the front in mind. Where possible, make cuts on the back side of the trunk or a branch to hide the scars from view.

Studies by the USDA Forest Service, spanning more than a ten-year period, are changing old concepts about what constitutes a correct pruning cut, a tree's response to pruning, and the use of tree wound dressings. The findings indicate that trees possess a self-healing mechanism against infection and decay caused by pruning cuts and other wounds. Alex Shigo, chief scientist of the Northeastern Forest Experiment Station in Durham, New Hampshire, describes the tree's response to wounds in this manner:

> **Trees survive wounds and infection because they are highly compartmented plants that compartmentalize the injured and infected tissues**. Trees have evolved over a period of 200 to 400 million years while being under the constant stress of wounding. Even with this stress, they still have evolved to be the largest and longest lived organisms ever to inhabit the earth. And yet trees have no **wound**

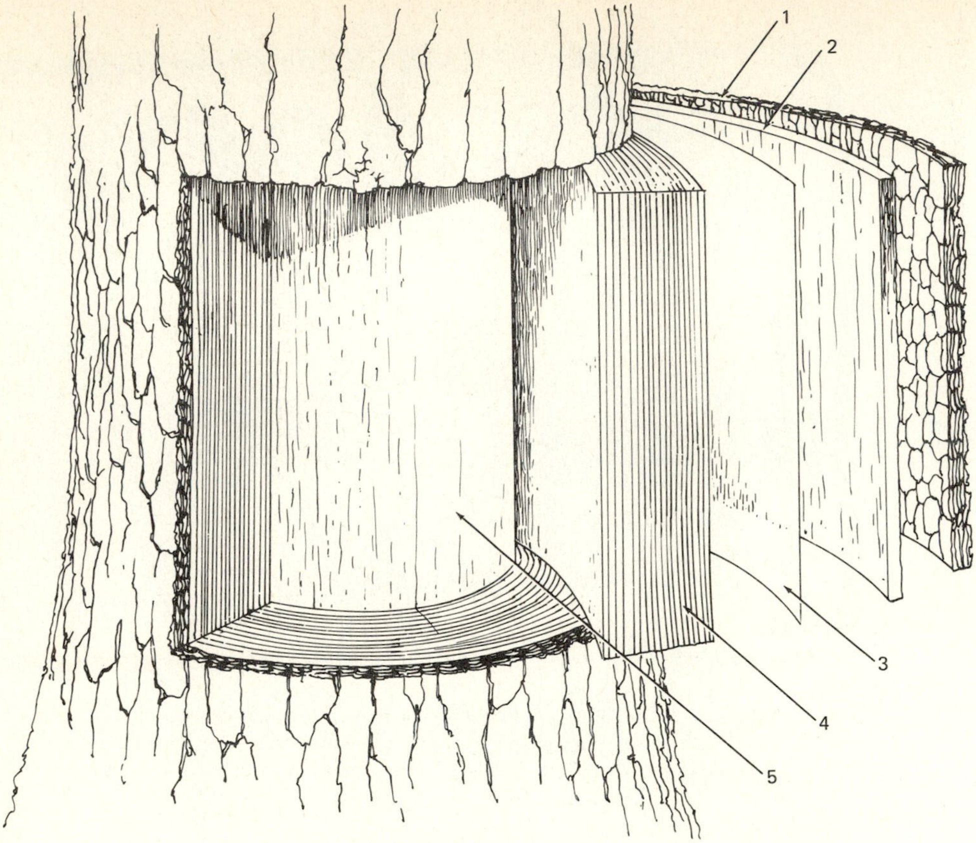

Figure 4-8 Location of the tree's cambium layer. (1) *The outer bark* insulates the tree against heat and cold, prevents moisture loss, and wards off many insect pests. (2) *The inner bark,* or phloem, is the conduit through which food is distributed to the tree. Each year, part of the inner bark dies and is fused to the outer bark. (3) *The cambium* is a thin cellular layer that produces new bark on one side and new wood on the other and seals the tree against infection and decay from wounds. (4) *Sapwood* is new inner wood that serves as the tree's pipeline for water. Each year the innermost cells lose their vitality and turn into heartwood. (5) *Heartwood* is the strong, supporting pillar of the tree. Although the cells are dead, the heartwood will not decay or lose its strength while the outer layers are intact. Adapted from a drawing, "How Does a Tree Build a Trunk?" by St. Regis Paper Company, New York.

healing process—healing in a sense of **replacing** or **repairing** injured tissues. Heal means to restore to a previous healthy state. It is impossible to heal injured and infected xylem. Trees have evolved as highly ordered, **compartmented** plants, that instead of healing, **compartmentalize** in an orderly way the injured and infected tissues. [Emphasis by the original author.][2]

[2]Ibid., p. 12.

Dr. Shigo goes on to explain that trees seal the area around their wounds by plugging the cells above and below the wound with resin and other substances. To prevent the spread of possible decay, cells from the cambium (a thin layer of living cells between the bark and the sapwood of the trunk, shown in Fig. 4-8) build a wall inside the trunk that separates the tissue present at the time of the wounding from tissues that form afterwards.[3] The cambium also develops a callus over the wound to close it to further infection or decay from bacteria, viruses, or fungi.

Because of the tree's own compartmented process of sealing wound damage, treatment of pruning cuts with wound dressing is not necessary. According to a study by Forest Service scientists, asphalt-based materials, orange shellac, and polyurethane varnish have no proven beneficial effect on callus closure, the prevention of decay, or the elimination of decay fungi. Some trees closed wounds rapidly, others more slowly, regardless of the treatment. The least damage occurred on untreated wounds. Favorable wound closure was effected most by the activity of the tree's cambial layer. This is considered possibly to be the result of a genetic factor and the overall health and vigor of the tree.[4]

Applied to bonsai, a sharp, clean cut facilitates callus closure. Good health, proper care, and fertilizing enable a bonsai to minimize wound damage. These studies suggest that wound dressings appear to have little value other than cosmetic appeal and a comforting psychological effect on the user.

Preserving the Callus Collar

The callus collar can be recognized as a raised ring, or collar, encircling the base of a branch where it emerges from the trunk or a larger branch. The collar contains the cells that are capable of growing over the pruning cut and sealing the wood against decay-causing organisms. Therefore, do not cut the callus collar when pruning a branch. (Where a callus collar is not present, make the cut smooth, flush with the remaining wood.) Retaining this collar results in a slightly raised scar on the trunk, which may be considered by some as unsightly, by others as a natural formation. Aesthetics aside, the evidence is clear that retaining the collar protects a bonsai against disease and decay. In the interest of the tree's longevity, it is important for the bonsai grower to cut directly above, not through, a callus collar when pruning.

Directional Pruning

During the spring and summer, a bonsai is shaped by selectively shortening shoots that have formed buds for future growth. This is a way of channeling the tree's natural growth for bonsai purposes. All new shoots emerge from buds.

[3]Ibid., p. 13.

[4]Alex L. Shigo and Charles L. Wilson, "Wound Dressings on Red Maple and American Elm: Effectiveness After Five Years," *Journal of Arboriculture,* 3, no. 5 (May 1977), 81-87.

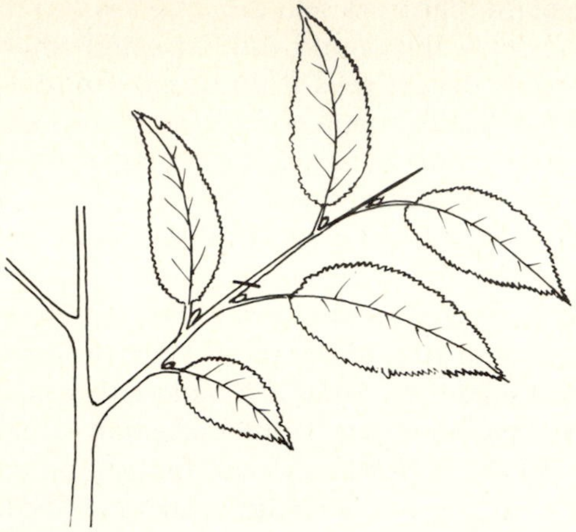

Figure 4-9.1 A zelkova shoot is cut at an angle slightly beyond the second bud on the right.

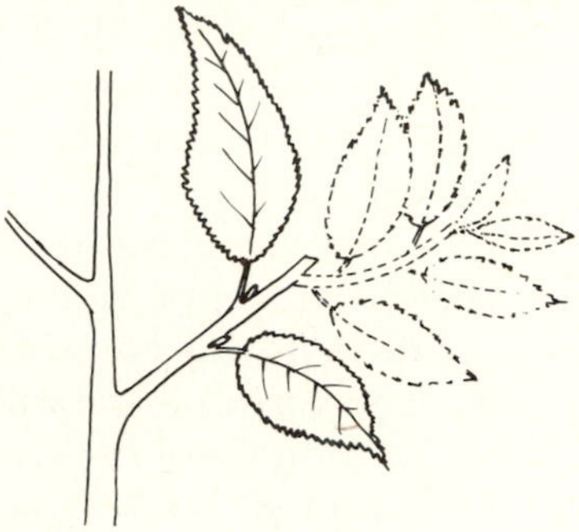

Figure 4-9.2 The replacement shoot that emerged from the bud is smaller and more compact than the original.

When a shoot is pruned (or broken by a natural cause), the remaining bud closest to the break will send out a replacement shoot. By selecting which bud will be next to the cut, the bonsai grower (like a traffic controller) is able to determine the direction of the bonsai's growth. For example, when growth is wanted to the right of a shoot, the shoot is pruned a short distance beyond a bud on the right-hand side, as shown in Figs. 4-9.1 and 4-9.2.

To use directional pruning effectively, the bonsai grower must be able to recognize buds and their location on the shoot. On trees with leaves (this includes deciduous trees and broad-leaved evergreens), a bud is always formed at the base of each leaf stem, or petiole. Buds begin to form early in spring as the new leaves start to harden. They vary in size and shape. A wisteria leaf, which is subdivided into leaflets (called a compound leaf), forms only one bud, located where the main petiole of the compound leaf joins the shoot. An example is shown in Fig. 4-10. On maples and other trees with leaves in pairs on opposite sides of the shoot, buds form also in pairs, at the base of each leaf petiole, as shown in Fig. 4-11.

On most needle evergreens, buds do not appear at the base of each needle but are scattered among the needles and at the tip of each shoot. Certain pines, however, form buds only at the top of each shoot. On others, new growth may sprout from buds beneath the bark. These are called adventitious buds, and they occur on a number of deciduous as well as evergreen species.

The buds at the tip of each shoot are called terminal buds. Growth from these buds causes the shoot to extend in its established direction. When a longer branch is desired, the terminal bud is retained.

A bud is the embryo of future leaves or shoots. Trees and bonsai require time and favorable conditions to form healthy, vigorous buds for their continu-

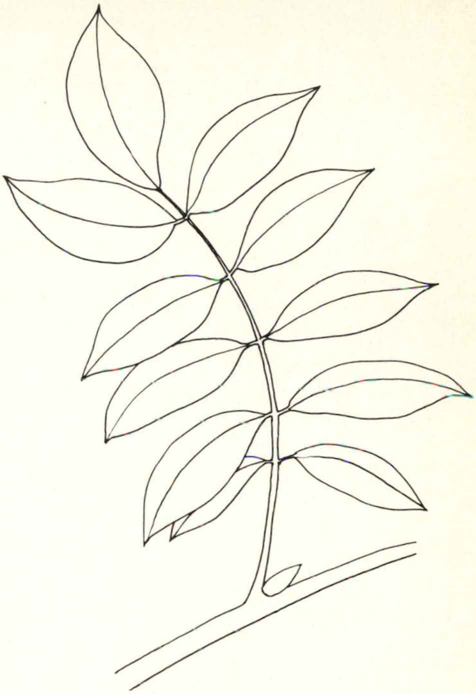

Figure 4-10 On a compound leaf consisting of two or more leaflets, only one bud forms, and its location is at the bottom of the main stem, as shown here on a wisteria leaf.

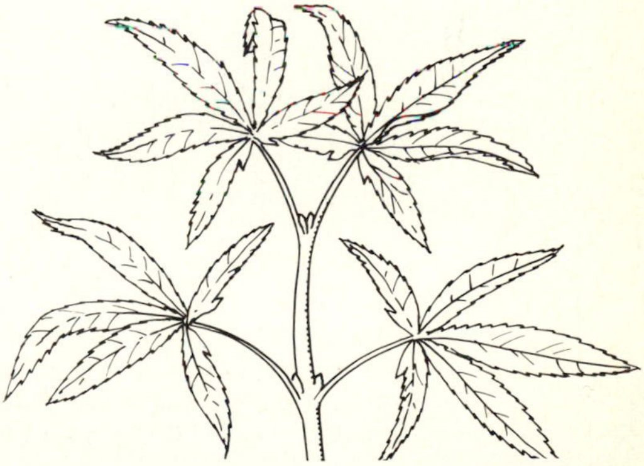

Figure 4-11 Leaves and buds are in pairs on Japanese maples.

ing growth. Pruning a shoot in the early part of the growing season allows ample time for the replacement shoot that emerges to develop buds for the following year.

Five Bonsai Pruning Cuts

The following pruning techniques are among the few "tools of the trade" needed for bonsai. Study each technique carefully. The first, on shortening a shoot, is an application of directional pruning. Practice for these techniques is provided at the end of the chapter.

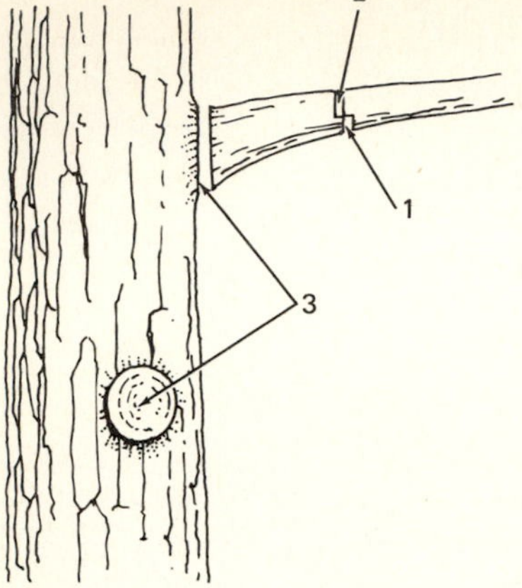

Figure 4-12 Correct pruning technique to preserve callus collar: (1) Undercut. (2) Upper cut to remove branch. (3) Branch stub cut flush with callus collar. Cambial cells gradually will grow over wound. Drawing adapted from an illustration by Dave Carroll in *Rx for Wounded Trees,* USDA Forest Service, p. 9.

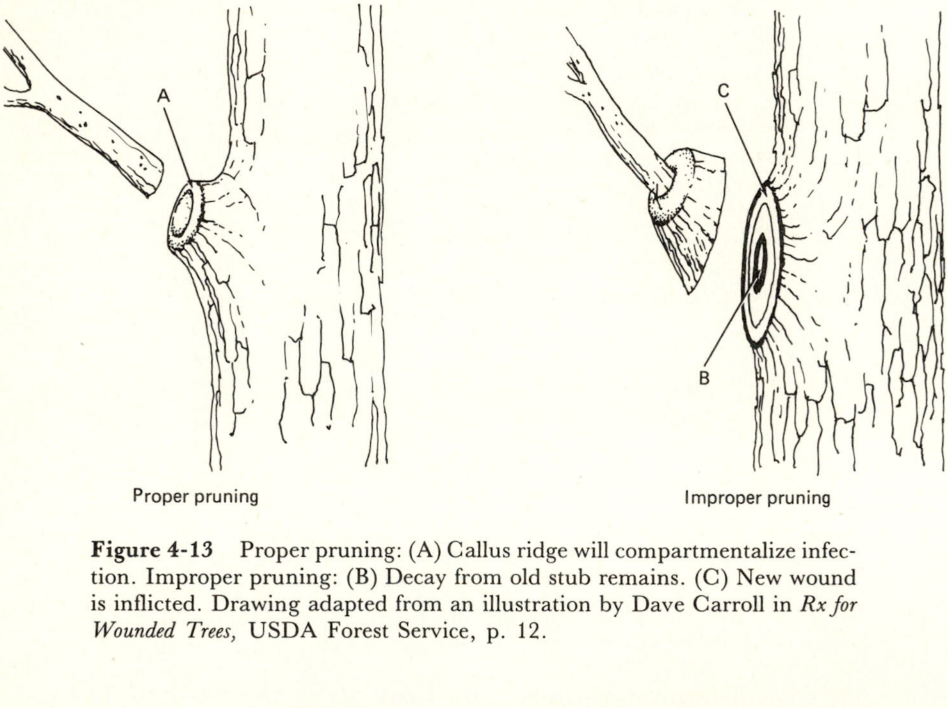

Figure 4-13 Proper pruning: (A) Callus ridge will compartmentalize infection. Improper pruning: (B) Decay from old stub remains. (C) New wound is inflicted. Drawing adapted from an illustration by Dave Carroll in *Rx for Wounded Trees,* USDA Forest Service, p. 12.

1. To Shorten a Shoot.

Tools. Trimming shears (Fig. 4-4) or small household scissors.

How to Prune. A shoot is the youngest woody growth on a tree. It is usually rather straight and thin, with a number of buds and leaves. Shoots in winter are shown in Fig. 2-2. Cut the shoot at a slant slightly beyond a bud. Make the cut fairly close to the bud, but not so near that the bud is damaged nor so far that an unslightly stub remains. A small stub about ⅛ inch long is satisfactory.

2. To Remove a Branch from the Trunk.

Tools. Hand pruners (Fig. 4–2), Japanese shears (Fig. 4–3), or a small saw.

How to Prune. When using hand pruners, place the sharp cutting blade alongside the wood that will remain after the cut. During pruning, only the section that is removed comes in contact with, and is compressed by, the heavy, blunt blade of the shears. Because the two cutting blades of the Japanese shears are identical and cross each other, either one is placed next to the wood that is to remain.

If the branch to be cut has a callus collar at its base, make the cut flush with the surface of the callus formation, as shown in Fig. 4–12. To remove a dead branch (Fig. 4–13), cut it back carefully to the collar. On large cuts, the wood inside the collar may be hollowed out to form a slight depression. If this is done, take care not to cut or damage the collar.

3. To Shorten the Trunk.

Tools. Hand pruners, Japanese shears, or branch nippers.

How to Prune. This cut, in principle, is similar to pruning a shoot except the shoot has now become a large trunk and the buds have grown into branches. To remove an upper section of the trunk, make the cut at a slant, as shown in Fig. 4–14.1. This will form a transition between the original trunk and the replacement branch, which becomes the new top, as seen in Fig. 4–14.2. On a small trunk, branch nippers may be used. On larger trunks, a flat cut may be hollowed to a slightly concave surface with a chisel. Nippers are especially useful when the trunk and replacement branch are both growing in an upward direction and form a close angle at their juncture.

Figure 4-14.1 Shortening a young trunk.

Figure 4-14.2 The nearest branch becomes the continuation of the trunk.

4. To Shorten a Branch.

Tools. Hand pruners, Japanese shears, or nippers.

How to Prune. Whenever possible, prune a branch at the fork of another branch or shoot, preferably where the cut will not be seen from the front view. If no callus collar is present, make a clean, sharp cut flush with the remaining wood. Otherwise, cut directly above the edge of the callus collar.

5. To Eliminate Unwanted Branches. Branches that do not conform to a pleasing bonsai pattern because of their size or location are pruned whenever and as soon as they are found. It is helpful to detect and remove such branches as shown in Figs. 3-8.1 through 3-8.7. They are the only branches that may be pruned with certainty before the composition and shape of the bonsai are determined. Their removal provides a clearer view of the remaining trunk-branch structure.

Tools. Sharp pointed shears, nippers, hand pruners, or a saw.

How to Prune. Take care to avoid cutting the callus collar, if present, or nicking the bark. With these precautions, cuts are made flush with the remaining wood.

TIMING

Winter Pruning: Old Wood

Late winter, shortly before spring, is the preferred time for pruning growth formed in earlier years. Timing is important. Do not rely on the calendar. The annual transition from winter to spring fluctuates from year to year. Look outdoors for signs that plants in the ground are resuming growth. In southeastern Pennsylvania, for example, willow trees in the landscape change from brown to yellow before their leaves appear; the pointed leaves of skunk cabbage break through the snow; crocuses and snowdrops flower. They signal that winter is ending and spring will soon arrive.

This is the time for late winter and early spring pruning. In spring, bonsai experience their most vigorous growth and adjust easily to changes in their size and structure. Start work with deciduous trees when their buds begin to swell. They are the first to break winter dormancy and will resume growth in a few weeks as they slip into spring. Delay pruning conifers and other evergreens until warmer weather, because these trees are slower to return to active growth.

Deciduous Bonsai. For deciduous bonsai, late winter is an ideal time for:

1. Shaping or restyling a bonsai.
2. Removing unwanted or damaged branches.
3. Trimming last summer's shoots, which were left undisturbed in the fall.
4. Grooming the bonsai for spring.

Early Spring: Old Wood and New Shoots

Old Wood. Old wood can be pruned in the spring. However, as new buds open, take care to avoid damaging tender new leaves on the remaining branches.

New Shoots.

Deciduous trees and broad-leaved evergreens. Pinch back the tip of each new shoot after three to six leaves have formed. Use fingers or small, pointed shears. Always retain several nodes with leaves where buds will develop for the next round of growth.

Coniferous evergreens. To trim the new growth of needle evergreens, except pines, pinch back the cluster of emerging needles as each bud opens. Remove about half of the needle cluster. The size of the remaining portion determines the length of the new shoot. Where a long shoot is wanted, take only a small section of the cluster. Do this as the clusters open or a few days later when the needles have separated slightly. New needle clusters on a yew, *Taxus* sp., before and after pinching are shown in Figs. 4–15.1 and 4–15.2. Among spruce and other needle conifers in this group, buds do not form if the new shoots have already hardened.

To pinch the needles, hold the bottom of the emerging bud tightly with one hand and twist the top section with the fingers of the other hand. Squeezing the bottom of the clump between the fingers will spread the needles apart and make them more accessible. Not all the needle clusters emerge at the same time on a tree or a bonsai. A week or two may elapse between the time the first and the last cluster opens. Continue to pinch the needle clusters until the last bud has opened.

Figure 4-15.1 Clusters of new needles emerge on the tip of last year's shoots.

Figure 4-15.2 New needles remain after a portion of each cluster was removed.

Figure 4-16 A pine bud at the tip of the branch elongated into a candle.

Pines. As pine buds begin to grow, they extend into "candles" (Fig. 4–16) before the needles form. It is easy to pinch the candle. Hold the lower end with one hand and remove a portion of the upper part with a snappy twist, or cut it with small shears. To eliminate an unwanted shoot, remove the entire candle or break off unwanted buds before they develop into candles.

As needles lengthen and the candles become shoots shorten the shoots, by pinching or trimming them with shears. Do this before the stems become hard. Take care to avoid cutting across the needles when shortening a shoot. Retain some needles on each shoot.

Late Spring and Summer: Old Wood and New Growth

Old Wood. The preferred time for extensive pruning of old growth has now passed. When a bonsai is extensively pruned in summer, protect it for several weeks from the drying effects of wind and sun.

New Growth.

Deciduous and broad-leaved evergreens: Soft Shoots. Scattered soft shoots will continue to appear throughout the growing season. Trim or pinch them as in early spring.

Shoots That Have Hardened. Cut back overly long shoots with hard stems. Make the cut immediately beyond the bud selected as a replacement shoot.

Conifers Other Than Needle Evergreens. Junipers, arborvitae, chamaecyparis, and similar conifers are in this group. They are the last to resume growth in the spring. The new shoots, light in color, are easily distinguished from the darker foliage of previous years.

Soft Growth. To remove the tender new growth, hold it with one hand where it emerges from the older foliage and pluck or pinch off the outer portion. Do this by hand. Cutting the overlapping cordlike foliage of these species with shears causes browning along the area of the cut.

New Growth That Has Hardened. As the new growth develops and matures, in many of these evergreen species it forms attractive fanlike whorls. To shorten the foliage, make the pruning cut at a fork in the whorls. Awl-shaped foliage, found on many junipers, is soft while it is young, but as it matures it forms points on each tip that are sharp to the touch. Cut the stem of mature shoots carefully between the awl-shaped pointed foliage.

Fall: Cessation of Pruning

As the growing season ends, the tree distributes food manufactured by the leaves during spring and summer to all parts of the tree, including the trunk, branches, buds, and roots, where it is stored until the following spring. It is the source of energy for the tree's new growth in spring and the only source of energy for deciduous trees until next year's leaves are capable of photosynthesis. For this reason, do not prune bonsai in the fall. Pruning a full-size tree in the ground at this time robs it of needed food stored for the winter and spring. This affects a bonsai even more. Prune bonsai in the fall only to remove dead or damaged branches.

PRACTICE AND REVIEW

These exercises provide experience in bonsai pruning techniques. Use expendable material. Substitute cut branches for bonsai plant material to be pruned and shaped into bonsai forms.

Materials: Use any one or more of the basic pruning tools described in this chapter, including hand pruners, Japanese pruning shears, nippers, or scissors, and a turntable, if available.

Select evergreen or deciduous branches 12 to 18 inches long and approximately ¼ to ⅜ inch thick, preferably from trees and shrubs with short internodes and small leaves. Look for branches with shoots distributed around all sides as opposed to a flat linear pattern of shoots only on two sides. Provide a support to hold the branches in an upright position, such as a large wooden carpenter's clamp or other device, so that both hands will be free to work on the material. A concrete block about 3 inches deep and 3 inches wide with a hole in the center (Fig. 4–17.1) is handy for pruning and wiring practice. It can easily be made with prepackaged concrete mix. For a mold, use a small milk carton cut to size or a plastic flowerpot with a covering over the bottom holes. When the concrete is slightly set, but before it hardens, insert a round pencil or dowel straight down into the form to make a hole 1½ to 2 inches deep and ¼ to ⅜ inch wide. Remove the dowel before the mix hardens. The block is ready to use after it is cured for a few days.

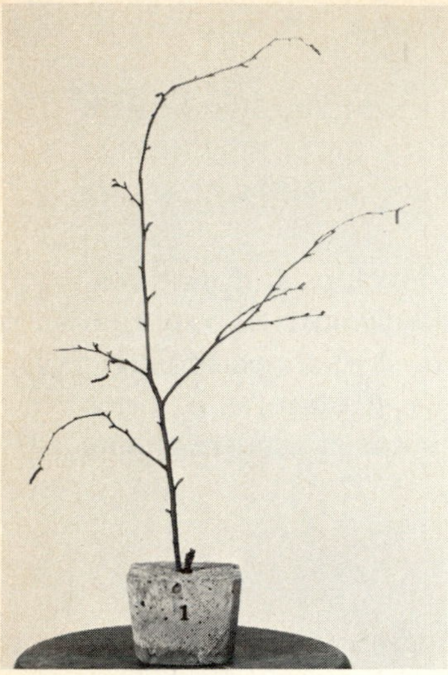

Figure 4-17.1 A branch for practice pruning wedged tightly in a concrete holder.

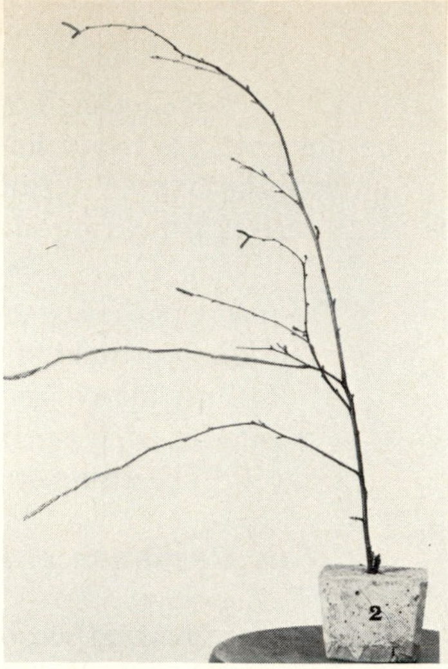

Figure 4-17.2 View from the left side.

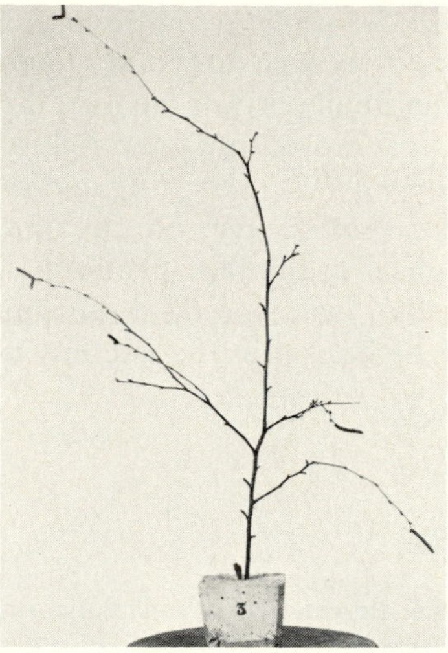

Figure 4-17.3 View from the rear.

Figure 4-17.4 View from the right side.

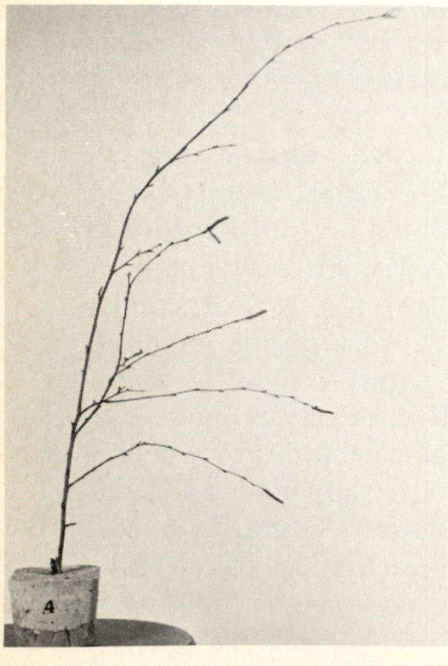

Figure 4-17.5 The view in Fig. 4-17.3 was selected as the front and the branch pruned to a small tree-like form.

How to Shape Material to a Bonsai Form by Pruning

1. Place the selected branch securely in its concrete holder, as shown in Fig. 4-17.1. If the branch wobbles, stabilize it with a wedge.

2. Examine the branch from all sides as seen in Figs. 4-17.2, 4-17.3, and 4-17.4. Consider the branch a trunk and remove nonconforming shoots and branchlets that may be present. (If necessary, review the list of unwanted branches in Chapter 3.)

3. When the branch is cleared of unwanted growth and opened to view, select a pleasing trunk line; you will probably find several. Check the location of the bottom branches in relation to each possible trunk line. From the available choices, select the view that provides the best combination of a pleasing trunk and strong, well-placed bottom branches. In the illustrations, Fig. 4-17.3 was chosen as the front view.

4. Prune the trunk and branches to a treelike shape. First, shorten the major branches (make each pruning cut slightly beyond a bud) and remove any remaining unwanted branches on the trunk. Project the height of the finished bonsai in relation to the length of the branches. The trunk should be taller than the combined span of the longest branches on either side of the trunk. Finally, shorten the trunk to a bud, a small shoot, or a branch that will continue the upward growth of the trunk. Make the cut at a slant as shown in Fig. 4-17.5.

Inspect the bonsai. Were any of the cuts made in the fork of another branch? If so, are they at a location that is not seen from the front? At any juncture of the trunk and branch, is the branch thicker than the trunk? If it is, remove the branch unless it is vital to the shape of the bonsai.

Consider how pruning can change an ordinary branch into a little treelike bonsai. Finding the potential ''little tree'' for bonsai—its trunk line and a few major branches—is the first and major step in creating a bonsai. Repeat this exercise several times to train the ''inner eye'' in discovering a bonsai shape in undefined plant material.

Pruning Larger Plant Material

To develop further skills in pruning, locate and obtain permission, if necessary, to prune trees, shrubs, and/or vines growing in the ground. Look for material that either needs pruning or is in the path of a bulldozer or a construction project.

Use garden hand pruners or, for lighter cuts, Japanese-type bonsai shears or branch nippers to shorten branches, remove a branch from the trunk or from another branch, and eliminate unwanted branches. Work carefully and prune slowly. Before making a cut, check to see if a callus collar is present. If so, do not cut into it.

Based on the information in this chapter, how large a diameter will each tool cut easily and without being forced? Is the maximum cut the same for all species? If garden hand pruners are used, which blade is placed nearest the wood that will remain? Do you prefer a particular tool for certain cuts? If so, explain. After pruning, clean each tool as described in the text and store it in a damp-free place until needed.

ADDITIONAL READING

DR. ALEX L. SHIGO, chief plant pathologist at the Forest Service's Northeastern Station, and his colleagues have done pioneer scientific work that provides new knowledge on tree decay and the effect of pruning cuts. Their findings are of benefit to bonsai as well as normal-size trees; a few titles are listed below.

SHIGO, ALEX L., *Tree Decay: An Expanded Concept*, Agriculture Information Bulletin No. 419, Forest Service, USDA. Washington, D.C.: Superintendent of Documents, 1979.

SHIGO, ALEX L., AND CHARLES L. WILSON, "Wound Dressings on Red Maple and American Elm: Effectiveness After Five Years," *Journal of Arboriculture*, 3, no. 5 (May 1977).

SHIGO, ALEX L., AND OTHERS, *Internal Defects Associated with Pruned and Nonpruned Branch Stubs in Black Walnut*. Forest Service Research Paper NE-440, Forest Service, USDA. Broomall, Pa.: Northeastern Forest Experiment Station, 1979.

SHORTLE, WALTER C., "Tree Care: A New Look, 1979," *Journal of Arboriculture*, 5, no. 12 (December 1979). Presented at the annual meeting of the Penn-Del Chapter, International Society of Arboriculture in King of Prussia, Pa., February 1979.

5

Wiring

PURPOSE

Wiring a bonsai, in principle, is similar to placing orthodontic braces on teeth. It offers the bonsai grower considerable control over positioning a trunk or branch to affect the final shape of the tree. The technique is widely used in the refinement and shaping of the magnificent bonsai of Japan. It consists of wrapping malleable wire around a section of the bonsai and bending it permanently to another position. After a period of time, the wired wood becomes set, and the wire, no longer needed, is removed. Hands-on wiring and the simulation of a bonsai in the Practice and Review section are an essential and integral part of this chapter.

Methods Used Before Wiring

Wiring is relatively new to bonsai. It came into use during the latter part of the nineteenth century and is far more precise than earlier training methods of repositioning branches with sticks or ties. Even today, however, bonsai growers may reposition a branch by tying it to a fixed location, such as the trunk or the bonsai container (Fig. 5–1), until it becomes set in its new position. Or weights, such as lead sinkers or stones wrapped in string, may be hung on a branch to lower it. Twine and weights continue in limited use, particularly where a change is a simple matter of one direction—up or down, right or left. By contrast, a wired branch can be moved in several directions, elevations, and angles along its entire length.

Figure 5-1 Branches on an ancient pine (rear view) held in a lower position by wire. Japanese white pine, *Pinus parviflora,* at the U.S. National Arboretum.

Tools

Strong, sturdy tools are needed to cut wire. Never use the thin-edged blades of pruning shears or ordinary scissors. Household pliers, on the other hand, make convenient and satisfactory wire cutters. Japanese tools include small, heavy, scissorlike cutters for thin wire and a special long-handled wire cutter with hard, strong cutting blades at the tip for heavy wire. Both tools (Fig. 4–7) greatly facilitate removing wire wrapped around a bonsai.

Copper and Aluminum Wire

Both copper and aluminum wire are malleable, easy to apply, reusable, not disfiguring, and sufficiently rigid to hold a wired trunk or branch in the desired position. Contact with the metal does not harm the bonsai. Pliable steel wire is usable but rarely seen on fine bonsai because it rusts.

Copper wire is stronger than aluminum wire of equal thickness. As it ages, its original bright shining color turns a soft brown, which blends with the tree. The thickness of copper wire is specified by gauge. The smaller the gauge number, the thicker the wire. The thickest wire generally used for bonsai starts with #6 or #8 gauge and the thinnest is #22 or #24. Aluminum wire is measured not in gauges but in millimeters. As an aid in identifying wire sizes, Table 5–1 lists copper wire by gauge and millimeters and aluminum wire by millimeters. The table indicates, for example, that #12 gauge copper wire is the same diameter as 2.0 mm aluminum wire. When switching from either copper or aluminum

TABLE 5-1 DIAMETERS OF COPPER AND ALUMINUM WIRE

Copper		*Aluminum*	*Millimeter Size*
Gauge	*mm*	*mm*	
		6.0	
		5.0	
#6	4.1		
		4.0	
#7	3.65		
		3.5	
#8	3.25		
		3.0	
#9	2.9		
#10	2.6		
		2.5	
#11	2.3		
#12	2.0	2.0	
#13	1.8		
#14	1.6		
#15	1.5	1.5	
#16	1.3		
#17	1.1		
#18	1.0	1.0	
#19	0.9		
#20	0.8		
#21	0.7		
#22	0.65		

wire to the other, do not match their sizes exactly but allow for a larger diameter of aluminum wire. For instance, aluminum wire of 3.0 mm rather than 2.0 mm is the working equivalent of #12 gauge copper wire. Actual sizes of a cross section and a short length of aluminum wire 1 through 6 mm are shown in the right hand column of the table.

With the thin, strong copper wire it is possible to obtain precise, complicated arrangements of branches and twigs for delicate or sophisticated effects. While the thicker and softer aluminum wire is less suited to intricate manipulation, many bonsai enthusiasts feel that aluminum wire results in a more natural look for bonsai.

Annealing. Heat is applied to make thick copper wire (#14, #12, or heavier) more pliable. The process is called annealing. Annealed wire prepared for industrial use is sometimes available, or the wire may be annealed at home. A temperature range between approximately 850° and 925°F. is critical.[1] A fire that is not sufficiently hot will not soften the metal, while too high a temperature (such as that produced by a coal fire) will cause the wire to become brittle and break when it is bent. A fire of paper and light wood provides the proper amount of heat. One method of preparing the wire is to coil it into six or eight loops, 8 to 12 inches in diameter. Place the loops on a wood fire that is burning steadily. When the copper emits a glow, it is sufficiently heated. Remove it from the fire and allow it to cool. (If the copper fails to glow, heat the loops over a hotter fire.) Small quantities of wire are sometimes annealed on top of a kitchen range.

Annealed wire retains its pliability until it is bent or flexed, which causes it to harden. The soft wire is easy to wrap around a branch or trunk, and in the process it regains its original hardness. Copper wire may be repeatedly annealed and reused.

For most bonsai, copper wire requires no preparation other than annealing the thick, heavy strands. However, for maples, *Acer* spp., azaleas, *Rhododendron* spp., and other species with thin bark, wrap copper wire in paper or floral tape before applying to lessen the chance of damaging the bark. Cut soft tissue paper or similar material in long strips about one-half inch wide and wind the strips in spirals around the wire. Tape the paper at either end to hold it in place.

Aluminum wire is a more recent introduction to bonsai. Although similar to copper in many ways, aluminum wire is softer and does not need annealing or paper wrappings. Copper wire continues to be preferred where thinness and strength are wanted. Aluminum wire is desirable for species with especially tender bark and for its ease of handling. Aluminum wire packaged for bonsai is coated with a thin layer of copper or is anodized to a brown color to resemble copper. The coating has no purpose except to make the wire more attractive. The most used widths of aluminum wire, measured in millimeters, are from 1.0 to 6.0.

To reuse strands of copper and aluminum wire removed from a bonsai, hold the wire taut and pull it back and forth against a stationary pipe or other hard rounded edge to straighten the loops. Heavy strands of copper wire may need to be annealed again.

Wire Sources. Wire suitable for bonsai is available in large quantities from copper or aluminum wholesalers. Hardware, craft, and bonsai shops supply smaller quantities. It is sometimes possible to obtain scrap wire left from electrical wiring installations. First remove the insulation by stripping or burning, then handle the wire as other copper wire of the same size.

TECHNIQUES

Apply wire from the front, side, or back of a bonsai, whichever is convenient, but place it in a manner that looks good from the front view. Keep both hands

[1]Masakuni Kawasumi, *Bonsai with American Trees* (Tokyo, New York, and San Francisco: Kodansha International Ltd., 1975), p. 74.

close to the trunk or branch being wired. Hold the section to be wired and guide the wire with one hand while coiling the wire onto the surface of the bonsai with the other hand. Direct the pressure caused by bending the wire to the hand and fingers rather than letting the wire exert pressure against the bark.

This is the wiring sequence that most growers find effective: Wire the trunk first, branches next, and twigs last. Wire a bonsai from the bottom upward and the interior outward. Apply the heavier wire before the lighter wire. Where more than one strand of wire will be needed on the same part of the bonsai, use the heaviest wire first, followed by successively thinner wire. Keep all additional wire parallel and close to the first wire. Coil the wire directly on the surface of the branch or trunk without pressing leaves, needles, or small shoots beneath the spiral.

Wrap the wire as tightly as possible without bruising or pressing into the bark. Loosely applied wire with space between the wire and trunk is unsatisfactory because it has little holding power. Use the following method to feel the amount of pressure required: Apply a piece of malleable wire in spirals ¼ inch apart around one of your fingers. If the wire presses into the finger, it is too tight; wire that is not in contact with the finger is too loose. Properly applied wire touches the finger along its entire length without causing indentations.

Try to keep the spirals evenly spaced for a pleasing appearance and uniform pressure. At times, it may be necessary to modify the spacing. This occurs, for instance, when branches or shoots are in the direct path of the approaching wire. If this happens, adjust the span of the spiral to pass under, above, or around the obstacle, rather than to pass over it, as illustrated in Fig. 5–2.

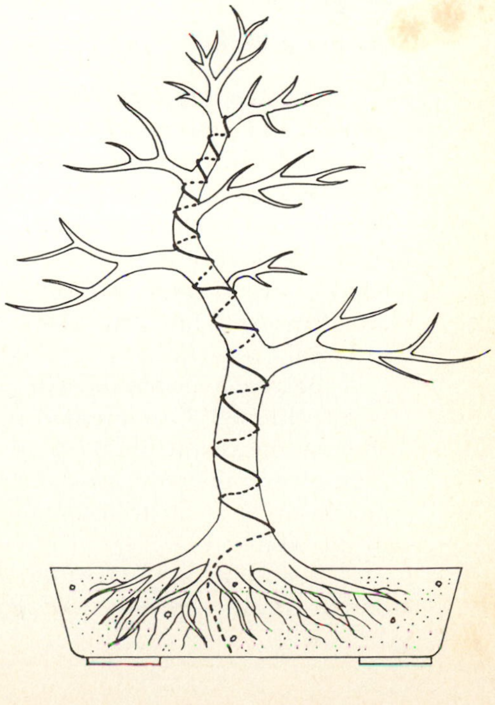

Figure 5-2 Wire is spiraled at a 45-degree angle to the axis of the trunk.

Clockwise or Counterclockwise. It often makes little difference whether the wire is applied to a trunk or branch in a clockwise or counterclockwise direction. However, when a wired section is to be twisted either clockwise or counterclockwise, wind the spirals in the same direction. This will strengthen the grip exerted by the wire as it is twisted. On the other hand, if a wired trunk, for example, is turned in an opposite direction to the spiral of the wire, the spirals become loose and unwound. As a result, their effectiveness is destroyed.

The Role of the Cambium

When wiring a bonsai, take special care to protect the cambium layer beneath the bark because it is the life center of the tree. As indicated in Chapter 4, when a tree is wounded, cells from the cambium expand to seal off the wound and prevent the spread of decay-causing organisms. In addition, this thin cambial layer, only a single cell thick (Fig. 4–8), is the material that forms the tree's wood, bark, and food conduits. As the cambium cells harden, the wired section of the bonsai becomes fixed in its new position.

At the start of the growing season, the cambium cells begin dividing to add rows of wood cells to the sapwood on one side and additional cells to the inner bark on the other side. The formation of new wood each year by the cambial cells occurs not only on the trunk but on all branches and shoots that are covered with bark. (They are seen in the annual rings on a cross section of a tree.) These new wood cells become part of the hard inner structure of the tree. During the hardening of the sapwood, especially in fall and winter, a wired branch or trunk becomes set in its new position.

Wiring a Trunk

The first step is to select wire of adequate length and thickness for the job. The length can be estimated at 1½ times the linear distance to be wired. The thickness of the wire is more difficult to determine. It varies according to the stiffness, as well as the diameter, of the wood. Sometimes this can only be found by trial and error. Use wire that is not considerably longer or thicker than required to do the job. For beginners working with young, supple plant material, copper wire of gauge #18 or #16 and aluminum wire of 1.0 or 1.5 mm should be adequate. Thin wire aids in learning wiring techniques because it is easy to handle.

Be sure to fasten the wire securely to keep it from slipping when the trunk is repositioned. One method is to bend the end of the wire and insert it into the potting mix at the back of the trunk. This does not hurt the root system. However, if the wire slips and is loose as it is wound on the trunk, remove it and insert it again to a greater depth until the bottom section is tightly held in the soil.

Beginning at the bottom of the trunk, wrap the wire around and upward on the trunk in spirals at an angle of 45 degrees. Keep the spirals angled and about ⅜ inch apart, as shown in Fig. 5–2. If the wire is wrapped in a flat, horizontal circular pattern instead of at an angle, the effect of a coiled wire spring is created. Such coils have no holding power and, when moved, spring back to their former position.

Continue the wire as far upward as the trunk is to be repositioned, provided the wood remains hard. If the top of the trunk is thin and requires wiring, change to a lighter wire. Anchor it first by running the wire for 3 or 4 inches closely parallel to the spirals of the larger wire. When the wiring is complete, it is not necessary to make a hook or bend of any kind to hold the end in place. If the wire is longer than needed, simply cut the extra length flush with the trunk.

When thick, annealed wire is required, determine the path of the wire beforehand in order to place it on the outside of proposed bends and around, instead of over, obstacles. Unlike thin wire, which is easily removed and reused, heavy annealed wire becomes hard and rigid as it is applied, and it is not readily usable for another try.

Bending the Wired Section

The sequence of steps in wiring and repositioning a section of the tree varies according to the flexibility of the wood and the preference of the bonsai grower. When the new position of a thin branch is determined, it is possible to move and hold it to that position as it is wired. Alternately, a heavier branch is often wired first and then repositioned. With a trunk, first determine the location and direction of any planned bend or curve before applying the wire. As an aid to reaching a decision before wiring, tentatively move the trunk or branch to this or that position, then choose the most pleasing arrangement. Once the trunk or branch is wired, carefully move it to the predetermined location and stop; moving it around to alternate positions will seriously damage the cambium cells wherever the wire exerts strong pressure through the bark. A bend in one direction only has a limited effect on the cambium. However, bending a wired section first one way and then another bruises and may destroy the cambium in many places.

To bend the trunk or branch, start at the thickest section, work outward, and slowly inch along. If a branch occurs where the trunk is to be bent, make sure the wire is placed immediately above and below the branch, as shown in Fig. 5–3. Hold the trunk tightly and bend it with a slow, steady pressure. Do not force the wood beyond the limit of its flexibility. This varies among species. Azaleas and maples are quite brittle, whereas junipers and pines are among the most pliable species. If the wood does not bend readily, make only a partial bend and bend further at intervals of two or three weeks.

If the bending is not successful because the wire is too thin to exert sufficient pressure, add another wire or rewire the trunk with a heavier wire.

To make a trunk more flexible prior to wiring, move it back and forth, as in a limbering-up exercise. This is helpful on wood known to snap easily when

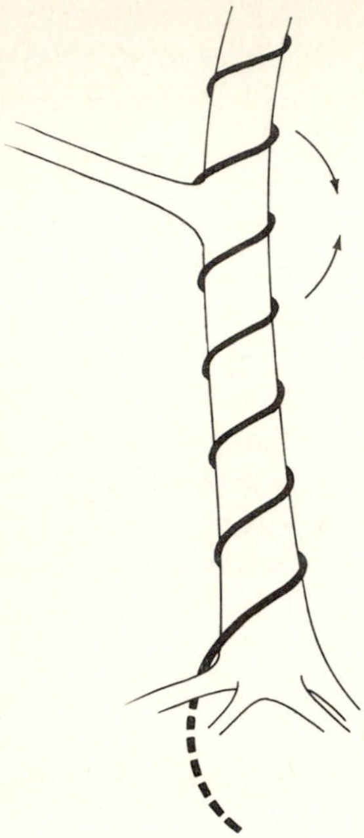

Figure 5-3 When bending a trunk, the branches are kept on the outside of the bend.

bent. The flexibility in most species also may be increased by withholding water for a few days prior to wiring. A reduction in the amount of moisture in the woody tissues causes the cells to shrink and become less turgid. The bonsai begins to wilt in the same way as flowers in a vase without water. In this condition the wood is far more pliable and easier to bend. Partial dehydration prior to wiring is recommended where considerable bending is anticipated or whenever species with notably stiff wood are to be wired.

Removing the Wire. After a bonsai is wired, inspect it several times a month to check for signs of the wire pressing into the bark. This is noticeable when the bark begins to swell slightly beneath the wire. If this occurs, remove the wire immediately. Where wire is allowed to become embedded, cambium cells are damaged, the surface of the bonsai is disfigured, and the wire is hard to remove.

In cold climates, wire that is not pressing into the bark may safely be left on the bonsai until early spring. By then, sapwood formed during the previous summer has hardened, and the repositioning of the bonsai has become fixed. In warm climates where dormancy is not complete, new growth hardens most during the tree's period of rest, or partial dormancy. The rest cycle can be recognized by the absence of new shoots or new foliage.

When it is time to remove the wire, if it is thin and flexible, simply unwind it by hand. When a length is freed, cut it with pliers or wad it into a small ball and continue unwinding. Use the special wire cutters with strong cutting blades previously described for heavy, stiff wire that is difficult to lift off manually without damaging the bark. Cut the wire into short lengths starting at the top or bottom of the trunk. By dividing every spiral into several small pieces, each piece is readily removed or falls free of its own accord. After removing the wire, if the new position is not yet set, rewire the same trunk or branch along a course slightly above or below the previous wire.

Wiring a Branch

Wire a branch on the lower part of the trunk in the same manner as the trunk. After securing the wire by inserting one end into the potting mix at the rear of the trunk, spiral it upward on the trunk and onto the branch. If wire is already on the trunk, keep the second wire closely parallel to the first. If it is necessary to cross the second wire over the first, make the crossover at the rear of the trunk where it will not be seen.

The wire must touch the trunk lightly at all times. When the branch is reached, coil the wire around the fork of the trunk and onto the branch without lifting it from the bark. It is not an acceptable practice to span the wire through the air when moving it from one part of the bonsai to another.

To bend a branch downward, place the wire over the top of the branch at its juncture with the trunk. If the branch is to be raised, bring the wire beneath the branch. On each branch, continue the wire outward beyond the section to be changed.

Wiring Two Branches. Two branches on the same trunk can be wired with one piece of wire if they are far enough apart for five or six spirals of wire to be wound on the trunk between them. As shown in Figs. 5-4.1 through 5-4.4, place a length of wire midway on the trunk between the two branches. Spiral one section upward and out along the upper branch (Fig. 5-4.2) and the other

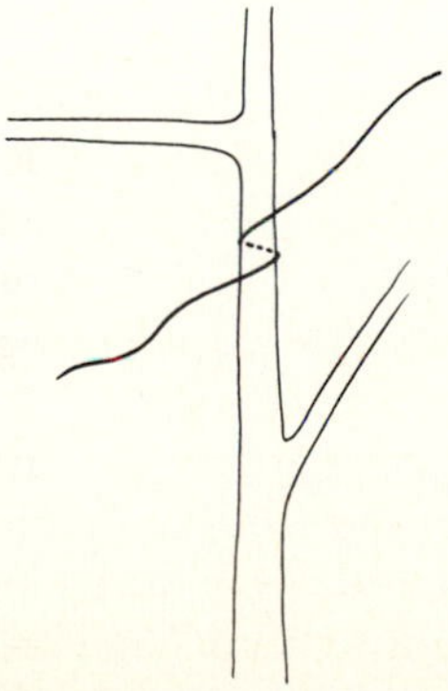

Figure 5-4.1 Wire is started midway between the two branches to be wired.

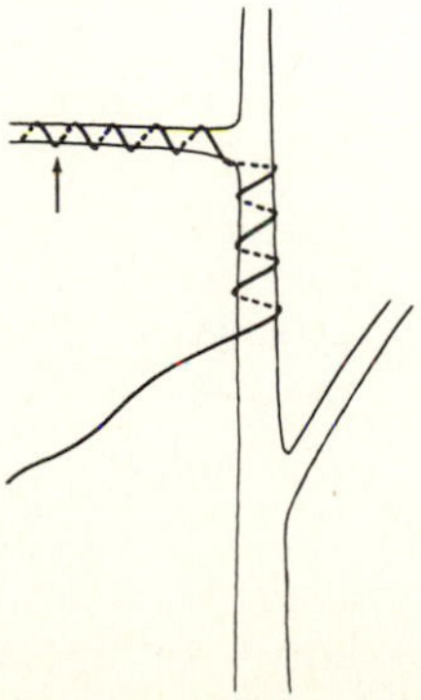

Figure 5-4.2 Wire is placed along the underside of the left branch, which will be moved upward.

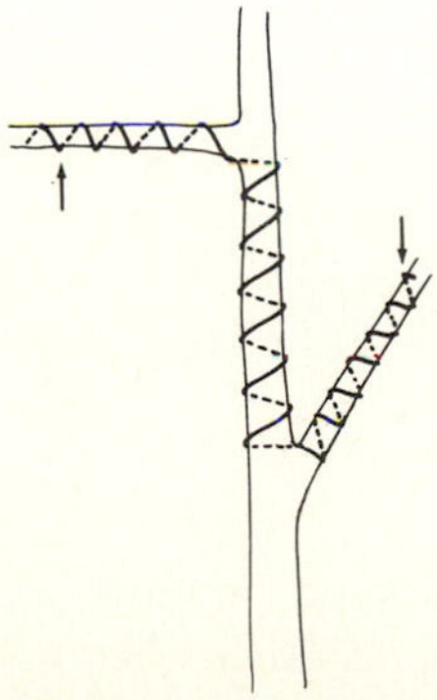

Figure 5-4.3 At the juncture of the lower branch, wire is placed on the top side of the branch, which will be lowered.

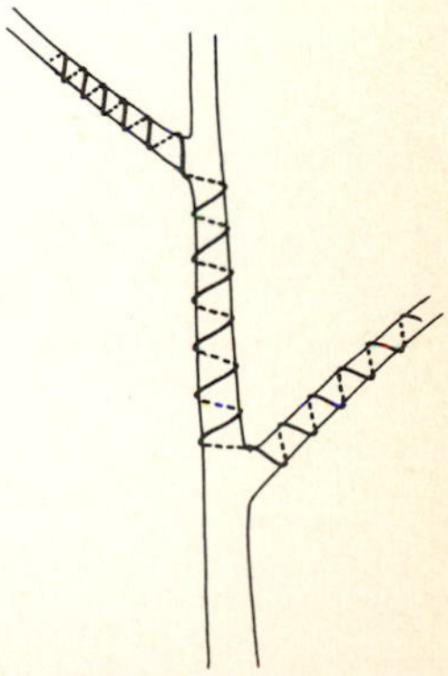

Figure 5-4.4 The top branch is moved upward, the bottom one downward.

(Fig. 5–4.3) downward on the trunk and onto the lower branch. Then reposition the two branches (Fig. 5–4.4).

This method proves most effective when the fork of one branch is at right angles on the trunk. Wire this branch first; the 90-degree change in direction will lock the wire in position. By contrast, where the two branches are opposite each other or separated by only a short distance on the trunk, a single piece of wire produces a seesaw effect. In such instances, it is necessary to wire each branch independently.

Crossing the Wire in a Loop. As an alternative to anchoring one end of the wire in the soil, a strand of wire may be fastened securely in a loop formation by wrapping the wire completely around the trunk so that it crosses itself, as shown in Fig. 5–5. Place one end of the wire on the back of the trunk, pointing in the direction to be wired, and hold it firmly. Continue the wire around the trunk until it crosses itself as it arrives at the starting point. Then hold the loop securely with one hand and spiral the wire upward around the trunk. After five or six spirals, the loop and spirals will be firmly positioned on the trunk, and the wire can be used to bend the upper trunk.

A method of wiring a branch starting with a loop on the trunk is shown in Fig. 5–6. With this handy technique, the wire may be fastened in a loop and used directly where it is needed.

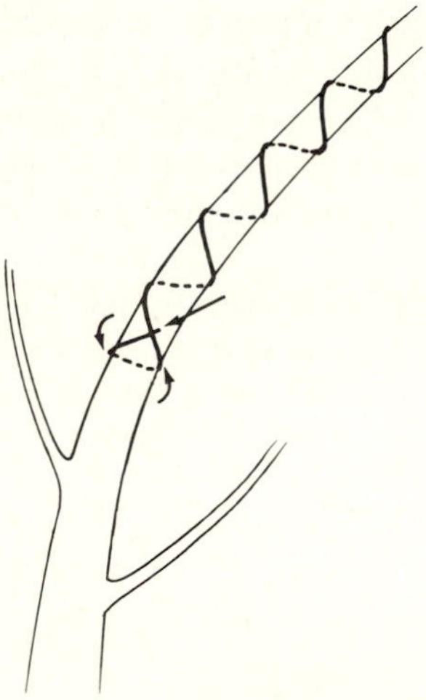

Figure 5-5 Wire secured in a loop formation on the trunk.

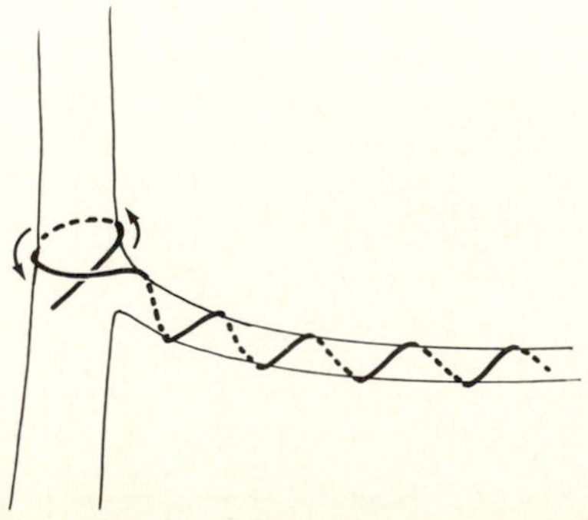

Figure 5-6 Wire fastened in a loop on the trunk, then wound along a branch.

TIMING

Early spring, before buds open, is an advantageous time for wiring deciduous trees. Their bare branches make them more accessible during this season than at other times. And the section of trunk and branch that is repositioned will have the benefit of an entire growing season to produce new shoots and foliage in the area chosen by the bonsai grower. Remove the wire the following winter or early spring unless it becomes embedded. In that event, remove it immediately and apply new wire, if needed. When rewiring, avoid placing the new wire on the same surface as the previous wire.

Generally, a bonsai can be wired at nearly any time. The few exceptions are a brief period in spring when the newly emerging soft growth would be easily damaged, later in the season when a bonsai is in flower, in autumn when fruit is hanging on the tree, and during cold winter weather when the wood has become brittle.

Other times to avoid wiring are periods following heavy rains or excessive watering when the tree's turgid cells make the trunk and branches prone to snap if they are bent.

PRACTICE AND REVIEW

Repeated practice of the first few exercises helps to develop proficiency and skill in wiring. A mastery of wiring techniques for bonsai is comparable to the skills and dexterity required in other art forms. If necessary, review the information given in this chapter on the selection of wire as to its width and length, methods of fastening wire, correct techniques of application, and the subsequent bending of the trunk and branch. Use the concrete branch holder in the pruning exercises in Chapter 4, or a similar support, in these practice exercises.

Lessons in Wiring Techniques

Select flexible branches approximately 18 inches long and ¼ inch thick from several species and a strand of wire for each branch. Tools needed are pruning shears and pliers or a bonsai wire cutter.

To prepare the branch for wiring, remove all growth within 4 or 5 inches of the bottom. This includes leaves, shoots, twigs, and dead wood. If necessary, thin dense growth occurring higher on the branch to clear space for the wire. Choose a front view and do all the work with this view in mind.

When the branch is ready to be wired, wrap one end of the wire around the bottom of the branch and insert the branch and wire in the concrete base as described in the Chapter 4 practice exercises.

1. Wiring a Branch. With the wire and branch fastened securely, wire the branch in spirals as described previously. When finished, evaluate the wiring as follows:

a. Was the wire applied with moderate pressure, thereby preventing it from indenting the bark? Was an even pressure maintained so that no spaces between the wire and the bark were formed by loosely wound spirals?

b. Were all the spirals at a 45-degree angle, evenly spaced, and no more than ½ inch apart?

c. Did the wire avoid pressing foliage or shoots against the bark? If the wire was not completely used, was the surplus cut flush with the branch?

If the answer to each question is yes, the wiring is well done. If any answer is no, repeat the exercise by wiring other branches until the evaluation is affirmative.

2. Bending a Branch. Prepare and wire another branch as described in the first exercise. After the branch is correctly wired, bend a section of the branch to the left; then find another location to bend it to the right.

a. Were both hands used to bend the branch?

b. Is the inside of the bend free of shoots or other branches?

c. Will the branch remain in the position to which it is bent? If not, add a second wire closely parallel to the first. Was the bending successful with the second wire? If the answer is no, consider whether the branch is too thick or the wire too thin to do the job effectively.

When every answer is satisfactory, proceed to the next exercise. Otherwise, repeat the wiring and bending until it is done correctly.

3. Straightening a Branch. Select a branch with one or more curves. Prepare and wire it as described in the first exercise. This time, after the branch is wired correctly, change it to a straight vertical position starting at the bottom and working upward.

a. Were both hands used, with a gentle, even pressure?

b. If the wire was inadequate to hold the branch straight, was a second wire added? Was it alongside and parallel to the first? Did the second wire remain parallel without crossing over the first wire at a point visible from the front?

If all answers are yes, you have acquired the fundamental technique of wiring and may proceed to the next exercises, which are variations of wiring techniques.

4. Wiring Two Smaller Branches. Select a branch with a number of well-developed smaller branches at least 3 or 4 inches apart. Insert the bottom of the branch and wedge it securely in the concrete holder. To facilitate the wiring, remove small or surplus growth on the main stem of the branch. Choose two smaller branches to be wired with the same piece of wire. Plan to move the higher branch upward and bend the lower one slightly downward. After the two branches are wired and repositioned, consider the following questions:

a. Are the two branches 3 or 4 inches apart?

b. Was the wiring applied correctly as evaluated in the previous exercises?

c. Was the wire kept close to the bark at the fork of each smaller branch without creating spaces between the wire and the branches?

d. At the fork of the higher branch, was the wire placed on the underside of the branch? At the fork of the lower branch, was the wire on the top side of the branch?

5. Wiring with a Loop. Select and prepare a branch to be wired and place it firmly in the holder. Plan to wire the middle and upper section of the branch. Cut a piece of wire about two-thirds the length of the branch. Make a wire loop, as described previously, at a location one-third of the way up the trunk. When the loop is fastened securely, continue the wire to the top of the branch. Gently bend the wired trunk where a small branch would be positioned on the outside of the curve; make a similar but less pronounced curve in the opposite direction, higher on the trunk.

Repeat this exercise, if necessary, until wiring, bending, and forming a curved trunk line comes easily. Remember, it is not necessary to have a branch at every curve in the trunk. When a branch is present on a curve, its preferred location is on the outside.

Simulating a Bonsai

This practice exercise combines pruning and wiring techniques to shape a cut branch into a mock-up bonsai with a front view, a bonsai trunk and branch pattern, and a treelike form.

The tools and concrete holder are the same as those used in exercises 1 through 5. However, wire in a wider choice of thickness may be needed here. Give special attention to the selection of a branch. Look for one with the characteristics described for bonsai in Chapter 2. These include short internodes, smaller branches distributed at diverse points around the main stem, and, whenever possible, shoots growing on the small branches. To have branches that are easy to wire and bend, reject species with stiff wood (such as azaleas, *Rhododendron* spp., and boxwood, *Buxus* spp.) and avoid plants with thorns or spikes.

Use expendable material. An excellent source is the branches removed from trees and shrubs in the normal process of pruning. At the start, choose branches about 18 inches or more long and ¼ to ⅜ inch thick. They will be shorter after pruning and shaping. Anchor the branch in a holder, as shown in Fig. 5–7.1. Use a wedge, if necessary, to hold it securely. If for any reason during this practice the tree appears to be unsuitable as it is, look for a usable section higher on the trunk or discard the material and start over with another branch.

Cleanup. Remove any small, dense growth that clutters the trunk. For example, many species of junipers, such as *Juniperus virginiana* shown in the illustrations, tend to produce tiny shoots on the trunk, often in the forks of branches. Eliminate all branches and shoots below the lowest major branches, as in Fig. 5–7.2.

Choosing the Front. Next, examine the trunk from top to bottom and from all directions for a pleasing trunk line and branch placement. In Fig. 5–7.2, the three long bottom branches are too far apart for a bonsai of this size. In this and similar instances, remove the bottom section of the material and work with the upper section shown in Fig. 5–7.3.

Figure 5-7.1 Practice material in its original condition.

Figure 5-7.2 The material partially cleaned of unwanted shoots and branchlets.

Figure 5-7.3 The lower portion of the practice material in Fig. 5-7.2 is discarded and replaced with the upper section.

Figure 5-7.4 The view chosen as the front.

Figure 5-7.5 Superfluous growth is removed; major bottom branches are selected for the simulated bonsai.

Figure 5-7.6 The trunk is shortened; the bottom branches are wired and trimmed.

Figure 5-7.7 The small, treelike form achieved after pruning and wiring.

The taper and harmony of the trunk are other important features to consider. Inspect the trunk from all sides. Follow each possible trunk line without interruption from the bottom to the top. If necessary, use a pointer and mark each view of the trunk line with a piece of chalk. Keep the options of modifying the upper trunk by wiring and using branches to replace the upper portion of the trunk. The view selected as the front in the practice material is shown in Fig. 5–7.4.

Shaping the Material. Remove superfluous growth (Fig. 5–7.5) for better visibility and to select the bottom branches. Next, shorten the trunk, if necessary, to a height more than twice the distance of the lower trunk (measured from the lowest branch to the bottom of the trunk). When shortening the trunk, look for an upward-growing branch on which the pruning cut can be made at the back, where it will not be seen. The branch that replaces the trunk may require wiring to appear as a natural continuation of the trunk. Keep the width of the bonsai less than the height of the tree as measured by the two bottom branches. Consider the branches higher on the trunk. Thin the branches that are clustered closely together and eliminate branches that are thicker than the trunk at the juncture where they meet. In Fig. 5–7.6, the top of the trunk has been pruned, most of the branches shortened, and the major bottom branches wired.

A Treelike Form. To create the suggestion of a treelike shape, project an imaginary arc or oval for deciduous trees and a triangle for needle conifers from the top of the mock-up bonsai to the tip of the longest branches on either side. Shorten branches that extend considerably beyond this periphery. To add a finishing touch, wire and reposition the upper branch to fill large gaps in the tree and adjust all branches to give each one its own territory. This is shown in Fig. 5–7.7.

Additional Practice. Repeat this exercise with different branches as often as possible to acquire a headstart in learning techniques for creating a bonsai. Because this practice does not involve roots, soil, or living trees, it can be done conveniently indoors or out at any season of the year.

ADDITIONAL READING

KAWASUMI, MASAKUNI, *Introductory Bonsai and the Care and Use of Bonsai Tools.* Tokyo and San Francisco: Japan Publications, Inc., 1971. The manufacturer of the famous Masakuni bonsai tools in Japan describes Japanese bonsai techniques and the use of bonsai tools.

———, *Bonsai with American Trees.* Tokyo, New York, and San Francisco: Kodansha International Ltd., 1975. A continuation of *Introductory Bonsai* featuring the author's photos of American trees used for bonsai taken during a visit to the United States. Kawasumi's books are a detailed, outstanding source of information on bonsai tools and their use.

6

Bonsai Container Mixes

The potting mix in a container is home and food for the bonsai's roots. It provides a cupboard of minerals that the tree utilizes for growth and energy. Small open spaces in the mix form conduits for the circulation of air and moisture, while the weight of the mix prevents the tree from being uprooted by the force of strong wind and rains. The mix usually consists of a few, rather than many, materials and is not difficult to prepare. A mix as simple as decomposed rock (which contains organic matter) is satisfactory. It may be used as it is found, or if an excessive amount of organic matter or humus is present, coarse sand may be added.

FUNCTIONS OF THE GROWING MEDIUM

In the past, it was believed that different mixes were required for various species of bonsai. Now, the test of a good mix is not how few but how many species can grow in it. A prepared mix must be used rather than natural soil because soil taken from the ground and placed in a container loses its normal function.

Natural Soil and Potting Mixes

After a rain, the force of gravity pulls water from the surface of the ground through long, narrow pores to the substrata. As the pores are drained of water, they become filled with air, which supplies oxygen to the roots. When the soil around the roots becomes dry, water moves upward through pores from the substrata by capillary action. This complex process, reaching far into the ground, provides alternately moisture and air to the roots, but it cannot operate within the limited space of a small container. A bonsai potting mix, therefore, uses ingredients that provide an effect similar to the drainage, aeration, and water retention that occur in the ground.

American potting mixes for bonsai are based on the principles of mixes formulated at universities and land-grant colleges for commercial production of container-grown plants. Plant scientists indicate that a mix should contain approximately 50 percent solids and 50 percent pore space, with half the pore space filled with air and the other half with water. The mix will then consist of 50 percent solids, 25 percent air, and 25 percent water.

Roy L. Donahue and his coauthors describe in *Soils: An Introduction to Soils and Plant Growth* how the size of the pores affect plant growth:

> Pore spaces are occupied at all times by air and water. "Tortuous pathways" best describe soil pores; soil particles have irregular shapes and thus leave the spaces or pores between them very irregular in size, shape and direction. Sands have large and continuous pores. In contrast, clays, although containing more total pore space because of the minute size of each clay particle, have very small pores, which transmit water slowly. Small "bottlenecks" in the pores fill with water and block air movements through them. Air exchange may be inadequate for plant growth in such clayey soils. The most rapid water and air movement is in sands and strongly aggregated soils, whose aggregates act like sand grains and pack to form many large pores.[1]

After explaining that where pores are too small, water does not drain and the soil becomes waterlogged, and when the pores are too large, the soil is overly dry, Donahue states that "*to the growing plant pore sizes are of more importance than total pore space*. The best balance of water retention (smaller pores) plus adequate air and water movement (larger pores) is in medium-textured soils such as loams."[2]

Pore space that provides for both aeration and water retention is required in a bonsai potting mix.

Aeration

Although the need of roots for air is not readily apparent, it is equal to their need for water. Roots depend on a continuous supply of oxygen from the air for respiration. During this process the root cells take in oxygen and release

[1]Roy L. Donahue, Raymond W. Miller, and John C. Shickluna, *Soils: An Introduction to Soils and Plant Growth*, 4th ed. (Englewood Cliffs, N.J.: Prentice-Hall, © 1977), p. 62. Reprinted by permission of Prentice-Hall, Inc., Englewood Cliffs, N.J. 07632.

[2]Ibid., p. 63.

carbon dioxide. Carbon dioxide wastes and other gases set free in the exchange are diffused through the open pore spaces and returned to the outside air.

Roots suffer injury if oxygen is insufficient; when levels drop too low, the roots cease to function and die. To assure a supply of air in the pore spaces, the pores must be sufficiently large to allow water to drain rapidly through the mix. Large-size aggregates in the mix, such as granules of coarse sand (round or sharp) will provide this. Other large particles that create open pore space include gravel screenings, crushed granite or shale, and basic slag from smelting operations. These ingredients are called mineral aggregates. For a container mix, they should be chemically inert and sufficiently hard to retain their shape as long as they are present in the mix.

Moisture Retention

In addition to air, roots require a constant minimum amount of moisture. Trees, which are composed largely of water, obtain much of their food in liquid form. They will die if dehydrated. From water, tree roots absorb minerals transported in soluble forms. Water also acts as a solvent in the transfer of mineral nutrients from the roots to other parts of the tree.

The ingredients that retain moisture in the potting mix consist primarily of organic matter. Peat moss heads the list, especially sphagnum peat moss and Michigan peat. Soil and compost also have moisture-retaining qualities. Fine sand and clay, which hold moisture, are not used in large amounts because their small particles compact so tightly that air cannot enter.

Support

Strong, thick roots that extend many feet outward from the trunk and deep into the ground provide a secure support for the tree's trunk and branches. Such a root system enables a tall tree in the ground to withstand the force of winds and heavy rains.

The bonsai in a container is held securely by its own intricate spreading network of slender roots interspersed among hard, heavy aggregates in the mix. A root mass firmly anchored by the weight of ingredients in the potting mix is able to hold and support the bonsai tree. The mineral aggregates listed previously to form pore space are the heaviest ingredients in the mix and provide the required weight. By contrast, perlite and other lightweight aggregates contribute too little weight to hold a bonsai securely in its shallow container.

Summary of Ingredients

Ingredients frequently found in a bonsai potting mix are listed in Table 6-1 according to their primary function in the potting mix; several ingredients overlap and serve more than one purpose.

TABLE 6-1 MAJOR POTTING MIX INGREDIENTS BY FUNCTION

Aeration and Drainage	*Water Retention*	*Weight*
Coarse sand and gravel screenings	Sphagnum peat moss	Coarse sand and gravel screenings
Crushed granite or shale	Michigan peat	Crushed granite or shale
Basic slag and slag by-products	Humus	Basic slag and slag by-products
	Soil	Soil
	Prepackaged soilless mix	

Choosing the Ingredients

With the many materials available, there is no need to use ingredients that are expensive or hard to obtain. While those found in one area may not be available in another, this is not a problem. The two essential ingredients can be found nearly anywhere. One is a hard aggregate for weight and pore space, and the other is material for water retention. The third ingredient, soil, may be omitted, if necessary, with the use of supplemental fertilizers.

The following characteristics are desirable for ingredients in a bonsai potting mix:

1. Availability. Look for readily available ingredients, either natural material found in the area or commercial products distributed locally. This will assure convenient supplies at reasonable prices.
2. Uniformity. Use uniform ingredients and standardize the potting mix. This produces a reliable mix time after time.
3. Cleanliness. Make certain the ingredients are sanitary and free of harmful salts, insects, and pathogens. Avoid materials such as sewer sludge, which may contain chemicals in amounts toxic to bonsai.
4. Identifiable ingredients. Use only materials of known ingredients. Where the contents of packaged material is not clearly labeled, obtain this information from the distributor or manufacturer.
5. Durability. As bonsai are repotted at intervals of one or more years, insist on ingredients that will hold their structure over long periods of time. Some prepared mixes, which are excellent for starting seedlings, are formulated to last only a few months. They will not likely retain their structure in a bonsai mix.

Combining the Ingredients

In the following statement from *The U.C. System for Producing Healthy Container Plants, bonsai* can be substituted for *plants*: "If the mix is a good one, nearly all plants may be grown in it. If it is a poor mix, only those which are tolerant of the poor features may be grown in it."[3]

Using one mix has many advantages. It simplifies the procurement and preparation of materials. It may be stored in quantities to be available as needed. If the mix requires modification for certain species of plants, this is easily accomplished by adding the required ingredients. Soil with a persistent high moisture content is injurious to a number of trees. Pines, for example, do not long survive in a soil (or a container mix) that retains water. For such bonsai, rapid drainage after rain or watering is essential, so a mix with large aggregates is generally used. Alternatively, a standard mix with average drainage and longer intervals between watering is also satisfactory.

A basic mix that is suitable for a wide range of plant material in one climate will not necessarily be satisfactory in all parts of the world or in different climatic regions of a single country. For example, in dry areas, a mix with high moisture-retention capabilities is needed, while in damp, humid areas, a mix with more rapid drainage is preferred. The best mix is one suited to the local environment and the needs of the bonsai grower.

BASIC BONSAI CONTAINER MIXES

Tools and Equipment

Depending on the quantities being prepared, the following tools and equipment will be needed:

A trowel, shovel, hoe, or concrete mixer for combining the ingredients.

Gallon cans, buckets, or other containers for measuring the ingredients.

Covered waterproof cans or bins for storing the mix.

Scoops that may be cut from strong plastic bottles with molded handles.

Sieves. Have on hand at least three sieves with wire mesh of ⅜, 1/16, and 1/32 inch. Additional sieves of ¼ and ½ inch may also be useful. Sieves are available from bonsai suppliers or may be constructed from hardware screening.

Preparations. For the average bonsai potting mix, use particles between ⅜ or ¼ inch and 1/16 inch. (The maximum particle size may be increased to ½ inch for bonsai in extra-large containers and reduced to 1/16 inch for small bonsai in tiny containers.)

Sieve all ingredients separately before measuring, starting with the largest mesh, to remove debris and oversize particles. Discard the material that does not pass through this screen. Then sieve with the next largest screen and dis-

[3]Kenneth F. Baker, ed., *The U.C. System for Producing Healthy Container-Grown Plants* (USDA: University of California, 1957), p. 101.

card the small particles that pass through. Make a final screening with a 1/32-inch mesh to eliminate dust and other minute particles. It is important to remove these fine particles from the mix because otherwise they fill the open pore spaces so essential for aeration and drainage. Because sieving is a dusty operation, plan to prepare the mix outdoors, if possible. This eliminates much of the cleanup and the hazard of breathing the resulting dust.

It is helpful to measure the ingredients in standard units such as a cubic foot, cubic yard, or cubic meter or, for smaller amounts, by liters or gallons. With known, uniform units, fertilizers or other supplements may be added in specified amounts.

Combine all ingredients in a dry condition and use a dry mix for potting.

The following four basic mixes, containing different ingredients, are suitable for a range of climates and growing conditions. Substitutes can be used when a listed material is not locally available. The first two contain soil; the others are soilless.

1. Soil, sphagnum peat moss, and coarse sand in equal parts.
2. Soil, Michigan peat, and coarse sand in equal parts.
3. Michigan peat or sphagnum peat moss 40%, crushed granite 60%.
4. Prepackaged mix and aggregates in equal parts.

1. Soil, Sphagnum Peat Moss, and Coarse Sand in Equal Parts

This bonsai mix, suitable for many parts of the country, was formulated in the 1960s and has been used in many areas of America over a long period of time.[4] The soil provides support, mineral nutrients, possibly trace elements, and moisture retention. Coarse sand creates open pore space for aeration and drainage, and its physical weight holds the roots of the bonsai in the container. Sphagnum peat moss contributes both aeration and moisture retention. A bonsai growing in this mix is shown in Fig. 6-1.

Take soil from areas free of nematodes and harmful residues of herbicides and from beneath the grass and weeds that may be present. Work it through a 1/4- or 3/8-inch mesh screen to remove stones, leaves, roots, twigs, and other debris, then spread the soil out to dry. Sieve the dried soil through a 1/16-inch mesh to remove small particles. Discard whatever passes through the mesh and use the soil that remains in the sieve. Sometimes other ingredients, particularly hard aggregates, are sieved a third time to eliminate fine particles that pass through a 1/32-inch mesh. With soil, the benefit of a fine screening is questionable because the soil particles tend to break down and disintegrate in the mix as soon as it is watered.

[4]Dorothy S. Young, "Getting Started with Bonsai: The Potting Mix," *Journal of the American Bonsai Society*, 2, no. 2 (Summer 1968), 17–18.

Figure 6-1 Climbing hydrangea, *Hydrangea anomala,* in a mix of equal parts of soil, sphagnum peat moss, and coarse sand.

Pasteurization and Fumigation. For soil that is apparently free of undesirable organisms and substances, the individual grower may decide whether the additional treatment of pasteurization or fumigation is warranted. The commercial grower considers such treatment essential.

Small amounts of soil may be pasteurized to destroy insects and harmful organisms by heating it for 20 minutes in an oven with the soil at a temperature of 170°F. Set the oven for 180°. Spread the soil in a clean, shallow pan to a depth of ½ to 1 inch and insert an oven thermometer into the soil. Stir the soil several times during the baking to distribute the heat evenly. An oven temperature below 200° is critical. Higher temperatures may kill all the living organisms that are present, leaving a partially pulverized, lifeless soil of no value.

Soil may be chemically treated before use to control nematodes, fungi, other pathogens, and weeds with specially formulated fumigants such as Vapam and similar products. Handle these fumigants with extreme care and caution according to the manufacturer's directions. Use them out of doors. They are not intended for use in a greenhouse or in an area where plants are growing.

Sphagnum Peat Moss. Sphagnum peat moss, also called highmoor peat, is derived from species of sphagnum moss that have turned into peat. It is found in bogs in Europe, Canada, and parts of the northern United States. Canadian sphagnum peat moss (Fig. 6–2) has a uniform fibrous structure that resists further decay and is long-lasting in a potting mix. Its average pH level is 3.5 to 4.5. It is essentially sterile, odorless, and free from harmful salts, chemicals, and insects. Its fibrous structure provides greater aeration in a container mix than other peats that are more decomposed. For a potting mix, use sphagnum peat moss cut in short lengths and packaged in 4- or 6-cubic-foot bales (which expand when loosened) or bagged in smaller quantities.

Figure 6-2 Canadian sphagnum peat moss.

To prepare sphagnum peat moss, rub it across a coarse screen to find and discard bits of roots and twigs that may be present. After it is sieved, compress it slightly in the measuring unit. And, of course, handle sphagnum moss in a dry form.

Sand. Sand is available from many sources. Builder's sand and concrete sand of mixed particle size may be obtained in large and small quantities from building suppliers. Examine a sample for the prevalence of particle sizes that are wanted. Avoid sand that contains mostly fine particles. For example, a fine-particle sand used for refractory bricks is not suitable for bonsai mixes.

Sieve the sand three times, first to remove overly large particles, a second time to eliminate grains less than 1/16 inch, and a third time with a 1/32-inch mesh to remove the residue of dust that may remain. If the sand consists mainly of fine particles less than 1/32 inch, most of it will have to be discarded. Sand bars along freshwater streams and lakes are a natural source of sand. Sand from these deposits may require washing as well as sieving to remove clay and other sediment. Do not use sand from the shores of salt water or any sand containing salt; the salt will kill the bonsai.

Industrial sand, such as sandblasting sand, is excellent for container mixes because it has been cleaned and graded. This is a sharp silica sand available in washed, uniform-particle size. Grade labeling is not nationally uniform. For bonsai, use a grade containing particles from about 1/16 to 3/16 inch. It is usually marketed in large quantities. When only small amounts are needed, clean sand of similar size packaged as aquarium sand or parakeet gravel may be used.

Substitutes for Coarse Sand. In areas where coarse sand is not available, the following substitutes provide the same function in the potting mix. They are hard, heavy aggregates, long-lasting and chemically inert.

1. Gravel Screenings. Small particles of lake or river gravel (Fig. 6-3) are available as gravel screenings from sand and gravel distributors or may be found in natural deposits. Screen the gravel to remove overly large aggregates, then sieve again to obtain granules between 1/16 and 1/4 or 3/8 inch. Wash the gravel

Figure 6-3 Gravel screenings.

to be used thoroughly or sieve it with a 1/32-inch mesh to remove the fine particles and dust.

In localities where crushed clay brick is available, this can be used as a substitute for sand. Prepare crushed brick for a bonsai mix by screening or washing as described for gravel screening.

2. *Crushed Granite or Other Hard Rock.* This excellent ingredient is available from natural deposits or from sand and gravel distributors. Any hard rock that does not contain lime is satisfactory. Usually, sieving and washing are required to obtain clean particles in the sizes wanted.

3. *Poultry Grit.* Crushed granite sold by the bag at farm supply houses as chicken or turkey grit (Fig. 6–4) is another good substitute for sand. Grading of particle sizes may vary among distributors. In the Middle Atlantic states, "starter" grade contains 1/16- to 5/16-inch particles. Sieve and wash bagged grit to remove fine particles and dust. But read the label. Crushed oyster shells and limestone are also marketed as poultry grit. Their high lime content is not suitable for container mix.

4. *Basic Slag.* This, too, is a good substitute for coarse sand, especially in areas near iron-ore or aluminum-smelting operations. The basic slag produced

Figure 6-4 Poultry grit (crushed granite).

Figure 6-5 Basic slag.

at steel mills contains hard, uneven granules from minute particles to clinkers 1 inch or more thick. Sieved and washed slag granules are shown in Fig. 6-5. Be sure to wash the granules thoroughly to remove all traces of the dust and powder that are always present. In powdered form, basic slag is a liming material that has no place as a major component in a container mix.

When using basic slag, test the mix first on other plants to make sure that the procedures used for removing the powdered lime are effective. Because of the possible presence of free lime, basic slag is not recommended in a mix for acid-loving plants, such as azaleas.

5. *Expanded Slag.* Expanded slag, marketed under the names Haydite, Waydite, and others, is formed as highly heated slag is sprayed with streams of water. The resulting "puffed" granules, produced for cinder-block production, are available from suppliers to cinder-block manufacturers. A similar hard, expanded cinder-block aggregate is Arka-lite (Fig. 6-6), made from special clay called "gumbo," which is fired at 2,000 °C. Gumbo clay deposits are found in the Arkansas-Tennessee region and at scattered locations elsewhere in the country.

Figure 6-6 Arka-lite, a form of expanded slag granules.

Remember to sieve and wash all basic and expanded slag granules before adding them to a bonsai container mix.

Combining Ingredients. After sieving and preparing the soil, sphagnum peat moss, and sand or a sand substitute, combine them in equal parts by volume: one measure of sieved soil, one measure of prepared sphagnum peat moss, and one measure of clean, sieved sand. Stir the dry ingredients together until they are thoroughly mixed. The container mix may be used immediately or stored in a dry place until needed.

2. Soil, Michigan Peat, and Coarse Sand in Equal Parts

This is a mix (Fig. 6–7) for climates and species that require more than average moisture-holding capacity in the growing medium. Substitute Michigan peat for sphagnum peat moss. Where coarse sand is not available, switch to a similar coarse aggregate.

Michigan Peat. Michigan peat, also known as hynum peat or lowmoor peat, is formed from decomposed hynum moss, reeds, sedges, and cattails. It is more finely textured than sphagnum peat moss, contains smaller pore spaces, and retains water longer. Its variable pH level ranges from 3.5 to 7.0. Michigan peat is marketed moist in plastic bags or bales. To prepare, simply spread it out to let the moisture evaporate and follow the directions for sieving sphagnum peat moss. Prepare the soil, coarse sand, or sand substitute as described for the first mix. Measure the three ingredients in equal amounts. Combine and blend them thoroughly. The mix is ready to use; in a dry condition it may be stored for long periods.

For a container mix without natural soil, select a hard mineral aggregate for weight and aeration and another ingredient for moisture retention. Combine the two and use with a regular program of fertilizing. Soilless mixes are a convenience for growers who do not have ready access to soil or are in areas where harmful organisms are present in the soil. Other growers prefer not to use soil because of its high variability and favor ingredients that are more uniform.

Figure 6-7 Left to right, soil, Michigan peat, and coarse sand.

3. Michigan Peat or Sphagnum Peat Moss 40% and Crushed Granite 60%

Prepare the ingredients in the manner described for the first two mixes. This is a basic mix containing no soil for areas of average humidity where the climate is neither excessively dry nor excessively humid. In dry climates, substitute peat humus, which is decomposed Michigan peat with a high water-retention capability, for Michigan peat. If the peat is highly acidic, add two tablespoons of powdered limestone per gallon. Because fine particles in the humus tend to compact, coarse organic material such as pine, fir, or hardwood bark may be added for increased aeration. In especially humid areas, use sphagnum peat moss; its stronger fibers will provide better aeration than Michigan peat.

Crushed granite is a superior aggregate because it is neither strongly acid nor alkaline, contains no chemicals harmful to plants, and does not break down in a mix. Other aggregates may be used. Cleaned, graded industrial sandblasting sand is also among the most desirable aggregates where it is available. Many growers combine basic slag or slag products with Michigan peat or other acidic peats to neutralize the possible lime content of the slag.

4. Prepackaged Mixes and Aggregates in Equal Parts

When soil, sphagnum peat moss, or other peats are not obtainable, it may be necessary to use a prepackaged mix. Beyond its availability, a prepackaged mix offers no advantage over the organic material previously described, and it contains several disadvantages. Prepackaged mixes are not made for bonsai. More often than not they contain ingredients such as perlite or vermiculite, which, although excellent for many horticultural purposes, are too light to provide the weight needed in a bonsai potting mix. Avoid bagged mixes with such labels as "topsoil", "sterilized soil" or "compost" unless all the ingredients are listed. The name on the label is not a list of the ingredients. Any name may be placed on a bag filled with sewer sludge or muck. Sludge may contain chemicals in amounts harmful to plants, while muck consists mainly of fine particles and is unsatisfactory in a bonsai mix.

Among prepared mixes, the best are those packaged and marketed for commercial plant production. Several of these are available in small quantities with the ingredients clearly labeled. For example, Metro-Mix Growing Medium 500 and similar prepared mixes formulated for growing pot plants contain sand, bark, and peat moss. These mixes are longer-lasting than mixes formulated for seedlings and safe when combined with coarse aggregates for a bonsai mix.

When a prepackaged mix is selected, air dry it, if wet, then sieve it in the same manner as soil to remove both overly large and overly small particles. Add an equal volume of clean, sieved mineral aggregates containing 1/16- to 3/8-inch granules. Use any of the aggregates previously described. If the mix tends to compact, add coarse leaf mold or finely cut bark (after removing fine particles). A prepackaged mix usually contains more than enough moisture-holding materials for a bonsai mix. In areas of either pronounced humidity or dryness, it may be necessary to raise or lower the proportion of organic ingredients to the mineral aggregates.

Miscellaneous Ingredients and Mixes

Nature's Mix. Nature's mix is composed entirely of decomposed rock, which contains organic matter. Where deposits of decomposed granite or shale can be found, they provide a complete and satisfactory container mix. Minimum preparation is required; simply sieve the decomposed rock through a ⅜-inch mesh screen to remove overly large pieces and add coarse sand if large amounts of humus are present.

Calcined Clay. Calcined clay granules are made from fuller's earth or montmorillonite (an aluminum-silicate clay) fired at high temperatures. They have been used in bonsai container mixes with reports ranging from excellent to poor. The hard, porous granules (Fig. 6–8) are marketed as a soil conditioner for lawns and golf courses. They may be difficult to obtain in small quantities. In a bonsai container mix they add weight, create pore space, and retain water. It is not known how slowly or rapidly they release water in the mix or, if the mix becomes dry, whether the granules may absorb what little moisture is available for the roots. Calcined clay may be combined in various ways with one or more of the following ingredients: soil, sand or other hard aggregates, sphagnum peat moss or other peats, and organic materials. The Japanese deciduous holly in Fig. 6–9 is growing in a mix containing calcined clay.

Before incorporating calcined clay in a container mix, sieve the granules to remove the many fine particles that are present, then rinse them thoroughly to wash off the dust. Hard calcined clay granules fired at high temperatures are distributed as Turface by International Minerals and Chemical Corp. and as Terra-Green by Oil-Dri. Grades labeled "soil conditioner" contain granules up to 3⁄16 inch in size. "Mulch" and "jumbo" grades contain slightly larger granules. Clay granules that are air-dried or baked at low temperatures and marketed as absorbents for oil or pet litter are not recommended. These granules are not sufficiently hard to retain their structure in a bonsai container mix.

Figure 6-8 Calcined clay granules.

Figure 6-9 *Ilex serrata* at the U.S. National Arboretum in a container mix of one-third mulch-size calcined clay granules, one-third crushed granite (poultry grit), and one-third equal parts of sphagnum moss and peat moss. Photo courtesy of USDA.

Testing and Adjustments

Occasionally, a mix is unsatisfactory. This may be caused by a harmful substance in the ingredients, but more often it is the result of poor drainage and lack of aeration. Such conditions are produced by excessive amounts of water-holding ingredients or fine particles in the mix. A faulty mix may be improved by a change in the ingredients to increase open pore space or by improved sieving to eliminate fine particles. At times, it may be necessary to replace the ingredient that holds too much water or contains a large proportion of fine particles with a better material.

When a mix gives poor results and the cause cannot be determined, testing may be required to check the level of acidity or alkalinity or the amount of mineral elements such as lime or magnesium. In many states, a soil-testing service is provided at a nominal charge by state agricultural colleges and universities or through county offices of the USDA Agricultural Extension Service.

The pH Level. The pH level is a designation of relative acidity or alkalinity from 1.0 (highly acid) to 14.0 (highly alkaline); 7.0 is neutral. Bonsai and most other plants grow best in a slightly acid or neutral growing medium with pH levels between 5.5 and 7.0. Excessively high or low pH levels interfere with the plant's absorption of minerals in the soil. Ground limestone, pulverized to pass through a 100-mesh sieve, is a safe soil conditioner for reducing acidity; to lower acidity by one pH unit, add it to the mix at the rate of 4 or 5 pounds per cubic yard, or about 2½ ounces per cubic foot, and mix thoroughly.

Finely powdered limestone is effective within a short time. Calcitic limestone consists almost entirely of lime, while dolomitic limestone contains lime and up to 50 percent magnesium. Coarsely ground particles require from one to three years to dissolve and are not recommended when immediate results are wanted. Slaked lime and quicklime are highly concentrated and should not be used in a container mix.

It is seldom necessary to reduce the alkalinity of a potting mix because most of the ingredients are below pH 7.0. If the mix is overly alkaline, replace the ingredient causing the high pH level with peat moss or other materials with a low pH reading. To modify a mix already prepared, add ground sulfur at the rate of 1½ to 2 pounds per cubic yard, or approximately 1 scant ounce per cubic foot, to lower the pH level one unit. Blend the sulfur thoroughly with the other ingredients to eliminate the danger of high concentrations in a portion of the mix, because concentrated sulfur is toxic to plants.

PRACTICE AND REVIEW

1. Locating Suppliers and Sources

Which of the following ingredients for bonsai mixes are available from commercial or industrial sources in your area?

Sphagnum peat moss, Michigan peat, peat humus.
Prepackaged potting mixes for commercial plant production.
Builder's or concrete sand.
Gravel screenings.
Crushed granite.
Poultry grit.
Industrial sandblasting sand.
Calcined clay particles.
Basic slag from smelting operations.
Expanded slag used in cinder block production.

Which of the following materials may be obtained from natural sources in your area?

Soil.
Crushed or decomposed rock.
River or lake sand.
Gravel deposits.

2. Preparing a Mix

Select ingredients from the available materials in your area and, as described in this chapter, prepare a sample bonsai container mix. With local climatic conditions in mind, choose one of the mixes listed below for a 3- to 6-gallon sample.

Soil, sphagnum peat moss or Michigan peat, and a large-particle aggregate in equal parts.

Michigan peat or sphagnum peat moss 40%, large-particle aggregate 60%.

Peat humus or prepackaged commercial mix 30% to 40%, large-particle aggregate 60% to 70%.

Use the mix for potting plant material in Chapter 8 and creating a bonsai in Chapter 9.

ADDITIONAL READING

BAKER, KENNETH F., ed., *The U.C. System for Producing Healthy Container-Grown Plants*, Manual 23. University of California and the Cooperative Extension Service in Agriculture of the United States Department of Agriculture, 1957, and many reprints. The first manual on potting mixes for container-grown plants describes the purpose, principles, and methods of formulating mixes. Valuable for its basic information.

BOODLEY, J. W., "Media and Small Containers," *Journal of the American Bonsai Society, Inc.*, 12, no. 3 (Fall 1978), 64–65. The author, cooriginator of the Cornell University Peat-Lite Mixes, relates growing media in small containers to bonsai use.

DONAHUE, ROY L., RAYMOND W. MILLER, AND JOHN C. SHICKLUNA, *Soils: An Introduction to Soils and Plant Growth*, 4th ed. Englewood Cliffs, N.J.: Prentice-Hall, 1977. This text on soil by plant scientists contains technical and up-to-date information on the composition, function, and chemistry of soils.

ROGERS, MARLIN N., "Soil Moisture and Aeration for Plant Growth," *Journal of the American Bonsai Society, Inc.*, 10, no. 3 (Fall 1976), 58, 67–68. A plant scientist at the University of Missouri at Columbia discusses adapting soil functions for growing dwarfed trees in containers.

7

The Container

A small bonsai container is indispensable in miniaturizing a bonsai. At the same time, it heightens the aesthetic effect of the tree. A tree is not chosen for the container; a container is selected to complement and enhance the tree. There are aesthetic and traditional guidelines for using certain container sizes and shapes for different forms of bonsai, but the final choice is a personal decision, reflecting the preference of the bonsai grower. Bonsai exhibits offer an opportunity to see a large variety of containers and how each is matched to a particular bonsai. When the two are combined successfully, a synergetic effect is achieved, and both the tree and the container are at their best.

BASIC CONSIDERATIONS

Bonsai containers must be made of durable, chemically neutral, inert material that will not react with the soil. They must have holes at the bottom for water drainage. They are nearly always footed to facilitate drainage and create a layer of air beneath the pot. In cold climates, containers should be able to withstand damage from freezing temperatures. The container must be stable when placed on a flat surface.

Materials

Natural. Clay, used in ancient times for bonsai containers, meets all the specifications and continues to be the material most frequently used. Ceramic bonsai containers may be porcelain, stoneware, or earthenware, depending on

Figure 7-1 Sargent juniper, *Juniperus chinensis* var. *Sargentii,* planted on a stone. Courtesy of Marion Gyllenswan.

the composition of the clay and the temperature of firing. Most clay pots are hard earthenware or stoneware fired at temperatures between 1,100° and 1,200°C. and may be glazed or unglazed.

Stone containers are durable and attractive but difficult to produce. They are not commonly seen outside of China, Hong Kong, and other countries of East Asia, where shallow marble and soapstone containers, from several inches to more than four feet in length, are popular for rock and tree landscapes. Hexagonal containers of thin, polished stone slabs are occasionally seen among Chinese bonsai. Natural rough stone slabs are popular in many countries as bonsai planters. A planting of junipers on a stone slab is shown in Fig. 7-1. Plastic slabs with a natural look, as well as natural stone, are used for bonsai plantings in Japan.

Since the 1970s, Japan and, later, the United States have produced plastic bonsai containers that appear identical to ceramic ones. Plastic pots meet the requirements for durability, are chemically inert, and have drainage holes. In every respect, only close inspection will distinguish a well-made plastic container from a ceramic one. Although they cost less than ceramic pots, the synthetic aspect of plastic may be the cause of their limited acceptance for bonsai, where a close affinity to nature is emphasized.

Homemade. Wood and concrete containers are popular, especially for group plantings and saikei, and may be easily made at home. Choose a wood such as white cedar, redwood, or cypress for durability and rot resistance. Space the bottom slats slightly apart to allow for drainage. For increased durability, treat the wood with zinc naphthenate, a colorless preservative that is not harmful to plants. Copper naphthenate, although safe, is not satisfactory for containers because of the dark green stain it leaves. Avoid using preservatives with a pentachlorophenol base; it is lethal to plants.

To make a concrete container, use a wood frame. Add wire mesh for reinforcement and nail corks to the bottom for drainage holes. Before the concrete has completely hardened, remove the frames and rub the outside walls with a wire brush to obtain a natural-looking texture. Either make the containers from scratch by mixing sand and cement, or for convenience use a prepared dry ready-mix.

Horticultural Effects

Growing a plant in a container causes smaller leaves and shorter internodes. It slows the plant's rate of growth by inducing the formation of a small, rather than a large, root system. A restricted area for root growth is important to bonsai, and using the container is considered a basic bonsai technique.

The effect of the container on bonsai differs from other container-grown plants only by degree. All plants in containers experience a reduction in their rate of growth and have slightly smaller than normal leaves and shorter internodes. In bonsai, the unusual smallness of the container makes the effect pronounced. The size of the container should be as small as possible, large enough only to allow the bonsai to grow and survive.

Aesthetic Effect of the Container

In few instances are function and beauty combined so well as here. The bonsai container, essential to dwarfing the bonsai, also heightens the beauty of the tree it has dwarfed.

A bonsai container is no ordinary pot. It has a unique shape and purpose, which is to house the bonsai. It also isolates the bonsai from distracting elements. In a sense, the container personalizes a bonsai and prevents it from being lost in a crowd. It would be difficult to see a small bonsai planted in the ground, surrounded by other foliage. Its beauty would be lost in the greenery. The container is somewhat like a stand on which sculpture is placed, but it is also much more. It gives the bonsai definition and space.

A bonsai may be outstanding in a number of ways. A container is always selected to match the outstanding feature, or features, of the bonsai. This is generally the most conspicuous aspect, such as the flowers on a bonsai in bloom. For example, the container may be selected to harmonize with an azalea or crab apple covered with pink flowers. Or a grower may want to reinforce an active trunk line; this, too, can be accomplished by the container. Likewise, a con-

Figure 7-2 Blue Atlas cedar, *Cedrus atlantica* cv. Glauca, in a small, round, shallow container. Courtesy of Don Lem.

tainer can be used to call attention to a bonsai's soft, curved lines or to harmonize with the hue or texture of the bonsai's trunk or foliage.

Generally speaking, traditional container usage to complement a bonsai may be summarized as follows:

Oval and rectangular containers: for trees with vertical, curved or slanting trunks (Figs. 1–1 and 2–1).

Deep square or round containers: for cascade and semicascade trees (Fig. 3–2).

Small, round, shallow containers: for trees with long, thin trunks in unusual styles (Fig. 7–2).

Large shallow containers: for rock and forest plantings and saikei (Fig. 2–6).

GUIDELINES ON CHOOSING A CONTAINER

Bringing the bonsai and its container together is like mixing colors on an artist's palette. Results count more than academic rules. The following guidelines are offered as an aid. Use them as general indicators rather than regulations.

Single Upright Trunk: Vertical, Curved, or Slanting

Shape. For these trees, the container is usually a rather low oval or rectangle. Square, round, or hexagonal containers are also used. Containers with angled corners (such as a rectangle or hexagon) emphasize an angled or straight trunk, sharp needles, or strong, straight lines, as seen in Fig. 3–1.

An oval or round container complements a bonsai with a curved trunk, a rounded crown, or soft foliage (Fig. 2–9) and is often seen with deciduous trees.

Sometimes a bonsai has both strong and soft features. The same bonsai may have a mix of sharp needles and a curved trunk, or a strong trunk and soft, rounded foliage. When opposite characteristics are fused, a hybrid container with both straight and curved forms is frequently used. In Fig. 2-8, the container is a rectangle, but the sides are curved to harmonize with the curved trunk.

Depth. For a bonsai with a thick trunk, a deep container provides support and visual balance. The depth of the container is usually proportional to the thickness of the trunk and sometimes matches it exactly. However, for trees with thin trunks, the container is not necessarily as shallow as the trunk's diameter. Usually a low container has a minimum depth of ½ inch or so to hold the potting mix in place.

Length. Try to have the longest dimension of the container longer or shorter than the height of the bonsai, rather than the same length. Usually the container is shorter when the trunks are tall. For a group of short trees, the container is most often longer than the tallest tree.

Single Trunk: Cascade or Semicascade

Shape. For this style of bonsai, use a heavy, deep, round container or one with equilateral sides, such as a square or a hexagon.

Width. The width of the container is much less than the longest dimension of the bonsai.

Depth. The depth will vary. It is never the same height as the longest dimension of the bonsai and is usually, but not always, smaller. It must be sufficient to counterbalance the visual weight of a cascading bonsai as shown in Fig. 3-2.

Literati

Shape. This unconventional bonsai (Fig. 7-3) is most often displayed in a small, round, shallow container that serves as a pivotal point from which the

Figure 7-3 A literati bonsai in a saucerlike container.

trunk emerges. Unlike a cascade style, in this example, the literati bonsai is sufficiently light in weight to be self-balancing, as the small, shallow, round container indicates. On containers of this type, the sides may be flared, straight, or rounded, with or without molding.

Twin Trunk or Double Trunk

When selecting a container for a bonsai with two trunks, match the container to the line or size of the dominant trunk and the mass of the foliage.

Shape. When the trunks are close to each other and the foliage of the two merge, consider them as one tree and choose the container accordingly.

Length. Proportions of tree to container are the same as for a single trunk.

Depth. Consider closely placed trunks as one trunk when selecting the depth of the container.

Three or More Trees

The overall shape formed by a small group of trees is treated as a single tree.

Shape. Simple oval, round, or rectangular containers are usually chosen (Fig. 7-4). If the container is longer than it is wide, its length is proportional to the height of the tallest trunk, as for a single trunk.

Depth. The thickest trunk of the group is usually used to determine the container's depth. For a group that contains a number of large, prominent trunks, increasing the depth slightly may add stability to the planting.

Figure 7-4 The straight lines of the five Japanese maples, *Acer palmatum,* at the U.S. National Arboretum harmonize with the straight sides of the rectangular container.

Figure 7-5 Forest planting of *Portulacaria afra.* Courtesy of James J. Smith.

Forest Planting of Five or More Trees

Shape. A low, shallow container is effective for this type of planting. For straight, angular, or slanting trees, a rectangular pot is often used; oval containers are pleasing for trees with curved trunks, soft foliage, or gently molded silhouettes. For trees with thin trunks, an unusually narrow container is sometimes used to help the trees fill the container comfortably.

Length. In relation to the height of the tallest tree, the container is longer or shorter but never the same length. When the trees are tall, select a container shorter than the height of the tallest tree, as shown in Fig. 7-5.

Depth. Most forest plantings are in containers between ½ and 2 inches deep. The size and shape of the planting affects the depth of the container as much as the width of the trunks. Usually, well-balanced vertical trees are in containers of less depth than trees with slanting or large trunks. Visual weight is also a factor. Evergreen trees with dense, dark foliage are in deeper containers than deciduous trees of the same size with airy leaves and branching.

Texture

The surface finish on a container may be used to complement the texture of the bark, foliage, or flowers. With this in mind, choose a container with a smooth surface for a bonsai with shiny leaves or a trunk that has a sheen rather than wrinkles. A slightly rough surface on an unglazed container serves to accent a trunk with rough and fissured bark. In Chinese bonsai, a container may be selected to harmonize with the color or tone of the trunk.

Color and Glazes

Nowhere is a bonsai grower offered a greater choice than in the color and glazes of bonsai containers. Traditional Japanese bonsai imposes a different usage for glazed and unglazed containers. Unglazed containers, primarily brown, terra cotta, and gray, are considered suitable for nearly all forms and species of bonsai and are preferred for pines and other conifers. They are also viewed as more formal than glazed containers.

Growers often select glazed containers for flowering and fruiting bonsai and for deciduous trees with colorful fall foliage. Soft pastels are deemed appropriate for spring flowers and other lightly colored flowers or foliage. However, the color of the flowers, except possibly white, rarely duplicates the color of the container. Glazes of deeper colors are suitable for autumn fruit or flowers with vivid, bright colors. Dark glazes are sometimes used for conifers.

When considering texture or color as well as shape in selecting a container, it is possible to emphasize more than one outstanding feature of the tree. For example, a light blue glazed container will enhance the color of a pink flowering azalea bonsai. The flowers are surely an outstanding feature. If the tree also has a curved trunk or gracefully rounded masses of flowers, an oval-shaped container may be chosen for harmony. The bonsai will be complemented in several ways by a light blue glazed oval container.

The Rim

The rim, or lip, around the top of a container takes many forms. A container has no rim when the sides are cut flush at the top. Usually, however, a rim is present; it may be barely noticeable, a slight thickening no more than ¼ inch in width along the top edge, or a highly visible wide, flat band. The rim may be flared, rounded, beaded, scalloped, cordlike, or otherwise molded and embellished. Examples may be seen in photographs throughout this book.

There are no set rules regarding the use of a container with or without a rim. One way of deciding whether a rim is wanted is to look at the rim as additional staging. A highly visible rim accents the bonsai and attracts the eye to the planting; it is well matched with an active or dramatic bonsai. As the rim becomes smaller, its impact is reduced. Because of its horizontal character, the rim will enhance a bonsai with beautiful horizontal branching. A band of raised studs around the side of the container gives a powerful impact (Fig. 12–3). It is used with trunks that convey motion and strength.

Uses for a container without a rim are equally varied. A pot with strong lines and no rim is appropriate for a bonsai that is self-contained—a bonsai whose ancient appearance, massive trunk, or special beauty will speak for itself. Use a container with a small rim or none at all where a conspicuous rim would be overpowering. Low-keyed bonsai in this category include attractive group plantings of trees with slender trunks and started bonsai whose training is not yet completed.

Decorative Overlays and Indentations

A basic oval, rectangular, or equilateral container may be overlaid with molded forms or indented with grooves and panels. Such additions enable the container to emphasize strength and movement in a bonsai.

Molded fancy feet, for example, or indentations at the four corners of a container reinforce the strong trunk and fine detail of a mature, well-developed bonsai. They are also effective where arborization has produced dense branching and a pattern of many small twigs and shoots. The intricate branching of such a bonsai is matched with the addition of grooves and molding on the container. For young bonsai, a less pretentious container is a better choice. Pressed panels on the side of a container add interest in some ways, but, less emphatically, they have the same effect as a rim in drawing attention to the planting.

Use special containers for bonsai with delicate lines. An exquisite porcelain container or an earthenware container with thin walls and intricate molding is ideal for bonsai with fine features and a graceful form. This kind of container is not suitable for coarse, rugged bonsai.

Reserve a rare antique container for special use, perhaps an exceptionally old bonsai. A young bonsai or one that requires development is out of place in an antique container. There is a saying in Japan, "The container should never be more valuable than the tree." In the Japanese tradition, the tree is given predominance in every way, and the container is always subordinate.

Chinese Bonsai Containers

In China, ceramic art has flourished for thousands of years. Bonsai containers have been and continue to be admired and used for their own beauty. Their role is not considered less important than the tree's. The two are equal partners.

Chinese bonsai containers may differ in a number of ways from those in Japan. While many plain glazed and unglazed oval or rectangular containers are used in China, those working with Chinese bonsai will find containers decorated with flowers and landscapes in many colors or with poetry inscribed in calligraphy. To viewers accustomed to the understated Japanese container, such decorations and inscriptions may appear distracting. However, in China the container is used to harmonize and complement the aesthetic characteristics of the tree and, at the same time, to add a philosophical or poetic meaning. Thus, the Chinese container serves an additional purpose. A line of poetry or a picture on the side may bring to mind a historic or legendary episode that is also suggested by the bonsai. In China, container and tree together may tell a story, depict a scene, or evoke an emotion.

Surface decorations as well as other features of the container are taken into account as it is harmoniously matched to the tree in shape, size, and impact. The grower selects a container with an active form or pattern for a tree that is equally active, as seen in Fig. 7-6. An unadorned, simple container is used

Figure 7-6 The shape and decorative pattern of this Chinese container complements the active lines of the bonsai, a Chinese hackberry, *Celtis sinensis*. Courtesy of Wu Yee-sun.

for a tree that gives a feeling of equilibrium and repose. At times, the container may seem as prominent as the bonsai tree, and this is acceptable.

American Containers

Since the 1960s, American bonsai growers, along with other artists and hobbyists, have been making ceramic bonsai containers for their own use or to sell either as handicrafts or through small commercial outlets. A great variety of ceramic bonsai pots are now produced in America, including ones of great beauty.

PLACEMENT OF THE TREE

After a container is selected, consider the placement of the tree. It is usually planted in an area to the left or right of center and midway between the front and back of the container. Rarely is the tree placed exactly in the center. The design of the tree and the shape of the container will influence the tree's location, as shown in the following examples.

Single Trunk: Vertical, Curved, or Slanting

Oval or Rectangular Container. The prime planting area for a bonsai is within a band midway between the front and rear of the container and about one-third of the distance from either side. This is shown in Fig. 7–7 for an oval or rectangular container. The tree will appear especially well balanced within this area when the trunk is slightly to the rear rather than the front of the container.

When locating the tree, tilt the trunk if necessary to bring the mass of the foliage above the surface of the container. When a tree has a pronounced side branch or a secondary trunk, place the main trunk to the right or the left of center, whichever will bring the branch above the container, as seen in Fig. 7–8. Such a placement visually unites the tree and the container. To see the reverse of this effect, make a tracing of this bonsai with the tree moved from

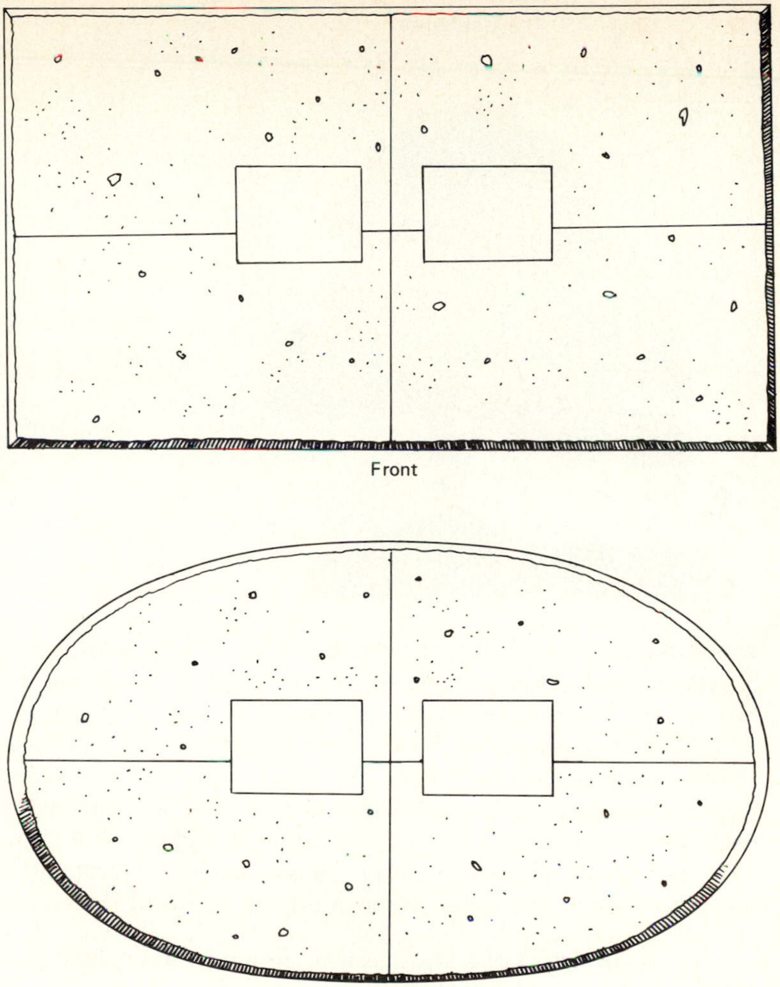

Front

Front

Figure 7-7 Prime planting areas for single upright trunks are to right and left of center in an oval and a rectangular container.

the right to the left side of the container and notice how the branches projecting out into space create a feeling of imbalance. Similarly, consider a vertical slanting trunk. Try to keep the trunk and the mass of foliage over, rather than beyond, the container, as seen from the front and side view.

Elevation of the Trunk. The bottom of the trunk is usually raised slightly above the top of the container, and the potting mix slopes gently downward to the side of the container. This establishes a pleasing line between the edge of the container and the trunk of the tree.

Bonsai growers may select a slightly deep oval or rectangular container for certain trees with an old trunk, as in Fig. 1-1. Rather than elevating a thick

Figure 7-8 Japanese white pine, *Pinus parviflora.* Courtesy of Lynn R. Perry.

trunk that has only a minimum number of surface roots, the base of the trunk is placed slightly below the rim of the container. The smoothed and leveled surface of the soil may be covered with sand, other granules, or moss.

Round, Square, or Hexagonal Container. A well-balanced tree with a single trunk is positioned slightly off center in a low, round container or in one with equilateral sides, as indicated in Fig. 7–9. As with oval and rectangular containers, the mass of the tree occupies the space above the container (Fig. 7–10) whenever the design of the bonsai permits. Here, the base of the soil is mounded above the container around the trunk of the trident maple.

Figure 7-9 Left to right, planting areas near the center of round, square, and hexagonal containers.

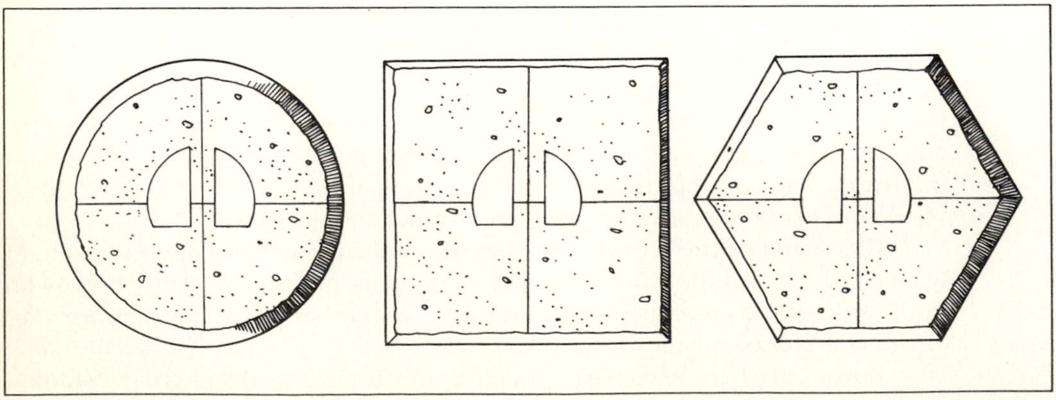

Figure 7-10 Trident maple, *Acer Buergeranum,* centered above a low, round container. Courtesy of J. Nakahara.

Placement of a Symmetrical Tree. While most bonsai are asymmetrical, on rare occasions a bonsai may be almost symmetrical. Such a tree is placed close to, and sometimes in, the center of the container. The container is usually smaller than the span of the longest branches on either side of the trunk.

Single Trunk: Cascade or Semicascade

Equilateral Container. When the trunk of a bonsai tree extends far beyond or below the base of the trunk, a deep container is required for counterbalance. The tree is placed at or near the center of a deep round, square, or hexagonal pot.

On a cascading bonsai, expose surface roots on the side of the trunk opposite to the direction of the cascade. These roots are a tremendous asset. They act as visual anchors holding the tree to the container. If necessary, move the trunk to one side of the container to allow space for the roots.

Multitrunk: Vertical or Slanting (Straight or Curved)

Containers. Shallow containers—oval, rectangular, or equilateral—are used for multitrunk plantings.

Placement of the Trunk. With two or more trees, the major trunk is placed in the same general area alloted to a single trunk, toward either the right or the left side and about midway between the front and the back of the container. Factors affecting the location are primarily the slant or line of the trunks and the shape formed by the top growth of all the combined trees. The mass of the branches and foliage is directly above the container, as seen in Fig. 13-12.

Figure 7-11 A ceramic container without holes containing Fukien tea, *Ehretia microphylla,* planted on sandstone. Courtesy of Wu Yee-sun.

Elevation of the Trunk. In a low, shallow container, the bases of the trunks are elevated above the rim of the container, and the potting mix slopes from the base of the major trunk downward to the edges of the container.

Trays

A tray or a low container without drainage holes (also called a *suiban*) is used for bonsai trees planted on a rock and for rockery landscapes, as in Fig. 7-11. Rocks may be surrounded by water or a layer of sand. Low containers for this purpose are traditionally made of stoneware, metal (especially bronze), or stone. Plastic trays are also available. The bottom of ceramic trays is thicker than usual to support the weight of the stones and rocks. Shallow trays of plywood may be constructed at home and waterproofed with a plastic coating.

Purchasing Bonsai Containers

A well-made bonsai container is an investment. With proper care it can be used again and again and will last indefinitely. However, it is not necessary, or even advisable, for the beginner to use pots of the finest quality. Attractive, less expensive containers will serve well during the novice's learning period.

PURCHASE AND CARE OF CONTAINERS

When acquiring a high-quality pot, the sides should be uniform and free of excessive warping, whether mass-produced or homemade. Except for shallow trays for heavy rock plantings, the sides and bottom of the pot should be of uniform thickness. To determine this, feel both the sides and the bottom. A bottom thickness that is considerably greater than that of the sides lowers the value of the container.

The bottom on the inside of the pot should be flat, level, and free of hollows, which are caused by poor-quality clay or faulty firing. The outside surface should be uniform and without stained or rough areas.

On a glazed container, variations in color often occur during firing and are not considered a fault. Sometimes an unusual variation is especially pleasing and adds to the value of the container.

The pot should sit firmly on a level surface without wobbling.

Sources of Bonsai Pots

The largest retail selection of bonsai containers is found at specialized bonsai nurseries and the sales areas at national and regional bonsai conventions. Containers are also available at some botanical gardens, horticultural institutions, and arboretums. An increasing number of garden centers and retail nurseries offer bonsai containers. Other sources include Oriental shops and large import outlets.

Bonsai or horticultural firms that sell containers by mail often advertise in bonsai publications. As a service to their members, local clubs may order containers in quantity from importers and wholesale distributors. The addresses of local and regional bonsai clubs and information on their publications may be obtained from the national bonsai societies listed in Appendix A.

Care of Bonsai Containers

Handle bonsai containers carefully to prevent cracking and chipping. Wash and clean them after using them and store them in a safe area to avoid breakage.

To remove a buildup of white salts from hard water deposits or fertilizers, soak the affected area in vinegar or wash it with a diluted acid solution. Use a small brush to remove the deposits. Handle the acid with extreme care.

A high-fired container will not crack during freezing temperatures unless the soil freezes and breaks the container as it expands. This is not likely to happen in a container with straight or outward-sloping sides; if the soil freezes it simply expands upward, as frozen ice rises in a bucket. When the sides of the pot curve inward or the top of the container has a lip extending over the soil, the roots and soil are blocked in position, as in Fig. 7-10. Such containers may crack if the root ball freezes. In winter they should not be placed where temperatures would cause freezing.

PRACTICE AND REVIEW

1. Keeping in mind that a bonsai may be enhanced by any one of several containers, look at the photographs of bonsai in this chapter. Are there instances where another container could be substituted for the one in the photo? Select a few bonsai, and for each one describe the size, shape, and possible surface finish of an alternate container you would choose.

2. Attend bonsai exhibits whenever possible to study the design of the tree and the container in which it is planted. In the combinations that you especially like, what aspect of the bonsai does the container complement or emphasize?

3. Figure 7-12 shows thirteen containers, eight of which belong to bonsai shown in Figs. 7-13.1 through 7-13.8. Make and cut out a tracing of each container and place it under the bonsai for which it was used. In your opinion, will any of the extra containers also be suitable for some of the bonsai? (The containers originally chosen are indicated in Appendix D.)

Figure 7-12 Eight containers that have been removed from their bonsai plus five additional bonsai containers.

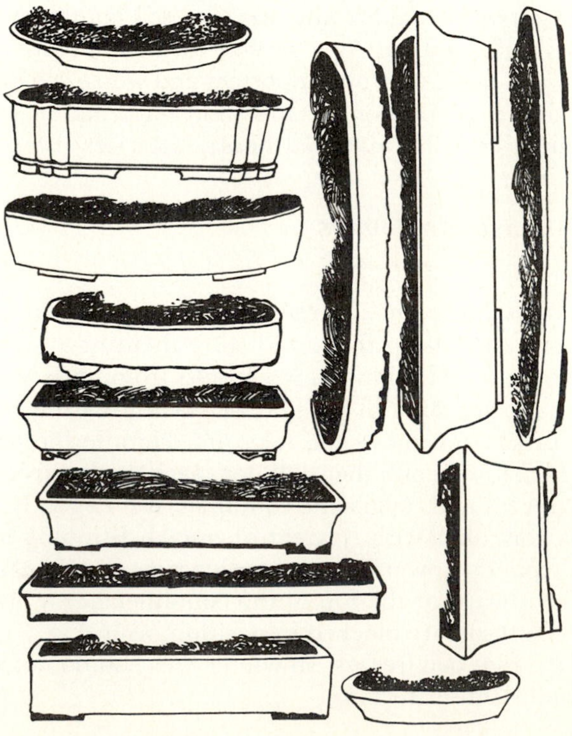

Figure 7-13.1 Bonsai A

Figure. 7-13.2 Bonsai B

Figure 7-13.3 Bonsai C

Figure 7-13.4 Bonsai D

Figure 7-13.5 Bonsai E

Figure 7-13.6 Bonsai F

Figure 7-13.7 Bonsai G

Figure 7-13.8 Bonsai H

8

Bonsai Potting Techniques

Transplanting a tree grown and prepared for bonsai to its first bonsai container is a milestone for both the grower and the tree. It signals that the tree is ready to be designated as a bonsai. This occurs only when the roots have formed a compact mass large enough to support the weight of the tree and the top growth has attained a semblance of bonsai characteristics. Most bonsai, not only those started as seedlings, spend the early part of their life in pots larger and roomier than bonsai containers. Regardless of the size of the container, the timing and potting techniques are essentially the same.

BASIC CONSIDERATIONS

Timing

The preferred time for potting bonsai and bonsai material is early in the growing season, when buds are beginning to enlarge but before new growth appears. At this time, the greatest danger in potting—desiccation or drying of foliage—is minimized. A most unfavorable time, except in the hands of a skilled grower, is the brief period when newly emerging soft leaves are unfolding but not yet functioning. The delicate tissue-thin leaves are highly susceptible to water loss and will collapse if the flow of moisture from the roots is interrupted during transplanting. In an emergency, such as a broken container, when it is necessary to repot a bonsai at an unfavorable time, use a similar or slightly larger pot and disturb the roots as little as possible.

In cold climates, fall is acceptable, but not preferred for potting bonsai. After top growth ceases, root growth continues at a reduced rate when soil temperature is above freezing. Confine fall planting to vigorous, healthy plants. Keep the pruning of roots and top growth to a minimum and protect the roots from freezing. While fall planting is not as critical in warm climates or for indoor bonsai, spring or summer potting is preferable.

Relation of Root Pruning to Top Growth

The functions of a tree above and below ground are closely related. Through photosynthesis, leaves manufacture and supply the tree and roots with energy in the form of carbohydrates. In turn, the roots furnish the leaves and other sections of the tree with water and mineral nutrients. However, it is an erroneous belief that when part of the tree above ground is pruned, the roots must also be pruned. This does not occur in nature. For instance, a large section of a tree may be torn off in a storm without corresponding reduction in the root system. The tree does not succumb to this imbalance; rather, when top growth has been reduced, the tree itself slows the growth of new roots until the balance is restored. Likewise, the new shoots and leaves on a bonsai may be trimmed frequently without reducing the root mass.

When shortening the top growth excessively, for example, from a 3-foot to a 1-foot tree, reduce the root system to prevent the stimulation of unwanted rank new shoots.

In reverse, however, trimming the roots on a potbound bonsai does not automatically require a similar reduction in the top growth. Corresponding pruning of the top growth will be needed only if the roots are severely cut back. This usually occurs during the initial pruning, when plant material is shaped to a bonsai form.

Prune the root mass more cautiously than the top growth. A bonsai will suffer from excessive root pruning if the remaining roots are insufficient for providing the moisture and nutrients needed by the trunk, branches, and foliage. The effect of root pruning varies among species and according to age. Young trees, with "seedling vigor," produce new roots more quickly than older trees, and species known to root readily from cuttings are able to develop new roots soon after pruning.

Work Area and Tools

For potting bonsai, choose a work area that is well lighted and protected from wind and direct sun. To prevent the roots from becoming dry, keep a hand sprayer with water nearby to mist the roots. If the potting is interrupted, be prepared to cover the exposed roots with damp newspapers or cloth. Shallow plastic work trays are handy receptacles for potting mix and other materials.

In addition, have on hand plastic or metal screening with 1/16- or 1/8-inch mesh (window screening is satisfactory) to cover the drainage holes, a prepared

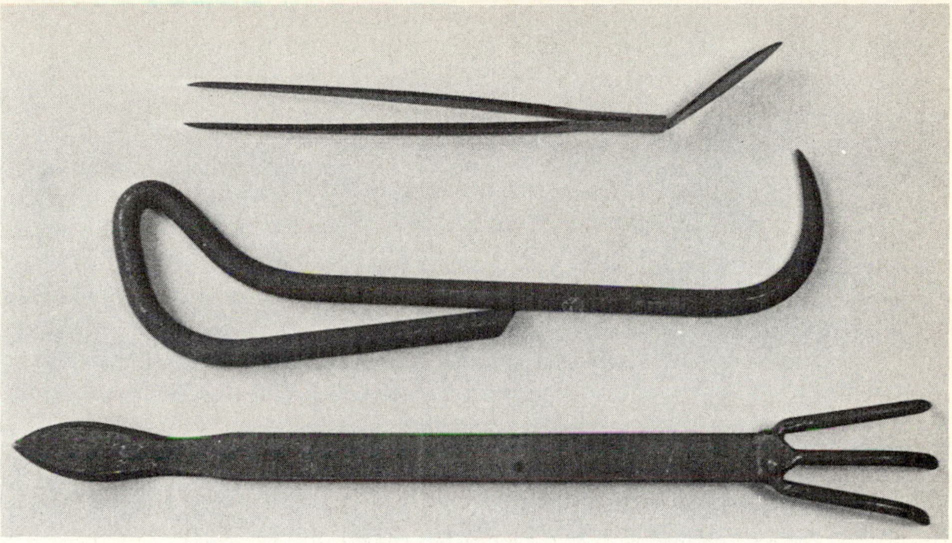

Figure 8-1 Bonsai potting tools: a small rake for loosening soil in a root ball, a root hook for separating heavy roots, and multipurpose tweezers.

dry potting mix as described in Chapter 6, and a watering can or hose with a nozzle that sends out a fine, soft spray. Such nozzles, attachable to a regular garden hose, are available at hardware or garden centers.

Tools. Set aside a pair of old pruning shears for pruning roots. Hard aggregates in the potting mix can nick the sharp blades of fine shears. Other useful tools are tin snips for cutting wire screening (their hard blades, unharmed by aggregates in the potting mix, are also suitable for pruning roots), a hand trowel, a small brush, and one or two round, slender wooden planting sticks. These may be chopsticks, special Oriental bamboo planting sticks, or simply dowels or pencil-size sticks shaped to a taper.

A metal hook or rake is used to separate a massive root ball or roots tightly massed together, and tweezers with a flat blade at one end or a small trowel are helpful for firming the surface of the soil. These three tools are shown in Fig. 8–1. A turntable is a valuable addition for rotating the bonsai to view it from all sides. Strong turntables are available where bonsai tools are sold or may be constructed at home. Inexpensive lazy susans found among kitchenware are satisfactory for light or medium-weight bonsai material.

Pots

Before it reaches a bonsai container, a bonsai is usually grown in a variety of pots; a container used for this purpose is called a training pot. The relatively large size of the pot provides space for root growth. Training pots may be made of plastic, metal, wood, clay, or other materials, with holes provided for drain-

Figure 8-2 Bonsai material growing in training pots: Left to right, *Ficus benjamina, Gardenia* sp., *Cryptomeria japonica, Chamaecyparis obtusa,* and *Acer Buergeranun.*

age. Simple wooden boxes constructed with slats at the bottom (spaced slightly apart for water drainage) and a few short narrow strips of wood nailed underneath to provide a layer of air space make excellent training pots for large plants.

A sampling of training pots is shown in Fig. 8-2. For most prebonsai plants, plastic or clay flowerpots are satisfactory. Plastic pots offer the advantage of light weight, easy cleaning, and convenient storage. They tend to hold moisture in the potting mix for longer periods of time and consequently require less frequent watering than trees in clay pots. Clay pots, although harder to clean, heavier, and subject to cracking, are preferred to plastic by many growers. Clay pots allow moisture and air to permeate through the porous walls and offer the advantage of being an earth material appropriate for bonsai. Plants, including bonsai, will grow in either type of pot. The choice is a matter of personal preference.

POTTING BARE-ROOT SEEDLINGS AND PLANTS

Instructions on potting start with seedlings and proceed to larger and older plants. This planned progression is designed to acquaint the beginner with simple potting techniques that are transferable to bonsai. At the same time, it provides information on handling prebonsai plants, which are the major source of plant material for bonsai.

Seedlings One to Three Years Old

Sources. Look for seedlings anywhere in the vicinity of mature trees—in yards, gardens, vacant lots, fields, and along the side of roads. Select species from maples, figs, hornbeams, spruce, juniper, pines, and others known to be suitable for bonsai. When gathering seedlings, use a trowel to loosen the soil, then lift each one gently, taking care not to break the tender young roots. If the seedlings are to be planted immediately, simply cover the roots with loose soil to prevent drying. If replanting will be delayed for a day or two, wrap the roots in a protective covering such as damp newspaper or sphagnum moss to keep them moist.

One- to three-year-old seedlings (called liners or lining-out stock) are produced in large numbers and shipped bare-rooted by commercial nursery growers. Minimum orders, usually a hundred of a kind, may contain more seedlings than an individual can use but are manageable as a combined order for a club or group. The seedlings are graded by age and by size; in each age group, the smaller sizes are best for bonsai and saikei. Not all nurseries sell to the general public. Those who do will appreciate your cooperation. Read the conditions of sale set forth in the price list. To facilitate processing, enclose a sufficient amount to cover sales tax (if any) and shipping charges as well as the cost of the plants.

Unpack the seedlings immediately upon arrival and immerse their roots in a bucket of water or an emulsion of clay and water. If they will not be planted for a few days, remove them from the water after an hour or two, rewrap them in the packing, and store them in a cool place out of the wind and sun. If planting is delayed and the weather is cool, ''heel in'' the seedlings, as follows: Prepare a shallow trench (dig one side at a slant) in a shaded area protected from wind and spread the seedlings along the trench. Cover the roots and lower trunk with loose, damp soil and keep moist. The seedlings may safely remain in the trench for a week or two unless new growth appears; if this occurs, pot the seedlings as soon as possible.

When working with seedlings germinated in a low, flat container, remove them a few at a time to minimize the amount of time that their roots will be exposed to air.

Containers. Plant the seedlings in the smallest container that will accommodate the roots without crowding. Usually a 2½- or 3-inch round or square pot is satisfactory. Depending on the size of the seedling and the extent of the roots, select a larger or smaller pot. Pots considerably larger than required are not satisfactory. Plants grow best when their roots fill the pot comfortably and are well distributed toward the sides and bottom. When roots occupy only a small portion of the pot, their growth is less vigorous.

Place a piece of screening over the drainage hole at the bottom of round plastic or clay pots to prevent the mix from falling through the hole. Use a section of screening larger than the hole so that even if the screening is accidentally dislodged, part of it will remain over the opening. Screening is not required over the small holes in each corner of a square plastic pot.

Bonsai Potential of Seedlings. In bonsai, potting is more than planting the roots. It involves positioning the plant. Before each seedling is potted, examine it for visible swelling on the lower trunk, which is the first indication of the thick area that forms the bottom trunk. Look also for the presence of roots in this area. The roots may be thin as a thread, but they will become strong supporting roots on the trunk of the future bonsai. A thickened trunk with roots is often found buried beneath the soil, hidden from sight until the seedling is transplanted. As shown in Fig. 8-3, A is the current soil line and B the base of the trunk, which has been covered with soil. If part of the trunk that was

Figure 8-3 A seedling for bonsai. (*A*) Trunk width seen at soil level. (*B*) Thicker trunk uncovered below the soil will become the bottom of the trunk.

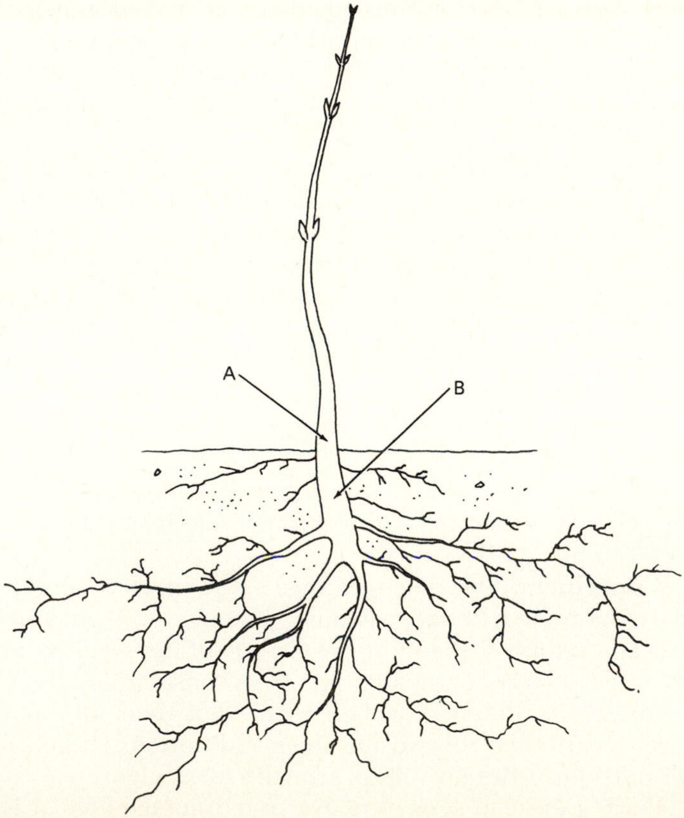

previously buried is used as the base, cut off roots higher on the trunk flush with the bark.

Root Pruning. Next, shorten heavy, long roots, using the same technique used to prune branches. Prune a root with a clean, slanting cut at the fork of another root and immediately beyond the fibrous roots that are to be retained.

Thick roots are anchors that secure the tree in the ground and the conduits through which water and nutrients reach the trunk. Fibrous roots, with many minute root hairs, are the roots that actively absorb and transfer moisture and nutrients to the tree. Large roots are not needed on trees grown for bonsai in a small container. Therefore, even on a seedling, cut them off to encourage the development of fibrous roots that will nourish the tree. Fibrous roots may be recognized as the tiny, tender, nearly white rootlets on the surface of the woody roots. When pruning the heavy, unwanted roots, take care to make the cuts at locations that will not, at the same time, remove the feeder roots. For example, in Fig. 8–4.1, most of the fibrous roots are located at the end of a long taproot which cannot be shortened without removing the feeder roots. By contrast, root growth in Fig. 8–4.2 is suitable for bonsai. Several long roots may be shortened without jeopardizing the mass of feeder roots near the base of the trunk. Although not all seedlings develop roots suited to bonsai, most species popular for bonsai produce fibrous roots under favorable growing conditions. Examples of preferred roots on a seedling for bonsai are seen in Fig. 8–5.

Potting. When the seedlings are ready for planting, sprinkle about a ¼ inch of potting mix on the bottom of the container. During the potting, hold the little tree in the pot with the base of the trunk approximately ½ inch below the rim. Use a planting stick to arrange the roots evenly throughout the container. Place them in a lateral or slightly downward position, and do not permit them to recurve upward toward the top of the container.

Gently pour dry potting mix from a trowel into the container from all sides to fill the spaces between the roots to ¼ inch from the top of the container. When the potting is finished, tilt the container slightly to see whether the seedling is firmly in position. If so, tap the pot a few times on a flat surface to settle the mix. In the process, a little more mix may be needed.

If the tree is not steady in the container, place the pot on a flat surface and hold it firmly. With the other hand, gently thrust the planting stick systematically throughout the container to a depth of several inches. Whenever the mix seems to give, keep the end of the stick in that area and with short, even motions pivot the top of the planting stick back and forth a few inches. This will cause particles in the mix to slip and fall into empty spaces that may be present. Although air pockets, as they are called, occur more frequently with large material than with seedlings, the same method is used to eliminate them. It is a handy bonsai technique to learn now.

When using a dry mix, if the potting is not satisfactory, pour out the mix and repot the tree. The fluidity that permits the mix to be reused is lost when it becomes wet. For this reason, check each planting carefully before watering it.

Figure 8-4.1 A poor root structure for bonsai, with fibrous roots at the far end of a long taproot.

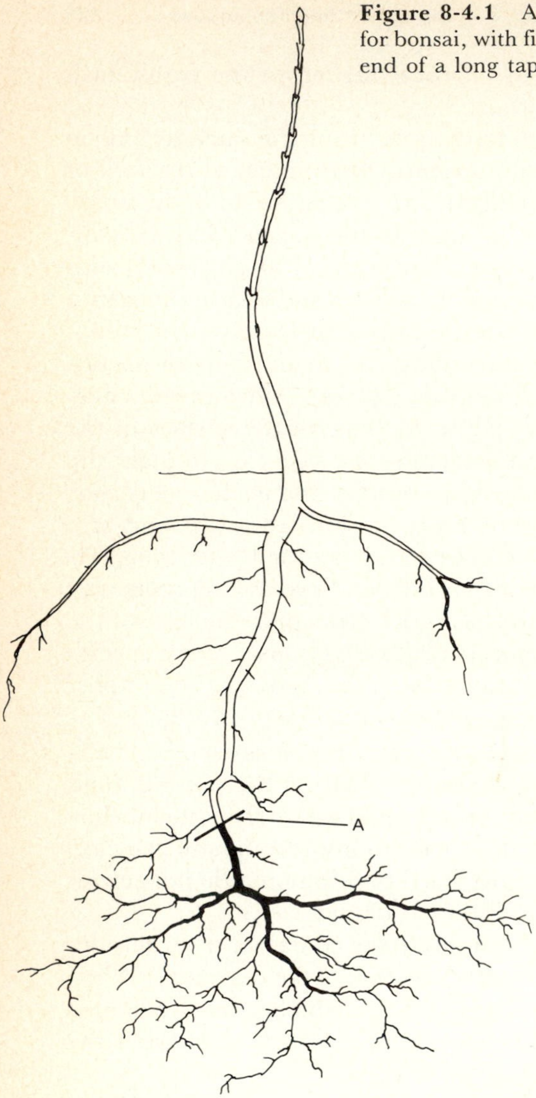

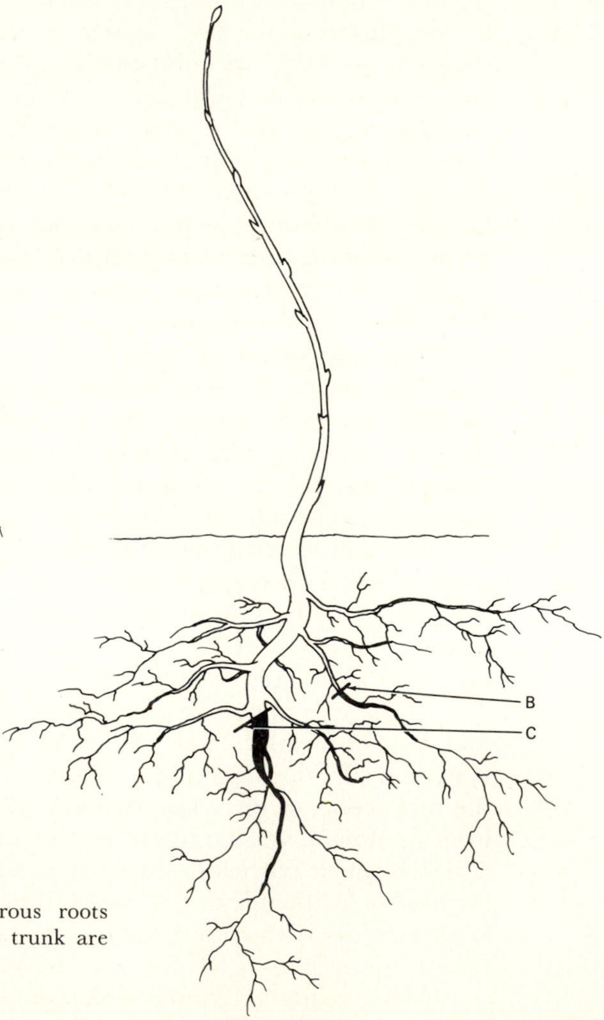

Figure 8-4.2 Many fibrous roots close to the bottom of the trunk are more suitable for bonsai.

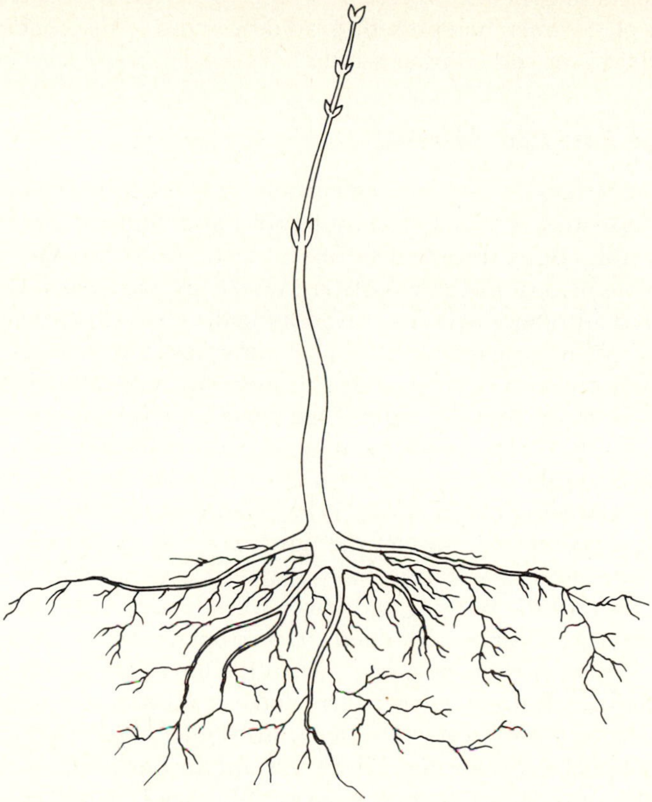

Figure 8-5 Excellent root distribution for bonsai purposes.

Watering. Water the seedlings shortly after they are planted with a gentle spray from a watering can or hose. Pass the spray back and forth over the containers until the potting mix is saturated and water drains from the holes at the bottom of the pot. Thorough watering from the top is preferred (especially when using a dry mix) to placing the newly potted plants in a tray of water to soak. When the container is immersed in water, the pressure of water rising upward through the drainage holes tunnels into the dry mix and may dislodge the planting.

Place the thoroughly watered seedlings in an area protected from sun, wind, and frost. Water regularly when the top of the soil becomes slightly dry. After two weeks, and when there is no danger of freezing, move the seedlings to a permanent growing area.

Small or tender seedlings will do best under partial shade. In a sunny area, place them beneath protective screening or lathe or other material. When the heat of summer has passed, gradually remove the shade cover to harden the seedlings for the coming winter.

Large Bare-Root Material

Sources. This group consists of trees and shrubs approximately 2 to 3 feet tall. As nursery stock, it may be sold and shipped bare-rooted. For learning material, young trees and shrubs hit by a mower or otherwise damaged are also suitable if most of their roots are intact, as are trees in locations that must be cleared for other purposes. An additional source of practice material are marked-down plants at garden centers or nurseries. Plants with slightly damaged top growth are usable so long as the roots are not damaged.

Remove the soil around the roots by shaking the root ball. If clumps of clay or soil remain, break them up with a wooden planting stick. The roots should be sufficiently free of soil for a clear view of the complete root structure.

Handling the Trunk. When handling old bonsai or advanced material for bonsai, always protect the aged bark on the trunk. This is bark that has begun to form a fissured, flaky surface characteristic of old trees and appears first around the bottom and lower trunk. Such bark is one of a bonsai's most valued assets; once dislodged, it is irreplaceable.

Injury occurs most often when the lower trunk is handled during potting. Therefore, from the very start, make it a habit not to grab or hold a bonsai tree by the lower trunk. Hold the trunk higher toward the top among the branches where the bark is young. It is important for beginners to acquire this habit now while working on expendable material; once learned, correct handling will become routine.

Examining the Tree. Keep the roots moist while examining and pruning the tree; spray them with water or wrap them in damp newspaper or cloth. Use a turntable to rotate the plant and observe the trunk and branches from all sides. If the plant wobbles, set it in a container temporarily or wedge the root ball to hold it steady.

Trunk and Branch Pruning. Prune the top growth as described in Chapter 4. Remove all unwanted (nonconforming) branches as well as shoots at the base of the trunk and in the fork of the trunk and branches. Until a front view is selected, little additional pruning is required at this time other than shortening excessively long trunks or branches.

Root Pruning. Uncover the roots and examine the bottom of the trunk to find the widest base that may be present with surrounding roots. Do not ignore or remove small, thin roots in this area. Handle them carefully; they will develop into large, strong surface roots. Inspect the roots beneath the trunk to determine the extent and location of feeder roots. A larger plant naturally requires more feeder roots than a seedling. Their preferred location is the area around and directly under the trunk. Try to shorten or remove thick taplike roots and retain as many fibrous roots as possible. This is also the time to eliminate roots that, like unwanted branches, are nonconforming: roots that are girdling other roots or growing upward toward the surface and are too stiff to reposition.

In choosing between a lateral or a vertical root, give priority to the lateral root because it will fit later into a shallow bonsai pot. However, flexible vertical roots, especially those with feeder roots attached, are worth bending and moving to a horizontal position during potting. Remove dead and damaged roots. When large roots cannot be reduced without destroying an undue number of fibrous roots, it may be necessary to plant the tree in a large container for a while to encourage other fibrous roots.

Potting. After pruning, select a training pot that will hold the roots comfortably and place the pot on a turntable to rotate it during potting. Or it may be more convenient to set a small pot directly on the mix in the tray, where it can be easily turned. (Any mix that spills during the potting will remain in the tray.) Mound the mix in the bottom of the training pot to fit the underside of the roots, as shown in Fig. 8–6.1. Press the roots on the mound and, with a short back-and-forth motion, work them into close contact with the mix, as seen in Fig. 8–6.2. Fill the spaces between the roots with mix. Use a planting stick to move the mix into small crevices. For larger pots, keep the soil level at the bottom of the trunk ½ inch or more below the top of the container. The inside of the container extending above the mix collects water when the plant is watered. If the mix is level with the top of the container, much of the water immediately runs down the outside of the container instead of penetrating the potting mix. When the tree is firmly planted in the container, check again for air pockets to complete the planting as seen in Fig. 8–6.3.

Although it has been a customary practice in horticulture, findings by plant scientists indicate that placing a layer of broken clay pots, coarse gravel, or other such material in the bottom of the container before potting does not facilitate drainage, as is commonly believed. Instead, it forms a thin layer of water called a perched water table (Fig. 8–7) that remains in the container immediately beneath the potting mix. A perched water table hinders drainage and reduces the amount of growing area that otherwise would be available to the roots.

During the planting, give particular attention to flexible roots around the base of the trunk. Arrange them in an outward direction, like the spokes of a wheel, before covering them with a layer of mix. Prior to watering, test the plant for its stability in the container. Use the wooden planting stick to check for air pockets. Provide a protected environment for several weeks before moving newly potted plants to their permanent growing area. If potting is done in hot weather, make the transition to a sunny exposure gradually.

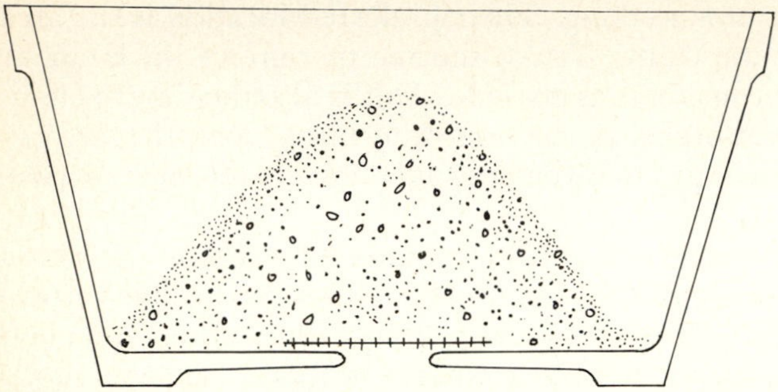

Figure 8-6.1 A mound of mix placed in the container (the amount may vary).

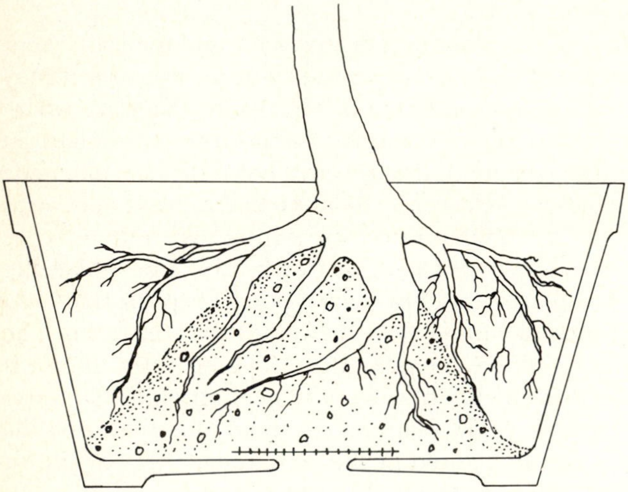

Figure 8-6.2 Roots placed over the mound.

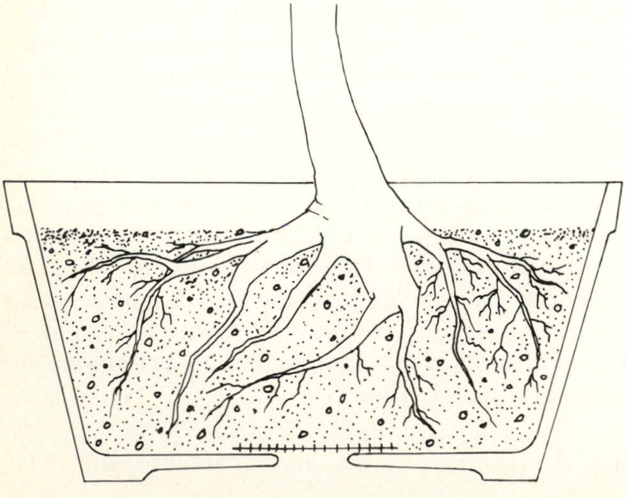

Figure 8-6.3 The completed planting.

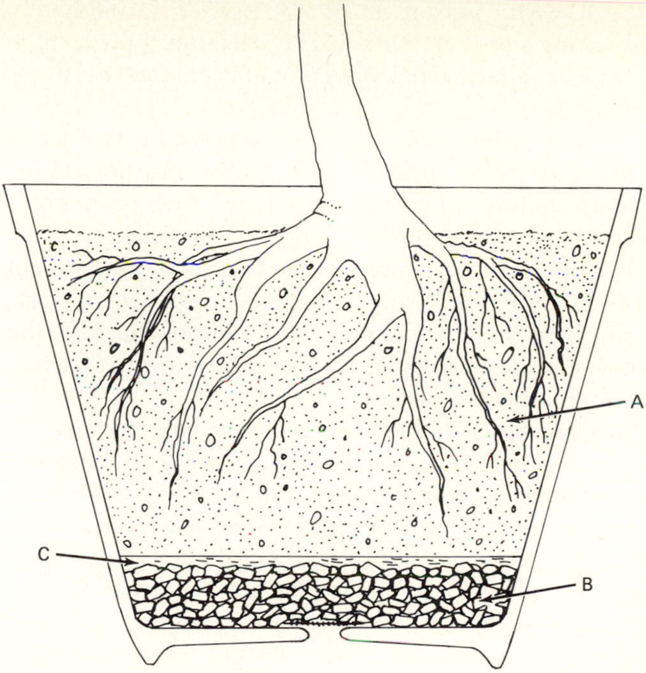

Figure 8-7 Perched water table. (*A*) Potting mix. (*B*) Large aggregates. (*C*) A layer of water between the large aggregates and the mix.

POTTING PLANTS WITH SOIL ON THE ROOTS

Let the soil become partially dry before potting bonsai and plants growing in containers or taken from the ground. Avoid working on a root mass in a wet, clayey soil.

Sources

Most plants used for American bonsai are nursery-grown, in containers or in the ground. Plants dug with the roots surrounded by soil and wrapped in burlap are called B&B, meaning ''balled and burlapped.'' Another source is trees and shrubs removed from mountains or other places. These ''collected'' plants for bonsai are described in Chapter 17.

Trees for bonsai taken directly from the ground demand more skill in handling than those growing in containers. For this reason, the use of container-grown material is recommended for beginners.

Container-grown Stock. Mass-produced and nationally distributed container-grown plants range in size from a few inches to several feet and already have proved their ability to grow in the confines of a container. A container-grown plant usually has a well-developed root mass and may be transplanted throughout the growing season or, if not needed immediately, may be kept in its container for a period of time. The selection, however, may be limited because large-scale standardized production concentrates on popular species with a high survival rate.

A more serious disadvantage for bonsai is faulty root growth, which occasionally occurs when bottom roots are forced upward in the nursery container during mechanical planting operations. Such roots may become too stiff to be moved and flattened to fit a shallow container.

A closely related problem arises when plants are kept in containers for long periods prior to marketing. The root mass becomes choked by its own roots encircling the inside of the pot. As these roots harden, they are difficult to separate and reposition. Responsible nursery growers take measures to prevent these undesirable root formations.

Removing the Plant. Plants are easily removed from a round metal or plastic pot. Turn the pot over and tap the rim smartly on the edge of a table or bench to separate the ball of soil from the container. Occasionally, a root ball does not come out and must be freed by cutting the can. Make a vertical cut from top to bottom with strong cutters, such as tin snips (not bonsai pruning shears). Wear heavy gloves for protection against the sharp metal edges of tin containers. If requested at the time of purchase, many nurseries will split the side of the container with a cutting tool made for this purpose.

Removal of Excess Soil. Place the root ball on a turntable and examine it to find the thickest part of the lower trunk. As indicated previously, although a trunk may be thick at soil level, another, thicker base may sometimes be found beneath the soil. To remove the top layer of mix, hold the root ball firmly, insert the wooden planting stick at the base of the trunk to a depth of about ½ inch, and pull the stick gently through the soil outward to the edge of the ball. Rotate the turntable and continue the process around the trunk until a thick bottom area on the trunk is uncovered or until a depth of several inches is reached. Remove all loose soil to bring the uncovered trunk and roots to view. Loosen hard, compacted soil or matted roots with a metal hook or rake. Use this tool with care to prevent its sharp point from tearing the bark or breaking the roots.

Next, loosen the roots on the outside of the ball. If roots are entangled at the bottom of the ball, separate them. It is not necessary to remove all the soil, only enough to see if there are long roots that should be shortened or removed. Loosen the root ball gently and examine the roots by hand. A plentiful supply of fibrous roots means that a large portion of the long, heavier roots may be eliminated. Depending on the extent of fibrous roots, the root mass may be reduced to one-half or even one-third of its original volume. Roots are often entangled and difficult to distinguish from one another. Before removing a root, trace it along its entire length, beginning at its origin at the trunk, to make certain that a desirable root is not cut by mistake. During this pruning, keep as much soil as possible in the root ball.

When selecting roots to be pruned, shorten or remove the vertical ones to reduce the height of the root ball.

Compatible Mixes. While pruning the root mass, carefully observe the texture of the soil surrounding the roots. It is extremely important that the new mix and the old have particles and pore space of similar size. For example, match an old mix consisting of small particles with another small-particle mix; repot roots growing in a coarse mix of large aggregates and open pore space in a mix of similar-size aggregates.

The cohesion and adhesion of water prevent the normal exchange of moisture between mixes of widely different consistency. A fine-particle clay soil, surrounded by a large-particle sandy mix, absorbs water from the more open mix, even when the clay soil already contains water. As a result, the coarse sandy mix is almost permanently dry and cannot support root growth, while roots in the compact mix, which cannot release water, are in danger of being waterlogged.

This condition is found, for instance, when azaleas, growing in a root ball containing a compact mix of fine sand and humus, are repotted in a mix consisting of coarse sand or other large particles. When the plants fail to grow and gradually suffer a decline, examination will reveal that no new roots have grown in the coarse-particle medium and that old roots within the compact root ball are rotting from excessive moisture. The problem is remedied by entirely removing all old potting mix from the roots and repotting the plant bare-rooted in an entirely new mix.

The process operates in reverse. Plants in a root ball of a large-particle mix will not receive adequate moisture when potted in a container with a fine-particle, compact mix. The compact mix will draw water and moisture from the looser mix. This condition is easily avoided by using mixes of like composition in the same container. The ingredients need not be identical so long as they are similar in aggregate size, pore space, and texture.

Potting. It is easy to repot a root mass that remains intact in its growing medium after pruning. Apply the preceding potting instructions with the following modifications: After trimming the roots, knead the underside of the root ball into a slightly concave hollow. Build a mound of mix in the container that will fill this space. Press the root mass over the mound and wiggle it to bring the roots in touch with the potting mix. Work more mix around and under the sides of the root ball. Fill any spaces between the roots with mix. Check for air pockets during the potting. Keep the soil level ½ inch or more from the top of the container. Water thoroughly when the potting is completed.

Roots without Soil. When potting bonsai material with little or no soil remaining on the roots, trim and arrange the bare roots to fit into the container. Without a soil covering, the long roots and small fibrous roots are easy to see. Move crowded roots into the open areas and rearrange the root mass in other ways as needed. During the potting, take extra care to prevent the roots from drying and to fill all spaces between the roots with potting mix. Otherwise, potting procedures are essentially similar to those for roots with soil.

Moss

A green cover of moss will hold the potting mix in place and protect the surface of the soil from erosion during rain or watering. Moss suitable for bonsai is not always obtainable when needed. Keep a supply handy by placing moss in training pots around prebonsai trees. The experience in gathering and using moss will give the beginning bonsai grower a head start in applying moss later to a first bonsai.

Although most mosses prefer shade and moisture, those that are partially sun-tolerant are best for bonsai. Two such mosses are the gray-green *Bryum argenteum*, called silvery thread moss, and *Barbula unguiculata*, yellow-green beard moss. Look for any low, compact, sun-tolerant moss. Gather moss wherever it is found—on a wall, along a walkway, at the base of a tree, at the edge of a garden, on a golf course, or in a parking lot. Accept woodland moss if no other can be found, although it soon browns when placed in the sun.

Use a trowel or flat-bladed tool to lift moss from the ground with a thin layer of soil attached. Large sheets of moss are convenient, but small pieces are equally usable. Trim the moss of surplus soil and remove twigs, leaves, and other debris. If it is not used immediately, moss can be stored for a while if kept damp and in the shade.

When applying moss, moisten the surface of the mix in the container with a fine spray and either spray the bottom surface of the moss or place it in a shallow tray of water. The moss will adhere to the mix readily when both the moss and the mix are moist. Immersing the moss in water will also increase its pliability. Place the moss on the surface of the mix and mold it to the contour of the planting with the flat end of tweezers or a small trowel. Small pieces close together create a slightly uneven mosaic surface that suggests a distant field or slope.

For an irregular area, it may be necessary to trim the moss to the required shape with a knife or old scissors. Mosses do not have roots; only thin, cellular threads hold them to the soil.

Moss may be used in innovative ways. Treat moss as pigments in a painting or as textures on sculpture. When a variety of moss is available, apply some in large swathes and others as small accents around a tree or rock. Light green mosses at the base of trees in the interior of a planting bring the eye into the bonsai, while darker moss on the outside and back form a subtle frame or backdrop to the bonsai.

Occasionally, moss covers only a portion of the container, such as the area around the base of the tree, in contrast to the exposed soil elsewhere. Great freedom is enjoyed with the use of this lowly material so long as the results appear natural, low-key, and in keeping with the overall effect of the bonsai. Moisten newly applied moss with a fine spray of water and then water thoroughly.

Dried Moss. When moss is plentiful, it may be dried, ground, and stored for future use. Select low-growing moss with only a thin layer of soil. Clean it of all foreign matter and dry it in the sun, then grind it to a powder in a mortar or force it through a fine sieve. To reconstitute it on a bonsai planting, first water the potting mix in the container thoroughly with a fine spray, sprinkle the moss over the moist surface, press it lightly into the soil, and cover it with a nylon net. Keep the container moist and in the shade. Within a week or two, depending on the moisture and humidity, the cells and spores of the dried moss will rejuvenate and form a new moss cover.

Moss in a bonsai container has a relatively short life span, especially in sunny areas of low humidity. Under these conditions, it must be replaced periodically.

Liverwort. Liverworts are primitive plants that resemble moss. They are not mosses, however, and may be harmful to bonsai. Liverworts form small green rufflelike growth that hugs the ground. A few are attractive, but, if unchecked, they develop extensive colonies that cover the surface of the soil, sealing it against the entrance of air and preventing the evaporation of moisture. On a bonsai, this causes root rot and decay. Remove liverworts with tweezers or a trowel.

PRACTICE AND REVIEW

Starting with Seedlings

Many of the finest bonsai in the Orient were started from seedlings. Although years are required to develop a single seedling into a specimen bonsai, young seedlings are suitable for miniature bonsai, group plantings, and saikei.

Materials: Small seedlings (about 4 to 8 inches), potting mix, small pots, shears, trowel, planting stick, and a watering can or hose. Self-germinated seedlings are found everywhere: gardens, lawns, fields, roadsides, forests, and vacant lots. Use a small trowel to remove seedlings from the ground, and protect the roots from drying. Follow this procedure to plant the seedlings:

1. Examine the lower trunk. Remember, the trunk of a one- or two-year-old seedling is often thickened where roots have emerged. Are lateral surface roots present in addition to a longer taproot? Continue the examination and decide which section of the trunk will be planted at soil level.

2. Next, evaluate the root growth and the extent of the fine feeder roots, which must be retained when other roots are pruned. Shorten the taproot and other long roots as much as possible.

3. Consider the angle where the trunk emerges from the soil. Will the trunk be vertical or slanting? If slanting, tilt the trunk to either side or the rear of the container and select the most pleasing trunk line as the "front" of the seedling. Shorten overly long trunks or branches before potting.

4. Plant each seedling in a small container. As seedlings grow, trim and prune them for use as future bonsai material.

Repotting a Plant in a Pot

Obtain a plant with one or only a few stems growing in a container from a garden center, a supermarket, a friend, or some other source. Assemble the tools and materials used for potting a seedling and follow the procedures described in the chapter for potting a plant with soil on the roots. After pruning the roots, repot it in the original container or a slightly larger pot. Remember to use a mix that is compatible with the soil that is on the roots, or remove all the old soil. This is excellent practice for gaining skill and confidence in potting. As a learning aid, use plants in a variety of sizes for practice material.

A Moss Landscape

This exercise is an introduction to the many uses of moss in bonsai and saikei.

Materials: Several varieties of moss, including low-growing species; a waterproof ceramic tray, or other low "containers" such as a slate tile, a slab of stone, bark, or a plastic supermarket tray for packaging produce; peat moss, potting mix, and sand (optional); and a trowel, tweezers, and utility scissors.

1. Moisten the peat moss or potting mix and form it into a contoured landmass on the tray. Include several elevations with hills, mountains, valleys, and hollows. Add rocks if desired.

2. Follow the previous directions for applying moss to a planting. Use taller mosses to portray a distant woods and shorter moss for fields and pastures; other effects may also be achieved.

3. Add sand as a finishing touch to suggest a stream or a body of water. If the planting is in a tray with a rim, use tweezers to press the edge of the moss a quarter of an inch or so below the top of the tray.

4. When completed, spray the planting with a fine mist of water. It will last for several weeks, indoors or outside, if it is kept moist and out of direct sun.

9

Creating a Bonsai

SELECTING THE MATERIAL

Finding Suitable Material

A beautiful bonsai is the result of the grower's skill plus the potential of the plant material. All bonsai growers develop the ability to distinguish good plant material from poor.

By Species. Great variation exists among plants within a species. In selecting material, it may be necessary to examine many plants of a species to find one with a trunk and branch structure suitable for bonsai.

Examine each plant from all sides to determine its bonsai potential. Where growth is thick, spread the branches apart to inspect the interior trunk and branching. Be sure the light is good, and take time to make a careful selection. The most important areas to consider are the bottom of the trunk, the lower trunk, and the first usable bottom branches. This area contains the focal points of the future bonsai; much of the upper portion of the plant material will be cut away. The search for bonsai material can be time-consuming and may require an examination of numerous plants at a nursery or garden center. As an aid to bonsai growers, specialized bonsai nurseries offer plants preselected and grown for their bonsai configuration.

Preliminary Eliminations. When looking for plants at a general nursery or plant center, adopt a process of elimination to reduce the time required to select suitable material. From the very start, consider only healthy plants with foliage of a good color. Do not give ailing plants or those with any sign of pests or disease a second glance.

Inspect the plants quickly one by one to eliminate those with strong structural defects that cannot be easily concealed. Pay particular attention to the following areas for features that are unwanted and hard to change or ignore.

Trunk. First look at the base and lower trunk. This area consists of the tree's most rigid wood. It is harder to change than any other section of a tree. Promptly eliminate a trunk that is badly damaged or scarred. A hooked trunk, that is, one with a sharp angle near the base, disqualifies the tree. Such an angle is displeasing in a bonsai.

On older trunks ½ inch or more thick, if there is no thickening at the base, no evidence of surface roots, however thin, and no suggestion of a taper along the first 12 inches of the bottom trunk, reject the plant. On young trunks ¼ inch or less, make allowances for the possibility of future development.

Branches. By now, the number of plants has been greatly reduced, perhaps by well over half. Inspect the branching next.

The point at which a branch emerges on the trunk or shoots grow from a branch cannot be easily changed, if at all. Examine these junctions quickly. Experienced bonsai growers will choose a pattern where new growth appears at various locations around the perimeter of a trunk or branch. By contrast, branches that emerge along parallel lines on either side of the trunk create a flat linear pattern not easily adaptable for bonsai. Reject such plants.

Eliminate plants whose largest and thickest branches are clustered at the top of the trunk with thin branches at the bottom or whose branch growth is so dense on the trunk that extensive thinning will be required. After pruning, many unsightly scars will be visible. Such plants are disqualified as bonsai material.

Identifying Favorable Features. After plants with unalterable defects have been screened from the potential bonsai material, examine the remaining plants for positive features.

Trunks. Again, the inspection starts with the trunk. Set aside plants with one or more of the following characteristics for further examination and eliminate the others:

A pronounced wide base at the bottom of the trunk.

Visible surface roots.

A taper.

A lower trunk emerging from the soil in a straight or slightly curved manner.

Branches. Examine the plants for a favorable branch structure, including the following:

Distribution around all sides of the trunk.

Spacing of no more than several inches apart.

Most of the largest branches on the lower half of the plant.

Thin branches on the upper portion of the trunk.

If needed, one or more branches to replace the trunk for increased taper.

When making this examination, it is important to remember that the location of a branch on the trunk is permanently fixed. Sinews of woody cells bind it to the trunk at that exact spot. Widely spaced branches, which often appear on larger material, cannot be brought closer together on the small bonsai trunk. At the start, branches on the plant material should be closely spaced (but not crowded) and distributed at various elevations on the trunk.

In the same manner that a trunk with many branches is preferred, so are branches with many smaller branches. Each branch increases the options of how a bonsai is shaped and where the trunk may be cut back. Likewise, each small branch, or branchlet, forms a fork on the larger branch and adds to the choice of exactly where a branch may be shortened and how far back or on which side the cut is made.

Leaves or needles are only a covering; do not consider them a structural element. Furthermore, most of the original foliage is usually cut off in the process of making the plant into a bonsai. Nevertheless, a bonsai grower may be tempted to select material because of a dense, beautiful mass of leaves. Never do this. Among all the components involved in the formation of a bonsai, none is replaced more easily or more quickly than the leaves. Often new foliage will sprout in a matter of weeks, or at the most, one growing season, while five or more years may be required to develop a new branch. Look for the structural features; the trimmings are renewable.

Plant Material for the Initial Bonsai

The Plant. For the first bonsai, select a container-grown plant about 10 to 16 inches high with an upright trunk and lateral branches. It will most likely be in a gallon or half-gallon container, but the container size may vary. The demonstration plant in Fig. 9-1.1 (found at a garden center) is a Torulosa juniper.

Timing. Because of the extensive pruning and repotting involved, the preferred time for starting a bonsai is spring, when the plant is at the peak of its vigor. Moreover, it will have a full growing season to produce new shoots and foliage to embellish the bonsai design.

In warm climates with extended growing seasons, it is possible to prune and repot plants for bonsai throughout most of the year. In cold winter climates, however, a plant may be weakened by severe pruning immediately prior to its winter dormancy. Except for indoor bonsai, in cold climates, postpone bonsai work until the end of winter or early spring.

STRUCTURING THE BONSAI

The tools, work area, and materials are the same as for potting prebonsai material, as explained in Chapter 8, plus wire, wire cutters, pruning shears, and a suitable container.

Figure 9-1.1 *Juniperus chinensis* cv. Torulosa, juniper from container-grown nursery stock.

Figure 9-1.2 The top of the trunk is pruned, and small branches near soil level are removed.

Figure 9-1.3 The bottom trunk is examined for roots near the surface.

Figure 9-1.4 A thicker trunk with many roots is found below the soil level.

Figure 9-1.5 The juniper is tilted to obtain a different view of the trunk.

Figure 9-1.6 The trunk is shortened; wire is applied to the trunk and lower branches.

Figure 9-1.7 Rear view showing where the trunk was pruned at a juncture of a branch.

Figure 9-1.8 The juniper wired and pruned to a bonsai form.

Place the plant on a turntable to remove all brown leaves or needles, dead twigs, debris, and weeds or grasses at the base of the trunk. Remove unwanted branches to open the interior structure to view, and shorten an overly long trunk or branches, as shown in Fig. 9-1.2.

Evaluating the Trunk and Branches

The Bottom of the Trunk. First examine the bottom of the trunk. If it shows little thickening and few surface roots, as in Fig. 9-1.3, explore the area beneath the soil level. Carefully remove the top level of soil as described in Chapter 8 to bring the buried trunk to view. Stop the probe after several inches if the trunk appears disfigured or if it is shrinking in diameter and return the soil to its original level. If a wider trunk is uncovered, inspect it with these questions in mind: How extensive are the surrounding roots? Does the trunk rise from its base without a pronounced curve or sharp angle? Is the newly found section harmonious with the section immediately above? After viewing it from all sides, if the trunk that was buried is an improvement over the other, use it as the base of the tree. Remove any roots along the new trunk that will be above soil level. On the demonstration juniper, a thicker trunk and roots were found beneath the surface, as shown in Fig. 9-1.4.

The Trunk Line. Next, examine the plant material for a harmonious, tapered trunk line. Place a wedge under the container to tilt the trunk (Fig. 9-1.5) and view it at various angles. Often there will be a choice of desirable trunk lines. Keep the best alternatives in mind while evaluating other aspects of the plant.

When making a small bonsai from large material, the original trunk is usually shortened, and in the process, its taper is destroyed. Inspect branches on the upper trunk as possible substitutes for the trunk. Then later, if necessary, choose the branch that will form a natural continuation of the trunk.

Major Bottom Branches. The two major bottom branches are commonly referred to as the first and second branch, or branches one and two. Select them as a pair. One of the two will usually be the longest and strongest branch on the bonsai. Their preferred location is on alternate sides of the trunk, fairly close together and at different elevations from the top of the container. If they are too low, they obscure the view of the lower trunk; if they are too high on the trunk, they create a bare, monotonous area that lacks interest. When the major branches are not in an ideal position, remember that they are but one aspect of the tree, and an attractive bonsai can nevertheless be created when the placement of these two branches is less than perfect.

After choosing the first and second branches, look for a short branch on the rear of the trunk between the first two. This branch gives the bonsai three dimensions and depth.

The two side and one rear branch form a group of three, a branch arrangement frequently used in bonsai design. Rotate the turntable to locate other possible bottom branches seen from different views of the trunk. This will offer a choice of branch arrangements when selecting the front of the bonsai. The two side branches are most pleasing when they extend slightly toward the front. This happens automatically when they emerge on the side of the trunk a bit toward the front. Often, a branch originating toward the rear of the trunk may be wired and brought forward. Do not use a branch formed directly on the front of the trunk. (After the front is selected, remove such branches.)

Selecting the Front

The front view is the ''best'' combined view of the roots, trunk, and major branches. Select it in the same manner as in the practice exercise in Chapter 5. Weigh all the factors and choose the best combinations. Consider the trunk and branches not only in their present state but as they will appear after several years of development. Nearly all bonsai techniques are applied for their future effect. Many bonsai growers develop a form of dual vision that enables them to superimpose the future image of the bonsai on its present form.

The choice of the front is a value judgment involving a personal appraisal of the plant and its bonsai potential. Unlike a mathematical equation with one correct answer, the ''best'' view of the bonsai may be but one of several possibilities.

One approach is to choose the front according to established criteria, with a wide bottom trunk and surface roots ranked first in importance, a prominent tapered trunk second, and a closely related 1-2-3 branch arrangement third. The presence of all these features emphatically assures a well-structured bonsai. However, only a small proportion of plants meet these specifications, which if applied rigidly would fault or downgrade much otherwise attractive plant material.

Most bonsai are made from ''imperfect'' plants. The grower emphasizes the plant's strong points to distract from the less desirable ones. Be selective when choosing the front; examine the plant material for its treelike features and determine which ones will be most effective in transforming the plant into a convincing bonsai. For example, shrubby plants such as spreading juniper or boxwood are not trees; if used for bonsai, these shrubs will need a pronounced trunk and surface roots to appear as trees. On the other hand, when the plant material is a flowering or fruiting tree, a hawthorn or crab apple, for instance, the easily recognizable flowers and fruit are vivid tree-identity features that indicate that the bonsai is truly a tree. For such bonsai, a trunk and branch structure able to support the flowers and fruit is adequate. Although a wide bottom trunk with surrounding surface roots will always strengthen and enhance a bonsai, many beautiful bonsai lack this feature.

After evaluating the possible front views, select the one you prefer for your bonsai. On the demonstration juniper, the view seen in Fig. 9–1.5 was designated the front. It is helpful to mark the front view while working on the tree and to make a simple sketch of the trunk and branch structure of the bonsai as you envision it.

Shaping the Bonsai

Return the plant to the container to keep the root ball from falling apart while wiring and pruning the top growth. Place a layer of crinkled newspaper on the bottom of the container to raise the top of the root ball flush with the rim. This will make the plant more visible and accessible. Start work at the bottom of the trunk and continue upward.

1. Overview. While looking at the plant from the front, take a moment to review its most important features: the extent and location of roots around the trunk, the angle of the trunk's emergence from the soil, the entire trunk line from bottom to top (including a replacement for the upper trunk), and the location of the major bottom branches.

2. Lower Trunk. Remove any shoots remaining on the trunk beneath the two lowest major branches. For the time being, retain rear branches that may be present behind the two major ones. If a portion of the lower trunk is to be repositioned, wire and bend it now. Continue the wire on the upper trunk if it is to be repositioned later.

3. Major Bottom Branches. These branches may require wiring to move them slightly forward toward the viewer or to bring their line into harmony with the trunk. Straighten the branches if the trunk is predominantly straight; curve them to harmonize with a curved trunk.

To complete the group of three branches, select a rear branch located between the first two or in the general vicinity. If no rear branch is present, it is sometimes possible to use a rear branchlet on one of the two major branches. If so, wire and position it toward the rear of the trunk.

4. Trunk Height and Branch Length. As described in Chapter 5, a pleasing ratio between the total height of the trunk and the length of the lower trunk (measured from the bottom of the trunk to the lowest major branch) is approximately three to one. This ratio is not rigid, but avoid making the height of the trunk twice that of the lower trunk. On a newly started bonsai, the trunk is often shorter than its future projected height.

Keep the major branches less than half the height of the trunk, whenever possible. All other branches, of course, are shorter.

Work in progress on the juniper is shown in Fig. 9-1.6. The trunk has been wired and cut back to a replacement branch. The two lowest bottom branches are also wired and shortened, but not yet repositioned. A slight protrusion and small shoots on the lower trunk were removed. The rear view in Fig. 9-1.7 shows where the trunk was pruned to reduce its height.

5. Upper Trunk. Wire and position the replacement branch to appear as a natural continuation of the trunk. If necessary, bend the replacement to harmonize with the lower section. Generally, it is possible to trim the top of the trunk and shorten the bottom branches to establish a compact bonsai form.

6. Upper Branches. Use the first group of bottom branches as the starting point for selecting branches higher on the trunk. Choose well-defined branches on alternate sides of the trunk with small branches toward the rear. A pleasing effect is achieved when two side branches and one rear branch can be formed in groups of three similar to the major bottom branches. Whenever possible, avoid branches directly opposite each other as well as two branches close together on the same side of the trunk. While working within the limitations of the plant material, use these guidelines for branches ascending the trunk:

1. As they become higher on the trunk, choose progressively shorter and thinner branches that are smaller in diameter than the trunk.
2. Avoid one branch directly above another. If this occurs, wire one of the branches and move it to the right or left of the other.
3. Select branches that emanate from various locations on the sides and rear of the trunk.
4. Vary the spacing between branches to avoid the appearance of rungs on a ladder.

When the branch arrangement is finished, cut off unwanted branches. Where a callus collar is present, make the cut flush with the top of the collar. Trim the rear branches, if needed, to make them shorter than side branches at the same general elevation.

Examine the distribution of branches around the trunk by standing above the bonsai and looking. Are the branches distributed on both sides and the rear of the trunk?

7. Angle of Emergence. From the front view, observe the angle that each branch forms at its juncture with the trunk. When the major bottom branches are horizontal, they form a 90-degree angle at the trunk, as seen in Fig. 9–2. Several alternate patterns may be formed by the angle of branches on a trunk. In Fig. 9–3.1, the downward-growing branches move progressively closer to a horizontal position as they ascend the trunk. The bottom branch is slightly above horizontal in Fig. 9–3.2. The higher branches point more and more upward as they ascend the trunk. In Fig. 9–3.3, the lowest branch slants downward, the second branch (from the bottom) is closer to a horizontal position, and the third branch is horizontal. The next two branches slant increasingly upward.

These three sequential patterns establish continuity in the changing angle that each branch forms at its juncture with the trunk. The progressive changes introduce a pleasing rhythm to a bonsai and avoid unwanted crossing branches. A highly visible branch that fails to conform to an established pattern should

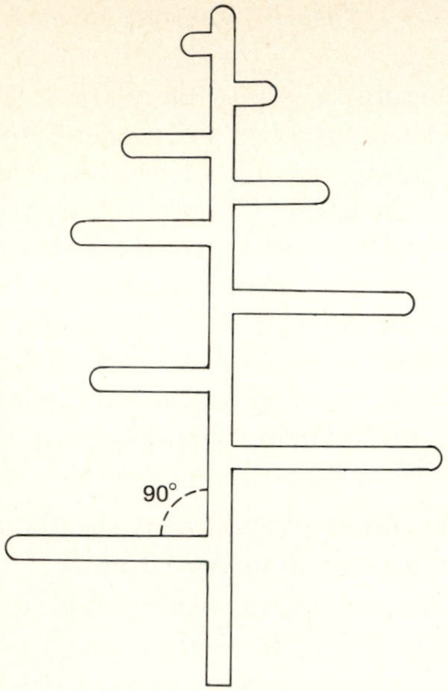

Figure 9-2 Diagrammatic drawing of horizontal branches on a bonsai.

be wired and matched to the others. As seen in the drawings, the major bottom branches form a line that is repeated or progressively modified as the branches ascend the trunk.

8. A Treelike Form. After wiring and shaping the trunk and branches, prune the plant to a treelike form by projecting an imaginary line from the apex of the trunk to the tip of each major bottom branch. On young needle evergreens, the lines are straight and form a triangle. On deciduous trees, the line is curved to form an oval or a rounded triangular shape. Cut back each branch that extends beyond the lines. Branches of somewhat uneven lengths give a more natural effect than ones trimmed flush like a hedge. The juniper shaped into a bonsai in Fig. 9–1.8 has a triangular form. Most of the trunk is visible. The branch replacing the top of the trunk appears as a natural extension of the trunk. The branches along the middle section of the trunk have been wired, trimmed, and positioned. The tree is now ready for a smaller training pot or a bonsai container.

9. Root Evaluation. Lift the root ball from the container and place it on the turntable for an examination. If the root mass consists of large roots with only a sprinkling of fibrous roots, repot it in a training pot for a few more years. Choose a pot the same width and half as high as the first container. When a mass of fibrous roots is present after larger roots are pruned, the tree is ready for a bonsai container

Preparing the Container

To minimize the time that the roots are exposed to the air, prepare the bonsai container beforehand. Place screening over each drainage hole and fasten it

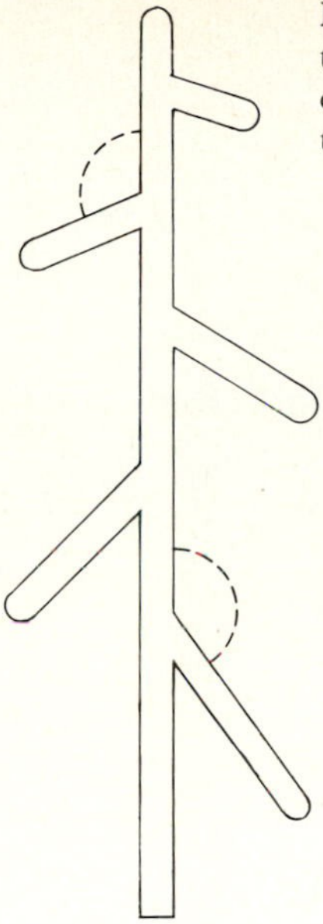

Figure 9-3.1 The downward direction of each branch is progressively increased from the top to the bottom of the trunk.

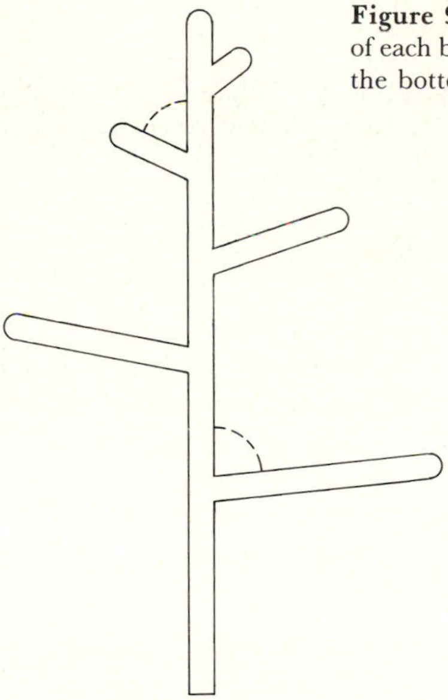

Figure 9-3.2 The upward direction of each branch gradually increases from the bottom to the top of the trunk.

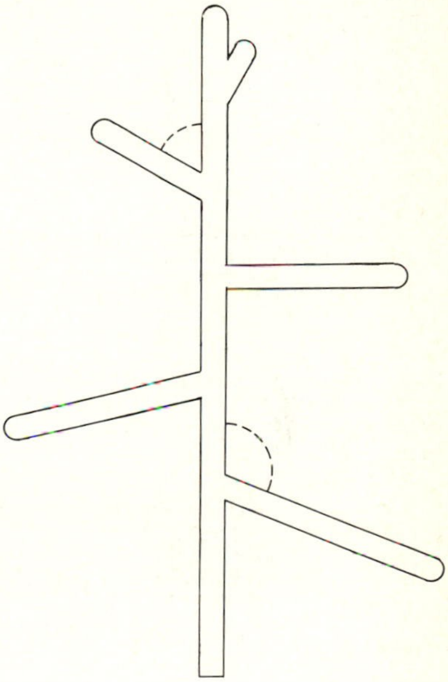

Figure 9-3.3 An example of progressive sequence in the angle formed by branches in opposite directions from the middle branch.

securely if the tree is likely to be moved here and there before its final position is chosen. Use the following method to prevent the screening from being dislodged:

1. Select a strand of 1.0- or 1.5-mm aluminum or #14 or #16 gauge copper wire about 6 inches long or longer, depending on the size of the hole. Bend the wire into three equal lengths (Fig. 9–4.1) sufficiently long to overlap the hole. Bend each end of the wire at right angles (Fig. 9–4.2) to fit snugly along the inside of the hole. Extend each loop ⅜ inch above and beyond the hole, as shown by wires A-a and B-b in Fig. 9–4.3.

2. A side and top view of screening secured by wire is shown in Fig. 9–4.4. The ends of the wire are bent tightly against the underside of the container.

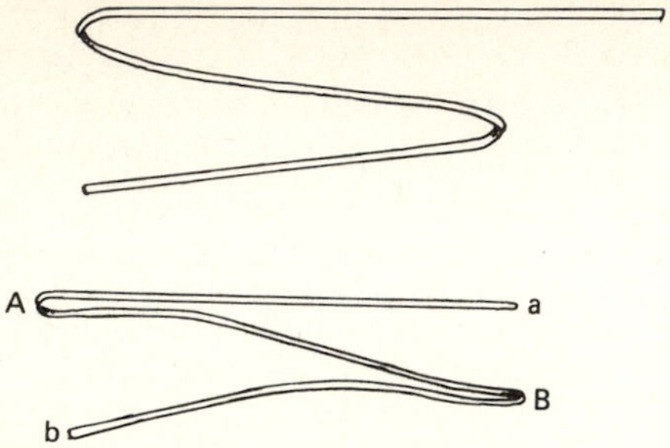

Figure 9-4.1 A strand of wire bent into three equal sections.

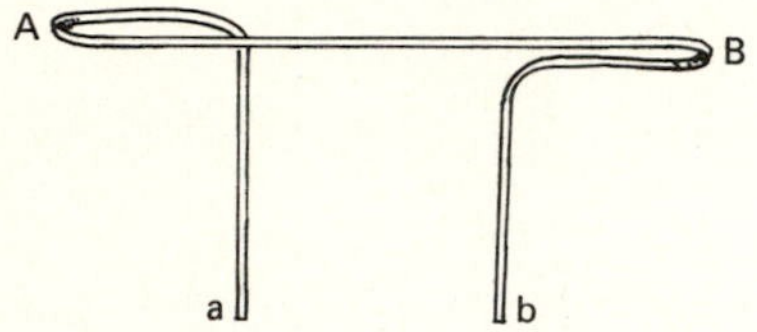

Figure 9-4.2 A right-angle bend is made at each end of the wire.

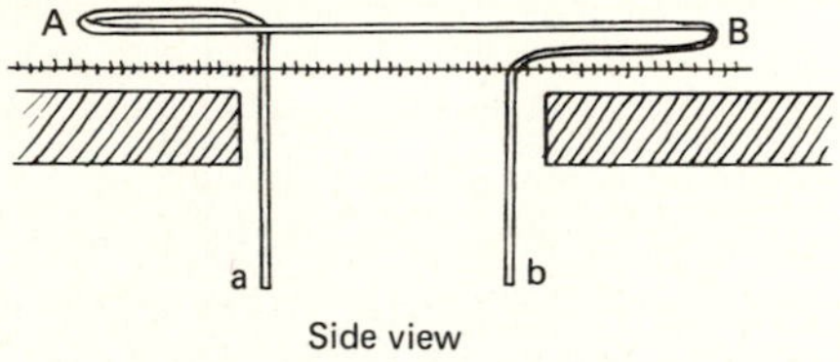

Figure 9-4.3 Wire is inserted through a hole in the container.

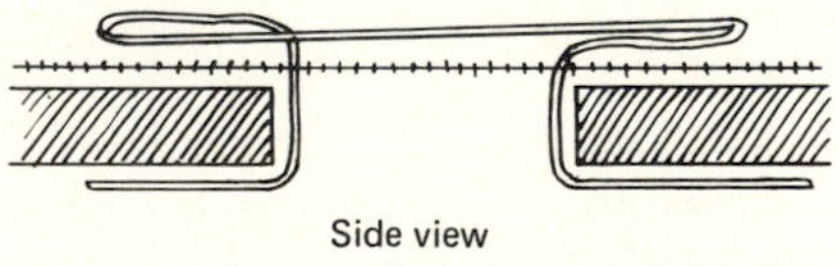

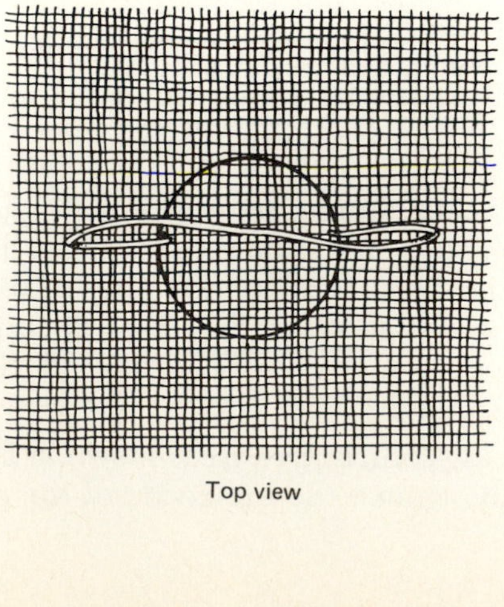

Figure 9-4.4 *Side view:* Both ends of the wire are bent flush against the underside of the container. *Top view:* Wire has secured the screening in the container.

Tying the Tree. Growers frequently tie the tree to the container to prevent it from being uprooted by strong winds, animals, or mishaps. This precaution is especially helpful for trees with weak root systems, top-heavy branching, or trunks with a pronounced slant. Trees with vertical trunks and extensive supporting roots tend to be well balanced and stable in their containers. Whether or not a tree requires tying is a matter for the individual grower to decide. To tie the tree, prepare the container prior to potting by inserting one or more long strands of thin wire or waxed string through the screening and drainage holes (Fig. 9–5.1). Drape the ends over the outside of the container (Fig. 9–5.2) until needed.

For a container with only one hole, anchor the wire by wrapping it around a piece of wood or heavy wire on the underside of the hole, as shown in Fig. 9–5.3. Later, when repotting the bonsai, cut the wire beneath the container before removing the tree. Waxed string gradually disintegrates and will not require further attention.

Adjusting the Roots. Moving a started bonsai from a nursery container or training pot to a shallow bonsai container will probably require flattening the root mass as well as shortening long, thick roots that will likely be present. To keep root pruning to a minimum, sometimes pruning can be combined with shaping the root mass to fit the new container. A root ball held together by intertwining roots may be kneaded to fit into the container. If the container is longer than it is wide, elongate the roots to that shape. Adjust the height of the root ball to bring the bottom of the trunk slightly above the rim of the container. Allow space for a layer of fresh potting mix on the bottom of the container. Trim and mold the root mass to a shape that will leave a 1-inch-wide band of continuous open space between the roots and the sides of the container.

Potting a Bonsai

1. Place the container on a turntable. As work progresses, rotate the tree to view it from all sides in each stage of the planting.

2. Before adding potting mix, hold the tree in its desired position and elevation in the container. Carefully note the space available for fresh potting mix between the root mass and the bottom of the container.

3. For roots that are loosely separated and not embedded in a mass of soil, place a layer of mix ¼ to ½ inch thick on the bottom of the container. Hold the tree in position for planting and gradually add more mix with a trowel. Direct the mix under, between, and around the roots from all sides of the container. Use a planting stick to coax the mix into gaps and empty spaces among the roots. Continue potting until the mix reaches the desired soil level at the bottom of the trunk.

For roots in a compact ball, use a trowel to place a layer of mix on the bottom of the container that will be as high as the underside of the root ball. If the bottom of the root mass is concave, mound the mix to fit the shape of the roots. Set the tree in the container with its root mass on top of the mix.

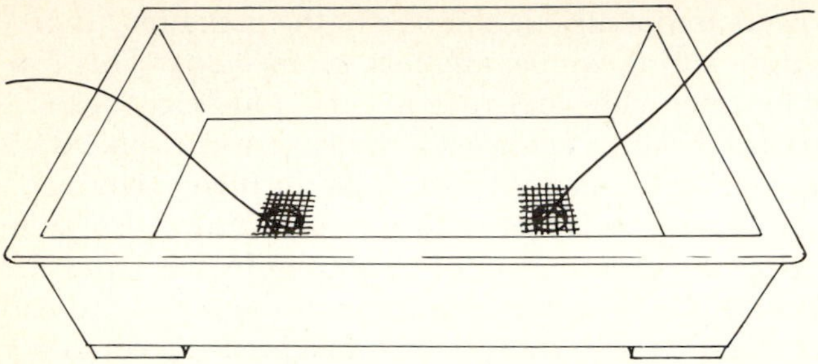

Figure 9-5.1 Wire to tie the bonsai in the container.

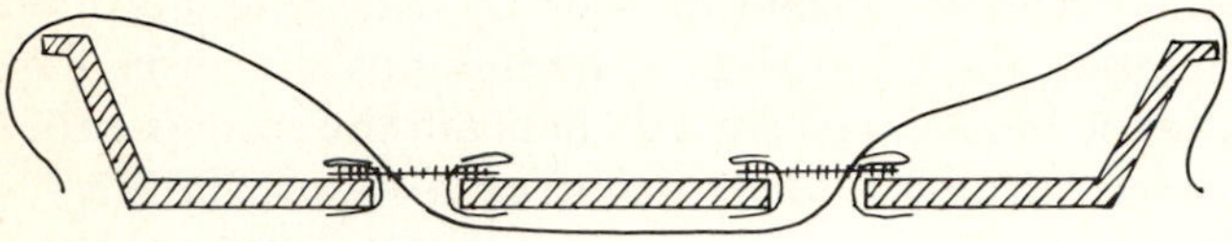

Figure 9-5.2 Side view.

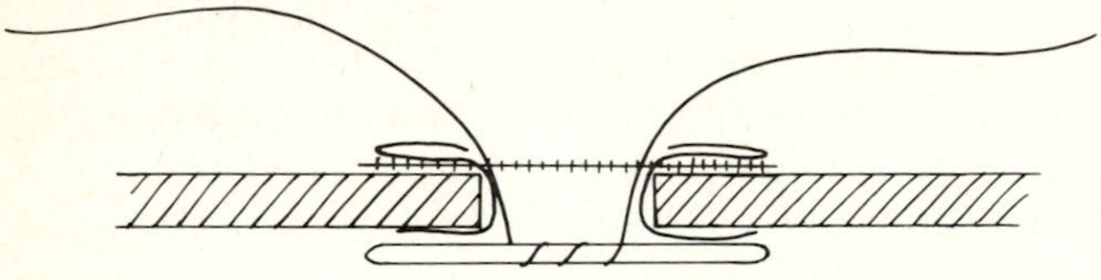

Figure 9-5.3 Anchoring the wire in a container with a single hole.

Wiggle the root ball back and forth with a gentle, firm motion to bring all the roots into close contact with the mix. Complete the planting with the aid of a planting stick. Work the mix into all crevices between the roots until all roots are surrounded by mix.

4. Examine the position of the tree from all sides. Is the bottom of the trunk in the preferred location in the container? Is it at the desired elevation? With the planting stick, separate and reposition roots that are tightly against or encircling the trunk. Inspect the tree from the top. Is the mass of the foliage over the container?

5. If the tree is to be tied to the container, this is the time. Cross the wires over the root mass and pull them taut near the bottom of the trunk. Knot the two wires together and tighten them with pliers. Add more mix, if needed, to restore the mix to its former level in the container.

6. With the tree tied in position, again check the mix for air pockets. A few small roots may appear above the surface of the soil. They will not survive in the air. Push them into the mix with the planting stick or simply clip them with shears.

7. Test the security of the tree by tilting the container. If the tree wobbles, search again for air pockets. Or has the wire or string tied to the roots become loose? If the tree cannot be steadied, pour out the mix and repot.

Figure 9-6 The Torulosa juniper potted in a bonsai container.

8. When the tree is securely planted in the container, shape and firm the surface of the potting mix with the flat blade of the tweezers or a small trowel. Form a smooth, slightly downward slope from all sides of the trunk to about ¼ inch below the rim on the inside of the container. In Fig. 9-6, the Torulosa juniper shaped earlier in the chapter is potted in a bonsai container.

This is the last chance to make changes that require wiring, pruning, or moving the tree. Before watering the bonsai, check it again and complete any work that may have been overlooked. After the bonsai is watered, the mix will settle around the roots. At that time, no part of the bonsai should be manipulated. Do nothing that will move or tilt the trunk. Altering part of the trunk or a branch at this stage pulls the newly planted roots from their close, direct contact with the potting mix. Postpone all further work and touch-ups for at least a month. This will allow time for the roots to become firmly embedded in the new mix and container.

9. Apply a moss cover, if available, and water the bonsai thoroughly. Keep the bonsai in partial shade and away from strong wind for the next ten to fourteen days. Water thoroughly when the mix becomes slightly dry; do not keep the soil constantly moist. If foliage is present, misting it several times during the day is helpful in reducing water loss from the leaves by evaporation.

10. After two weeks, if the bonsai shows signs of health and renewed growth, move it to its permanent growing area. Loss of foliage, limp leaves, or absence of emerging new growth are signs that more time is needed in the recovery area. Do not fertilize until at least a month after repotting.

The care and growing conditions that each species prefers as bonsai are described in Part Two. Consult this section for additional information concerning particular species used for bonsai.

PRACTICE AND REVIEW

Additional Bonsai

Repeat this chapter, beginning with the selection of plant material, as often as possible. Try to use a variety of species to create several more bonsai. Making a bonsai is a complex procedure for the beginner because many factors must be considered and coordinated at the same time. But bonsai is no more complex than learning to drive a motor vehicle, to dance, or to play a musical instrument. As with all activities requiring skill, mastery comes with practice.

Study Bonsai Examples

Methods used by bonsai growers to handle the placement of major bottom branches, incorporate taper and harmony in the trunk, or establish proportions between trunk height and branch length may be found among the bonsai illustrations in Parts One and Two. Notice also how often the ''rules'' are bent. If possible, discuss your observations with bonsai colleagues and other growers.

10

Bonsai Care

Bonsai and other plants have a remarkable ability to generate their own growth and in many ways to care for themselves. There is no need to fuss over a bonsai when its basic requirements are met. These include a good growing medium and adequate levels of water, air, light, and supplemental fertilizer. Favorable growing conditions and care make a bonsai healthy, attractive, and less susceptible to pests and disease.

Because bonsai are living, growing plants, they change from day to day. The change is gradual, but sometimes the recognition is sudden. An unexpected change may be alarming to an inexperienced but perceptive bonsai grower. One of the most frequent inquiries a bonsai teacher receives concerns browning of evergreen foliage: "The needles on my pine are turning brown! What should I do?" A brief discussion usually indicates that the brown needles are old ones close to the trunk in the interior of the bonsai. It is natural for conifers to slough off these needles. Despite their name, evergreen trees are not "ever green," as the carpet of pine needles in a pine forest reveals. Evergreens shed portions of their old foliage at intervals rather than all at the same time. In this connection, the owner of a bonsai nursery once described how a customer arrived at the nursery one day, walked directly to an area of pine bonsai, looked at them intently, turned around with a pleased expression on his face, and promptly left. Later, the customer explained to the owner that the needles on a pine bonsai he had bought recently were turning brown and he wanted to see if this was normal. The customer acted wisely in checking the condition of his bonsai against others. Where bonsai are not available for comparison, it is worthwhile to inspect similar species that are prevalent in the area at plant centers, nurseries, or nearby gardens and wooded areas.

As these incidents suggest, bonsai care is based mainly on common sense and careful observation. Many "problems" involving day to day care may be avoided by treating bonsai essentially as trees planted in small containers.

WATERING

In Japan, bonsai masters say it takes seven years for an apprentice to learn to water correctly. In America, with younger bonsai and simplified growing methods, it does not take nearly so long. Watering is, however, an essential bonsai skill that must be learned. More bonsai are lost from improper watering, either too little or too much, than from any other single cause.

Watering is part of a cycle during which moisture and air circulate in the potting mix. The maxim is: Water a bonsai thoroughly and not again until it becomes partially—but not completely—dry. During these cycles, the pore space in the potting mix is alternately filled with water or with air. On hot, drying days in late spring and summer, the average bonsai requires watering at least once and sometimes twice a day. Bonsai in small pots need more frequent watering.

Watering Techniques

Nozzles. Water bonsai with a nozzle that produces a fine spray. This may be a watering can with a rose (as the nozzle is called) containing many tiny holes or a hose with a nozzle that can be adjusted to a fine spray. Add a turn-off valve between the hose coupling and the nozzle to regulate water pressure and to turn the water off when it is not needed. A turn-off valve and a variety of nozzles are shown in Fig. 10-1. The special Japanese nozzles for watering bonsai, de-

Figure 10-1 *Top:* Special Japanese hose nozzle. *Center:* Adjustable nozzle. *Bottom:* Left to right, misting nozzle, water turn-off valve, water breaker.

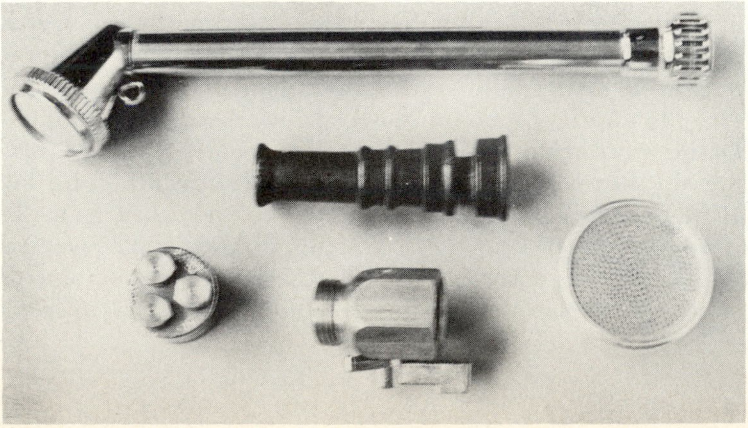

Figure 10-2 A well-watered bonsai drenched with a forceful stream of water. The hose is equipped with a turn-off valve and a Japanese nozzle.

signed to fit American hose couplings, project a fine yet forceful spray. Use the nozzle at full strength on large bonsai well established in their containers. Throttle it down to a gentle spray for other bonsai.

When watering (Fig. 10-2), direct the spray into the interior of the bonsai to dislodge insects and cleanse the foliage. Spray the trunk and branches as well. Move the spray slowly up and down into the foliage and back and forth over the bonsai to disperse the water evenly and gradually. Watering on a regular daily basis in this manner contributes to a bonsai's attractive appearance and healthy condition throughout the summer season.

With a watering can, follow this same procedure. Drench the trunk and branches first, then the potting mix.

Timing. The ideal time to water bonsai is in the early morning, as early in the day as possible. Avoid evening watering if other times are available. In the evening, water tends to remain on the bonsai, creating moist, humid conditions favorable to the spread of mildew and other mold. If the bonsai can be watered regularly only late in the day, set them apart from one another in a well-ventilated area to facilitate drying.

When watering bonsai on hot sunny days, take care to avoid wetting the leaves of thin-leaved trees, such as maples, when they are in the sun. The droplets of water act as lenses that cause the sun to burn the leaves and form disfiguring brown spots. This does not occur on conifers or broad-leaved trees with thick leaves.

A Watering Schedule. Bonsai can be conditioned to once-a-day watering. Early in the growing season, establish a regular time for watering each day and water thoroughly. Bonsai are able to adjust to the regularly available water during each 24-hour period. Only hot or drying conditions require more frequent watering.

Many factors affect the amount of water a bonsai needs each day. Consider the variables in the following lists and use your own judgment to determine where more or less water is needed.

Conditions Requiring More than Average Water

A dry, hot, sunny or windy day.
Small containers.
A grainy, loose potting mix.
Bonsai with many large or thin leaves.
Bonsai with extensive or potbound roots.
Porous containers.

Conditions Requiring Less than Average Water

Rainy days.
Cloudy, windless days.
Large containers.
A moisture-holding potting mix.
Bonsai with sparse foliage.
Glazed or plastic containers.

Several methods may be used to equalize the differences in the amount of water required by different bonsai in order to water all the bonsai at one time.

1. Group together bonsai with similar water requirements.
2. For bonsai that dry out quickly, provide extra protection from strong wind and hot sun.
3. Place bonsai that are in unusually small pots on a tray of sand, which will absorb and hold water for a period of time.
4. On hot, sunny days, set containers with species that normally require large amounts of water, such as bald cypress and wisteria, in shallow trays with a few inches of water, which will be absorbed during the day. Do not keep the pots in water constantly.
5. Plant bonsai that need less than average water, such as pines, in an especially porous mix and species that require extra amounts of water in a high-moisture-retention mix.
6. Substitute a glazed or plastic container for a porous one, or vice versa.

Providing Extra Humidity. Bonsai planted on a rock and species that require high humidity may be placed on stands or platforms above a tray of water or over a shallow pond. Such bonsai often prefer shade during the hottest part of the day.

Reviving Wilted Plants. Despite the best of care, occasionally a bonsai may wilt from lack of water. When this occurs, move the plant immediately into the shade and immerse the pot in lukewarm, not cold, water. Spraying the foliage with tepid water is also helpful. Remove it from the water the following day. Unless the plant was in a wilted state for a long time, it will regain its normal condition. Keep a wilted plant in partial shade for several days before placing it in the sun.

Automatic Watering Systems. An automatic watering system is necessary if manual watering cannot be provided daily. A variety of systems are available from horticultural and greenhouse suppliers.

Manual watering has an advantage, however, that no automatic system can match. Bonsai growers who water their bonsai by hand can see and inspect each tree daily. It is an opportunity to provide prompt treatment at the first sign of disease or insect infestation and to see what pruning, wiring, and other care may be needed. When using an automatic watering system, make a special point of inspecting the bonsai frequently.

FERTILIZERS

> One caution is necessary—the purpose of fertilizing bonsai is not to make them grow, but to keep them in good health. Heavy fertilization schedules will defeat the entire project of miniaturizing trees. If a diluted fertilizer is being used and the health of the bonsai is being maintained, it is sufficiently fertilized.[1]

All bonsai require fertilizing during their growing season. This is true whether or not the potting mix contains soil because frequent watering leaches mineral nutrients from the mix.

Mineral Nutrients

The major mineral nutrients, nitrogen, phosphorus, and potassium, operate as a team. A bonsai cannot effectively utilize one without the presence of the other two in adequate amounts. Nitrogen, essential for growth, reproduction, and respiration, is water-soluble and needs frequent replenishing. Adequate amounts of phosphorus, which is present in all living cells, are needed for growing tissue and the development of flowers, fruit, and seeds. A plant's utilization of potassium increases resistance to stress and disease and promotes root growth. This is especially important for bonsai. All three elements should be available in a fertilizer regularly used for bonsai.

Calcium, magnesium, and sulfur are three other minerals essential to plants. Calcium is usually present in plants in adequate amounts. For bonsai grown indoors, calcium may be depleted by a water softener. To replenish calcium, add gypsum at the rate of ½ teaspoon to 1 gallon of water or 1 level tablespoon to 6 gallons.

[1]Lynn R. Perry, *Bonsai: Trees and Shrubs, A Guide to the Methods of Kyuzo Murata* (New York: The Ronald Press, © 1964, reprinted 1975), p. 30.

Magnesium, which combines with phosphorus for plant growth, is also usually present in adequate amounts. If needed, it is readily added in the form of dolomitic limestone. Plants obtain sulfur more often from the decomposition of organic matter than from minerals in the soil. If additional sulfur is needed, it may be added as gypsum, which contains sulfur as well as calcium, at the rate given in the preceding paragraph.

Trace elements, iron, manganese, zinc, copper, boron, chlorine, and molybdenum, are called micronutrients because they are used by plants in exceedingly small amounts. They are not added to a fertilizing schedule or a potting mix indiscriminately. A University of California study found that micronutrients "can be quite toxic to plants if present in more than a few parts per million parts of the soil."[2] The report does not recommend their addition to the container mix.

The exact function of all the micronutrients is still unknown, according to Roy L. Donahue, professor of soil sciences at Michigan State University.

> The elements may limit plant growth either because there may not be a sufficient amount of them in the soil or, as is more often the case, because some condition in the soil reduces their availability. All the micronutrients except molybdenum are more soluable in an acid soil; molybdenum solubility increases with liming.[3]

Selecting a Fertilizer

Fertilizers are available in many forms. Slow-release fertilizers may be added during the preparation of the potting mix in amounts indicated by the manufacturer. They will be effective for the time specified on the package. Organic fertilizers such as rapeseed cake and fish emulsion may have trace elements not found in other fertilizers, but they contain only small amounts of the major mineral elements. If used, consider them a supplementary rather than a complete fertilizer. Rapeseed cake with bonemeal contains about 5 percent nitrogen and only 1 or 2 percent phosphorus and potassium, and the nutrients are released slowly.

The selection of a fertilizer is a matter of individual preference. Many growers find an inorganic water-soluble fertilizer convenient, odorless, easily measured in specified amounts, and suitable for both indoor and outdoor bonsai. It may be applied to either the soil or the foliage when the bonsai are watered. As the results are soon apparent, applications can be adjusted promptly according to the bonsai's needs. For bonsai, dilute inorganic fertilizers to half the strength recommended on the package and apply at regular intervals during the growing season. Avoid strong applications at long intervals.

[2]Kenneth F. Baker, *The U.C. System for Producing Healthy Container-Grown Plants* (USDA: University of California, 1957), pp. 106–107.

[3]Roy A. Donahue, Raymond W. Miller, and John C. Shickluna, *Soils: An Introduction to Soils and Plant Growth*, 3rd ed. (Englewood Cliffs, N.J.: Prentice-Hall, 1971), p. 232.

A fertilizer with, for example, 10-15-10 on the package indicates, in percentages, the amounts of nitrogen, phosphorus, and potassium, in that order. For bonsai, select a formula containing all three minerals without excessive amounts of nitrogen at the expense of phosphorus or potassium.

Application. After new leaves have appeared in the spring, fertilize bonsai once a week or every two weeks. As long as the bonsai are healthy, continue the schedule. If growth is either too weak or too excessive, adjust the strength or the frequency of application, or both. Make the changes by stages, one at a time, and with each change allow several weeks for the results to be seen. In cold-winter climates, stop fertilizing near the end of the bonsai's active growing season; this may be in August or September. In year-round warm climates, do not fertilize bonsai during their period of partial dormancy. At this time, growth ceases temporarily, and the plant is in a state of rest.

Mineral Deficiency

Signs of a mineral deficiency may be conflicting and are best diagnosed by an expert. The use of a complete fertilizer containing the three major minerals will often correct an observable deficiency. Before applying micronutrients, test the mix, or have it tested, for verification that the mineral is needed and in what amount. The following leaf symptoms are a general guide to mineral deficiencies:

Nitrogen: weak growth and yellowing of lower leaves.

Phosphorus: mottled brown or yellow leaf blades; petioles and veins may be red or purple.

Potassium: burn at the tip of the leaves; edges may be purple.

Manganese: older leaves are yellow; new leaves remain green.

Iron: new leaves are pale or yellow; small veins may turn yellow.

Magnesium: blotched yellow or light brown leaf blades; the veins remain green.

REPOTTING

Bonsai need repotting when their roots completely fill the container. In this condition, the roots soon become potbound. Spring, of course, is the best time for potting or repotting. A brief period during the summer when bonsai are not in active growth is also satisfactory. This temporary resting period occurs when fully formed but unopened buds are present on the tips of new shoots. The purpose of repotting is to reduce the size of the root mass and make space in the container for new root growth; the space gained by removing a portion of the old roots is filled with fresh potting mix, which provides a new growing area for the roots.

Most young bonsai require repotting at intervals of one to three years, depending on how rapidly their roots fill the container. The original size of the root mass and the unused space in the container largely determine when a bonsai will become potbound. The tree's vigor and growing conditions also influence root development. Healthy, fast-growing bonsai are the first to need repotting.

As bonsai age, the intervals between repottings lengthen. Older bonsai trained over a long period of time are repotted at three- to five-year intervals. A few species are repotted more frequently. Wisteria, with its thick roots, is repotted every year, and azaleas usually at two-year intervals.

Repotting Signals

A bonsai needs repotting before the roots have completely filled the container at the expense of the potting mix. When this occurs, the tree is under stress. The foliage gradually loses its healthy green color, small branches die, and new growth is weak. While these conditions may be caused by a lack of fertilizer or a poor mix, they generally indicate that repotting is needed. Other symptoms signaling that repotting is due include the following:

1. Only a small amount of water is absorbed when the bonsai is watered. Most of the water runs off the surface. With little or no moisture-holding material in the container, the roots soon become dry and require frequent watering.
2. Roots clog the drainage holes at the bottom of the container. This occurs when potting mix or growing space is no longer available.
3. The surface of the soil is raised above the rim of the container as crowded roots expand and push against the bottom and sides of the container.
4. The bonsai changes in weight. As the potting mix is replaced by roots, the weight of the container is reduced. A grower who is aware of the bonsai's normal weight is conscious of the change.

Figure 10-3 Potbound roots of *Wisteria* sp. and a small potbound Kingsville boxwood, *Buxus microphylla* cv. Compacta.

5. The final test is simple: Turn the bonsai over and lift the container from the root mass. If the roots are potbound, layers of roots will be seen encircling the outside of the root ball, as shown in Fig. 10-3. Such roots, grown under adverse conditions, are often abnormally thick and differ from the bonsai's normal roots.

Repotting Techniques

1. To separate the root ball from the container, first cut the wire that may be holding the tree to the pot. It is a simple matter to remove the root ball. Turn over the container, tap it sharply with your fist, and lift it from the root mass. On rare occasions when the root ball adheres to the container, run a knife along the inside wall or give the root ball a push through the drainage hole.

2. To prune the roots, place the root ball on a turntable or other flat surface. Remove the top layer of soil with a planting stick and loosen long roots that encircle the sides and bottom of the root ball. If the roots are unusually hard or matted, use a metal hook. Unwind and separate these roots for their entire length.

Inspect the roots at the base of the trunk for undesirable root formations. Look for roots that are binding the trunk, are bent and growing above the surface, cross one another, or are too large for the container.

Trace the entire length of an undesirable root to see how many fibrous roots are present. A long root that contains a multitude of fibrous roots may be essential to the bonsai's health. Rather than pruning it, try to find a place for it in the container.

Eliminate long, thick roots with few fibrous roots unless they are among the attractive surface roots at the base of the trunk. Shorten surface roots by cutting them beneath the soil at the fork of a smaller root that will be retained.

3. Before further reducing the roots, reexamine the root mass after long, unwanted roots have been eliminated. Will it fit comfortably in the container now with space to spare on all sides and the bottom? If so, no further pruning is required. If the root mass is too large, trim the roots around the sides and bottom to create about 1 inch of space between the root ball and the inner surface of the container. This is the approximate space needed in a 9- to 12-inch container. Increase or decrease this space according to the size of the container and the circumference of the root ball.

Repot the bonsai in the same container unless it has noticeably increased in size since the last repotting. Occasionally, a heavy root may have formed that is essential and cannot be trimmed or removed. Under these circumstances, select a container that will accommodate the root with ease. Later, as other roots develop, it is usually possible to shorten the long root and again use the original container.

The question is often raised as to how extensively roots may be pruned without jeopardizing the health of the bonsai. The vigor and age of the tree, how quickly the species grows new roots, and the time of the year are factors to be considered. On a well-rooted bonsai in healthy condition, it is safe to reduce the roots by one-fourth to one-third. On species that root readily, sometimes one-half of the root mass is removed.

4. After pruning the roots, keep them moist while preparing a container. Clean the original container if it can be used again, or select another. Fasten screening over each drainage hole and place the container on a turntable or flat work surface. Sprinkle a thin layer of potting mix in the bottom of the container and proceed with the potting as described in Chapter 8.

Wedge-Shaped Pruning

Over the years, as the outside of a root mass is pruned and trimmed during each repotting, the interior roots gradually enlarge and thicken into a mat of compact, intertwining roots far too dense to prune. When this stage is reached, instead of trimming the outside of the root mass, cut a pie-shaped wedge into the root ball. Use a saw rather than pruning shears to cut through the hard root mass. Repot the bonsai and fill the opened space with potting mix. It will provide a growing area for new roots.

Rhododendron and a few other species that quickly form dense root masses are pruned by the wedge method. Whenever used, this technique helps to prevent the formation of massive roots and enables the bonsai to develop a continuous supply of young, vigorous roots.

It is helpful to keep records of the date and location of the first and subsequent cuts. As shown in Fig. 10–4, wedge-shaped cuts are made over the years in alternate sections around the trunk. On an old bonsai, a wedge-shaped cut is usually made no more often than every three to five years.

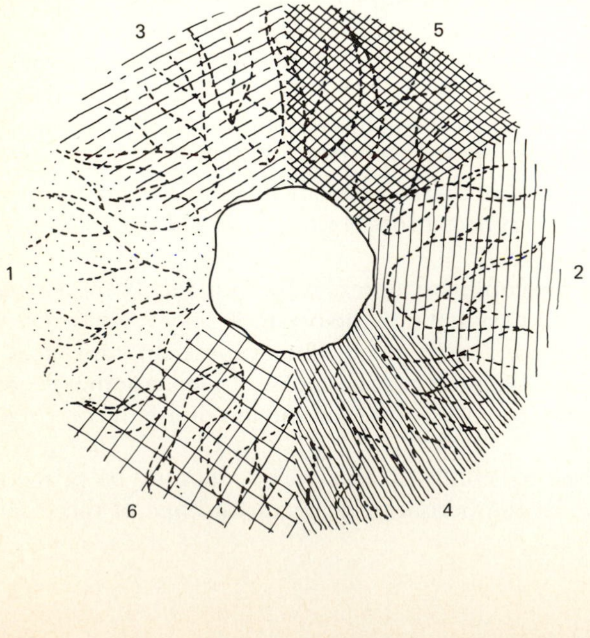

Figure 10-4 A diagrammatic drawing showing one sequence of wedge-shaped root pruning on an old bonsai. The cuts are numbered in sequence.

Mycorrhiza

Occasionally, a white fungus may appear on the roots or in the potting mix of pine and other bonsai. This is not necessarily a danger signal. More likely, it is a mycorrhizal fungus that lives in a mutually beneficial relation with the fine roots of nearly all green plants, including bonsai. The tree supplies the fungus with carbohydrates, and the fungus in turn provides the tree's roots with nitrogen. Such fungi are most effective in soils of low fertility. They are not ordinarily found, or needed, in well-fertilized soil or container mixes. Occasionally, they appear in a bonsai container.

INSECT PESTS

Insects and plants have coexisted for ages. The elimination of all insects in the vicinity of the bonsai is not necessary. Many beneficial insects are destroyed by an overkill approach, including insect predators such as ladybugs, praying mantises, assassin bugs, and minute parasites that prey upon harmful insects. The reasonable aim of the bonsai grower is to confine insect damage to a negligible amount. It is impossible for every leaf on a bonsai to be perfect during the entire growing season.

As mentioned earlier, insects are controlled most effectively by prompt action at the first sign of their arrival. At that time, many of them may be eradicated manually. Otherwise, months of treatment may be required to destroy entrenched infestations.

A forceful spray of water directed daily into the foliage and the interior of the bonsai, as described in the section on watering, will dislodge aphids, caterpillars, white flies, and other insects and mites before they obtain a foothold. Bonsai watered in this way generally remain free of leaf damage from chewing insects during the summer. To be effective, the forceful sprays of water must be applied regularly on a daily basis. This will ensure hitting the pests at their most vulnerable stage regardless of their life cycle. All insects and mites are most defenseless when newly hatched. As they mature and enter the adult stage, they develop protective mechanisms, such as the hard covering of scale, that enable them to withstand assaults.

Manual Control

A number of troublesome insects on bonsai may be eliminated manually. To dislodge Japanese beetles, for example, place a container of water under the branch where they are found and give the branch a light tap. They will drop into the water. Pluck gypsy moths, measuring worms, and other caterpillars from bonsai with tweezers or by hand. Where gypsy moths and Japanese beetles cause noticeable damage, the use of traps often proves beneficial. Sweet, sticky deposits, called "honeydew," on the surface of leaves or stems indicate the presence of sucking insects. Close examination will reveal scale, mealybugs, or aphids feeding on leaf surfaces or stems. These can be removed with a cotton swab dipped in alcohol or by scrubbing the bonsai gently with soapy water and a small, soft brush. Regular weekly treatment for at least a month is needed to eradicate adults and newly emerging young.

Pests On and Under the Ground. Bonsai are sometimes troubled by snails, slugs, earthworms, and ants that are attracted by aphids feeding on the stems and leaves of a bonsai. Controlling the aphids as described in the preceding paragraph should eliminate the problem. If the ants are operating from the potting mix in the container, they may be isolated, and eventually destroyed, by placing the container on bricks or other supports in a tray of water.

To bring earthworms to the surface, apply a solution of dry mustard and water (1 teaspoon of mustard per gallon of water). Remove the pests as the irritant causes them to surface. Although earthworms are beneficial in the ground, they cause havoc in a container by creating air pockets in the potting mix and clogging the drainage holes with their castings.

Slugs and snails disfigure leaves as they feed on the foliage at night. The thin, shiny trail they leave is a sure sign of their presence. During the day they lodge in moist, dark recesses under stones, flowerpots, or similar cover, where they may be found and destroyed. Other effective remedies are commercial slug bait or trays filled with beer set out on wet boards or burlap during the evening. A sprinkling of dry material, such as sand or ashes, around the bonsai will create a dry barrier that slugs are not likely to cross.

Sprays

A dormant oil spray, applied in the fall after deciduous bonsai have dropped their leaves or on a warm day in early spring before the buds have opened, is an effective control for two common pests, scale and mites. Dormant oil sprays are safe to use on a great many plants; however, some evergreen species may suffer discoloration. Be sure to read the label first to learn which species would be harmed, and apply the dormant oil spray according to information contained on the manufacturer's label.

In some cases of established insect infestations, treatment with a chemical pesticide may be necessary. Do not use chemical pesticides on bonsai that are in a weak condition, under stress, or pot-bound. Avoid spraying when air temperatures are above 90 °F. or on cold, humid days. Early morning spraying is best during the hot summer. Before using chemical pesticides, read carefully the manufacturer's information on their handling and application and follow the label instructions explicitly.

The agriculture and forestry departments at state universities and county offices of the USDA Extension Service are valuable sources of information on controlling plant diseases and pests in various regions of the country.

ADDITIONAL READING

Titles on plant disease and insect control in the following list were provided by Dr. Ann F. Rhoads, plant pathologist, Morris Arboretum, University of Pennsylvania.

BROOKLYN BOTANIC GARDEN STAFF, S. H. Davis, ed., *Gardening Without Pests*, Handbook No. 89. Brooklyn, N.Y.: Brooklyn Botanic Garden, 1979.

CARR, ANNA, *Color Handbook of Garden Insects*. Emmaus, Pa.: Rodale Press, 1979.

HORST, K. R., *Westcott's Plant Disease Handbook*, 4th ed. New York: Van Nostrand Reinhold, 1979.

JOHNSON, WARREN T., AND HOWARD H. LYON, *Insects that Feed on Trees and Shrubs*. Ithaca, N.Y.: Cornell University Press, 1976.

PIRONE, P. P., *Diseases and Pests of Ornamental Plants*, 5th ed. New York: Wiley, 1978.

11

Bonsai Growing Areas

OUTDOOR GROWING AREAS

Enjoy your bonsai. Whenever possible, select a combined growing and display area that is convenient and easily seen from the home. This may be a table on an uncovered porch, a shelf outside the window, or a raised platform in the yard or garden. Depending on the number and sizes of the bonsai, it could be a small shelf a few feet in length or rows of many long platforms.

The best growing area for a tree trained as a bonsai is one that approximates its natural environment. Some species prefer sun while others like shade. Although most bonsai are able to survive under less than optimum conditions, successful growers select an outdoor environment that matches the growing needs of their bonsai. When growing conditions are limited, select species that will grow reasonably well in the available space.

Light

Place bonsai above, rather than on, the ground in a location where they will receive direct overhead light, as in Fig. 1-5. This light contains far more radiant energy (the energy required for plant growth) than light rays that reach the bonsai at a slant or through a pane of glass.

Sun and Shade. To accommodate species with diverse environmental needs, look for a location with both sun and shade during part of the day. The growing needs of trees vary. Pines and junipers require at least several hours of sun each day for healthy growth. Spruces and maples, on the other hand, prefer partial shade. Where natural shade is not available, the addition of a latticed roof or shade cloth will provide the necessary shade.

Three or four hours daily of full sun is usually sufficient for bonsai that like direct sun. Avoid overexposure. Hot summer sun for long periods may cause the soil in the container to become so dry that it must be watered several times a day.

If available, morning sun is preferred because it produces better growth with less heat than afternoon sun. Strong, direct sunlight results in the short internodes and reduced leaf size wanted in bonsai, whereas shade causes longer internodes and larger leaves.

When a plant receives light from one direction only, such as the east, all the leaves and new shoots lean in that direction. Bonsai growers use this response to light advantageously by turning a portion of a bonsai that requires more growth toward the source of light.

Under normal conditions, light from all sides is the most beneficial. This is obtained by rotating the bonsai a quarter turn each week consistently in a clockwise or counterclockwise direction.

Temperature

When trees and shrubs common to the local region are grown as bonsai, they will be suited to the outdoor temperatures during the growing season. On account of their small containers, however, they will need extra shade and more frequent watering than their counterparts in the ground.

Trees and plants normally experience a drop in temperature of ten degrees or more at night. This is essential to their health and well-being. Lower night temperatures occur automatically for bonsai that are outdoors and in the open air. Therefore, during the warm spring and summer months, do not confine bonsai in a greenhouse or other enclosed structure.

Water

An area open to the sky also provides refreshing, life-giving rain. Natural rainfall washes the leaves, waters the soil, and invigorates a bonsai far more than water from a hose or watering can. With this in mind, avoid placing bonsai under a structural overhang where rain does not fall.

Wind and Ventilation

Another consideration in site selection is obtaining the beneficial effects of wind. A bonsai's trunk, branches, and new shoots are strengthened and thickened as they are moved to and fro by light winds. Breezes bring fresh air and oxygen to the leaves for photosynthesis and respiration. However, protect bonsai from strong winds, which may overturn the tree and container, and from persistent wind, which has a drying effect. Strong winds are easily diverted by a wind barrier. This may be the side of a building, a wall, a hedge of trees, or some other natural or constructed windbreak, as shown in Fig. 11–1.

Fig. 11–1 Bonsai on wooden shelves open to the sky and protected from the wind by a wall, a fence, and trees.

Small Ground Plots

Many bonsai growers set aside a small parcel of ground as a growing area for young plant material and a convalescent ward for weak or ailing bonsai. Roots and trunks develop far faster in the ground than in a container. Lift the plant from the ground every year or two to prune the thick roots. Also, trim the top growth regularly to prevent the formation of large, heavy branches that would destroy the projected bonsai conformation. The growing site should be open to both sun and shade and convenient for watering.

SITE SELECTION AND CONSTRUCTION

All bonsai share the requirements for light, temperature, water, and fresh air described in the preceding section. Place bonsai on supports above the ground to protect them from insects, animals, and accidental damage and to enhance their visibility. And for convenience, select a site that is well drained and free of wet areas.

Shelves for bonsai are generally made of wood, with space between the boards for ventilation and drainage. The number and sizes of the bonsai will determine shelf depth, which is usually from one to three feet. The height of the shelves from the ground varies from 18 to 38 inches. When placed as cross-pieces over lengthwise supports, 1-by-4-inch boards (Fig. 11–1) are satisfactory. When run along the length of the bench, heavier 2-by-6- or 3-by-6-inch boards are used (Fig. 11–2).

Fig. 11–2 Portion of the growing and display area for a large bonsai collection. Courtesy of Associates at Shoppons' Run.

Redwood, cypress, cedar, and other rot-resistant wood is long-lasting but may not be available in all areas. To extend the life of these and other woods, apply one or two coats of a wood preservative such as colorless zinc naphthenate or the copper form, which is green; neither is harmful to plants. Prior to construction, soak the portion of all posts that will be below ground in a wood preservative. In areas where the ground freezes, place the posts below frost level. Other supports for the shelves include old utility poles, cinder blocks, and sections of large ceramic flue or sewer pipes.

WINTER QUARTERS

Dormancy

As a survival mechanism, cold-climate trees are genetically structured for complete dormancy. If moved to warm climates or into heated buildings for the winter, such trees survive only for a limited time. Complete dormancy is built into the life process of all woody plants native to areas where average annual minimum temperatures are between 0° and 10°F. or less. In North America, these regions include Zone 7 and colder zones on the USDA Plant Hardiness Zone map in Appendix D.

When a tree is completely dormant, all growth above ground is suspended; buds developed during the summer remain tightly closed; respiration is at a low ebb. The condition of dormancy in a tree is comparable to hibernation in certain mammals and reptiles. It is a process that enables trees in cold climates to survive winters of freezing and below-freezing temperatures.

Trees are signaled in the fall to prepare for winter dormancy not by a drop in temperature, which is variable, but by changes in day length, which occur with precise regularity year after year. As the days become shorter, the glucose produced in the tree by photosynthesis is distributed throughout all parts of the tree to be assimilated and stored as a reserve of energy for the winter months. The bark thickens as the cambium cells build a new layer of inner bark. As temperatures drop, the tree covers all its buds and the needles that will remain during the winter with layers of a waxy secretion. Before winter arrives, the tree has completely sealed and insulated its exterior from the cold. With this built-in protection, the above-ground structure of a tree in nature is able to withstand winter temperatures of −30°F. and lower.

Roots confined to a container cannot survive the same low temperatures as the tree's top growth. In nature, a tree's roots are protected from damaging cold temperatures by their location below the frost line, where the ground does not freeze. Roots in a bonsai container, however, are vulnerable to below-freezing temperatures with no built-in insulation against the cold. Such roots require protection from severe cold during winter dormancy.

Care Preceding Dormancy

Healthy bonsai that have received good care during the spring and summer have a head start in preparing for dormancy. Such trees are in excellent condition to survive the winter. Bonsai growers can assist their trees' preparations for winter in the following ways:

1. Stop all fertilizing high in nitrogen in late summer to avoid stimulating soft new shoots that will not harden before winter. Because roots are alive and somewhat active during the winter, give them one application of fertilizer that contains phosphorus and potassium and little or no nitrogen. Do this in late fall, after all the leaves have dropped and before the bonsai are moved into winter quarters.
2. Postpone all but emergency pruning until late winter or early spring.
3. Reduce watering. After leaves and temperatures drop, the potting mix dries more slowly than in summer.
4. Keep the bonsai outdoors during early fall to allow them to prepare for winter. Light frosts and even early snow are not harmful to winter-hardy trees.

Clean-up Before Winter Storage

When night temperatures drop below freezing (in the northeastern United States, for example, this varies from September to November), move the bonsai into protected winter quarters. Be sure that deciduous trees have dropped their leaves; remove remaining ones by hand.

Inspect each bonsai prior to storage. Look for cocoons or webs where insects may be wintering. As a sanitary measure, clean the containers of dead leaves, twigs, weeds, and debris, which are favorite nesting grounds of harmful insects and pathogens. Watch for bonsai that may be badly potbound. Such trees are especially susceptible to freezing because their roots are no longer surrounded by a protective layer of soil inside the container. Temporarily repot bonsai in this condition by lightly trimming the roots and adding potting mix. Or move the bonsai to a larger pot with space for mix around the sides and bottom of the root ball. This will hold the tree until spring, when it can be properly repotted.

SELECTING WINTER QUARTERS

Unless the bonsai collection is large, it is not hard to find satisfactory quarters. Many choices are available. For care-free wintering, choose a location that meets the criteria discussed here.

No Direct Sun

This is important. Sun and fluctuating temperatures are winter's greatest threat to bonsai. On a cold winter day, the warming heat of the sun causes the plant's cells to fill with water. When this occurs, a quick drop in temperature can be fatal. At temperatures below 32 °F., water within the cells of a woody plant freezes and ruptures the cell. To avoid this, nature increases the permeability of the cell's wall as temperatures drop, thus enabling water to leave the cells. When temperatures decrease gradually, there is sufficient time for water to move through the cellular walls. With a sudden temperature drop, water trapped within the cell freezes, and the cell is destroyed. Prevent this by wintering bonsai out of the direct sun.

Fresh Air and Moisture

Choose a place that is convenient for watering and that can be opened for fresh air on clear, warm days. In winter, as in summer, do not allow bonsai to become either completely dry or constantly wet. Water only when the soil in the container is not frozen. After the bonsai are placed in winter quarters, inspect them periodically for an indication of how often watering is necessary, which may be every few weeks, every month, or at even longer intervals. It is not unusual for a few bonsai to require watering more frequently than the others. If so, place them together where they can easily be watered as needed.

To replenish fresh air and oxygen, open a tightly enclosed or sealed shelter on days when the temperature is above freezing. Ventilation helps to prevent mold. Should mold appear, take the affected bonsai outside on a mild day and remove the moldy growth. As mold tends to develop when the potting mix or the enclosure is too wet, examine the container for evidence of faulty drainage or overwatering, and as a precaution, provide more ventilation.

Accessibility

Choose a winter shelter that is not isolated. "Out of sight" may well be "out of mind." A cold attic may provide an ideal environment, but the location is poor. It is likely to be unfrequented for long periods of time, and bonsai placed there may be forgotten. A corner of an unheated garage with daily traffic in and out is a far better choice.

Is Light Necessary?

Because of differences in winter climates, confusion sometimes arises concerning a bonsai's need for light when it is dormant. In the regions of Japan where most bonsai are grown, the winters are mild and bonsai are placed in shelters with one side opened to the air and light. The opening is temporarily closed when temperatures drop below freezing. Meanwhile, at Arnold Arboretum in Massachusetts, where the climate is far colder than the Tokyo-Kyoto area of Japan, deciduous and coniferous bonsai are wintered in an unlighted building with no windows at controlled temperatures of 35 °F. The need for light is directly related to the extent of dormancy. At an average temperature range of 40° or higher, where bonsai are not completely dormant, slight growth may occur and light will be beneficial. Bonsai that are completely dormant at temperatures below 35° do not require light.

A bonsai grower in New Hampshire built a small woodland version of the bonsai wintering quarters at Arnold Arboretum. The insulated frame structure, shown in Fig. 11-3, has no windows or artificial light. It contains a thermostat and a small electric heater to provide heat when temperatures drop below 35°. In the fall, the bonsai are removed from their pots and placed fairly close together on the earth floor. The root balls are covered with a mulch. Periodically, the door is opened for fresh air and ventilation.

Fig. 11-3 A winter bonsai house in New Hampshire. Courtesy of William Smedley.

SUGGESTED WINTER QUARTERS

Indoors in Existing Structures

Depending on the number of bonsai, many existing buildings have suitable space for wintering bonsai. These include unheated structures and cold areas in heated buildings. They offer easy storage with a minimum of preparation. The following ready-made storage areas are frequently used by bonsai growers:

Tool houses and sheds.
Barns.
Garages.
Springhouses.
Unheated basements.
Window wells and cellar doors opening to the outside.
Cold areas in heated basements.
Enclosed unheated porches.
An unheated room in the home.
Recessed north and east windows.

Out of Doors

When wintering bonsai on the ground, choose a location out of direct sun and with natural drainage away from the bonsai. This may be next to a building, along a wall, under a hedge, or in some other area protected from the wind. Cover the bonsai with chicken wire to discourage rabbits, and set out rodent bait to avoid damage from mice and moles. To keep the poisonous bait from dogs and birds, place a small amount in used tin cans and leave only a small opening at the top. Lay the cans on their side under the wire mesh.

To protect the roots, the containers may be partially buried in the ground or mulched with pine needles or salt-marsh hay. Sometimes, the undersides of the containers are covered with foil or plastic to keep them clean. If so, punch holes in the bottom of the wrapping to allow for water drainage and keep the tops of the containers open for air and water. Peat moss is not a satisfactory winter mulch for bonsai because its high water-holding capacity tends to keep the roots permanently wet. Furthermore, if the wet peat freezes and expands, it may cause the containers to crack.

In windy areas, a layer of cut branches or a simple lean-to will protect the bonsai from drying. Where the site is open to precipitation, rain and snow will reduce the need for watering; however, bonsai should be checked periodically for dryness, especially after a period of dry, windy weather.

Growers in climates with a permanent snow cover during the cold months of the year, have the option of wintering their bonsai under a blanket of snow. In the fall, choose a safe, well-drained site where the bonsai will not be disturbed.

Bury or mulch the containers as described previously. Add rodent bait, and chicken wire to keep out animals. If deep drifts are likely, cover the bonsai with branches to prevent damage from the weight of snow and ice. The bonsai will not require watering or other attention until the snow has melted.

Cold Frames and Sun Pits

A cold frame, used for centuries in farming and gardening, is a low structure with four walls and a sloping top, usually of glass, to trap the heat of the sun (and to allow rain to run off). It is used for its greenhouse effect to grow seedlings or tender plants. As a winter storage facility for bonsai, place the cold frame on a well-drained site out of the sun and build the walls high enough to accommodate the bonsai. For added protection, excavate the ground inside the frame and mulch the containers and bonsai roots with pine needles or salt-marsh hay. Where winters are severe, cover the cold frame with old rugs, plastic, or other weatherproofing materials.

In mild climates, glass sash or sheet plastic is an adequate cover. Lift the cover slightly on warm days to provide fresh air and to prevent high temperatures from unseasonably warming the bonsai. On warm days, water the bonsai as needed.

A sun pit is a deep cold frame. The bottom, built well below the frost line, is covered with pebbles for drainage. The pit is insulated from freezing temperatures by the surrounding soil four to six feet below the ground. A sun pit for bonsai may be a simple excavation lined with boards or cinder blocks or a permanent structure with a walk-in entrance. Selecting a site at or near the top of a gentle slope with natural drainage away from the pit is of the utmost importance. A pit located on level or low ground may become filled with several feet of water, causing the loss of the bonsai that are wintered there.

Cover the pit in the same manner as a cold frame. On sunny days, lift a glass sash cover slightly to prevent a rise in temperature from the sun's heat. Bonsai in a deep pit do not require frequent watering unless the pit is opened during repeated spells of warm weather. In cold climates, a covering of plastic or old carpets provides additional protection. Open tightly covered pits and cold frames on warm days to give the bonsai fresh air and ventilation.

Under Plastic

Bonsai may also be wintered directly on open ground where water does not accumulate, preferably out of the sun. A method described by James E. Klett,[1] Department of Ornamental Horticulture, University of Colorado, uses Du Pont's Microfoam, available in large sheets that can be cut to size. Klett recommends watering the bonsai the day before they are moved to the site and placing a

[1]James E. Klett, "Storing Woody Plants," *Journal of the American Bonsai Society*, 15, no. 3 (Fall 1981), 51–53.

Fig. 11–4 A winter bonsai shelter opening on a basement window. Courtesy of William F. Reed.

light frame of wood and chicken wire over the assembled plants to protect them from the weight of snow and ice. A rodenticide is also suggested. For extra strength, sandwich the Microfoam between two sheets of white polyethylene and stretch the thermal blanket snugly over the frame. Allow sufficient width and length for an extra foot on the surface of the ground, then add soil or gravel to seal and hold down the covering. If the area does not receive direct sun, the internal temperatures will not rise rapidly on warm, sunny days. An accumulation of snow on the covering is helpful—it provides another layer of insulation. During the winter, the bonsai require no attention other than periodic inspections to make certain that the covering remains tightly sealed.

Many other ingenious arrangements for wintering bonsai have been devised with plastic. In the cold climate of northern Pennsylvania, for example, a resourceful bonsai enthusiast erects a rectangular frame covered with black plastic outside a basement window, as shown in Fig. 11–4. On cold nights, opening the window from the inside prevents the bonsai from freezing. Other growers enclose the space between house and garage with plastic. The top may be left open or covered with a slatted board or snow fence. Another simple shelter is a plastic enclosure erected outside the window of a heated house or apartment. Attractive displays can be made at windows that receive no winter sun. Place the bonsai on outside shelves and enclose them in clear, heavy plastic. They can easily be watered from indoors.

Wintering Bonsai in Mild Climates

In Zone 7 and warmer zones, the necessity for special wintering arrangements decreases as the median winter temperature increases. In subtropical climates, "winter care" is unknown. An expert bonsai grower from Hawaii, during his first visit to bonsai growers in the northeastern United States, was amazed to see the cold frames, sun pits, and toolhouses used to winter bonsai. He remarked repeatedly that he had no idea it could be necessary to move a complete bonsai collection, bonsai by bonsai, from summer to winter quarters—and back—year after year.

In warm climates, a tree's dormancy is only partial. This means that light is essential during the winter. And, of course, less protection from cold is required. During this time when bonsai are experiencing a period of rest, reduce the amount and frequency of watering and stop fertilizing.

Where sudden below-freezing temperatures are possible, be prepared to protect the bonsai from freezing. Warm-climate plants do not develop protective measures against cold. They are as dependent on their owners as the bonsai in cold-winter climates.

12

Development

The bonsai started in Chapter 9 with a basic framework of a trunk and a few branches is now ready for training and shaping into a compact, beautiful specimen. A large part of this is done by pruning the new growth.

SHAPING NEW GROWTH

Trimming the new shoots dwarfs and shapes a bonsai. Its growth each year can be limited to a few inches, and in some instances to a fraction of an inch, by shortening each new shoot. (Untrimmed shoots, by comparison, may grow a foot or more.) The bonsai's shape can be controlled by cutting each shoot to a selected bud to determine the location and direction of the replacement shoot. The question is no longer *how* to prune but rather *where* to prune for the desired bonsai effect.

The first step is to look at the started bonsai and form a mental image of it as a mature specimen. It is often helpful to make a simple outline or diagram showing the future trunk, the major branches, and the tree's periphery. Again, examine the started bonsai, this time with the future bonsai in mind. Then ask these questions: How much, if any, additional height is wanted on the trunk? Are any of the branches already too long? Or does a major branch require lengthening? Are there locations where a new branch would embellish the projected pattern? The answer to these questions will indicate where to prune and where not to prune. Before pruning each shoot, consider its future. Where more length is wanted, remove only a small portion, or none at all. Where the shape of a branch is already established, trim most of the shoot to produce more compact growth.

Where a taller trunk is wanted, before shortening the shoot that will become the new top of the trunk, let it grow until it forms a pleasing taper with the trunk beneath. At the same time, fill gaps in the periphery by trimming the tips of new shoots to stimulate side shoots. Keep in mind at all times the overall shape that is wanted and orchestrate the pruning cuts accordingly.

Timing

The thickness and vigor of the replacement shoots may be regulated further by the timing of the cut. When a new shoot is cut back early in the season, the second shoot, benefiting from a long period of growth, will be comparatively large. But if the first shoot is not trimmed until late spring or early summer, the replacement shoot will be thinner.

Developing a New Branch

To obtain a new branch from a young shoot, allow it to grow and send out side shoots. In early summer (whether or not side shoots are present), remove the terminal bud at the top of the primary shoot to encourage lateral growth. The following spring, cut back the major and the lateral shoots to fit the bonsai pattern, and continue the process as the branch develops. Results are obtained in a few years on specimens that form numerous buds with short internodes, such as species of maples, azaleas, zelkova, and holly.

Twiggy Growth

The repeated division of a branch into smaller branchlets, shoots, and twigs is an undisputed sign of its tree identity. To induce this on a bonsai, trim the new growth as often as possible during each growing season. New shoots on many species of maples and elms can be trimmed at least twice and on zelkova three times during one season. This produces the effect of two or three years' growth in one year.

The Cloud Effect

As branches develop twigginess, they create a smooth periphery on the bonsai, as seen in the more than 150-year-old thorny elaeagnus in Fig. 12–1. To achieve this effect in a minimum of time, follow a plan. Determine the contour desired along the tip of the branches and keep an outline of it in mind. Trim each new shoot to fit into the proposed periphery. Remove all new growth that extends beyond the desired shape. After shaping the foliage into a smooth, contoured form, maintain this shape by allowing only a minimum of growth each year.

Fig. 12-1 Thorny elaeagnus, *Elaeagnus pungens,* at the U.S. National Arboretum. Photo courtesy of USDA.

Effect of Climate

In warm climates, quick results are obtained by the repeated trimming of new growth. With a long growing season, bonsai are able to send out numerous cycles of new growth in one year. Regular trimming of these new shoots produces a dense network of fine branchlets within a short time. The same results in colder climates require a longer period of time.

STABILIZING GROWTH

Stablized growth and a smooth covering of foliage are associated with mature bonsai whose form and branching have been established. On some trees, such as maples, the finished form can be maintained by a special pruning method. To stop the growth of shoots on mature bonsai, follow this procedure: In early spring, as the first pair of leaves emerge and while they are tender, wrinkled, and not fully opened, a new shoot, thin and wispy, will begin to form between the leaves. This is the shoot that usually is not trimmed until it has lengthened and begun to harden. With this method, remove the shoot but not the two tender leaves. This will prevent further growth. Timing is critical. Trim or pinch the shoot while it is soft and flaccid. The original leaves will mature and remain on the tree for the entire season. Buds for next year will form at the base of the petioles, but no additional growth will occur beyond the first two leaves. Next spring, the buds will send out normal growth. This technique can be used on healthy maples but not on bonsai in a weak condition. As it limits growth severely, do not apply it to a bonsai every year.

On needle conifers, apply this technique by plucking the new needle clusters at their earliest stage of emergence. Permit only a bit of the cluster to remain. To shorten new pine shoots further for the following year, remove the largest bud at the tip of each shoot in late fall.

FLOWERING AND FRUITING BONSAI

Special pruning techniques are used for flowering and fruiting bonsai, which are divided into two groups. Most are in the first group, consisting of species that flower in the spring from buds produced during the previous growing season. Bonsai found in this group include flowering quince, *Chaenomeles*; *Cotoneaster*; hawthorn, *Crataegus*; *Forsythia*; apples and crab apples, *Malus*; almonds, apricots, cherries, and plums, *Prunus*; azaleas, *Rhododendron*; and *Wisteria*.

In early spring before flowering, prune these bonsai sparingly to remove damaged or disfiguring branches. Immediately after flowering, prune drastically wherever needed. Then, as new shoots elongate and harden, trim each one back to one or two buds. Let the replacement shoots develop and form flower buds. Do not prune again during the summer except to remove damaged or unwanted shoots and branches.

On species such as quince that produce flower buds along the length of a new shoot, snap off the terminal bud in midsummer to direct strength into the lateral flower buds. After flowering, azaleas form flower buds at the tip of the new shoots, which emerge in whorls. Remove all but two or three shoots in every whorl and shorten each remaining shoot early in the season to allow time for flower buds to form for the following spring.

For flowering bonsai that produce fruit, delay pruning after flowering until the fruit has set, then prune as described in the preceding paragraphs. If the fruit is large, allow only a small number to mature. Remove the others to preserve the vigor of the bonsai. Picking the fruit when it is ripe rather than letting it remain on the tree will help the tree to direct its energy into buds for the coming year.

The second group of flowering bonsai includes species of *Citrus*; andromeda, *Pieris*; orange jasmine, *Murraya*; *Stewartia*; many *Ilex*; and other genera that flower in late spring or in the summer from buds on the current year's growth. Prune these species as though they were deciduous bonsai. In late winter or early spring, cut back last year's shoots to a few buds. Let the new shoots grow, elongate, and form flower buds. After flowering, prune only to shape the bonsai or remove unwanted branches. Postpone other pruning until late winter or early spring.

REDUCING LEAF SIZE BY DEFOLIATION

Defoliation is patterned on a phenomenon that occurs in nature when deciduous trees, stripped of their foliage by gypsy moths or other pests, are able to survive by producing a second growth of leaves. There are two reasons for defoliating, or removing the leaves, on a bonsai. The leaf size in the second growth is smaller. In addition, the new leaves show brighter color in the fall and less signs of wear and tear than foliage that has been around for an entire growing season.

Bonsai that respond most favorably to defoliation include species of maple, *Acer*; elm, *Ulmus*; and *Zelkova*. Defoliation is applied sparingly to species of beech, *Fagus*; hornbeam, *Carpinus*; *Ginkgo*; and other trees that do not readily produce a second set of leaves and buds after the first leaves have been removed.

As an alternative to complete defoliation, many growers follow a less drastic method and remove individual oversize leaves during late spring and early summer. This benign procedure replaces the large leaves with smaller ones. However, over a period of time, without defoliation, the leaves of most bonsai will reduce in size as a result of bonsai training. Defoliation accelerates this process, but it places a bonsai under strain. Do not defoliate the bonsai every year. Allow intervening years of regular growth.

Techniques

Defoliate only healthy, well-developed bonsai. It is, of course, counterproductive to defoliate young bonsai trees that are being grown to strengthen their trunks, branches, and roots. The best time to defoliate is late spring or early summer, when the first set of leaves is mature and buds are present at the base of the petioles. This allows adequate time for new leaves and buds to form for the following year.

Fertilize a bonsai regularly during the spring before defoliating it. The defoliation need not be complete; it may be done selectively. Skip branches that display weak growth. After defoliating a branch, remove the terminal bud to direct the new growth into the leaves rather than toward extending the branch.

By Species. Most species of maples respond well to defoliation, including trident maple, *Acer Buergeranum*; Amur maple, *A. Ginnala*; Japanese maple, *A. palmatum* (except thread-leaf and lace-leaf varieties); and American red maple, *A. rubrum*. To remove the leaves with a long petiole, such as found on maples, simply cut the petiole in half. The bit remaining will drop later of its own accord.

Elms frequently defoliated include American elm, *Ulmus americana*; Chinese

Fig. 12-2.1 A shoot of *Zelkova serrata* before leaf trimming.

Fig. 12-2.2 *Zelkova serrata* after leaf trimming.

elm, *U. parvifolia*; and Siberian elm, *U. pumila*. The petiole on an elm is so short it is hard to find at the base of the leaf. Therefore, cut the leaf by running the scissors along the side of the shoots. So long as half or more of the leaf is removed, the remaining section will drop before the new leaf emerges.

Japanese gray-bark elms, *Zelkova serrata*, are pruned in the same manner as *Ulmus* elms. The technique applied to a zelkova shoot is shown in Figs. 12-2.1 and 12-2.2.

ACCELERATING AGING

''How old is that bonsai?'' is a question commonly heard at bonsai exhibits. Age adds a special quality to a bonsai. It testifies to the daily care the bonsai has received over a long period of time. During all its years and decades as a bonsai it was watered every day. It was trimmed several or more times each year to maintain its small size. And it was repotted many, many times during its lifetime.

Yet age in itself is not a valid basis for evaluating a bonsai. Age offers no guarantee that a bonsai is well designed or carefully trained. A handsomely trained bonsai less than twenty years old may have greater beauty than one five times that age.

Age, however, augments a bonsai's beauty. It makes a beautiful bonsai more beautiful. Age is responsible for the gnarled limbs, furrowed bark, spreading roots, dense foliage, and contoured silhouette of old trees in nature. Bonsai growers have discovered methods of implanting the appearance of age on a bonsai. The following techniques help to age a bonsai beyond its years.

Driftwood

What looks older on a bonsai than the silvery sheen of driftwood sculptured by the elements? Driftwood, which is produced in nature over a long period of time, is characteristic of old trees. This is seen in the old California juniper in Fig. 12-3.

Techniques. Confine driftwood to portions of a mature bonsai where it would naturally occur, such as on the top or the side of a trunk or a branch that has died. Remove the bark when the tree is in active growth. After determining the extent of the driftwood, mark the boundary with chalk or a pen. With a sharp knife, cut along the line through the bark and cambium to the sapwood beneath. To facilitate stripping the bark, shorten overly long branches, but keep a few side branches. Loosen the bark first by squeezing it with pliers along the length and all sides of the branch. Then, if the wood is young and flexible, pull the bark from the branch with a strong tug. Otherwise, peel it off in strips. Check to be sure no remnants of the cambium adhere to the wood. Smooth rough areas

Fig. 12-3 California juniper, *Juniperus californica,* collected near Palmdale, California, and trained as a bonsai for fifteen years. Courtesy of Ben Oki.

by sanding or scraping. Retain small twigs and branches that are present. They give a convincing touch to the driftwood. For a natural effect, break long branches by hand instead of cutting them, or partially cut one side of the branch (or trunk) and tear it with a quick jerk.

Shaping the Driftwood. A section of a bonsai that has been stripped can be wired and moved to another position while it is supple and flexible. Remove the wire after the wood hardens, and sand the trunk or branch to a smooth finish as though polished and sculptured by the wind.

Preservation. Untreated driftwood darkens naturally, but fungi may cause unsightly blotches. To create and maintain an attractive sheen, coat the surface with lime sulfur, available as a ready-to-use solution at plant and garden centers. Place a protective waterproof cover over all areas of the bonsai as well as the surface of the potting mix where the lime sulfur may drip. Apply the solution with a soft brush in warm weather. Start at the edge of the cut and work away from the live wood. If the solution accidentally comes in contact with other parts of the bonsai, flush immediately with water until it is completely removed.

After treating the wood, place the bonsai in partial sun to be dried by the air. After several days, return it to its regular growing area. Apply a second coat, if needed, in a week or so. Thereafter, repeat the treatment every few years as required.

Aging the Trunk

No lovelier sign of age can be found on a bonsai than beautiful old bark, whether it is the tautly stretched covering of a beech (Fig. 12-4) or the shredding bark of an ancient trident maple (Fig. 12-5). Over the years, each species, according to its nature, develops beautiful, distinctive outer bark. This process cannot be accelerated on a bonsai, but it can be aided by carefully handling and protecting the existing bark.

To add a veneer of age on a trunk without harmful effects, press bits of lichen onto the bark. Look on boulders or sunny banks for patches of silver lichen with a touch of red (called British soldiers) or for a shade-tolerant silvery green lichen found on the trunks of trees. Lichen is easily transferable to bonsai. Use a small spatula, a knife, or the flat end of tweezers to place the lichen on the trunk of the bonsai and press it gently into crevices on the bark.

Aging the Apex

A simple technique for giving a relatively young bonsai an aged appearance is to modify a pointed apex into a rounded crown. The triangular apex, characteristic of many young trees and certain conifers, is not a permanent aspect of most species. With age, the majority of trees develop a round crown. Many growers help their bonsai age by rounding the apex. This can be seen on four Japanese bonsai at the National Arboretum shown in Fig. 12-6, and it is characteristic of nearly all specimen Japanese bonsai.

Fig. 12-4 Bark on an old European beech, *Fagus sylvatica,* at the Morris Arboretum of the University of Pennsylvania. Photo by Paul W. Meyer.

Fig. 12-5 Peeling bark on an ancient trident maple, *Acer Buergeranum,* at the Morris Arboretum. Photo by Paul W. Meyer.

Fig. 12-6 Four Japanese bonsai with well-developed contoured forms: left to right, trident maple, *Acer Buergeranum* (60 years old), planted over a rock; Japanese white pine, *Pinus parviflora* (120 years old); a dwarf Japanese maple, *Acer palmatum*, a yatsubusa (30 years old); and another trident maple (80 years old).

To induce a rounded apex, shorten the trunk below the top of the surrounding branches. Be sure to make the cut at the fork of another branch. If this causes a temporary gap in the apex, wire and rearrange the nearby branches to fill the empty space. Trim the new growth that develops to conform to the new shape. Within a few years, this will add decades to the appearance of a bonsai.

Age Indicators on Roots

On a bonsai, thick spreading roots spell age. To thicken roots, bury them slightly below soil level while they are young. After they have enlarged, bring the upper surface, not the entire root, slightly above the soil level. Bark will gradually form on the surface exposed to the air. Meanwhile, keep the sides and underside of the roots immersed in the soil for additional growth and thickening. Apply this treatment during a bonsai's early years. Later, visible, aged surface roots will be present on the mature bonsai.

STRENGTHENING THE DESIGN

The foregoing techniques provide opportunities to improve the composition and appearance of a bonsai. Bonsai growers find also that they are able to induce harmony and negative space while working on the bonsai's structure and foliage. As a trunk becomes taller, for example, harmony may be increased by pruning and wiring the new section to conform to the established trunk line. In the process, keep the lower trunk open to view. To add a subtle touch, create windows in dense foliage surrounding the upper trunk to suggest the uninterrupted continuation of the trunk from bottom to top. On a bonsai with an upright trunk, remove upward-growing branches that compete with the vertical thrust of the trunk. Curtail the length of long branches to keep the branches noticeably shorter than the trunk.

Use every opportunity when wiring or pruning a branch to improve the resulting negative space. Be aware of the pleasing empty space that may be formed between the branches whenever a branch is repositioned. A slight change of the branch in one direction or another may create beautiful negative space.

These detailed considerations require time for their full impact to be evident, but even during the early years they bring a touch of unmistakable beauty to a bonsai.

13

Creating Additional Bonsai

This chapter introduces two new American styles based on native trees in North America and Hawaii and describes older styles from Oriental bonsai. When creating a bonsai, use the silhouettes, line drawings, and photographs in this and other chapters for examples of trunk lines, branch placement, and negative space. The single-trunk styles can be created with the techniques already described. Where needed, additional information on design and techniques is provided. Specific plant material is not required. Any species with the characteristics needed for bonsai and a growth pattern similar to the proposed style will be suitable.

BONSAI STYLES

Formal Upright Style

All other bonsai styles can be derived from this style. It was inspired by the tall, straight trunks of magnificent conifers found in the mountains and the forests of Japan. Its beautiful composition, however, is not easily replicated in bonsai because appropriate plant material is hard to find. An example is shown in Fig. 3-1 in Chapter 3.

Trunk. The design calls for a vertical, straight, tapered trunk. If the trunk is curved, straighten it by wiring. Where a natural taper is lacking, prune the trunk to a replacement branch that will increase the taper.

Branches. Arrange lateral branches (which are straight except on a bonsai

Fig. 13–1 Informal upright style, Lodgepole pine, *Pinus contorta* var. *latifolia*. Courtesy of J. Nakahara.

suggesting an ancient tree) on the trunk in sets of three. Follow instructions in Chapter 9 regarding their length and location. A formal upright bonsai is usually conical, triangular, or, occasionally, oval.

Informal Upright Style

This popular, flexible design is used for a large number of deciduous and evergreen bonsai. The informal upright description is also a catch-all designation for bonsai that do not fit into other patterns.

Trunk. Position the straight or curved trunk in an upward direction with the top of the trunk above the surface of the container, as in the excurrent lodgepole pine in Fig. 13–1.

Branches. The arrangement of branches on an excurrent tree are detailed in Chapter 9.

Slanting Style

Trunk. For the slanting style, position a straight or somewhat curved trunk upward and outward at a pronounced angle from a line perpendicular to the bottom of the trunk. Extend the apex beyond the rim of the container. The stunning shimpaku juniper in Fig. 1–1 is an outstanding example of this style.

Branches. In branching, this style differs from the informal upright style. Here, the strongest bottom branch is on the side of the trunk opposite the direction of the slant to balance the counterthrust of the trunk. When the bottom branch is on the same side as the slant of the trunk, direct it downward toward the top of the container. It will appear as a prop supporting the trunk.

Roots. Contrary to the usual practice of showing surface roots on all sides of the trunk, in the slanting style their preferred location is on the side of the trunk opposite the slant. Rather than keeping them along the surface, thrust the roots abruptly into the soil within a short distance of the trunk. They will appear to be anchoring the slanting trunk in the container.

Fig. 13–2 Broom-style *Zelkova serrata*. Photo courtesy of *International Bonsai*.

Broom Style

The broom style is closely associated with *Zelkova serrata*, although other species with upward-growing branches, such as yaupon, *Ilex vomitoria*, are suitable. The trunk is usually less than half the height of the foliage. The branches, which are straight, form a vaselike shape.

The first broom-style bonsai officially recognized by professional bonsai growers in Japan was created with a zelkova. A Japanese broom-style zelkova is shown in Fig. 13–2.

Instructions for growing miniature broom-style zelkova from seed are given in Chapter 17. The information can be adapted to larger bonsai by letting the trunk grow taller before starting the training techniques.

Zelkova may also be trained to the broom style from large nursery stock. Do this in spring to allow ample time for new growth to develop during the current growing season. Select a tree with a straight trunk from 1 to 3 inches in diameter. Make a flat, smooth cut across the trunk about 8 or 10 inches from the bottom. Take care not to tear the bark. Chisel the top of the trunk into a saucerlike hollow. Reduce the root mass and plant the zelkova in a large training pot.

Place it in open shade in an area protected from direct sun and wind and convenient for watering. To promote sprouting, keep the surface of the cut covered with damp sphagnum moss or a cellulose sponge for the balance of the growing season. After the first month, fertilize regularly.

For a few years, many new shoots will sprout from the cambium layer where the trunk was cut. Select strong, straight shoots at various distances around the circumference of the trunk and remove the others. Eliminate shoots that may sprout on the lower trunk. As the shoots develop where the trunk was cut, trim them regularly to encourage branching. In a few years, after major branches are formed, move the tree to a smaller training pot and continue to develop the branches.

Banyan Style

This is a new American bonsai style. It originated with species of banyan figs in two widely separated states, Florida and Hawaii. The style was devised for warm-climate species, but it is also used in colder climates when these trees are grown as indoor bonsai.

Trunk. At a relatively short distance from the ground, the trunk of a banyan fig may divide into many trunks and strong bottom branches. The 30-inch-tall collected Chinese banyan in Fig. 13-3.1 has nine trunks. When selecting a banyan for bonsai, look for a specimen with a sturdy trunk and visible surface roots.

Branches. Choose strong branches to serve as the large bottom limbs. Because they often tend to become horizontal on old banyans, wire them to this position, if desired. (In this respect, the banyan style differs from the broom style, in which the major branches are shaped to an upright, vaselike form.) Train the branches into a spreading umbrella of foliage that will be far wider than it is tall. Dense growth is easily obtained by trimming the new growth during the growing season.

Roots. A close-up view of surface and aerial roots is shown in Fig. 13-3.2. To obtain this on a banyan fig, allow the roots to develop naturally; they will form fascinating patterns, as they do in nature.

Fig. 13-3.1 Banyan-style Chinese banyan, *Ficus microcarpa* cv. Retusa, by David W. Fukumoto. Courtesy of Fuku-Bonsai.

Fig. 13-3.2 Detail of surface and aerial roots. Courtesy of Fuku-Bonsai.

Fig. 13–4 Natural flat-topped crown on bald cypress, *Taxodium distichum.* Courtesy of Vaughn L. Banting.

Aerial roots drop from the branches to the ground, where they take root and grow into strong supporting pillars. To promote the same phenomenon on bonsai, provide warm temperatures, plenty of light, and high humidity.

Flat-Topped Style

The flat-topped style is another new bonsai style. It is inspired by bald cypress, *Taxodium distichum*, a forest tree that grows extensively in swamps and lowlands of the southern United States. The flat-topped design introduced by well-known bonsai expert Vaughn L. Banting of New Orleans reflects the natural trunk and branch growth of this species. Bald cypress is an unusual conifer. It is not evergreen but deciduous and sheds its needles every fall. In its native habitat, it lacks the Christmas-tree shape and pointed top of northern conifers such as fir and pine.

The flat top develops, according to Banting,[1] on mature trees as the top of the original trunk bends to one side and a strong branch grows into the opening formed by the curvature, as seen in Fig. 13–4. Other branches growing from this side branch create a series of small crowns, or apexes, which in time extend across the top of the tree. The flat crown is located high on the trunk, with few, if any, branches on the lower trunk.

Trunk. The magnificent tall, tapered trunk, supported by a wide buttressed base, is a prominent feature of the design. (The woody knees, which protrude above the water from the roots of bald cypress growing in swamps, sometimes appear on bonsai). Because years are required to develop bald cypress bonsai with buttressed tapered trunks, growers frequently start with old, stunted trees found in the wild. Younger plants and seedlings are excellent for group plantings. In choosing specimen material for bonsai, select a trunk that displays a wide base and a gradual, continuous taper.

[1]Vaughn Banting, "Bald Cypress: The Flat-Topped Style," *Journal of the American Bonsai Society*, 12, no. 3 (Fall 1978), 60–63.

Fig. 13–5 Flat-topped style, detail of branch structure on bald cypress bonsai. Courtesy of Vaughn L. Banting.

Branches. When pruning branches in late winter or early spring, do not remove all the crossing branches. They are characteristic of this species and the flat-topped style (Fig. 13–5). Rather, prune the exterior branches to the shape of a slightly rounded flat crown, and thin the interior sufficiently to open it to view.

The beautiful light green feathery leaves, which sprout from the trunk and branches in profusion, are another striking feature of bald cypress. Most remain as leaves until they drop in the fall. A few harden and become shoots. Nationally known expert bonsai grower E. Felton Jones of Atlanta discovered how to turn a featherlike shoot into a permanent twig. Removing the tip of a shoot while it is still soft will often cause it to harden and produce buds and side shoots. Such shoots remain on the trunk when most of the summer's growth drops in the fall. Timing is important. Pinch or pluck the tip of the feathery growth before it hardens. Throughout the growing season, eliminate the unwanted new shoots by hand or with light shears.

This style is also used for pond cypress, *T.d.* var. *nutans*, a close relative of bald cypress.

Weeping Style

The weeping style is for species with hanging branches, not trees and shrubs with upward growth. Species popular for this style include willow, weeping cherry, wisteria, cotoneaster (Fig. 13–6), hemlock, juniper, and chamaecyparis.

Fig. 13-6 Weeping-style *Cotoneaster* sp. Courtesy of J. Nakahara.

Trunk. An upright trunk is the mainstay for the hanging branches. Select a sturdy slanting, curved, or straight trunk taller than usual to provide ample space free of obstructions for the drooping branches. A tapered trunk is not of prime importance here.

Branches. Retain branches that emerge at diverse locations around the trunk to distribute the hanging branches or flowers throughout the available space. Wire them as needed to improve the arrangement.

Pruning Techniques for Weeping Bonsai.

For wisteria and other species that flower on last year's growth:

1. Immediately after flowering, cut back each branch to one or two buds (or leaves). As each replacement shoot hardens, trim it back to one or two buds; direct the new growth outward.
2. Observe the new growth during the summer and prune the shape or shorten overly long branches. Wire a branch, if necessary, to move it into space that can be filled with flowers (or other branches) next spring. Reposition branches that are crowding one another.

For willows and other deciduous species with inconspicuous or late spring and early summer flowers:

1. In late winter or early spring, severely prune last year's growth, leaving only one or two buds on each branch.
2. Do not prune the shoots that emerge. Let them elongate during the summer to produce flowers and a weeping form.

3. If necessary, wire or lightly trim the new growth to establish open, graceful branching. Postpone further pruning until late winter or early spring.

For conifers:

1. In spring, pinch or pluck the tip of the soft new growth that emerges from each bud. Remove unwanted and nonconforming branches at this time.
2. Thin excessive growth during the summer to eliminate crossing or crowded branches. Otherwise, conifers probably will not require additional pruning unless a shoot touches the soil in the container. When trimming an overly long shoot, cut it back to a branchlet or a replacement bud. Remove sufficient growth to eliminate the need for repeated pruning.

Driftwood

In bonsai, driftwood may appear as old, bleached wood on part of the trunk or branches. It is considered a bonsai style only when a vital or a large portion of the tree is made into driftwood.

Trunk. Driftwood is naturally found on old trees, such as large conifers with weathered trunks. For this reason it is associated with old bonsai, particularly juniper, but it is also seen on other species and on bonsai of all sizes. An example of how driftwood can strengthen the design of a trunk is seen in the California juniper in Fig. 12-3, where the sweep of the trunk is dramatically accentuated by curved ridges in the driftwood.

Branches. Driftwood works magic in making unwanted branches acceptable. Ugly branches, for example, may be shortened and shaped to a pleasing line and bleached as driftwood. Overly large branches, located far too high on the trunk, may be whittled to a smaller diameter, then sanded and bleached into an attractive remnant of their former size.

On a long expanse of trunk, instead of removing all the tiny branches and leaving a large empty vertical area, add a touch of interest by making one or two small branches into driftwood. Techniques for creating driftwood are described in Chapter 12.

Windswept Style

The windswept design for single- or multitrunk bonsai reflects the unrelenting force of strong, persistent winds, which could produce the one-sided branch formation on the white pine in Fig. 13-7. On a windswept bonsai, the trunk and branches are positioned (often by wiring) to suggest the impact of ravaging winds over a long period of time. This is a challenging style with a windward side (facing into the wind) that is all but denuded of growth. It leaves a stark, empty area on one side of the composition that requires ingenuity to introduce, in a convincing way, foliage and branches where few would normally be found.

Trunk. Place the trunk, either vertical or slanting, in the direction that

Fig. 13-7 A windswept style seen in nature on a white pine, *Pinus Strobus,* at the Morris Arboretum. Photo by Paul W. Meyer.

the wind blows. A trunk with a pronounced curve is rarely used except on a large old gnarled tree. Several branches and the upper section of the trunk may be changed into driftwood to suggest the abrasive effect of the wind.

In the windswept western hemlock in Fig. 13-8, the small trunk on the right seems to be pushed by the wind against the large trunk in the center. By contrast, the third trunk (on the far left) is sheltered beneath the larger trunk.

Fig. 13-8 Windswept-style western hemlock, *Tsuga heterophylla.* Courtesy of J. Nakahara.

Branches. The branches on the western hemlock are positioned to reflect the varying effects of the wind. Those on the windward side are bent, as though by the wind. The lower branches on the sheltered trunk (to the lee of the wind) rest horizontally in their protected environment.

When creating a windswept style, the branching on the lee side offers a chance to establish interesting patterns. Arrange them at varying distances from one another. This will form attractive areas of negative space. Whenever possible, include branches that vary in length and thickness.

Several ingenious methods are available to introduce branches in the barren area on the windward side. For example, use driftwood to suggest vestiges of former branches, or retain a few bent branches at the bottom of the trunk that appear to be struggling for survival.

The windswept style is sometimes suitable for trees with lopsided branches, sparse foliage, or defects that would be difficult to utilize in other designs.

Semicascade Style

The semicascade style falls somewhere between the slanting and the cascade styles.

Trunk. The tapered trunk (or a strong lower branch) extends outward beyond the rim of the container. It is predominantly horizontal, but it may drop slightly below the top of the container. Branching is confined to the top and sides of the trunk.

Branches. Alternatively, a strong lower branch may assume the role of a semicascading trunk when the original trunk forms a small tree above the container, as seen in the juniper in Fig. 13-9. On all semicascade bonsai, the branches on the major trunk become progressively smaller as they approach the apex.

Fig. 13-9 Semicascade-style *Juniperus chinensis* cv. Prostrata. Courtesy of Thomas G. Wright.

Fig. 13–10 A collected mountain hemlock, *Tsuga Mertensiana,* made into a cascade bonsai by Dan Robinson. Courtesy of Puget Sound Bonsai Association. Photo by Charles M. Gordon, Photojournalist.

Cascade Style

Cascade bonsai are cliff hangers. The container is a small crevice in the cliff, and the bonsai a tree trying to rise from the effect of crushing wind, snow, and ice. A mountain hemlock in this style, shown in Fig. 13–10, reflects the struggle between the downward pull of gravity and the upward thrust of the tree for light and growth. This style, closely related to semicascade, is distinguished by a trunk that extends well below the top of the container. Lengthening the long bottom branch on the semicascade juniper in Fig. 13–9 would change it to a cascade.

Trunk. This style generally features a single trunk. If the trunk emerges from the container at a slant, continue the slant in the same direction until it turns downward. The cascading trunk is tapered toward its growing tip in the same manner as a vertical trunk turned upside down. A pleasing effect may be introduced by bringing a portion of a downward cascading trunk partially across the front of the container.

When two or more cascading trunks are present, place the shorter trunk or trunks in the rear at a slight angle rather than parallel to, or directly under, the major trunk. When a cascade or a semicascade bonsai contains both an upright and a cascading trunk (as in Figs. 13–9 and 13–10), the bonsai will have two apexes. The top apex is formed by the stunted tree above the container. The other is the tip of the downward-hanging trunk.

Branches. When no part of the cascading trunk is directly in front of the container, it is often possible to move one of the side branches slightly over the front of the container. This will tend to soften the strong line of the pot and visually unite the container with the downward-growing trunk.

The branches, spaced on alternate sides of the trunk, become progressively smaller as they continue downward. Those at the very tip of the trunk are often bent into a horizontal position.

Roots. With a cascading trunk that slants as it emerges, surface roots located on the side opposite to the direction of the cascade are a tremendous asset. They visually support the downward-hanging trunk. However, when the lower trunk emerges vertically from the container, supporting roots on all sides are preferred. Plant the bonsai midway between the front and back of a round or square (or equilateral) container and to the right or left of center, depending on the root system.

Literati Style

This free form of bonsai (Fig. 13–11) is the opposite of the precisely structured formal upright style. As in English, the word *literati* means ''men of letters'' in Chinese; it refers to court officials in ancient China who left riches and high position to live as simple recluses in the mountains. Their quiet, noncompetitive life allowed time for calligraphy, poetry, painting, contemplation, and the

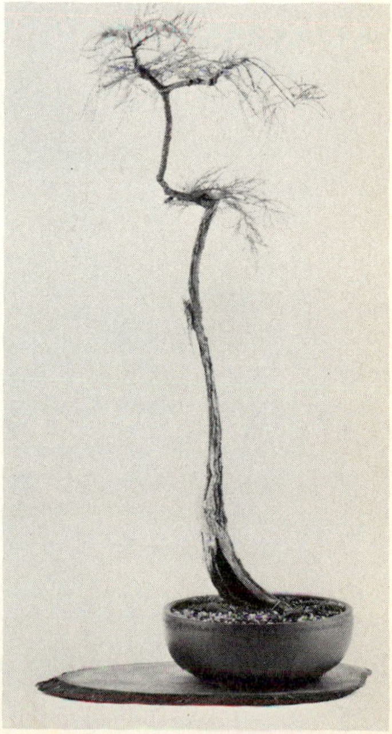

Fig. 13–11 Literati-style pond cypress, *Taxodium distichum* var. *nutans,* by Ruth Lamanna, exhibited at the 1982 Symposium of the Potomac Bonsai Association. Photo by Howard E. Clark.

pleasure of bonsai. Their bonsai became known for their unstructured yet beautiful form and in time evolved into the literati style (referred to as *bunjin* in Japan).

Conifers are frequently but not always used. There are no restrictions regarding species, size, or design. Although the style looks simple, that appearance is deceiving; it is difficult and requires a high degree of artistry.

Trunk. The single or multiple trunk is long and often thin and may have little or no taper. The tip of the trunk is not necessarily the highest point or the apex. For purposes of design, the highest point of the trunk, as shown in Fig. 7-3, is treated as the apex. The trunk may be straight, curved, or so irregularly bent as to seem almost contorted. In the best literati bonsai, however, the tree always has a natural appearance.

Branches. The few branches that are present may be widely separated. They have no prescribed placement. The foliage, often sparse and at the end of a branch, is not too heavy for a tall, slender trunk to support.

Literati bonsai are usually grown in small, shallow containers, but in keeping with the offbeat character of this style, unshaped slabs of earthenware or broken tiles are also used.

Negative space assumes an important role in this design and brings literati bonsai close to abstract art.

Two-Trunk Plantings

In these and other multitrunk plantings, the trunks are separate trees or trees growing from the same roots arranged into a single form with one periphery as in Fig. 13-12. Two trees from the same roots are called twin trunks. Whether

Fig. 13-12 Alberta spruce, *Picea glauca* var. *albertiana*. Courtesy of William N. Valavanis.

the trunks are from one or several trees, the styling is the same. Select two trees of the same species with similar trunks of different diameter and height. Start with the dominant tree; ideally, it has the tallest and thickest trunk. Examine it for its trunk line, taper, harmony, and branch structure. After determining the front, tentatively match the second tree to the first. Consider the two trees as one in their combined shape and periphery.

Before planting, try several tentative arrangements with the trunks close together at soil level. Gradually widen the distance between them as their height increases. If it is necessary to wire or prune one or both trunks, do this while they are in their training pots.

Plan to keep the major branches (which may also require wiring and pruning) on the outside of the planting. If a large root must be pruned in order to place the trunks close together, make certain that adequate fibrous roots will remain. Sometimes it is helpful to tie the two trunks with twine to keep them together when planting. Make the final adjustments before tamping the potting mix firmly in the container.

Three-Trunk Plantings

This is simply adding another tree to the design of a two-trunk planting. With three trees, place the largest or the smallest tree between the two others, as shown using Japanese white pine in Fig. 13–13. Arrange the trees to form unequal distances with pleasing negative space between the trunks. Plan to develop a unified periphery for the group. It need not be an unbroken line. Occasionally, the dominant tree will not fit comfortably between the other two. In that event, place the smallest tree in the center area and slant it toward the rear of the planting.

Fig. 13–13 Three-trunk-style Japanese white pine, *Pinus parviflora.* Courtesy of *International Bonsai.*

Cluster Plantings

Plantings of three or more trees with similar trunks are often arranged in a cluster style. The flaring trunks on the Japanese katsura tree in Fig. 13–14 exemplifies this beautiful, graceful style. Notice how the line of the low, near-horizontal trunks on the left are repeated in the near-horizontal branches on the right.

When planting trees in a cluster, duplicate the pattern of the katsura tree by placing the bottom of the trunks as close together as a tight fist and spreading the upper trunks into a fanlike arc. Rather than placing the trees in a straight row, tilt each one into a different plane, distributing them toward the front, side, or rear of the container. An example is seen in the cluster of seven Chinese elms (Fig. 13–15) planted by Jim Barrett, a nationally known bonsai professional in California, in a container that he made.

For this style, use a single species with similar trunks of different size. Choose evergreen or deciduous trees and shrubs with flowers, small fruit, or berries. Trunks may be curved or straight.

Fig. 13–14 Cluster style in nature, Katsura tree, *Cercidiphyllum japonica,* at the Morris Arboretum. Photo by Paul W. Meyer.

Fig. 13–15 Cluster-style Chinese elm, *Ulmus parvifolia*. Courtesy of Jim Barrett.

Forest and Landscape Plantings

Forest and landscape plantings, suggesting a scenic view of a few or many trees (Fig. A1-1 in Part Two), offer an opportunity to use young trees as well as specimen material. Use a roomy, low, shallow container. For each arrangement, choose trees of the same species with look-alike trunks in different sizes. Trunk height and thickness must be correlated (the tallest tree will have the thickest trunk), and one dominant tree must be the focal point of the planting.

Arranging the Trees. Design the planting while the trees are in their training pots or before removing soil from the roots. Determine the front of the dominant tree and match other trees to this one. Try several tentative arrangements with the dominant tree in the prime planting area of the container. Match the lower trunk of each tree to the trunk of the first tree and others in the planting. For a pleasing effect, pivot each tree to tilt its upper trunk slightly toward the outside of the container.

Avoid placing the trunk of one tree directly in front of or behind another or allowing one trunk to cross another when viewed from the front. Give each tree and its major branch its own space, clearly separated from that of other

Fig. 13–16 Five-trunk forest planting of *Cryptomeria japonica,* exhibited at Expo '70 in Japan.

trunks and branches. Direct large or low branches toward the outside, rather than the inside, of the container. Arrange all the trees (whether two or twenty) to form an overall shape of an arc, a crown, or a rounded triangle (Fig. 7–4), with the dominant tree providing the apex.

Prior to planting, wire and prune the trunk and branches as needed. Insert several strands of wire through the holes in the container to use, if necessary, for tying wobbly trees in position.

Angle of Emergence. Another key factor in a landscape planting is correlating the angle of emergence of each tree with the base of the dominant tree. (This is similar to the angle of emergence formed where a branch joins the trunk as described in Chapter 9.) Here, match all trunks to the slant or vertical position of the largest trunk. In the five-trunk planting of cryptomeria in Fig. 13–16, for example, the straight, dominant tree is positioned at a 90-degree angle in the container. All other trees are planted exactly at this angle. To add variety, the repetition of the angle may be progressively modified. This is seen in a landscape of Chinese elms in Fig. 13–17, where the trunks of the trees on either side of the two dominant trees emerge at a progressively smaller angle from the soil as their distance from the dominant trunk increases.

Fig. 13–17 Forest planting of five Chinese elms, *Ulmus parvifolia.* Courtesy of Wu Yee-sun.

Planting Techniques. Start with the dominant tree. Place a mound of potting mix in the container where the first tree will be planted. Spread the roots over the mound and press them down lightly. Add more mix and work it into the crevices between the roots with a planting stick. Plant the other trees in the same manner. When planting two trees close together, it may be necessary to shorten or remove several of the roots. This is not harmful if an adequate fibrous root mass can be retained. Otherwise, look for another tree that does not require extensive root pruning.

After the trees are planted, shorten or remove branches that are crowding one another. Gently slope the potting mix to the edge of the container and press it about ¼ inch below the container top.

Plantings of Two to Five Trees

A few trees are often more attractive as a multitrunk planting with their trunks close together than placed apart in a container. Where a small landscape of only a few trees is wanted, select trees with outstanding features—beautiful foliage or flowers, handsomely matching trunks—as in the forest planting of five Chinese elms in Fig. 13–17.

Plantings of Seven or More Trees

Large numbers of trees are frequently planted as a single group. One method of achieving a natural effect is to combine smaller subgroups into a single planting. Start with a group containing the largest tree. Add other groups on either side of the first. For one large planting, make the subgroups continuous. For a more open planting, place some of the subgroup slightly apart from the others. This breaks the monotony of a single group and offers opportunities to create highly visible empty space between groups and between trunks in a group.

PRACTICE AND REVIEW

Practice with Stick Trees

Skill in multitrunk plantings can be gained with a minimum of fuss by working with stick models. The stick trunks can be moved about at will without fear of damaging living trees or their roots, and the knack acquired in their placement is readily transferable to bonsai plant material.

Materials: Select a piece of rigid plywood, heavy cardboard, or similar material of approximately 10 by 15 inches and divide its length and width in half. Use the board as a container, with the intersection of the two lines marking the center. In each exercise, locate the domiant trees of the group within the interior area surrounding this intersection. Avoid planting a major tree in the exact center or at the edge of the container.

Assemble several sets of ten or more similarly shaped surrogate trees made from branches stripped of their foliage and trimmed to various lengths from 4 to 12 inches long. Samples are shown in Fig. 13–18.1. Look for matching branches with shoots or small branchlets from trees with compact growth such as selected

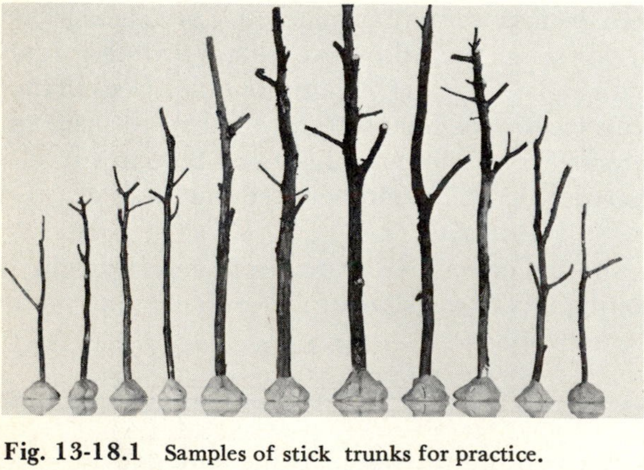

Fig. 13-18.1 Samples of stick trunks for practice.

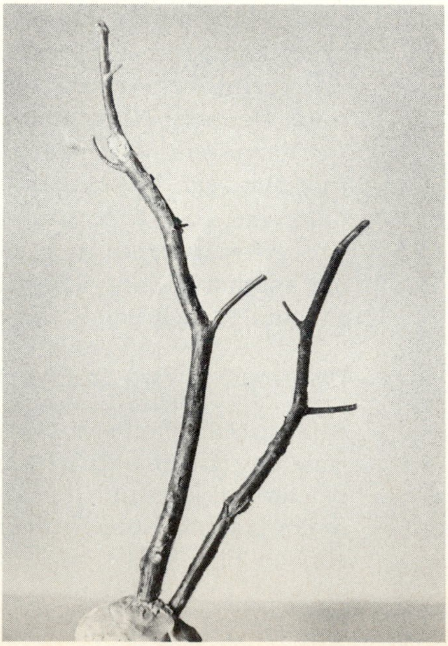

Fig. 13-18.2 Two-trunk style.

species of *Acer, Chamaecyparis, Juniperus, Thuja,* and other genera. The stick trunks illustrated in this chapter are from eastern red cedar, *Juniperus virginiana.*

For each set, prepare ten or more matched trunks containing one or two short branches. Extra trees will increase the number of options when a tree for a particular location is wanted. From here on in this practice, the instructional stick trunks will be referred to as trees. Have on hand about ¼ pound of reusable floral clay for each planting.

1. *Two trees.* Start with one large and one small tree with matching trunks. After inserting each trunk into a small ball of clay, arrange the trees with their trunks together at the base, as in Fig. 13–18.2. To find a pleasing space between the two trunks, turn them around and move them back and forth, this way and that, to view them from many different positions. Create continuous outward flow-

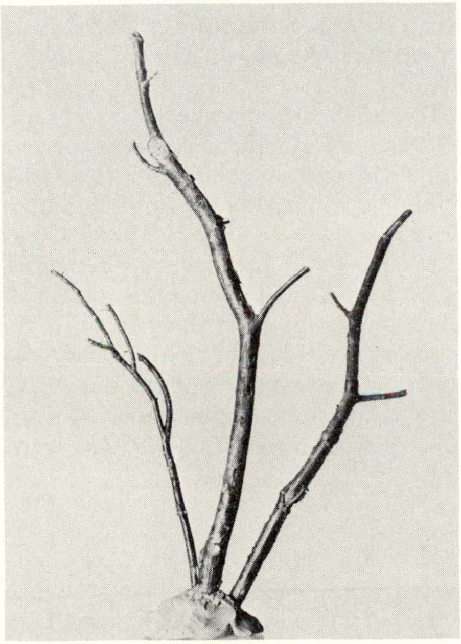

Fig. 13–18.3 Three-trunk style.

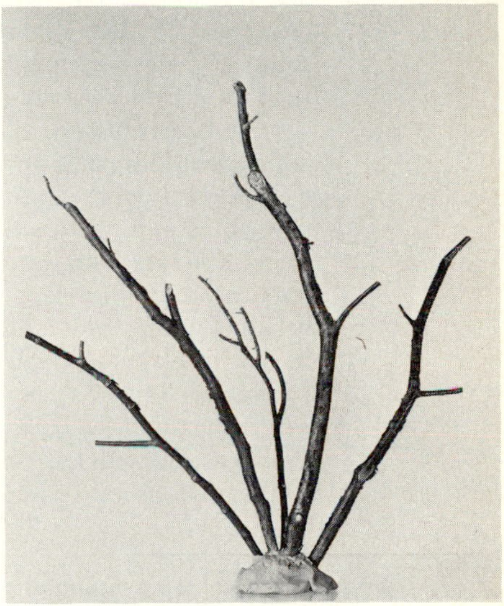

Fig. 13–18.4 Five-trunk style.

Fig. 13–18.5 Forest planting of twelve trees.

ing lines on the trunks by expanding the distance between them as they become taller. At the very top, point the tip of the two trunks in the same direction or slightly away from each other.

2. *Three trees.* For a group of three trees (Fig. 13–18.3), either add a third tree to the arrangement of two trees or start with three new trunks. Slant the trunks in different directions toward the front, sides, or rear of the container. Placing the dominant tree between the others forms an apex with a smaller tree on either side. Pay close attention to the trunk lines and the negative space they create.

3. *Five trees: a cluster.* Next, add two more trees to form a group of five, or start a new planting with five matched trunks. Follow the placement and techniques used for the two- and three-trunk plantings. An arrangement of five stick trunks is shown in Fig. 13–18.4.

4. *Five trees: a forest.* Place the dominant tree first. When adding other trees, arrange the trunk tops to form two sides of a triangle from the apex of the dominant tree to the right and left rim of the container; match the lower trunks and place them at unequal distances apart without letting one cross another from the front view. Give each tree its own territory without setting one trunk directly in front of or directly behind another.

5. *Seven or more trees: a forest.* To arrange a landscape of seven or more trees, either plant them as a unit or divide them into smaller subgroups of five and two, or three, two, and two. A group of nine is considered difficult to arrange; a three-three-three arrangement is monotonous, while a four-four-one grouping is too evenly divided; subgroups of five, three, and one are often used. Conclude the practice with a landscape planting of ten or more stick trees positioned at varying distances apart, with a forestlike periphery along the top of the trunks. To avoid the mechanical appearance of an unbroken slanting line along the top of the trunks, intersperse smaller trees among the large ones, (Fig. 13–18.5) and occasionally project the tip of the trunk slightly beyond the periphery. Allow time to try various arrangements with large and small, slanting and upright, and straight and curved trunks. Be innovative in placing the trunks to see what effects you especially like.

ADDITIONAL READING

A great variety of information on techniques, styles, and forms of bonsai will be found in the books listed at the end of Chapter 1. The following handbook is readily available and excellent for beginning and intermediate bonsai growers.

BROOKLYN BOTANIC GARDEN STAFF, Kan Yashiroda, guest ed., *Bonsai: Special Techniques*, Plant and Garden Handbook 22, no. 2. Brooklyn, N.Y.: Brooklyn Botanic Garden, 1966. This handbook, a frequently reprinted continuation of the BBG's popular *Dwarf Potted Trees: The Bonsai of Japan*, contains practical information on creating many forms of bonsai.

14

Saikei

Saikei are miniature plantings of trees and rocks and represent a major twentieth-century addition to Japanese bonsai. The word *saikei* (pronounced ''sigh-kay'') means ''trees and rocks'' in Japanese. Although based on bonsai design and composition, saikei are far easier to construct than bonsai. The appeal of saikei includes the following:

1. Freedom from the rigid requirements of bonsai.
2. A means of creating one's favorite landscape in miniature.
3. Inexpensive materials.
4. Immediate enjoyment; unlike the time required for the development of bonsai, a saikei may be enjoyed as soon as it is planted.
5. Easy care; the large planting area requires less frequent watering and repotting than bonsai.

Saikei was introduced by Toshio Kawamoto, an innovative Japanese bonsai master, during the 1960s. His father, Tokichi Kawamoto, also a noted bonsai master, a generation earlier introduced the now-famous broom style of bonsai. Kawamoto has detailed his bonsai-saikei techniques in four books, two of which are published in English and listed at the end of the chapter. An example of his saikei is shown in Fig. 14–1.

Saikei may be considered an extension of multitrunk plantings with the addition of rocks. The plant material, design, and planting methods are similar. The techniques for group and forest plantings in Chapter 13 can be applied

Fig. 14-1 Saikei of Japanese maples in early spring. Made ten years previously by Toshio Kawamoto during a teaching tour in the United States.

to saikei. Only the rocks are new, and they are treated as trees in terms of their similarity to one another, their arrangement according to dominance, and their location in the container.

PLANT MATERIAL

Most woody plants used in bonsai are also suitable for saikei. Preference is given to trees with small leaves, especially in distant landscape scenes where leaf size affects the scale and proportion. The greater freedom of saikei design expands the choice of plant material from the customary trees and shrubs to semiwoody herbs, succulents, cacti, and nearly anything else that will suggest a landscape scene. Most saikei, however, are planted with young trees.

As in landscape plantings, saikei uses trees of the same species, in assorted sizes, and with matching trunks. In size, the trees are ranked from the largest to the smallest and planted in this sequence. The tallest tree, ideally, also has the thickest trunk. In saikei this corresponding relationship of trunk height to width is continued down to the shortest tree, which will have the thinnest trunk. Where the height of a major tree is insufficient, the shortage may be overcome by planting the tree at a higher than normal elevation, thereby bringing the top of the trunk to the desired height. Trees that are excessively tall for their thin trunks are easily shortened by pruning. All trees for saikei should be compact and free of excessive or unwanted growth. Nonconforming trunks on supple young seedlings are easily corrected by wiring.

Occasionally, beautiful older trees, trained for bonsai, are seen in sophisticated saikei. But generally, when older trees appear, they are the faulty ones that fail to meet the exacting requirements of bonsai.

A sampling of plant material for saikei is listed here. Varieties and cultivars with especially small leaves are often preferred; a few are included in the listing. Many other species and cultivars can be used. The following trees and shrubs are also suitable for bonsai.

Suggested Trees and Plants for Saikei and Bonsai

Acer Ginnala Maxim. Amur maple

A. palmatum Thunb. Japanese maple and its varieties and cultivars

A. rubrum L. American red or swamp maple

Buxus microphylla Siebold & Zucc. Boxwood and cv. Compacta, Kingsville box

B.m. var. **japonica** Rehd. & E. H. Wils. Japanese box

B.m.. var. **koreana** Nakai Korean boxwood

B. sempervirens L. Common box

Carpinus caroliniana T. Walt. American hornbeam

C.c. var. **virginiana** Fern. Blue beech

C. laxiflora Blume Japanese hornbeam

Celtis sinensis Pers. Japanese hackberry

Chamaecyparis obtusa Endl. cv. Nana dwarf Hinoki cypress

C. pisifera Endl. Sawara cypress and cvs. Plumosa and Squarrosa

C. thyoides BSP. cv. Ericoides American dwarf white cedar

Cotoneaster microphyllus Wallich ex Lindl. Chinese cotoneaster

Cryptomeria japonica D. Don Japanese cedar, cv. Compacta and a yatsubusa form

Cupressus arizonica Greene cv. Compacta compact Arizona cypress

C. macrocarpa Hartweg Monterey cypress

Ehretia microphylla Lam. *(Carmona microphylla)* Fukien tea

Erica L. spp. Heath

Fagus crenata Blume Japanese beech

F. sylvatica L. European beech

Ginkgo biloba L. Maidenhair tree

Ilex crenata Thunb. Japanese holly and cvs. Helleri, Microphylla, and others

I. decidua Walt. American possum haw and cv. Warren's Red

I. serrata Thunb. Japanese deciduous holly

I. vomitora Ait. Yaupon holly and cvs. Nana and Shellings Dwarf

Juniperus chinensis L. Chinese juniper and cvs. Blaauw and Torulosa

J.c. var. **procumbens** Endl. cv. Nana *(J. procumbens nana)*, dwarf form

J.c. var. **Sargentii** A. Henry Shimpaku

J. squamata D. Don cv. Prostrata, similar to **J.c.p.** cv. Nana

Larix laricina C. Koch American larch
Malpighia coccigera L. Miniature holly
Picea glauca var. **albertiana** Sarg. Alberta spruce
P. rubens Sarg. Red spruce
Pinus Cembra L. Swiss stone pine
P. clausa Vasey American sand pine
P. leucodermis Ant. Balkan pine
P. parviflora Siebold & Zucc. Japanese white pine
P. Peuce Griseb. Macedonian pine
P. Strobus L. American eastern white pine
P. Thunbergiana Franco *(P. Thunbergii)* Japanese black pine
Podocarpus macrophyllus var. **Maki** Endl. Buddhist pine
Rhododendron indicum Sweet Japanese Macranthum azalea
R. kiusianum Mak. *(R. obtusum japonicum)* Japanese Kyushu azalea
R. serpyllifolium Miq. Japanese wild thyme azalea
Rosmarinus officinalis L. Rosemary
Serissa foetida Lam. Serissa and **S.f.** var. **variegata**, variegated serissa
Syzygium paniculatum Gaertn. *(Eugenia paniculata)* Brush cherry
Taxodium distichum L. Bald cypress
Ulmus parvifolia Jacq. Chinese elm and cvs. Catlin and Drake, evergreen with small leaves
U. pumila L. Siberian elm
Zelkova serrata Spach Japanese zelkova

ACCESSORY PLANTS

Kawamoto often adds charming small companion plantings at the base of the trees in his saikei. These tiny woody and herbaceous plants serve two purposes: Their flowers and foliage bring the eye into the composition, and they form an attractive transition from the rim of the container to the larger trees and rocks. Use the following list to search for these or comparable plant material in your own region. Experiment with indigenous small-leaved ground covers, creepers, wildings, and dwarf forms of cultivated plants. For best results, select accessory plants whose growing needs will match the growing environment of the saikei. The species listed here are also grown in small containers for display next to larger bonsai.

Suggested Accessory Plants for Saikei

Herbaceous

Acorus gramineus Ait. cv. Pusillus Grassy-leaved dwarf sweet flag
Asplenium Trichomanes L. Maidenhair fern
Carex L. spp. Sedge

Equisetum ramosissium Japanese dwarf scouring rush
Hedyotis caerulea Hook. *(Houstonia caerulea)* Bluets
Mazus reptans N. E. Br. A trailing ground cover
Sedum dasyphyllum L. and other low growing sedums
Selaginella caulescens Wallich ex. Spring Japanese golden fern
S. densa Rydb. A dark green, flat-growing form
Thymus Serpyllum L. Creeping thyme
Viola verecunda A. Gray var. **yakusimana** Ohwi. *(V. yakusimana)* Japanese dwarf violet
Woodsia ilvensis R. Br. Rusty woodsia fern

Woody and semiwoody:

Arctostaphylos Uva-ursi K. Spreng. Bearberry
Cotoneaster microphyllus Wallich ex. Lindl. and var. **thymifolia** Koehne Thyme cotoneaster
Gaultheria procumbens L. Wintergreen
Gaylussacia brachycera A. Gray Box huckleberry
G. dumosa Torr. & A. Gray Dwarf huckleberry
Leiophyllum buxifolium Elliott Box sandmyrtle
Rhododendron impeditum Balf.f. & W. W. Sm. A small-leaved rhododendron
R. kiusianum Mak. *(R. obtusum japonicum)* Japanese Kyushu azalea
R. serpyllifolium Miq. Japanese wild thyme azalea
Vaccinium angustifolium Ait. Low blueberry

ROCKS

In saikei, rocks are matched to the character of the tree. For harmony, match weathered, contoured rocks (Fig. 14-2.1) to trees with curved trunks and soft foliage. Select sharp, strong, and irregular rocks (Fig. 14-2.2) for angular or conical trees. The rock in Fig. 14-2.3 has both strong and soft aspects and is suitable for a variety of uses.

Choose rocks of different sizes with similar markings, color, indentations, or shape so that in the planting they will appear to be from the same geological formation. Plan to bury ugly or undesirable parts of a rock or cover them with moss. Expose only the attractive surfaces. Give preference to hard, durable rocks over soft ones and old-looking rocks to newly quarried stone.

Rocks in nature range from fantastic, exotic shapes to flat, undistinguished fieldstone. Irregular, asymmetrical shapes are most effective and easy to use in saikei, but even ordinary stones are acceptable. Rocks with a narrow width make efficient vertical walls to enclose a planting area. Their thinness takes relatively little of the limited planting space in the container, leaving more room for trees and roots.

Fig. 14-2.1 A weathered rock from the New York-New Jersey area.

Fig. 14-2.2 A pitted, sharp rock from Georgia.

Fig. 14-2.3 A rock from the Ozarks.

Sources

Natural rocks for saikei may be found in most areas; it is not necessary to purchase expensive specimens from rock shops or dealers. Look for rocks on the shoulders, ditches, and banks of country lanes or highways and farther from the road in rocky fields and woods, streams and river beds, lake shores and mountains. (Avoid rocks washed by salt water unless their harmful saline deposits are completely removed.) Construction sites where heavy equipment unearths buried rocks are worth investigating. In certain local areas where surface rocks are not present, stone and gravel distributors may have suitable rocks. Suppliers of landscape material are another possible source. But wherever the source, searching for rocks and finding them is part of the joy of saikei.

Oversize rocks also have their uses. Unwanted sections may be removed, or a large rock broken into pieces. A stonemason's hammer and chisel are useful for this. Wear goggles to protect the eyes from rock splinters. There is a special knack to splitting rocks. A stonemason, geologist, or knowledgeable hobbyist can demonstrate the technique.

CONTAINERS

The low, shallow containers used for group plantings are also suitable for saikei. Customarily, oval containers are preferred for trees with curved trunks or soft foliage and rectangular ones for needle conifers with straight trunks or sharp needles. To prevent warping, large containers are cured at the pottery for a month and placed at precise positions in the kiln for firing. When finished, they are strong, able to withstand freezing, and capable of supporting the heavy weight of a saikei with rocks. Equally satisfactory are inexpensive handmade containers including those described in Chapter 7.

MATERIALS

Materials and tools used for saikei are generally the same as those for bonsai. A turntable is especially helpful for rotating the planting, and a small 2- or 3-inch-wide brush is handy for smoothing the surface of the planting and cleaning the rocks of potting mix.

Moss is essential. It enhances the planting and prevents erosion of a sloping bank. To duplicate the appearance of the natural outcropping shown in Fig. 14–3, place moss over the edge of individual rocks and let only the rock's top surface appear above the soil.

Coarse sand or crushed rock is sometimes added to suggest a stream or a body of water. Avoid very fine sand; it is easily dispersed by rain and watering.

Three special materials not common to bonsai are used extensively in saikei: muck, floral clay, and styrofoam.

Fig. 14-3 Nineteen Catlin elms, *Ulmus parvifolia* cv. Catlin, on a sandstone slab measuring 22 by 28 inches. Saikei by Melba L. Tucker, California.

Muck

Muck is a natural plastic. In a saikei planting, it is molded into many shapes. It makes a planting pocket for the potting mix, it steadies the rocks in the container, and it creates contours on the surface of the potting mix. Muck is usually formed by combining a decomposed organic peat such as humus peat with a material that contains fibers such as sphagnum peat moss. Alternatively, clay can be combined with shredded twine or wool. The ingredients are mixed together until they form a homogenous puttylike substance.

Preparation. When using humus peat and sphagnum peat moss (both of which are clean, odorless, and of uniform consistency), start with approximately equal parts of each by volume. Gradually add water separately to each ingredient. Blend it by hand until the water is absorbed. Humus peat, which is often packaged in a moist condition, may require little additional water. By contrast, sphagnum peat moss will absorb a large amount. If either ingredient becomes too wet, drain the surplus water or add dry material to absorb it.

Combine the materials when they are thoroughly moist and knead them together. Long, continued kneading is the key to making muck that will hold its shape. It should be plastic yet firm. Test the mixture by squeezing a bit into a ridge about 1 inch high. If it has no texture and cannot hold its shape, add more fibrous material. If it crumbles, increase the water slightly and test it again. If the mixture is not pliable, add more humus peat. When the muck is ready, pat it into balls about 3 inches wide. In this form it may be kept for a long time in an airtight container, stored in a cool, sunless place.

When substituting other materials for humus peat, such as decomposed peat found at the edge of a marsh or natural deposits of clay, remove the bits of twigs, rock, or other foreign matter that may be present. Pottery clay that is free of chemicals has a uniform consistency and is usable as packaged. With clay, increase the amount of fibrous ingredients to 60 percent or more to compensate for the lack of air and pore space in clay.

As a substitute for the fibers in sphagnum peat moss, cut and shred into small pieces such coarse materials as hemp rope, untreated burlap, or heavy strands of wool. These and other natural materials will disintegrate and eventually merge with the potting mix. Always use materials that are not harmful to roots, for in time the roots often grow into the muck.

Floral Clay

Nontoxic floral or modeling clay is available at florist and craft shops. It is a malleable adhesive clay that is impervious to water and chemically inert. These qualities make it serviceable as an adhesive to hold rocks to the bottom of the container. Floral clay may easily be removed any time the saikei is rearranged or replanted.

Styrofoam

Styrofoam, a light polystyrene plastic may be inserted under a rock to increase its height. Unlike muck, styrofoam is capable of supporting a heavy weight in a saikei planting. It may be salvaged from packing material and easily sliced to the desired size and thickness with a knife. Styrofoam remains inert in the planting, unaffected by water or potting mix. When the flat side of a rock is placed on a piece of styrofoam, only a bit of floral clay is needed to hold it fast. If the rock is unstable, however, it is necessary to identify the uneven surface that causes the imbalance and to carve an indentation in the styrofoam to fit the rock. When the rock is balanced in the prepared hollow, it can be secured with floral clay, if necessary.

SAIKEI PLANTINGS

One Tree and One Rock

A saikei can be as simple as one tree and one rock. The two are always planted close to each other in the prime area of the container as seen in the diagram of the sample planting in Fig. 14-4. Crosses indicate a muck wall. The tree, rock, and container in the following exercise are for demonstration only. The rock is unusually large to emphasize its placement. Smaller rocks can be used.

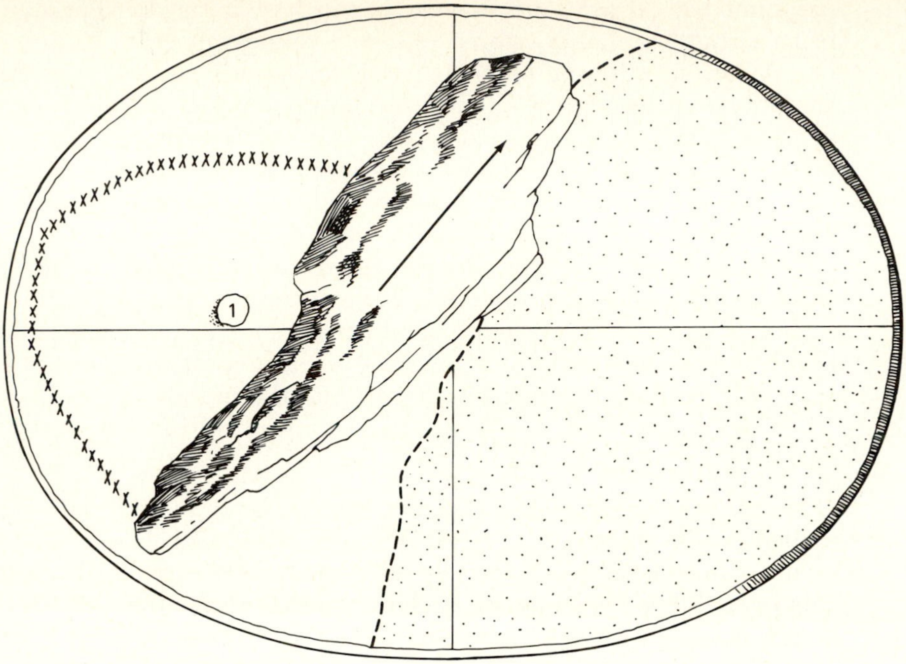

Fig. 14–4 Planting diagram: one tree and one rock. Arrow indicates long axis of the rock.

It is not necessary to duplicate the sample material. Select a combination that appeals to you.

Materials. One andromeda, *Pieris japonica*; one worn, irregular rock; one oval container (10 by 14 inches); and screening, as shown in Fig. 14–4.1. Choose a container that is longer than the height of the tree, with ample room for both the tree and rock.

1. Matching Tree and Rock. First, select the front of the tree. There may be several possibilities. Consider whether a strong branch can be placed over the rock or whether the tree can be slanted to lean above the rock. After the front is chosen, decide whether the tree will be planted to the right or the left in the container. (If the tree is on the opposite side shown in the planting diagram, make a tracing, turn it over, and work from the reverse image.)

Remove unwanted growth and shorten overly long branches. If necessary, change the line of the trunk by wiring. Postpone final pruning to shape the tree until the tree and rock are planted in the container.

Next, examine the rock for its best side, or "face." Keeping in mind the front of the tree, hold rock and tree together in various positions. Try matching them in different ways. Observe the long axis of the rock. Usually, the most pleasing position for a rock is diagonal to the front of the container. If the tree and the rock do not fit together comfortably, look for an alternate front on the tree or a different face for the rock. After experimenting, find an arrangement that you like. The view chosen in the sample is shown in Fig. 14–4.2. Before making a final decision, check the tree from the side. Do the trunk and major branch extend slightly toward the front of the container? If not, this can usually be adjusted by tilting or pivoting the trunk slightly.

2. Planting the Tree and Rock. Fasten screening over the drainage hole and place the rock in the container as indicated in the diagram. Is the best side visible from the front of the container? Is the rock stable and secure? If not, fasten it to the container with floral clay. When the rock is firmly in position, add the tree.

Use of Muck. In this example, and frequently in saikei, the tree is planted at an elevation higher than the top of the container. When this occurs, first build a wall of muck around the planting area to hold the potting mix, as shown in Fig. 14–4.3. Press a vertical strip of muck tightly to the bottom of the container about ½ inch beyond the root mass of the tree. Squeeze it into a ridge. To increase the height of the wall, add more muck. Make it no thicker than necessary to be free-standing and strong enough to contain the potting mix.

Sprinkle potting mix inside the wall where the tree is to be planted. After removing the tree from its container, scrape away the top layer of soil with the planting stick until supporting roots appear. If the uncovered lower trunk is satisfactory, let it serve as the bottom of the tree. Otherwise, here and elsewhere in saikei, bury that portion of the trunk if it is not pleasing.

Occasionally a root ball is too tall for the available space. When this occurs, carefully knead the root mass into a flatter shape. If the tree is too low, add more mix under the roots. It may be necessary to trim the roots on one side in order to place the tree close to the rock. Unless the roots obstruct the planting or are excessively large, root pruning is usually not required. There is ample space in a saikei container for roots.

Test the placement of the tree in the prepared area (Fig. 14–4.4) prior to planting. If the view is satisfactory from the front and both sides, proceed with the planting. When the tree is securely planted next to the rock, press the muck wall over the potting mix and smooth the surface into a natural slope toward the edge of the container, as in Fig. 14–4.5. Reexamine the shape and branching of the tree in its permanent position next to the rock. Remove unwanted branches and prune carefully to establish a pleasing periphery.

3. Finishing Touches. Water lightly and apply a covering of moss. Extend the moss slightly over the rock to create the effect of a natural outcropping. Beyond the planting area, use either moss or a ¼- to ½-inch layer of sand, as in Fig. 14–4.6. To create a different landscape, a smaller, matching rock may be added, as in Fig. 14–4.7. Water the finished saikei thoroughly and provide the care prescribed for bonsai.

Fig. 14–4.1 Tree and rock.

Fig. 14–4.2 A tentative arrangement —front view.

Fig. 14–4.3 Molded muck forms a planting pocket for the tree—rear view.

Fig. 14–4.4 Trial placement of tree in planting area—rear view.

Fig. 14–4.5 Tree planted next to rock—front view.

Fig. 14–4.6 Moss and sand added—front view.

Fig. 14–4.7 A second rock added—front view.

One Group of Five or More Trees

Choose look-alike trees of one species in assorted sizes and with similar trunk lines. Include one tree that is taller than the others and has the thickest trunk. Apply this trunk height-to-width relation to all the trees. Do not hesitate to shorten a trunk for this purpose. Plan to place the dominant tree and other major trees in the prime planting area and most of the smaller trees near the sides or at the rear of the planting.

In saikei, rocks are selected and ''planted'' as though they, too, were trees. The dominant rock is close to the dominant tree in the prime area of the container, and the smallest rocks are with the smallest trees. This association may be varied from time to time to add interest to a planting. However, no tree or rock is placed directly against the wall of the container.

A planting diagram is shown as a guide in Fig. 14–5. The crosses indicate the use of muck. Remember, it is not necessary to duplicate material. Choose matched trees, rocks, and a container that you like.

Materials. Seven American red maples, *Acer rubrum*; five or more irregularly shaped rocks; a low container; two muck balls; floral clay; and styrofoam, as shown in Fig. 14–5.1.

1. Preparation. Find the front of the largest tree. Rank other trees by size

Fig. 14–5 Planting diagram: seven trees and rocks. Arrows indicate the long axis of the rocks.

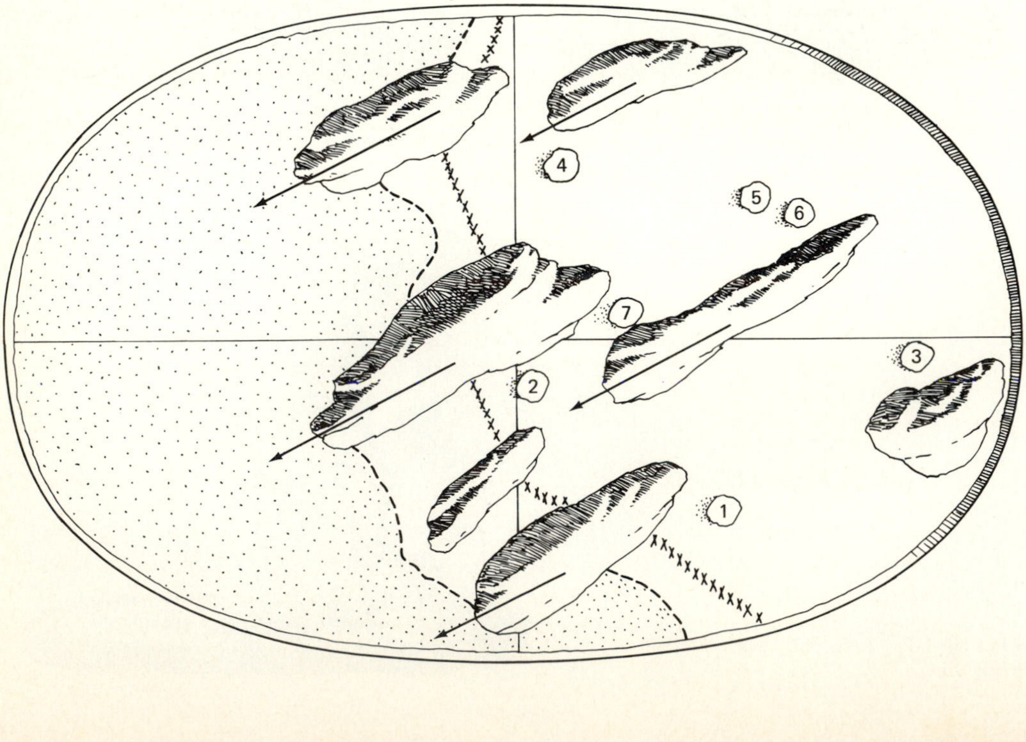

and match their trunks to the front view of the first tree. In Fig. 14–5, the trees are numbered according to the height of their trunks.

Select the face of the largest rock. Rank and match the other rocks to the face and shape of the first rock.

2. *Planting the Trees and Rocks.* Make several tentative arrangements of the trees and rocks in the container while the trees are in their training pots. Wire the trunks, if needed, to match them to the dominant trunk. The trial arrangement in Fig. 14–5.2 was later changed by moving the smallest tree to the rear of the planting and rearranging the rocks.

Plant the largest tree and rock first. Place the tree at the highest elevation in the planting. Then follow the planting diagram in Fig. 14–5 and plant the tree that is closest to the first. Continue to work outward from the dominant tree. Remember, do not let one trunk be directly in front of or behind another, and vary the spacing among the trees. Apply this also to the rocks: Place the long axis, or thrust, of each rock parallel to the first rock.

Place each rock firmly in the container. If it wobbles slightly, it may be steadied on a layer of potting mix. If it does not stay in position, find the cause and hollow a piece of styrofoam to cradle the projections that cause the imbalance. Fit the rock into the cavity and secure it with putty.

From time to time, check the trees and rocks from all sides. Are the trunks tilted slightly toward the outside of the container? Are the rocks parallel to the axis of the largest rock as seen in the planting diagram? If three trunks are in a straight line from any view, move one of the three to break this pattern. Make these adjustments while the planting is in progress. Notice in Fig. 14–5.3 that the trunk of a large tree is almost directly in front of another. It will be moved slightly to the left before the planting is completed. When it is finished, check the potting mix for air pockets and steady any tree or rock that is not secure. Replant trees that continue to wobble.

Examine the top of the trunks. Is the dominant trunk the tallest of the group? Will the top of its trunk form the apex of a triangle along the tree tops on either side? Trim the trunks, if needed, to establish a triangular form along the periphery. In the completed planting shown in Fig. 14–5.4, the trunks of the tree on the far right and on the far left were shortened to establish a triangular pattern.

3. *Finishing Touches.* When the trees and rocks are securely planted, moisten the surface of the potting mix and cover it with moss. If you wish, substitute sand for moss on part of the planting, and water thoroughly.

Two or More Groups

Saikei plantings are often divided into two or more groups of different size separated by water (sand) or a low valley (moss). Use trees of one species with matching trunks. Plant each subgroup as a separate saikei with one dominant tree and subsidiary trees of varying sizes. After making a tentative arrangement

Fig. 14–5.1 Materials for a saikei of five trees.

Fig. 14–5.2 A tentative arrangement—front view.

Fig. 14–5.3 Planting in progress—front view, before shortening trunks.

Fig. 14–5.4 Finished planting—front view.

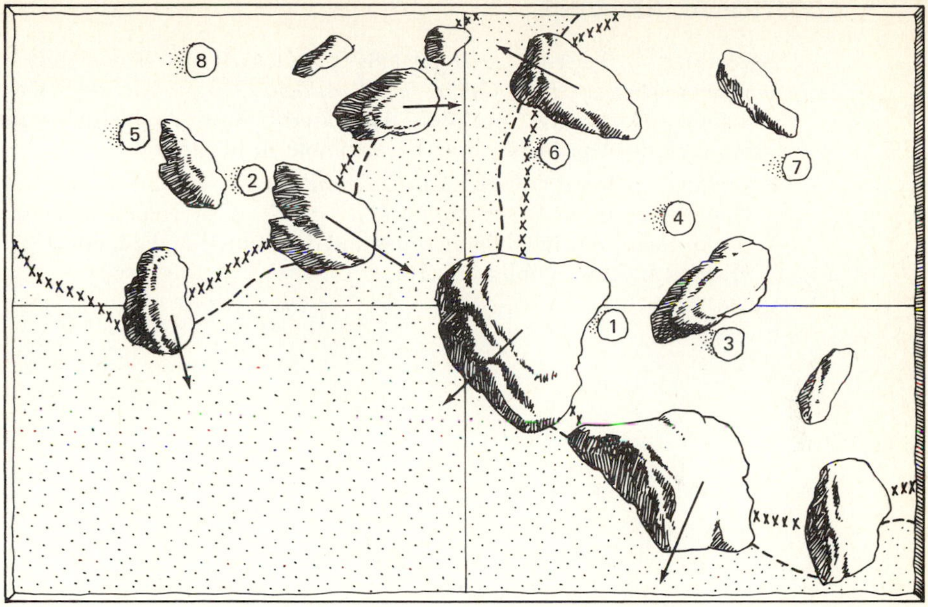

Fig. 14–6 Planting diagram: saikei divided into two groups.

of the complete saikei, plant the trees and rocks in the largest group first. Add satellite groups one by one to extend and strengthen the design of the first group.

Plan to unite the groups visually by a single overall periphery along the tree tops. Are the trunk lines similar? The trees in each group, for example, may all have straight, vertical trunks. Or the trunks in each group may slant in the same direction. Alternatively, with groups divided by a large body of water or a wide valley, the trees in each group may slant toward the dividing area (and one another).

A planting diagram for a saikei with two groups divided by a lake is shown in Fig. 14–6. Assemble eight similar trees and complementary rocks. From groups of five and three trees, with the dominant tree in the larger group.

Stage several trial runs to arrange the trees and rocks and select the design you especially like. Here, the rocks radiate outward like spokes of a wheel. Connect the large rocks bordering the water in each group with a wall of muck, and continue the wall to form planting pockets, if needed, for the major trees. Plant the first group at the highest elevation in the saikei. When the planting is nearly finished, add smaller rocks among the trees to suggest an outcropping. The banks and rocks along the edges of a divided saikei are a fine location for small accessory plantings. Thoroughly clean the surface of the container between the two groups by removing spilled potting mix and crumbs of muck before adding sand. If the area will be covered with moss, a cleanup is not necessary.

ADDITIONAL READING

KAWAMOTO, TOSHIO, AND JOSEPH Y. KURIHARA, *Bonsai-Saikei: The Art of Japanese Miniature Trees, Gardens, and Landscapes*. Tokyo: Nippon Saikei Co., 1963. This comprehensive, profusely illustrated book is a self-teacher for saikei. It is now out of print but may be available in libraries.

KAWAMOTO, TOSHIO, *Saikei: Living Landscapes in Miniature.* Tokyo and Palo Alto, Calif.: Kodansha International Ltd., 1967. A shortened, concise version of *Bonsai-Saikei*, reprinted many times and distributed in the United States through Harper & Row, Publishers, Inc.

15

Two Styles of Chinese Bonsai

THE LINGNAN GROW-AND-CLIP METHOD

The Lingnan method, one of the many forms of bonsai developed in China during the past two thousand years, exemplifies the close relation of bonsai to other Chinese arts. The Lingnan School (named after the area where it originated), and its grow-and-clip technique, achieves its effect by pruning alone. The trunk and branches of the bougainvillea in Fig. 15–1, for example, were developed by pruning, without the use of wire or other mechanical restraints.

Wu Yee-sun describes the origin of the style and technique in *Man Lung Artistic Pot Plants:*

> Toward the end of the Ching Dynasty and the beginning of the Republic of China, i.e. about 1900, dwarf tree trainers in Kwangtung Province introduced the ''Grow and Clip'' method, inspired by Chinese brush painting techniques. The result was a new layout and structure of dwarfed trees which have an ancient gnarled appearance as well as an easy grace. This method came to be known as the ''Lingnan School,'' and raised pot culture to the status of art. The other provinces adopted this method, which has since been universally employed by growers both north and south of the Yangtzekiang (the Long River).[1]

The grow-and-clip technique transforms a tree into bonsai by alternate pruning and growing. To develop a tapered trunk, for example, the trunk is pruned at the fork of the branch chosen as a replacement. This carefully selected

[1]Wu Yee-sun, *Man Lung Artistic Pot Plants,* 2nd enlarged ed. (Hong Kong: Wing Lung Bank Ltd. Art Publications, 1974), p. 63.

Fig. 15–1 *Bougainvillea spectabilis,* severely cut back, was grown as a bonsai by the grow-and-clip method. Courtesy of Wu Yee-sun.

branch is allowed to thicken until it is nearly reaches the size of the trunk immediately below and thus appears as a natural continuation of the trunk. It is then cut back severely to another small branch, and the process is repeated.

This is illustrated in the diagrammatic drawing in Fig. 15–2.1 where the trunk is pruned at point A, immediately beyond branch B. Branch B is allowed to grow until it appears as a natural continuation of the trunk, as seen in Fig. 15–2.2. When this branch has thickened, it is cut back to a smaller branch, C, as shown in Fig. 15–2.3. After branch C grows into another section of the trunk, it is pruned at branch D, and the process is continued. By this method, a trunk is built up in a succession of smaller and smaller sections until a tapered trunk of the desired height is obtained, as seen in Fig. 15–3.

The grow-and-clip method can be used anywhere. It is most effective with deciduous trees in climates that have a long growing season so that multiple layers of new growth can be obtained within a few years. The method may be applied to many styles of bonsai, from upright to cascade. Species that grow quickly and produce an abundance of new shoots respond especially well to this technique. The following are among the genera frequently used:

Acer
Bougainvillea (Fig. 15–1)
Celtis (Fig. 15–3)
Ehretia

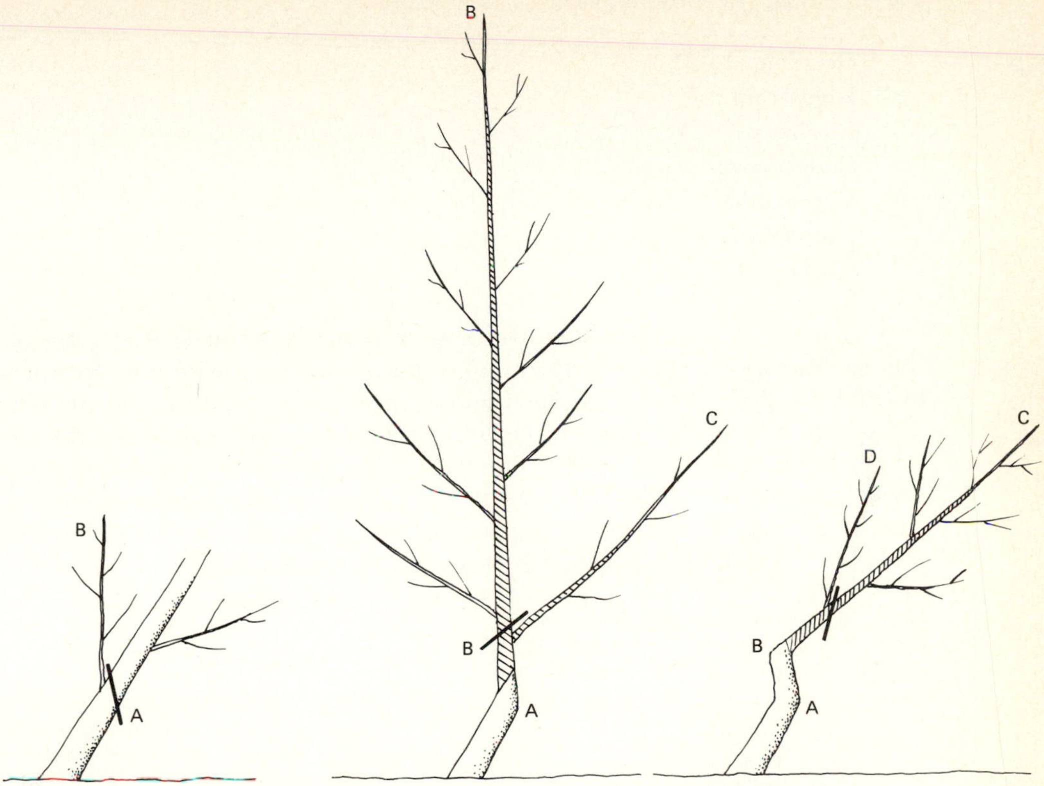

Fig. 15–2.1 The original trunk, A, is pruned directly beyond branch B, which will form the new trunk.

Fig. 15–2.2 After branch B has thickened to a continuation of trunk A, it is cut slightly beyond branch C; the trunk now consists of sections A and B.

Fig. 15–2.3 After branch C has developed, it will form the third section of the trunk; it will then be pruned at the fork of branch D, which will grow to be the fourth section.

Fig. 15–3 Chinese hackberry, *Celtis sinensis,* developed into a bonsai by pruning alone. Courtesy of Wu Yee-sun.

Ilex (Fig. 15-4)
Ligustrum
Lonicera
Podocarpus
Pyracantha
Sageretia (Fig. 15-5)
Ulmus (Fig. 15-6)

A plant with a fairly large trunk at the start is preferred to young plant material because it can be shaped into a specimen bonsai within a short period of time. Branches can be trimmed and shaped at the same time as the trunk. Trimming the new growth on the branches persistently will create the dense twiggy network seen on the sageretia in Fig. 15-5. Trees with a well-developed trunk may often be found growing in the ground or in a large container. On such trees, plan to remove the upper portions of the trunk and start the grow-and-clip training with a short, thick trunk, as in Fig. 15-6.

Fig. 15-4 Deciduous holly, *Ilex serrata* cv. Frosty Red, growing from the same roots and trained as bonsai using the grow-and-clip technique. Courtesy of Wu Yee-sun.

Fig. 15-5 This *Sageretia Thea,* with delicate branching on a gnarled trunk, is a product of the Lingnan School. Courtesy of Wu Yee-sun.

Fig. 15–6 Japanese elm, *Ulmus Davidiana* var. *japonica,* Lingnan School. Courtesy of Wu Yee-sun.

The grow-and-clip technique in sequence is illustrated in the following drawings:

1. Fig. 15–7.1: A two-trunk tree growing in the ground was selected. Although at first glance it appears to be a maze of branches without a dominant trunk, it has desirable features. For example, the natural taper of the trunk and branches is promising. The profusion of shoots and branches offer many choices where pruning cuts can be made to establish two new trunk lines. The dense growth indicates that compact foliage and branching can be expected. But most important, the lower portions of both trunks are well shaped for bonsai and placed in a pleasing position to one another.
2. Fig. 15–7.2: Clip. The tree is dug, and the roots, surrounded by a ball of soil, are wrapped in burlap. The point where each trunk will be shortened is marked by a slash in the drawing. Most of the branches will be removed, as indicated by the broken lines. The larger trunk, on the left, is pruned at four locations, while the smaller trunk is pruned twice. The roots are pruned (not shown) to remove those that will be too large to fit into the eventual bonsai container.
3. Fig. 15–7.3: After they have been pruned, the trunks are replanted in the ground for optimum growth with a regular program of watering and light fertilizing.
4. Fig. 15–7.4: Growth continues. New branches emerge; the lower trunks begin to thicken. One or several years later, when the formation has thickened, the tree is pruned again. The cut is made slightly beyond the replacement branch selected to continue the trunk. If only a few branches are cut, the tree is pruned

Fig. 15-7.1 Material selected for the grow-and-clip technique.

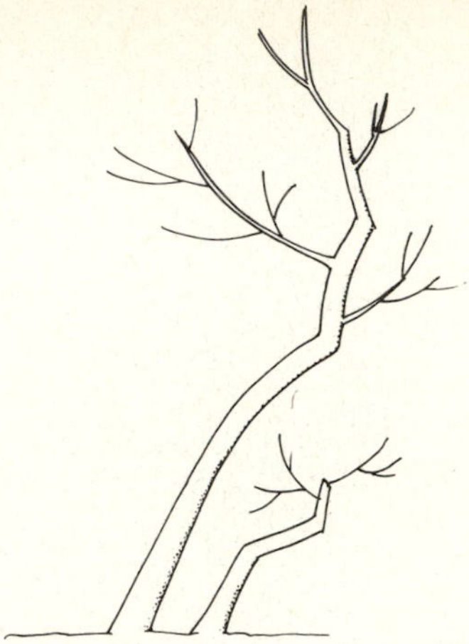

Fig. 15-7.3 The top growth and roots of the tree are drastically pruned before it is replanted.

Fig. 15-7.2 A twin-trunk tree, dug and wrapped in burlap; pruning cuts are indicated.

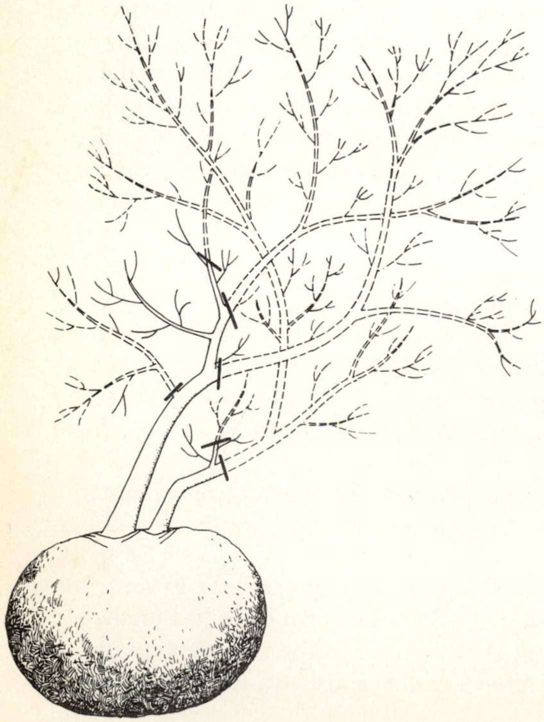

Fig. 15-7.4 Both trunks are then allowed to grow freely.

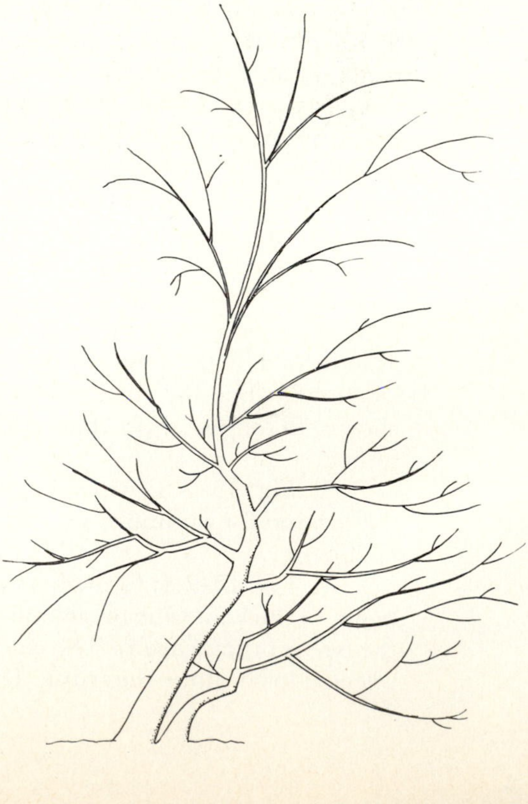

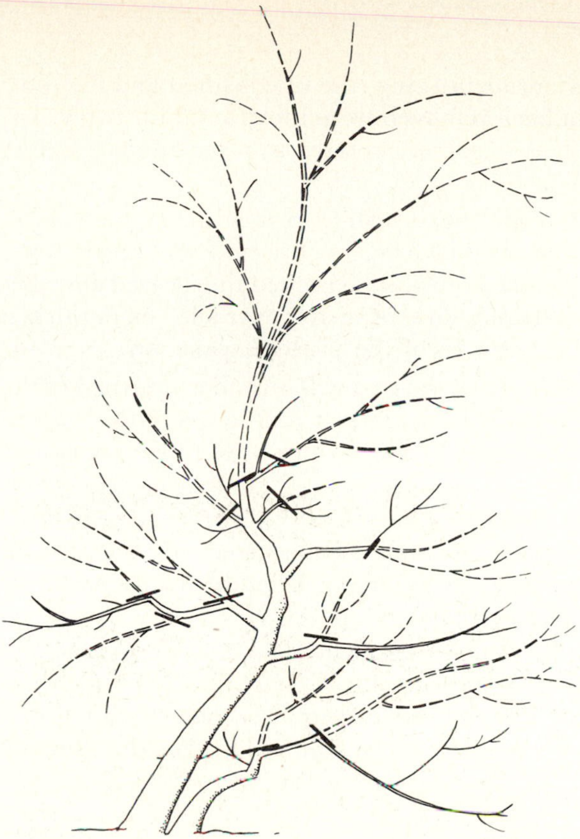

Fig. 15–7.5 Proposed pruning cuts are shown, growth to be removed is shown in dotted lines.

Fig. 15–7.6 After continual pruning, a bonsai shape is formed. When dense fibrous roots are present the tree will be moved to a bonsai container.

Fig. 15–7.7 After additional refinement by pruning, the tree is moved to a bonsai container.

while it is in the ground. For extensive pruning, the tree is lifted and the roots are also pruned. If a tree has not been removed from the ground for two years, it is dug, root-pruned, and, as it is replanted, rotated to place another side to the best source of light.

5. Fig. 15–7.5: Clip. Both trunks again will be pruned severely, as indicated in the drawing. In practice, individual branches are cut from time to time, whenever the diameter of a particular branch has reached the desired size. Because taper is wanted, neither the trunk nor a branch is ever allowed to thicken to the same diameter as the older growth of the preceding section.

6. Fig. 15–7.6: After clipping. Now the tree will be either returned to the ground to strengthen the roots or planted in a large training pot. Growing and clipping is continued in order to fill gaps in the periphery and increase twiggy growth.

7. Fig. 15–7.7: Completion. Within approximately six or seven years from the start of the grow-and-clip process, the tree is transferred to a bonsai container for further refinement and twig development. Both the trunks and their branches have developed to a pleasing taper.

The grow-and-clip technique creates bonsai with a harmonious trunk and branches because all sections of the tree are trained concurrently by identical techniques. The strong, angular lines in this example become rounded and gnarled with age, as seen in the photographs of bonsai developed by the Lingnan School.

ROCK PLANTINGS

Nowhere in the world are rocks used more extensively and skillfully than in China, a land of vast, majestic mountain ranges, rocky gorges, and fantastic karst formations. Rocks are an integral part of Chinese painting, philosophy, poetry, gardens—and bonsai. The beautiful miniature rockeries depicting mountains and rocky islands (Fig. 1-3) are a form of bonsai unique to China.

China excels in other forms of rock plantings consisting of one or a few trees planted over a rock (Fig. 15-8), with roots extending into the soil of the container, or on a rock (Fig. 15-9), where the roots are entirely confined to cavities in the rock. The following instructions for designing and constructing plantings on or over a rock are also applicable to rockeries and other rock plantings.

Use regular bonsai tools and equipment. A turntable is especially helpful. Additional materials include clay, sphagnum peat moss, thin wire, epoxy, netting, or burlap and moss to cover the planting. A rock chisel, hammer, and cement may come in handy. Before starting, make a clay slurry to spread on the planting area of the rock and mix equal parts of clay and sphagnum peat moss to use as potting mix.

Fig. 15–8 Chinese elms, *Ulmus parvifolia,* clinging to a Ying Tak rock with their roots growing in the container. Courtesy of Wu Yee-sun.

Fig. 15–9 Fukien tea, *Ehretia microphylla,* growing on an aquatic stone. Courtesy of Wu Yee-sun.

Rocks

The rock is the dominant feature. Select it first, then the tree. A hard, durable rock that does not crumble or split will be as permanent as a fine ceramic container. A rock of uneven surfaces with hollows, ridges, and pitted cavities creates interest and provides convenient planting areas.

In shape, rocks with one long and one short axis, as seen in Fig. 15–10, are preferred to round or square rocks. Placed in a vertical position, a long rock suggests a dramatic mountain peak. Turned horizontally, it has a restful air and may suggest a plateau or a flat ridge along a body of water.

Selecting the Front. Examine the rock carefully to select the side that presents the best view. This will be the face of the rock. It is comparable to the front of the tree and will, of course, be turned toward the viewer. If the front surface contains interesting holes and hollows, do not use them for planting pockets. Filling these attractive spaces with potting mix destroys their eye-catching appeal. Rather, plan to make the plantings on the rear or sides of the rock and bring the trunk and branches toward the front.

Stability. Check the rock for stability. It should be reasonably stable and well balanced. If it wobbles slightly, insert a thin piece of rock or other hard material to make it stable. If a rock requires additional support to keep it in

Fig. 15-10 Front view of a rock from the southern Appalachian Mountains stabilized on a cement base.

position, rather than fastening it to the container with epoxy or cement, add an extended base at the bottom. Prepackaged vinyl cement is fast-setting and easy to use. Place the rock on a flat board with supports that will hold it in position. Prepare the cement as directed on the package and build a pancakelike base around the bottom of the rock. Where a wide support is needed, make it thickest at the base of the rock, and smooth it to a thin edge as it spreads outward. The cement can be concealed beneath sand and water in the container that holds the planting, or it may be covered with small herbaceous plants. Occasionally, when a hard porous rock is found, the bottom may be sawed to a flat, even surface.

Plant Material

Plantings on a Rock. Choose trees with thin, flexible roots to fit the limited space available. Young trees are more vigorous and adaptable than older specimens, and their small size is in scale with the rock. The trees need not be specimen material; conceal unsightly features behind the rock and present the attractive aspects to view.

Popular material for planting on a rock include small-leaved species of *Buxus, Ehretia, Juniperus, Picea, Pinus, Rhododendron*, and other trees with fibrous, compact roots. In addition to the major tree or trees, small woody and herbaceous plants are often placed near the base of the rock.

Plantings Over a Rock or Clinging to a Rock. Here, trees with well-developed long roots are preferred, roots long enough to reach the container. To prepare the roots for planting over a rock, grow the tree for a few years in a tall, narrow container or a section of a ceramic pipe to give them an opportunity to elongate. Species of *Acer, Chamaecyparis, Juniperus, Pinus, Sageretia, Thuja,* and *Ulmus* are among the trees and shrubs popular for planting over a rock.

Wire Supports. Fasten wire supports around the planting area to hold the tree in position. These may be wire hooks or two strands of thin wire. Fasten the hooks or wire securely to the rock with a waterproof epoxy. Follow the instructions on the package and allow ample drying time. When the epoxy has set, insert thin lengths of wire through the hooks.

Placing the Tree

Tentatively hold each tree at a number of locations and different angles on the rock to discover its most pleasing position. When more than one tree is being planted, use or establish trunks of different heights. To duplicate the natural range of more than one species on a mountain, plant conifers near the top of the rock and deciduous trees at lower elevations.

PLANTING TECHNIQUES

On a Rock

Where several trees are to be planted, select their locations by tentatively placing them in various positions. Before removing a tree from its container, fasten wire to the rock where needed, as shown in Fig. 15-11.1.

1. Cover the planting area with a thin layer of wet clay. Work the clay into all crevices and rough surfaces of the rock. Slide the tree from its container and remove all loose soil from around the roots. Trim the roots into a small, compact mass the size of the planting pocket. If a thick or a long root is an obstacle, remove it unless it is essential.
2. Mold the root mass to fit the planting area and press it onto the prepared rock. Add a little more clay, if needed, to hold the roots fast, as shown in Fig. 15-11.2. (Avoid making the clay so thick that air cannot penetrate to the roots.) When planting on the side of a vertical surface, fasten burlap or soft screening between the wires to make a pocket that will hold the root mass.
3. Cover the roots with the prepared sphagnum peat moss and clay (or potting mix) and again tie the root mass with wire (Fig. 15-11.3) until it is held tightly to the rock. Before adding moss, trim any remaining strands of wire to one- or two-inch lengths. After the moss is applied, bend the short lengths of wire into the moss to hold it securely.
4. Follow this procedure until all trees are planted. For a finishing touch, insert small pieces of moss into one or two hollows on the rock or add tiny herbaceous plants to brighten a few crevices. The completed planting is shown in Fig. 15-11.4.

Fig. 15–11.1 Rear view of a rock prepared for planting *Ulmus parvifolia* cv. Catlin, left, and *Juniperus chinensis*.

Fig. 15-11.2 Rear view of the planting area in progress. The juniper roots, covered with clay and potting mix, are tied to the rock with wires; the roots of the elm are covered with clay and not yet tied.

Fig. 15-11.3 Rear view of a moss cover added over the plantings to hold the soil and conserve moisture.

Fig. 15–11.4 Front view of the completed planting, placed in a shallow tray.

5. Water the rock planting thoroughly and place it in a shady, protected area for a week or so. Then select a permanent location that is not exposed to hot sun or drying winds—with so little soil to hold moisture, the roots are very vulnerable to drying.

Over a Rock or Clinging to a Rock

For this type of planting, look for rocks containing hollows, shallow depressions, or ledges for planting the trees. A furrowed rock with vertical grooves (Fig. 15–8) will provide small trenches for the roots to follow on their way to the container.

Carefully map out the planting areas and paths for the roots prior to removing the trees from their containers. Use the materials and planting instructions for planting trees on a rock, modified as explained here.

Because the roots will be visible later, arrange them on the rock at different distances apart. Cover both the planting area and the path of the roots with clay to help them adhere to the rock. Press each root firmly against the rock along its entire length until it reaches the container. Occasionally, a few roots may be too short to reach the container. If so, plant them like the others, stretched as near to the container as possible.

When all the roots are arranged, cover them with the clay–sphagnum moss mixture. If the roots are long enough, tuck them into the mix beneath the rock. Cover the planting and the extended roots with a layer of moss. To prevent drying during the immediate postplanting period, add a cover of burlap or other porous material. Finally, wrap several strands of twine around the rock to hold the roots tightly in position, and fasten the rock to the container with twine, which will eventually disintegrate.

During the first year, keep the covering over the roots moist at all times. Remove it gradually over a period of years, starting at the top of the planting, but not until the roots have reached the soil in the container.

Follow the care instructions for plantings on a rock. When the roots are established in the container, this style of rock planting is less vulnerable than one entirely on a rock, and it may be moved safely to a more open growing area. As the roots on the surface of the rock become visible, they add a fascinating touch to the bonsai.

ADDITIONAL READING

BROOKLYN BOTANIC GARDEN STAFF, Kan Yashiróda, guest ed., *Bonsai: Special Techniques*, Plant and Garden Handbook 22, no. 2. Brooklyn, N.Y.: Brooklyn Botanic Garden, 1966, frequently reprinted. A continuation of the BBG's excellent *Dwarf Potted Trees: The Bonsai of Japan*, with practical information on creating many forms of bonsai, including rock plantings.

HU, YUNHUA, AND THE SHANGHAI BOTANIC GARDEN STAFF, Penjing, *The Chinese Art of Miniature Gardens*. Beaverton, Ore.: Timber Press, 1982. Useful material not found elsewhere on rock planting design and techniques from a major source of bonsai information and production in the People's Republic of China.

WU YEE-SUN, *Man Lung Artistic Pot Plants,* 2nd enlarged ed. Hong Kong: Wing Lung Bank Ltd. Art Publications, 1974. A valuable guide and reference with a wealth of photographs, many in color, illustrating various forms of rock plantings with a diversity of rocks and plant material as well as species shaped to bonsai by the Lingnan method.

16

Indoor Bonsai

When Americans had their first glimpse of Japanese bonsai, they wanted to enjoy these beautiful dwarfed trees in their own homes. At that time, few Americans were aware that Japanese bonsai are essentially cold-climate trees such as pines, spruces, and maples, which require several months of low-temperature dormancy in winter, and that attempts to grow, or even maintain, bonsai in a home or office are doomed to failure. To confuse the situation, in Japan bonsai were seen winter and summer in homes and other buildings. These reports failed to mention that the bonsai were indoors for only a few days at a time or that during the winter in the traditional unheated Japanese house there is little difference between the indoor and outdoor temperatures. Nor was it clear, when bonsai were new to America, that species grown as bonsai require the same year-round climate as their counterparts in nature.

Americans, especially in northern areas, persisted in their desire for indoor bonsai. They discovered on their own initiative that certain warm-climate trees and shrubs used as house plants could be trained as bonsai. Pruned and wired to bonsai shapes, house plants became the first indoor bonsai in the north.

Indoor bonsai received a great boost from bonsai enthusiasts in the south who had discovered that species used for bonsai in Japan cannot survive a warm southern climate. Southern growers then turned with outstanding success to their handsome native trees and shrubs for bonsai material. These species, such as silk oak (Fig. 16–1), have become the indoor bonsai of the north. Subtropical and warm-climate species used for bonsai in the southern United States are a prime source of plants for indoor bonsai. Other sources include the Caribbean islands, Hawaii, Hong Kong, southern China, and warm areas in other parts

Fig. 16-1 Silk oak, *Grevillea robusta,* a tall tree in central Florida, is grown as indoor bonsai in cold northern climates.

of the world. Indoor bonsai constitute an increasingly large proportion of American bonsai and are not limited to the north. Today bonsai with beautiful forms and colorful flowers brighten the interior of homes throughout the country.

MATCHING THE BONSAI TO THE ENVIRONMENT

Growing bonsai successfully indoors is simply a matter of matching the growing needs of the plant to the interior environment or changing the interior environment to suit the plant. Species are available for nearly every kind of home environment. A warm, sunny south window is ideal for most indoor bonsai, including many flowering species. East and west windows are suitable for nearly all foliage plants, and a few cold-climate species may be wintered indoors on cool windowsills that do not receive direct sun.

If necessary, the existing indoor environment may be easily modified to improve growing conditions: Where natural light is inadequate, fluorescent lighting may be installed; if a windowsill is too cold, it may be insulated with a second pane of glass or a layer of clear plastic. Is it possible to grow bonsai in a warm room where direct sun never enters without installing light fixtures for the plants? The answer is yes. A number of warm-climate species, such as the tropical-looking schefflera in (Fig. 16-2), are tolerant of low-light conditions the year-round.

This chapter explains how to use the indoor environment to best advantage for growing bonsai and suggests species according to their need for light, temperature, and humidity.

Fig. 16-2 Shade-tolerant schefflera, *Brassaia actinophylla,* can survive indoors without direct sun.

Light

The most important single requirement for growing bonsai indoors is adequate light intensity, which is expressed in footcandles. A footcandle is defined as the illumination on a flat surface from a standard candle at a distance of one foot. Several factors affect the intensity of natural light. One is the distance light must travel through the atmosphere to reach the earth. Light intensity is greatest at the equator, where the rays of the sun are nearly vertical and travel the shortest distance through the atmosphere. In northern and southern Temperate Zones, where light enters and travels at a slant through the atmospheric layer, the intensity is lower.

The seasonal tilt of the earth toward the sun also has a pronounced effect on light intensity. At noon on a clear day in summer, the light may register 10,000 footcandles in the northern United States and only 2,000 footcandles at the same hour and location in winter. In the north, winter light has but a fraction of the intensity of summer light and far, far less than the light in more southern latitudes. For example, during the winter, an indoor bonsai on a sunny windowsill in Chicago may receive up to 500 footcandles. At the same time, the same species outdoors on a sunny day in Pensacola, Florida, will receive 5,000 footcandles or more.

Indoor bonsai differ vastly in their light requirements. For those that need high light intensity, a location at a south or an east window in necessary. Light quickly loses intensity as it moves into the interior of a room; light that registers between 100 and 500 footcandles at a window may drop as low as 5 or 50 footcandles in the interior of the room.

Measuring Light Intensity. It is difficult for the human eye to gauge the level of light intensity. Special scientific light meters are required to obtain readings in footcandles. However, photographic light meters used by amateur photographers give readings of the relative amount of light intensity at various locations. They are helpful in indicating areas of highest light intensity in the home.

Bonsai that have been in the same location for a few months will indicate by their shoots and foliage whether or not they are receiving adequate light. In plant language, light deficiency is signaled by long internodes (formed as the cells stretch toward the light), yellowing of leaves (not enough light for food-producing photosynthesis), and thin, spindly shoots (the result of a weakened condition). Do not fertilize bonsai that are suffering from insufficient light. Under these conditions they are unable to assimilate the fertilizer, which will burn the roots if it remains in the soil. Move the weakened plant into better light, or replace it with a species that can tolerate existing light levels.

The Effects of Side Lighting. Light that reaches a bonsai from only one side, such as a window, will cause lopsided growth because the plant persistently reaches toward the light. Under these conditions, rotate the bonsai a quarter turn each week to expose all surfaces equally to the source of light.

Temperature

In light of the considerable span in temperature requirements among plants, it is easy to select species suited to the temperature where they will be placed. Most indoor bonsai grow well in a daytime range between 60° and 75°F. Plants are genetically programmed to nighttime temperatures of 10° or 15° less, and an occasional drop below that is not harmful. During the day, the heat of the sun through a glass window may raise the indoor temperature for brief periods to 80° or more. Such temporary daytime increases are normal and are not injurious to plants.

Temperature and Light. Temperature and light are closely related. Warm temperatures stimulate growth, which in turn increases the bonsai's need for light. High temperatures require high light intensities. At low indoor temperatures (55° or 60°F.), growth is minimal and high light levels are not needed. Many species used for indoor bonsai can adjust to either low or high temperatures. For example, mistletoe fig (Fig. 16–3) can be grown under moderate levels of light at moderate temperatures of 60° or 65°F. It will also thrive at higher temperatures (to 75°) with a corresponding increase in light intensity.

Humidity

The relative humidity in centrally heated houses and apartments is almost always too dry for bonsai. Although a humidifier may be built into a central heating system, it is usually best to increase the humidity in the immediate vicinity of the bonsai. Portable humidifiers range from high-output electrical units timed to go on at prescribed intervals to a fine mist of water produced by a hand sprayer. Here is a list of a number of popular practical methods of increasing the humidity in a small area.

Fig. 16–3 An indoor bonsai of mistletoe fig, *Ficus deltoidea,* planted on a rock. The small-leaved vine is *F. pumila* cv. Minima.

1. Group bonsai together. When close to one another, they share and retain each other's moisture and prevent its rapid dissipation over a larger area.
2. Place the bonsai on a tray of pebbles or an egg-crate grid (used in light fixtures) with a layer of water beneath. Make certain that the water level does not touch the bottom of the bonsai containers.
3. Set trays of water under radiators and in the vicinity of the bonsai.
4. Consider growing bonsai in rooms of the home where the humidity is highest—the kitchen or bathroom for instance.
5. Supplement these procedures by spraying the bonsai with a fine mist of water several times a week, more often if the indoor air is unusually dry.
6. Give the bonsai a weekly shower and leaf washing at a sink or tub.

SELECTING THE PLANT MATERIAL

Trees and shrubs for indoor bonsai may be divided into four groups based on their temperature requirements. Species tolerant of varied growing conditions will appear in more than one category. Remember that subtropical plants that require warm temperatures generally need high light intensities. Additional information on the following species suggested for indoor bonsai is provided in Part Two.

Species for Low Indoor Temperatures

A few species of cold-climate bonsai may be brought indoors for the winter and maintained in a condition of partial dormancy on a cold windowsill in an unheated room or on enclosed porches where the temperature remains above freezing. These are "borderline" plants at the northern limit of their range. They may be wintered in partial or nearly complete dormancy at daytime temperatures between 40° and 60°F. (For complete dormancy, treat them as other hardy cold-climate bonsai.)

For a winter of partial dormancy, bring the bonsai indoors prior to freezing and place them in a location that does not receive direct sun where they may be kept until the following spring. This process is not suitable for northern trees that require complete winter dormancy, such as *Abies*, fir; *Tsuga*, hemlock; *Picea*, spruce; and *Pinus*, pine.

Suggested Species for Cool Indoor Winter Temperatures

Buxus microphylla Siebold & Zucc. Boxwood, including many dwarf forms
B. sempervirens L. Common boxwood
Chaenomeles japonica Lindl. ex Spach Japanese flowering quince
Chamaecyparis obtusa Endl. Hinoki cypress and dwarf forms
C. pisifera Endl. Sawara cypress including dwarf forms
C. thyoides BSP. cv. Ericoides, Dwarf white cedar
Cryptomeria japonica D. Don Japanese cedar and many dwarf forms
Ilex crenata Thunb. Japanese holly, many forms
Juniperus chinensis var. **procumbens** Endl. Procumbent juniper and cv. Nana
J. squamata D. Don Prostrate juniper
Nandina domestica Thunb. Heavenly bamboo
Pyracantha angustifolia C. K. Schneid. Fire thorn
P. coccinea M. J. Roem. Everlasting thorn
Rhododendron indicum Sweet Japanese satsuki azalea
R. kiusianum Mak. Kyushu azalea
Thuja occidentalis L. American arborvitae, many dwarf forms
Ulmus parvifolia Jacq. Chinese elm

Species for Moderate Indoor Temperatures

Trees and shrubs in this group, which includes many popular indoor species, will thrive in winter with moderate daytime temperatures around 60° or 65°F. It is a mixed group of warm-climate species, such as serissa (Fig. 16-4), and Temperate Zone species, such as Chinese elm (Fig. 13-15). These plants receive sufficient light at an east or west window or within several feet of a south window.

Fig. 16-4 Serissa, or snow in June, *Serissa foetida,* produces sparkling small white flowers. Courtesy of I. Sawada and Puget Sound Bonsai Association. Photo by Charles M. Gordon, Photojournalist.

Suggested Species for Indoor Bonsai: 60° to 65° Daytime Temperatures

Araucaria heterophylla Franco *(A. excelsa)* Norfolk Island pine

Brassaia actinophylla Endl. Schefflera and a dwarf form, Arboricola

Calliandra emarginata Benth. Dwarf powder puff

Ceratonia Siliqua L. Carob tree

Chamaecyparis pisifera Endl. Sawara cypress, cvs. Plumosa and Squarrosa

C. thyoides BSP. cv. Ericoides Dwarf white cedar

Cotoneaster microphyllus Wallich ex Lindl. Chinese cotoneaster and cv. Cochleatus

C.m. var. **thymifolius** Koehne Thyme cotoneaster, a compact form

Cryptomeria japonica D. Don Japanese cedar and cvs. Compacta, Nana, and other dwarf forms

Cupressus arizonica Greene Arizona cypress

C. macrocarpa Hartweg Monterey cypress

C. sempervirens L. Italian cypress

Cycas revoluta Thunb. Cycad, Japanese sago palm

Ficus benjamina L. Weeping fig

F. carica L. Common edible fig

F. deltoidea Jack (*F. diversifolia*) Mistletoe fig

F. microcarpa L.f. (*F. retusa*) Chinese banyan and cv. Retusa

F. neriifolia Sm. *(F.n. regularis)* Willow-leaf fig, narrow-leaf fig

F. pumila L. Creeping fig

F. rubiginosa Desf. ex Venten. Port Jackson fig

Gardenia jasminoides Ellis Common gardenia, Cape jasmine

Hedera Helix L. English ivy, many forms

Ilex crenata Thunb. Japanese holly, many forms

I. vomitoria Ait. Yaupon holly, cvs. Schellings Dwarf, Stokes Dwarf, and many others

Juniperus chinensis var. **procumbens** Endl. Procumbent juniper, cv. Nana and other dwarf forms

J. squamata D. Don Prostrate juniper and dwarf forms

Ligustrum japonica Thunb. Japanese privet

Murraya paniculata Jack Orange jasmine or jessamine

Myrtus communis L. Greek myrtle

Nandina domestica Thunb. Heavenly bamboo

Olea europea L. European olive

Pithecellobium flexicaule J. Coult. Texas ebony

Pittosporum Tobira Ait. Mock orange and cv. Variegata

Podocarpus macrophyllus D. Don Podocarpus, Buddhist pine

P.m. var. **Maki** Endl. Yew podocarpus

Polyscias Balfouriana L. H. Bailey Balfour aralia

P. fruticosa Harms. Ming aralia and cv. Elegans

Punica Granatum L. Pomegranate and cv. Nana, dwarf pomegranate

Pyracantha coccinea M. J. Roem. Everlasting thorn

P. Fortuneana H. L. Li Chinese fire thorn

P. Koidzumii Rehd. Formosa fire thorn

Rhododendron indicum Sweet Japanese satsuki azalea

R. kiusianum Mak. Kyushu azalea

Sageretia Thea M. C. Johnst. *(S. theezans)* Sageretia

Serissa foetida Lam. Serissa, June snow

Severinia buxifolia Ten. Chinese box orange

Ulmus parvifolia Jacq. Chinese elm, especially the form Catlin

Species for Warm Indoor Temperatures

Subtropical and warm regions the world over offer a large selection of attractive trees and shrubs for indoor bonsai. A large number of figs are in this group including the strangler fig in Fig. 16-5 and many easily obtained species, such as the jade plant in Fig. 16-6. This group requires daytime temperatures between 65° and 75°F. or higher, with a drop of 10° at night. Most of these species need high levels of light intensity as found at an unobstructed south window.

Suggested Species for Indoor Bonsai: 65° to 75° Daytime Temperatures

Araucaria heterophylla Franco *(A. excelsa)* Norfolk Island pine

Bougainvillea glabra Choisy Paper flower, bougainvillea

Brassaia actinophylla Endl. Schefflera and a dwarf form, Arboricola

Calliandra emarginata Benth. Dwarf powder puff

Fig. 16-5 A strangler fig, *Ficus aurea,* found as a seedling and planted on tufa rock. Photo by Edmund B. Gilchrist, Jr.

Fig. 16-6 Ordinary jade plants, *Crassula argentea,* grown as bonsai in a Chinese container. Photo by Edmund B. Gilchrist, Jr.

Carissa grandiflora A. DC. Natal plum

Ceratonia Siliqua L. Carob tree

Citrus Limon Burm. f. Lemon, cvs. Meyer, Chinese dwarf lemon, and Ponderosa, wonder lemon

C. x limonia Osbeck *(C. taitensis)* Mandarin lemon, Otaheite orange

Crassula argentea Thunb. Jade tree and cvs. Tricolor and Variegata

Cuphea hyssopifolia HBK. Elfin herb

Cycas revoluta Thunb. Japanese sago palm, cycad

Ehretia microphylla Lam. *(Carmona microphylla)* Fukien tea

Ficus aurea Nutt. Strangler fig

F. benjamina L. Weeping fig

F. deltoidea Jack *(F. diversifolia)* Mistletoe fig

F. microcarpa L.f. *(F. retusa)* Chinese banyan and cv. Retusa

F. neriifolia Sm. *(F.n. regularis)* Willow-leaf fig

F. pumila L. Creeping fig and cv. Minima, dwarf creeping fig

F. rubiginosa Desf. ex Venten. Port Jackson fig

Grevillea robusta A. Cunn. Silk oak

Hedera Helix L. English ivy, many forms
Lagerstroemia indica L. Crape myrtle, and dwarf forms
Malpighia coccigera L. Miniature holly
M. glabra L. Barbados cherry
Myrtus communis L. Greek myrtle
Olea europea L. European olive
Pithecellobium flexicaule J. Coult. Texas ebony
Punica Granatum L. Pomegranate and cv. Nana
Pyracantha coccinea M. J. Roem. Everlasting thorn
P. Fortuneana H. L. Li Chinese fire thorn, many cultivars
P. Koidzumii Rehd. Formosa fire thorn, many cultivars
Sageretia Thea M. C. Johnst. *(S. theezans)* Sageretia
Schinus terebinthifolius Raddi. Brazilian pepper tree
Serissa foetida Lam. Serissa, June snow
Severinia buxifolia Ten. Chinese box orange
Syzygium paniculatum Gaertn. *(Eugenia australis, E. paniculata)* Brush cherry

CONDITIONING PLANTS TO LOW LIGHT LEVELS

When the available light is insufficient for growing a particular species indoors, it is possible to reduce its light requirements permanently by conditioning it to lower light levels. The process was developed in southern nurseries to condition plants to a marked reduction in light intensity before shipping them to northern markets. At commercial nurseries, "conditioned" plants are propagated from seed and grown in an enclosed structure under low, controlled light levels until they are ready for shipment. Such plants have proved to be as healthy as those grown outdoors in strong sunlight and far better prepared to survive northern environments.

For indoor bonsai, species that ordinarily require a warm, sunny south window can be grown at an east or west window or under fluorescent lamps. Species that ordinarily need medium light levels can be grown under even less light.

Use the following techniques to condition warm climate plants for indoor bonsai.

1. Propagate the plant from seed. (The process does not work with cuttings or vegetative reproduction.)
2. Germinate the seeds indoors under the same level of light they will receive as mature plants. For example, a plant to be grown under fluorescent lamps is germinated under identical lamps.

3. Maintain the same low light intensity after the seedling is transplanted and until it matures.
4. Take care to avoid crowding the plants. Make sure that the available light reaches all parts of each plant.
5. When using conditioned plants as bonsai, give them the same care and training as other bonsai.

The following genera include a sampling of species that are popular for indoor bonsai and may be propagated from seed: *Araucaria, Brassaia, Calliandra, Callistemon, Carissa, Ceratonia, Citrus* (for foliage only), *Cotoneaster, Cryptomeria, Cycas, Ehretia, Grevillea, Hedera, Ilex, Lagerstroemia, Ligustrum, Lonicera, Malpighia, Murraya, Myrtus, Olea, Pithecellobium, Pittosporum, Podocarpus, Punica, Pyracantha, Severinia*, and *Ulmus*.

The conditioning will not be detrimental for bonsai purposes. Charles A. Conover, director of the Agricultural Research Center, Apopka, Florida, has found that conditioned plants usually produce smaller and thinner leaves, and sometimes thinner trunks, than plants grown under high light intensity.[1]

CARE AND TRAINING OF INDOOR BONSAI

Indoor bonsai are dwarfed and shaped with the same techniques used for hardy outdoor bonsai—pruning, wiring, and confinement to a container. However, they may reflect the form of subtropical and warm-climate trees and differ in this respect from northern species and styles.

Pruning and Wiring

Ernesta D. Ballard, the first American to author a book with information about bonsai and a pioneer in growing bonsai indoors, points out that the timing of pruning and wiring is different for indoor bonsai.[2] She explains that with nearly year-round growth, indoor bonsai are repeatedly pruned throughout the year, whenever the tree is in active growth. This means more frequent pruning and wiring than for cold-hardy species. Ballard also points out that with their long growing season, indoor bonsai develop more rapidly than cold-climate species and are able to produce dense foliage in a relatively short time.

Wiring is applied and removed at any time during the year when it will not damage flowers or soft, emerging growth. Again, because of the rapid growth of indoor bonsai, the wire is checked frequently and is usually removed after a short period to avoid scarring marks on the trunk or branches.

[1]Charles A. Conover, "Plant Conditioning," *American Nurseryman*, August 15, 1978, pp. 16, 130–134.

[2]Ernesta D. Ballard, *The Art of Training Plants* (New York: Harper & Row, 1962), p. 39.

General Care

In midspring, when the weather has become mild and all danger of frost is past, move the bonsai outdoors, if possible, for rejuvenation during the summer months. Make their exposure to outdoor conditions gradual; place them first in full shade to permit their soft growth to harden, then into open shade. They will benefit from fresh air, sunshine, showers, and light breezes. Expose only plants that are native to hot or dry sunny regions, such as *Juniperus* spp., *Olea* spp., and *Pithecellobium* spp., to direct sun during the day. For the others, provide early morning sun.

In late summer or early fall, before cold weather and before the home heating system is in operation, move the bonsai indoors. Check each plant to be sure it is free of insects and disease; starting with clean healthy plants is a tremendous aid in maintaining disease-free and insect-free bonsai during the winter. An early return allows the plants to adjust gradually to the light, air, and other conditions indoors. When the heating system is turned on, the plants will need to adapt only to a decrease in relative humidity.

Partial Dormancy

When the days are short, from late November to the end of January, many bonsai indoors slow down their growth and enter a state of quiescence, or partial dormancy. The exact time and duration varies among species. During this period (observable by the absence of new growth), do not fertilize, and water bonsai less than normally. Postpone pruning, potting, and repotting until growth resumes.

Watering

As explained earlier, when watering bonsai, water them thoroughly, and for most plants allow the soil to become moderately dry before watering again. A number of species prefer soil that is slightly moist between waterings. This information is included for individual species in Part Two. To facilitate watering, group together plants with similar watering needs.

If indoor bonsai are moved outside for the summer, their watering needs will be constantly affected by changing weather. For example, on a cloudy, windless day, watering may not be necessary, while on a hot, breezy day in early May, bonsai may need watering once or even twice in a single day.

Potting and Repotting

A basic potting mix is suitable for most indoor bonsai. Species that require a special mix when grown outdoors will need the same mix indoors. Good drainage is essential. If the mix does not drain readily, repotting is recommended. Repot indoor bonsai prior to the start of and during their growing season. For many, this is late winter and early spring. Repot subtropical plants in midsummer, when the soil and air are well warmed by the sun.

Indoor bonsai are frequently planted with the surface of the soil leveled to slightly below the top of the container. This permits water to accumulate temporarily when the plants are watered and provides space for a covering of pebbles as described in the next paragraph.

Ground Covers

Moss is the preferred covering, but it is difficult to grow indoors except in areas with a high amount of moisture in the air. An alternate choice is a layer of washed pebbles about a quarter of an inch in size. An assortment in shades of white, cream, and beige forms an attractive natural cover at the base of a bonsai. Where small pebbles are not commercially available, they may be sieved from a batch of mixed sizes or found on sandbars along fresh-water streams and lakes. Pebbles from salt water will require repeated washings to remove saline deposits.

Herbaceous ground covers provide a decorative touch of green. Dwarf creeping fig, *Ficus pumila* cv. Minima, is a vine with small heart-shaped leaves. Young rooted shoots (it roots easily from cuttings) may be trained to grow along the surface of the potting mix by pinning them down with small pieces of U-shaped wire. For a tropical effect, allow the vine to grow upward on the trunk of a large indoor bonsai such as *Brassaia actinophylla* or other subtropical plants.

Corsican mint, *Mentha Requienii*, forms dense, low-growing mats that can be controlled by thinning. Two rampant growers, baby tears, *Helxine soleirolii*, and pearlwort, *Sagina procumbens*, become so compact that they choke roots of other plants in the same container. They are not recommended as ground covers for indoor bonsai.

Fertilizing

All indoor bonsai require regular fertilizing during their prolonged growing season. An inorganic, water-soluble fertilizer is odorless and convenient. Either a regular plant fertilizer or one formulated for house plants is suitable.

Apply the fertilizer every two or three weeks in a diluted solution—perhaps half the strength recommended on the package. If growth is excessive, decrease the amount of fertilizer in the solution; if the plants seem to require more fertilizer, shorten the intervals between applications.

Eliminating Pests and Disease

As with outdoor bonsai, the best method of preventing trouble from insects or disease is to keep the bonsai clean and healthy. Inspect and, for a week or two, isolate all new plants before placing them with the others. Spray each bonsai with water once a week at a sink or tub. Direct the spray into the foliage and under the leaves to dislodge pests before they become established. The water will also cleanse the foliage of accumulated dust.

Use a cotton swab dipped in rubbing alcohol to remove minor infestations of scale and slow-moving insects. To eradicate hard-to-see insect eggs and larvae, turn over the bonsai and dip the foliage into a basin of water to which a small amount of liquid soap or detergent has been added. For heavy infestations, wash the leaves and stems thoroughly. Insecticidal soap used according to directions on the label is effective as a wash or spray for aphids, mealybugs, and other soft-bodied insects. If chemical sprays are used, choose a warm day and move the bonsai outdoors for treatment.

Many homes and offices do not have ideal growing conditions for plants. In such situations, stick with regular species—the species of a genus is stronger than its unusual and rare cultivars. If it can possibly be managed, move the bonsai outdoors during the summer months. They will be revitalized by the fresh air, natural breezes, and increased levels of light and humidity.

BONSAI UNDER ARTIFICIAL LIGHT

Plant growth is no longer dependent on natural light. Bonsai in attractive settings are now grown under artificial light in homes, apartments, and other buildings where natural light is not adequate. A decorative display of bonsai grown under fluorescent light is seen in Fig. 16-7.

Indoor bonsai do not require the high-wattage incandescent or fluorescent lamps or high-intensity discharge (HID) lamps used in commercial plant production. Regular household fluorescent lamps and fixtures give excellent results without the need of special fittings or electrical installations. More important,

Fig. 16-7 A display of indoor bonsai and plants under flourescent light is visible through openings in an interior wall. Courtesy of William Smedley.

ordinary fluorescent lamps provide uniform illumination at a constant intensity in a wide range of low to high light levels.

The lamps are manufactured in many sizes and shapes. Round and U-shaped tubes are useful where space is limited, but long, straight, narrow tubes are more efficient. The strongest light in a fluorescent lamp is located in the center of the tube and drops sharply within nine inches of either end. Because the light is weak at the ends of the tube, one 48-inch lamp has a greater length of maximum light than two 24-inch lamps. Although one 96-inch tube is more efficient than two 48-inch tubes, space for installing an 8-foot-long tube and light garden usually is not available in the average home. For this reason, 48-inch lamps side by side are most frequently used.

Fluorescent Lamps for Plant Growth

Among the large number of fluorescent lamps available, including those designed especially for plant growth, the standard Cool White (CW), Warm White (WW), and Gro Lux (GL) lamps are effective for growing houseplants. Henry M. Cathey and Lowell E. Campbell, of the United States Department of Agriculture, made extensive studies to determine the effect of fluorescent lamps on plant growth. The following results of their findings are useful for indoor bonsai:

Lamps and Plant Response[3]

Cool White (CW) and Warm White (WW) Lamps

Green foliage expands parallel to the lamp.

Stems elongate slowly.

Multiple side shoots develop.

Flowering occurs over a long period of time.

Gro Lux (GL) Plant Lights

Deep green foliage expands but is often larger than on plants grown under CW or WW.

Stems elongate very slowly; extra-thick stems develop.

Multiple side shoots develop.

Flowering occurs late; flower stalks do not elongate.

Standard CW and WW lamps rank first in producing the growth wanted for indoor bonsai. Gro Lux lamps are a close second, with favorable deep green foliage and multiple side shoots. Extra-thick stems may be out of character on bonsai, and late flowering may be a disadvantage.

Unlike Gro Lux lamps, CW lamps give a grayed appearance to red and

[3]Henry M. Cathey and Lowell E. Campbell, *Indoor Gardening, Artificial Lighting, Terrariums, Hanging Baskets, and Plant Selection*, Home and Garden Bulletin No. 220 (Washington, D.C.: Agricultural Research Service, USDA, 1978), p. 16.

WW lamps emit light that has a grayed effect on red, green, and blue colors.[4] The colors are improved by switching to Deluxe Cool White and Deluxe Warm White or by substituting a Gro Lux lamp for one of the standard white lamps.

The Fixture. The most popular, convenient, and inexpensive fixture for indoor light gardening consists of two 48-inch lamps side by side, 3 to 6 inches apart, mounted about 24 inches above the support base for the plants. Preassembled utilitarian units, including lamps, lamp holders, a reflector, and the wiring, are available at electrical, hardware, and many other outlets. They are ready to use when fastened to an overhead support. A reflective back panel such as a mirror or a wall covered with flat white paint increases the amount of light the plants receive. If desired, the fixture may be concealed by valances.

Decorative fluorescent units especially designed for living areas in the home are also available at many outlets, including mail order. A do-it-yourself manual for growers who wish to design and build their own light garden, *Light Garden Construction* by Phyllis Wolff Banucci, is listed at the end of the chapter.

Lamp Life. The life of fluorescent lamps varies considerably. Information on life-hours is available from the distributor or manufacturer. Light that is effective for plant growth declines sharply after 70 percent of the lamp's estimated life is reached. Cool White and Warm White 40-watt lamps have a life of 20,000 hours. To figure the useful life hours of these lamps, multiply 20,000 by 0.70, which is 14,000 light-hours. If the lamp is on for 15 hours a day, divide 14,000 by 15. In this instance, the result is 933 days, or 2½ years before a replacement is needed. When installing a new lamp, many growers calculate its estimated useful life and make a written note of the replacement date. It is almost impossible for the human eye to notice when a reduction in the lamp's light intensity has occurred. On multilamp units, replace old lamps one by one at different times to avoid abrupt changes in light intensity.

The Timer. During every 24-hour period, indoor bonsai under light require from 12 to 18 hours of light, depending on the species. Flowering and fruiting bonsai need a full 18 hours; fewer hours are sufficient for foliage plants. Simple 24-hour timers eliminate the need for manually turning the lamps on and off each day. Timers are easy to use. For example, for 14 hours of light a day, set the timer to go on at a specific time, such as 8 A.M., and off 14 hours later, at 10 P.M. Connect the timer to the power source and the light fixture to the timer.

Reset the timer at any time for the number of hours required for the desired growth. However, do not keep the light on constantly. Plants cannot survive without a period of darkness every 24 hours.

Humidity. The light garden is easily humidified by setting the bonsai on a tray of pebbles with water beneath, as described earlier in the chapter.

Ventilation. To provide the fresh air that plants need, place the light garden in an area where air normally circulates; keep both sides and the front open

[4]Ibid., p. 13.

for ventilation. If the unit is installed in a recessed area or is enclosed, a miniature fan (available at hobby shops) is helpful in providing air movement.

Maintenance of the Light Garden. A fluorescent fixture requires little maintenance other than replacing old lamps. A monthly cleaning of tubes and reflectors will provide maximum illumination. Clean the trays and change the water from time to time as needed.

Arranging the Light Garden

Areas of High Light Intensity. The intensity of fluorescent light diminishes rapidly with the distance it travels from the lamp. The most effective growing area with the highest intensity is a band from 6 to 18 inches wide directly under the lamp, as shown in Table 16-1. Bonsai closer than 6 inches may be damaged by heat; below 18 inches the intensity drops abruptly and becomes too weak to produce the healthy, compact growth wanted for bonsai. Light intensity drops on either side of a perpendicular line 1 foot from the lamp. The footcandles in this area, toward the front or back of the long tubes, is shown in parentheses in Table 16-1.

Selecting the Plants

Suggested species for growing under light are included in the following list. Many others are suitable for both bonsai and light gardening. With limited growing space beneath the fixtures, look for compact plants with relatively small foliage. Dwarf forms that retain their treelike character are popular. In selecting plants, remember to match the temperature needs of the plant with the temperature in the area of the light garden. Choose plants with high temperature needs for a warm, well-heated room and species that prefer lower temperatures for cooler areas.

Table 16-1 ILLUMINATION IN FOOTCANDLES DIRECTLY UNDER 40-WATT COOL WHITE OR WARM WHITE FLUORESCENT LAMPS

Two Lamps	*Distance in Inches*	*Four Lamps*
700	6	900
400 (260*)	12	600
180 (150*)	24	330

*In areas to the front or the rear of the lamps

Source: Adapted from Henry M. Cathey and Lowell E. Campbell, *Indoor Gardening, Artificial Lighting, Terrariums, Hanging Baskets, and Plant Selection* (Washington, D.C.: Agricultural Research Service, USDA, 1978), p. 14.

The indoor light garden is excellent for using conditioned plants described earlier in the chapter. They can be germinated and grown directly under the lamps. Species marked with an asterisk in the following list may be propagated easily by seed.

Suggested Species for Indoor Light Gardens

Araucaria heterophylla Franco *(A. excelsa)* Norfolk Island pine

Buxus microphylla Siebold & Zucc. Boxwood and cv. Compacta, dwarf little-leaf boxwood, Kingsville boxwood

Calliandra emarginata Benth. Dwarf powder puff

Carissa grandiflora A. DC. Natal plum and dwarf forms*

Chamaecyparis thyoides BSP. cv. Ericoides Dwarf white cedar

Cryptomeria japonica D. Don Japanese cedar, many dwarf forms

Cupressus arizonica Greene Arizona cypress

C. macrocarpa Hartweg Monterey cypress

C. sempervirens L. Italian cypress

Ficus aurea Nutt. Strangler fig

F. deltoidea Jack *(F. diversifolia)* Mistletoe fig

F. neriifolia Sm. *(F.n. regularis)* Willow-leaf fig, narrow-leaf fig

F. pumila L. Creeping fig and cv. Minima, dwarf creeping fig

Hedera Helix L. English ivy, many dwarf forms

Ilex vomitoria Ait. Yaupon holly and cv. Schellings Dwarf

Juniperus chinensis var. **Sargentii** A. Henry Shimpaku juniper

J.c. var. **procumbens** Endl. cv. Nana Dwarf procumbent juniper

Myrtus communis L. Greek myrtle*

Podocarpus macrophyllus var. **Maki** Endl. Buddhist pine, Japanese yew

Punica Granatum L. Pomegranate and cv. Nana, dwarf pomegranate*

Pyracantha Fortuneana H. L. Li Chinese fire thorn*

P. Koidzumii Rehd. Formosa fire thorn

Rhododendron indicum Sweet Japanese satsuki azalea

R. kiusianum Mak. Kyushu azalea

Sageretia Thea M. C. Johnst. *(S. theezans)* Sageretia

Serissa foetida Lam. Snow rose

Severinia buxifolia Ten. Chinese box orange*

Ulmus parvifolia Jacq. Chinese elm, many dwarf forms including Catlin

Shape and Size. For best results, select bonsai that fit within the 12-inch band beneath the lamp (see Table 16–1). Compact plants are preferred to scrawny ones in order to minimize the change in light intensity from the top to the bottom of the foliage. The ideal form of a bonsai to be grown under fluorescent light may be a semicascade specimen whose entire horizontal trunk and foliage are confined within a short vertical distance.

Small and miniature bonsai of limited height also receive fairly uniform light intensity from top to bottom of the foliage. To bring such bonsai closer to the light, place them on an overturned flowerpot. Move a bonsai that shows signs of insufficient light into an area of higher light intensity.

A period of trial and error may be required to find the best location in the light garden for specific bonsai. To arrange the bonsai according to their light requirements, the relative differences in light beneath the fluorescent tubes can be compared to an outside garden. The area under the center of the lamps is comparable to direct sun outdoors; the distance within 6 to 12 inches of the lamps represents morning and afternoon sun; a greater distance, from 12 to 18 inches, suggests partial shade; the area beneath the ends of the tubes and the front edge of the light garden are in full shade.

Care of Bonsai Under Light

In addition to the care required by all indoor bonsai, those grown under light should be far enough apart so that each receives the full effect of light and adequate air circulation.

The bonsai will benefit tremendously from a weekly shower. It is an opportunity to wash the leaves of dust and insects. To keep the plants healthy, remove all the bonsai periodically for a thorough cleaning of the plants, the light garden, and the trays.

A Limiting Factor

Among the most handsome bonsai of warm climates are a number of species that are difficult, if not impossible, to grow indoors in cold-winter climates—even on warm, sunny windowsills or under fluorescent light. This group includes *Bucida buceras*, black olive, and *B. spinosa*, dwarf black olive; *Casuarina* spp., Australian pine or ironwood; *Coccoloba uvifera*, sea grape; and *Conocarpus erectus,* buttonwood, and other plants native to coastal subtropical areas of high temperature, high light intensity, and high humidity.

Although climatic differences between the subtropical and cold regions are too great for these plants to survive, because of their outstanding bonsai characteristics, persistent efforts are made to grow them indoors in cold climates. As transplants, they may survive for several years by utilizing their stored food reserves. However, exposed over a period of time to unfavorable conditions of low temperature, low humidity, and low light, only extraordinary growing skill or luck will ensure their survival.

It may be possible to acclimatize these species to lower light levels by propagating them from seed as conditioned plants. Otherwise, except where their needs can be met (i.e., a warm greenhouse with high light intensities), these subtropical coastal species are not recommended as indoor bonsai for cold climates.

PRACTICE AND REVIEW

Prepare a shopping list of six to eight plants to purchase as material for indoor bonsai:

1. In an apartment opening on a small terrace facing east with windows on the east and south. Daytime temperature range from 58° to 70°F.
2. A sunny, south-facing room where the temperature reaches 75° and more during the day and drops to 60° degrees at night.
3. For a friend who is starting an indoor light garden for bonsai. The temperature in the room where it is located reaches 68° during the day and drops to 55° at night.

ADDITIONAL READING

BALLARD, ERNESTA D., *The Art of Training Plants*. New York: Harper & Row, 1962; soft-cover edition, Barnes & Noble Books, A Division of Harper & Row, Publishers, 1974. A noted horticulturist clearly describes fundamentals of training and growing decorative plants. The author's companion book, *Garden in Your House*, is a valuable reference for hundreds of houseplants including species used for bonsai.

BANUCCI, PHYLLIS WOLFF, *Light Garden Construction*, Cultural Guide No. 7. New York: Indoor Light Gardening Society of America, Inc., 1978. A do-it-yourself manual by the ILGSA editor, containing twelve selected designs by members with specifications and information on construction, wiring, and installation. For publication list and membership information write: Indoor Light Gardening Society of America, Inc., 128 West 58th St., New York, N.Y. 10019.

BROOKLYN BOTANIC GARDEN STAFF, Constance T. Derderian, guest ed., *Bonsai for Indoors*, Plants and Gardens, 32, no. 3. Brooklyn, N.Y.: Brooklyn Botanic Garden, 1976. Twenty-one bonsai enthusiasts contribute extensive information on indoor bonsai. Well illustrated.

______, Jack Golding, guest ed., *Gardening Under Lights*, Plants and Gardens, 36, no. 3, 1980. A compilation of useful information on indoor light gardens with a glossary and many illustrations.

CATHEY, HENRY M. AND LOWELL E. CAMPBELL, *Indoor Gardening, Artificial Lighting, Terrariums, Hanging Baskets, and Plant Selection*. Home and Garden Bulletin No. 220. Washington, D.C.: Agricultural Research Service, USDA, 1978. Valuable for its basic information and descriptions of growing plants under artificial light.

CONOVER, CHARLES A., "Plant Conditioning," *American Nurseryman*, August 15, 1978, pp. 16, 130–133. Describes plant conditioning in southern commercial nurseries.

17

The Great and the Small

MINIATURE BONSAI

Miniature bonsai, or minibonsai, are bonsai no more than 10 inches tall. They are the miniatures of miniatures. In Japan, bonsai from three to six inches (measured from the top of the container to the tip of the tree) are referred to as *mame* bonsai. A collection of mame bonsai in the garden of a Japanese home is shown in Fig. 17-1. In America, however, the word *mame* (pronounced "ma-may") is often used for bonsai of 10 inches or less. These are the most challenging of all bonsai. But the rewards are commensurate. To minibonsai growers, the wonder of a bonsai is magnified as it becomes smaller.

The tiny bonsai in Figs. 17-2.1 through 17-2.3 were created by Yoshimi Itoh, a dentist by profession and an expert Japanese mame bonsai grower. One day in February when two American bonsai enthusiasts came to his home near Tokyo, Itoh escorted his guests to the balcony on the second story of his house to see in the distance a large zelkova whose bare branches formed a delicate fanlike silhouette in the winter sky. Then, taking his guests to his bonsai collection, he selected and placed on the palm of his hand an exceedingly small but perfectly formed zelkova, an image of the tree seen moments before. His message was clear: Minibonsai, in spite of their diminutive size, are able to capture the character and the form of their much larger counterparts in nature.

American interest is expanding in these wee bonsai, which require only a little space in the house or apartment and fit comfortably in an indoor light garden. Minibonsai are grown and given the identical care as other bonsai of the same species; pruning, wiring, and potting techniques are similar. However, they are watered more frequently than the average bonsai and must be

Fig. 17–1 An attractive growing and display area in Japan for mame bonsai. Courtesy of Yoshimi Itoh.

Fig. 17–2.1 Japanese black pine, *Pinus Thunbergiana,* 5 cm tall. Courtesy of Yoshimi Itoh.

Fig. 17–2.2 Spruce, *Picea* sp., 12 cm tall. Courtesy of Yoshimi Itoh.

Fig. 17–2.3 Japanese maple, *Acer palmatum,* 5 cm high. Courtesy of Yoshimi Itoh.

fertilized regularly to replenish nutrients leached from the small amount of soil that fills their tiny container. A special potting mix is not required. A basic mix suitable for other bonsai of the same species is quite satisfactory; screen out aggregates over 1/16 or 1/8 inch to prevent a few large particles from occupying an undue portion of the available space in the tiny container.

Containers

Beautiful containers for minibonsai are made commercially in China and Japan. Many others are produced by artist-potters, individual potmakers, and amateurs throughout the world. Such pots (and stands) often display an amazing amount of detail, as shown in Fig. 17–3.

Fig. 17–3 Old miniature bonsai pots. Round pot on left is less than 2 inches wide, the other is 1⅛ inch high.

Fig. 17–4 Mame bonsai of *Zelkova serrata* in a contemporary container by Japanese ceramist Teruko Tsugi. Courtesy of Zeko Nakamura.

But minipots need not be subdued. A popular Japanese saying, "The smaller the tree, the brighter the pot," is based on the commonsense observation that a decorative or innovative container is helpful in calling attention to a very small tree. The zelkova in Fig. 17–4, planted in a colorful Japanese minicontainer, is the work of internationally famous grower Zeko Nakamura, a former Zen Buddhist acolyte turned actor.

Display

Because minibonsai and their containers require such little space and are easily moved, a great deal of flexibility is enjoyed in their display. As with larger bonsai, avoid crowding; give each little bonsai ample space in its own territory. A display of a few small Japanese bonsai on a tiered stand arranged by Zeko Nakamura is shown in Fig. 17–5; Fig. 17–6 illustrates Chinese minibonsai in the People's Republic of China.

Minibonsai on a multilevel stand may be arranged in a variety of ways. One method positions trees according to their natural range in elevation from sea level to the mountains. Bamboo, grasses, zelkova, and other trees or plants

Fig. 17–5 Clockwise from bottom, dwarf bamboo; flowering apricot, *Prunus Mume;* and Japanese black pine, *Pinus Thunbergiana.* Courtesy of Zeko Nakamura.

Fig. 17–6 Minibonsai display at the Shanghai Botanic Garden.

that grow at low altitudes are placed on the lowest shelf, trees and shrubs found at moderate elevations, such as azaleas, maples, and crab apples, are on the middle tiers, and junipers, pines, and other mountain conifers are located on the highest levels.

Andrew N. Lenz, a nationally known bonsai grower and artist-potter, bypasses traditional Oriental staging to display bonsai on a stand (Fig. 17–7.1) made from American building materials.

1. The staging was contrived from two door panels, a section of a partially narrowed square beam, and other material discarded from a federalist-period restoration. The beam was sawed 3 inches from the top, and one of the door panels was inserted between the two pieces to form a two-level shelf. A small lower shelf was created 12 inches from the bottom on the narrowed section of the beam. This recessed area was enlivened by a tiny federalist door with its half-circle fanlight of spokes and a stack of three wine casks. The fanlight and casks repeat the circular pattern made by several knots on the beam.

2. The eye of the viewer, however, is drawn upward to a bonsai crab apple, the focal point of the display. The thick tapered trunk carries the eye to the top of the tree. From there, the long lower branch of the bonsai points to an accessory planting on the far right, shown in Fig. 17-7.2. The small statue next to the herbaceous planting arrests the movement at the end of the shelf.

3. The eye moves downward to a cascading bonsai on the middle shelf. We are attracted to this spot by the slant along the periphery of the bonsai and the unexpected Greek Revival column directly beneath. (It is the only large rounded structural component in the display.) The strong cascading branch is directly over an antique federalist-period model rowboat, which, sporting two fish and a turtle, suggests low ground and nearby water.

4. The other door panel forms the lowest shelf. Here the eye can turn in either direction. To the right is a small accessory planting placed on a black square, which, with the long legs of the pot and the mounded soil in the container, raises the eyes upward to the middle shelf and the cascading bonsai. Toward the left, a few thin blades of grass form a transition to the tiny door on the square beam and upward again to the crab apple. The cycle is completed.

Lenz's display suggests that the movement and composition so often seen in traditional staging can be effectively incorporated in contemporary displays.

Plant Material

For minibonsai, species with compact branching and root systems are preferred. Dwarf forms and cultivars are popular. The following species are among those with the ability to adjust to a great reduction in size and a limited area for root growth.

Popular Woody Plants for Minibonsai

Acer palmatum, Japanese maple

Buxus microphylla, dwarf boxwood and cvs. Compacta and Nana

Chaenomeles japonica, lesser flowering quince, var. **pygmaea** and cvs. Maulei and Sargentii

C. speciosa *(C. lagenaria)*, flowering quince and cv. Umbilicata Nana

Chamaecyparis obtusa, Hinoki cypress and cvs. compacta, Minima, and Pygmaea

Fig. 17-7.1 Minibonsai display contrived by Andrew N. Lenz at the Fifteenth Annual Symposium of the American Bonsai Society, College Park, Maryland.

Fig. 17-7.2 The lower branch of each bonsai directs the eye to another object in the display.

C. pisifera, Sawara cypress and cvs. Ericoides, Nana, and Pygmaea

C. thyoides, white cedar and cv. Ericoides, a dwarf form

Cryptomeria japonica, Japanese cedar and cvs. Compacta, Gracilis, Nana, and Vilmoriniana

Ficus neriifolia, willow-leaf fig and other figs with small leaves

Hedera Helix, English ivy and dwarf cvs. Jubilee, Needlepoint, and Pittsburgh

Ilex vomitoria, yaupon holly and cv. Schellings Dwarf

Juniperus chinensis var. **Sargentii,** shimpaku juniper and cvs. Blaauw and Nana

J. rigida, needle juniper

Malus Sargentii, crab apple with white flowers and ⅜-inch fruit

M. Sieboldii, a crab apple with bright pink flowers and $\frac{5}{16}$-inch fruit

Nandina domestica, heavenly bamboo and dwarf forms

Pieris japonica, Andromeda and cvs. Compacta, Pygmaea, and Variegata

Pinus parvifolia, Japanese white pine

P. Thunbergiana, Japanese black pine

Punica Granatum, pomegranate and cv. Nana, a dwarf form

Pyracantha angustifolia, fire thorn

Rhododendron indicum, Japanese azalea and satsuki cultivars

R. kiusiana, Japanese Kyushu azalea

Sageretia Thea, sageretia

Taxus cuspidata, yew and cvs. Brevifolia, Compacta, Minima, and Nana

Thuja occidentalis, American arborvitae and cvs. Compacta, Globusa, Pumila, and Tom Thumb

Ulmus parvifolia, Chinese elm and cv. Catlin, a small form

Zelkova serrata, zelkova and a Japanese form, Maki

In addition to woody plants, many grasses, bamboos, bulbs, flowering plants, and weeds are popular for minibonsai. There is no limit to the attractive herbaceous and semiwoody species that can be found.

Techniques

Other than working with naturally miniaturized dwarf forms, the two basic methods of reducing the size of established plant material are drastic pruning and starting with young material and trimming it repeatedly. For minibonsai, both techniques are used to the ultimate degree.

Reduction by Drastic Pruning. Select a plant growing in a container, or even shaped as bonsai, whose trunk can be pruned to one or more branches near the ground. This is quite similar to cutting back large material to create an average-size bonsai. Zeko Nakamura, affectionately known as "Zeko-san"

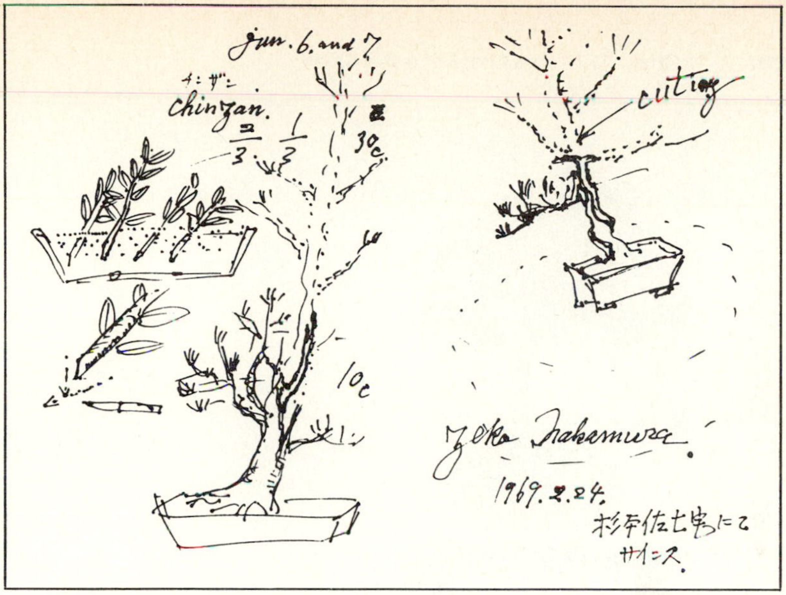

Fig. 17-8 Drawing by Zeko Nakamura showing a 4-inch minibonsai made from a 12-inch-tall Satsuki azalea, *Rhododendron indicum* cv. Chinzan; trimmed branches were rooted as cuttings.

to the bonsai world, demonstrated this technique to a visitor by quickly making the sketch shown in Fig. 17–8. The tall, 30-cm tree in the drawing is reduced to 10 cm. Notice that a portion of the trunk immediately above the cut was whittled away to form a taper with the remaining trunk. The branches will be shortened and positioned to develop a treelike form.

Figure 17–9 reveals Zeko-san's skillful sleight of hand in creating minibonsai. He removed the original tall trunk on a flowering quince so cunningly that the pruning cut is completely concealed on the finished bonsai. It is hard to realize that a tall trunk has been severed to within a few inches of its base to create this minibonsai.

Fig. 17–9 Skillful pruning removed the original tall trunk on this flowering quince, *Chaenomeles speciosa (C. lagenaria).* Courtesy of Zeko Nakamura.

Fig. 17-10 Minibonsai of dwarf Kingsville boxwood, *Buxus microphylla* cv. Compacta, in a container by Japanese artist-potter Hanyiu.

Dwarfing a Seedling. The second method starts with a young seedling or cutting whose new growth is repeatedly shortened. The following account describes how boxwood cuttings were made into minibonsai by an American hobbyist.

The Kingsville boxwood, *Buxus microphylla* cv. Compacta (Fig. 17-10), is one of several cuttings taken ten years previously. For the first few years, the cuttings were grown in regular training pots without pruning to produce healthy, well-rooted specimens. From the third year on, all new growth that protruded noticeably beyond the other foliage was removed, as were undesirable branches. The boxwood were placed among other young bonsai and did not require special attention. About every two years they were repotted and the roots were trimmed. During this period, the trunks and branches were examined, and each little boxwood was gradually shaped to a bonsai form. As each boxwood attained a pleasing shape, it was moved to a small bonsai container. Seedlings may be trained in essentially the same manner. It is often necessary, however, to remove or shorten the taproot.

Broom-Style Minibonsai

Zelkova serrata, a favorite species for a broom-style minibonsai in Japan, is often started from seed. Morihiko Tomita, exhibit manager of the Japan Bonsai Association, explained to a group of visiting American bonsai enthusiasts how to achieve this in only a few years. He prepared sketches of each step. The following account of Tomita's instructions first appeared in slightly different form in the *Journal of the American Bonsai Society*.[1]

Tomita provided special Maki zelkova seed, preferred for zelkova bonsai in Japan. Maki zelkova may be identified by the red color of their new shoots compared to green on other zelkova. The techniques described here, however, are applicable to all zelkova and may be adapted to other minibonsai grown from seed. The accompanying drawings by Morihiko Tomita are reproduced through the courtesy of the American Bonsai Society.

1. Planting the seeds (Fig. 17–11.1). Plant the seeds 1½ inches apart in a flat or shallow box filled with a mixture of sand and soil. (Make sure there are provisions for adequate drainage.) Fall is the best planting time, right after the seeds are collected. In cold climates, protect the seeds with a mulch during the winter.
2. First year, spring (Fig. 17–11.2). After the first branches have five or six leaves, cut each branch back to two leaves, then trim approximately two-thirds of each remaining leaf. This will promote new branching.
3. First year, summer (Fig. 17–11.3). Four branches have developed, one from each leaf that was trimmed. Allow these branches to grow.
4. Second year, spring (Fig. 17–11.4). This is the time to remove the seedlings from the box. Cut off the taproot and prune all the branches to two buds before replanting each seedling in a training pot. Spread the roots horizontally during the transplanting.
5. Second year, summer (Fig. 17–11.5). Cut all branches back to two leaves and trim two-thirds of each remaining leaf, as shown in Fig. 17–11.2.
6. Second year, fall (Fig. 17–11.6). After the leaves have fallen from the tree, gather the branches together close to the trunk and fasten them with twine. Keep them tied until the following spring.
7. Third year, early spring (Fig. 17–11.7). Remove the twine before new growth appears. Again, prune all of last year's shoots back to two buds. In summer, prune again as described previously. In subsequent years, continue similar spring and summer pruning to develop a tiny broom-style bonsai with many branches.

[1]Morihiko Tomita, "Broom-Style Zelkova in Three Years," *Journal of the American Bonsai Society*, 7, no. 2 (Summer 1973), 42–43.

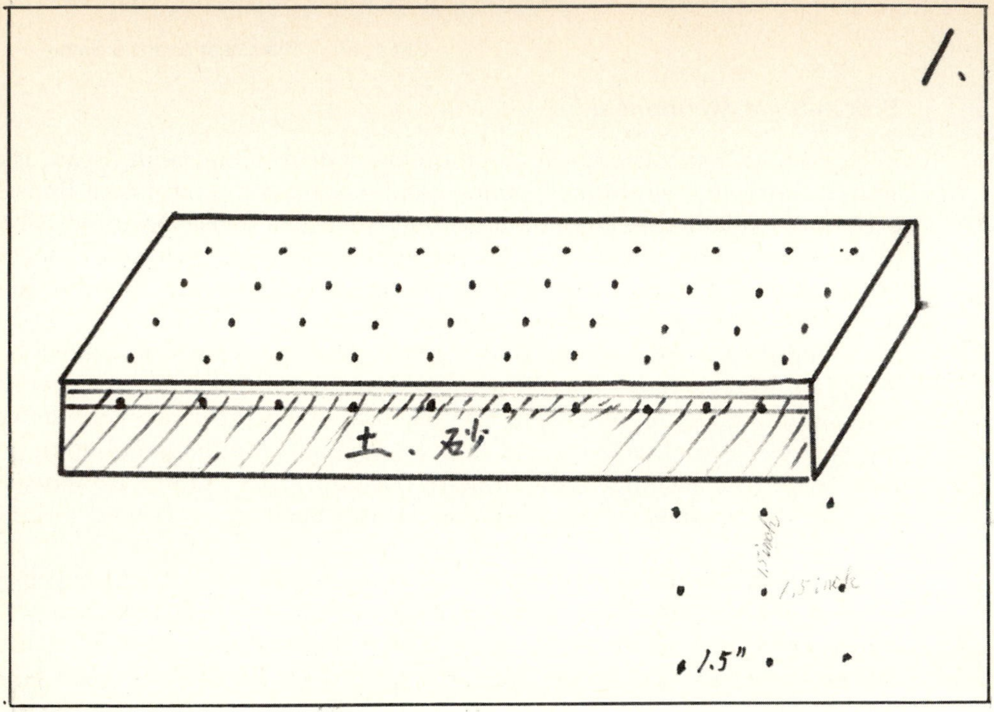

Fig. 17–11.1 Planting zelkova seeds.

Fig. 17–11.2 First year, spring.

Fig. 17–11.3 First year, summer.

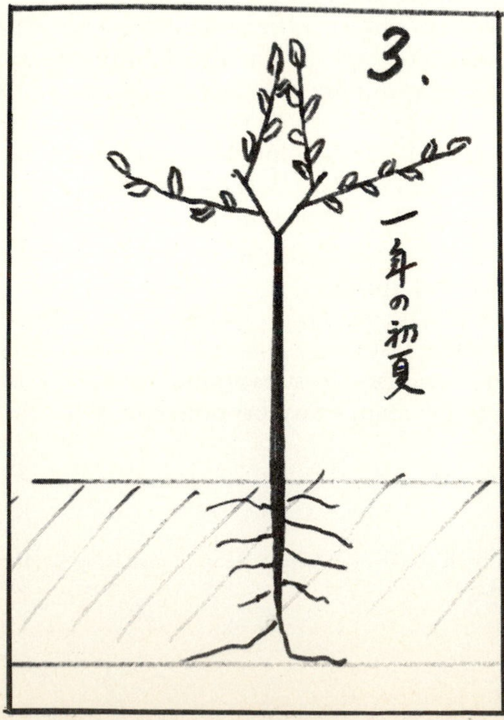

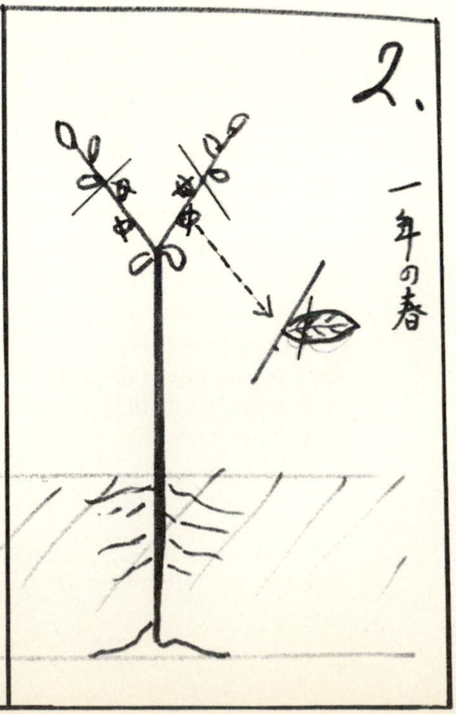

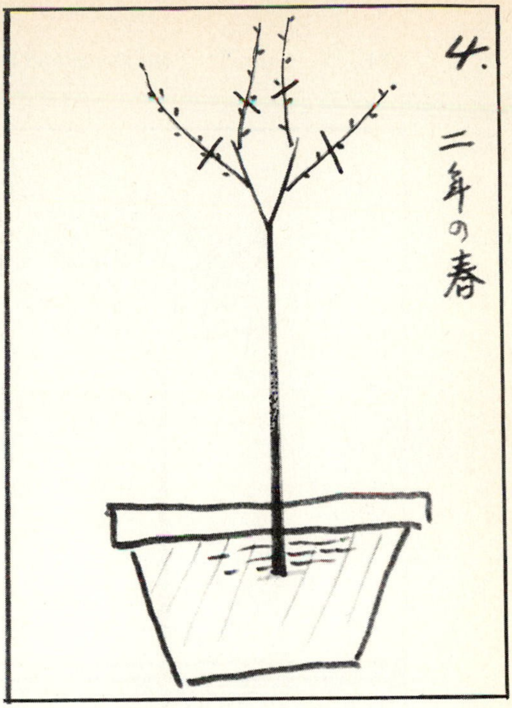

Fig. 17–11.4 Second year, spring.

Fig. 17–11.6 Second year, fall.

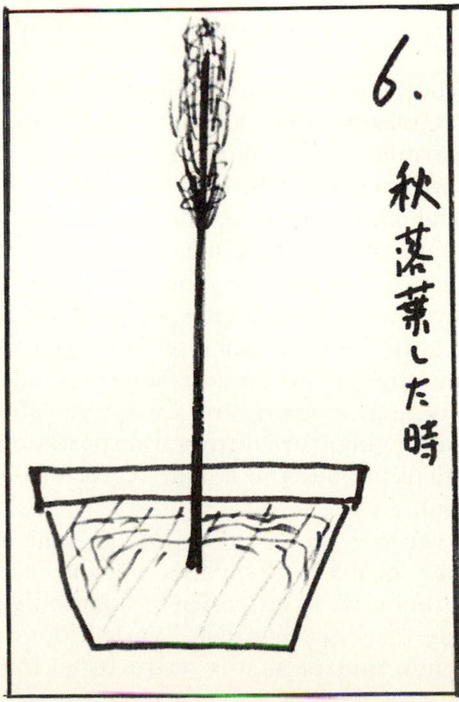

Fig. 17–11.5 Second year, summer.

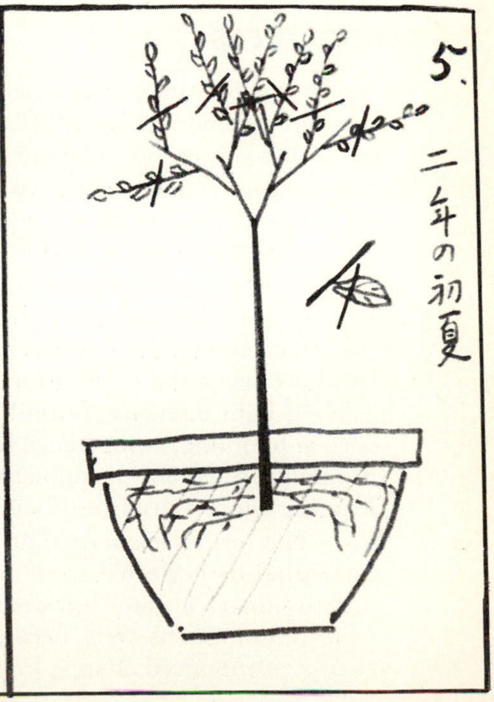

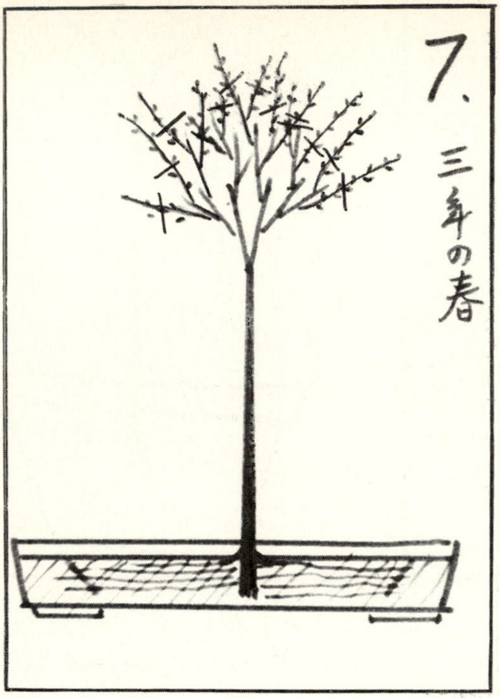

Fig. 17-11.7 Third year, early spring.

COLLECTED TREES

Many magnificant bonsai have been created from "collected" trees such as the ponderosa pine in Fig. 17-12. Collected trees are nature's bonsai. They are old, often stunted survivors of hostile environments in mountains, forests, and other terrains. Most are large as well as old and must be reduced in size for bonsai.

There is something special about collected bonsai. A marvelous old weathered trunk is not easily obtained by other means. And the very age of the tree can reach an awesome two centuries or more.

A tree collected from high mountain altitudes needs a period of acclimatization when brought to low elevations. This transition period may require intensive care when the roots resume growth and the tree adjusts to altered conditions of light intensity, humidity, and temperature. Such trees often demand special handling, competence in digging, care during transportation, attentive nursing throughout the adjustment period, and a high degree of skill in transforming the material into bonsai.

The term *collected trees*, however, is also used in another sense to describe unwanted or neglected trees and shrubs in backyards, vacant lots, and other nearby areas. Locally collected material is far easier to handle than old trees from mountainous areas because the "home-grown" variety does not experience a pronounced change in environment as it is restructured into a bonsai.

Fig. 17–12 Ponderosa pine, *Pinus ponderosa,* estimated to be 600 years old. Courtesy of Frank Takishita.

Techniques

Finding the Material. For the bonsai novice, the best hunting ground is the home territory. Look for shrubs—azaleas and junipers, for example—and small trees that have been trampled underfoot, outgrown their space in a crowded foundation planting, or are to be removed and replaced by new specimens. Anything growing in the path of a bulldozer is prime material. By starting with plants that have no future, an inexperienced grower can work comfortably with the hope of prolonging the tree's life.

To avoid needless digging, examine each tree or shrub for its bonsai potential before removing it from the ground. Look especially for a harmonious trunk line, well-distributed branches, and the configuration wanted for starting a bonsai.

Digging. When lifting a tree or shrub from the ground, use extreme care to preserve as many fine feeder roots as possible. The best time to move a plant is early spring. Follow these procedures:

1. Remove all grass, weeds, and their roots within an 8- to 12-inch radius around the trunk of the tree.
2. With a hand rake or trowel, loosen and scrape away the top layer of soil. Dig carefully around the tree to locate major roots at the bottom of the trunk.
3. Wherever a taproot is encountered, carefully remove the soil for a foot or so to see whether fibrous roots are attached. Widen the cleared area, if necessary. If none are found, examine other taproots to locate feeder roots.
4. Continue digging until a root mass sufficient to support the tree is uncovered. If fibrous roots are not present within 12 inches or so of the trunk, replace the soil and look for a tree with a root system closer to the trunk.

> Remove the root mass with as much soil around the roots as possible. Place the tree on a piece of burlap or heavy plastic. If the roots are bare, add soil, cover them with damp newspaper or sphagnum moss, and wrap them well. When a potential bonsai is found growing in a shallow indentation on bedrock or clay, it can often be removed easily with all its roots intact.

Keep collected trees out of direct sun after they are dug to prevent the roots and foliage from drying.

Shaping. Before replanting a collected tree, place it on a turntable and examine it from all sides. Unless the tree is in a weak condition or collected out of season, select the front and prune the tree immediately, perhaps severely, to its basic bonsai shape. Choose a design or style that brings out the tree's strongest assets and is similar to the line of the existing trunk and major branches.

Work facing the front of the tree. It will probably (but not always) be necessary to shorten the trunk. If the replacement branch for the trunk is thin, do not prune it; use the Lingnan method and allow it to grow and thicken into a natural extension of the trunk. If the branch is not harmonious with the rest of the trunk, wire it now to conform with the trunk's dominant line. An alternate method of handling an overly tall trunk is to save a portion and change it into driftwood, as seen in the Rocky Mountain juniper (Fig. 17–13).

After selecting the major branches on the trunk, remove the unwanted ones. Are the branches in proportion to the projected height of the bonsai? When shortening branches, cut them back sufficiently to allow for future growth. Use regular bonsai pruning techniques: Make the cuts at the fork of another branch or immediately beyond a bud.

Fig. 17–13 Rocky Mountain juniper, *Juniperus scopulorum,* estimated to be 650 years old. Courtesy of Frank Takishita.

Roots. When the trunk-branch framework is established, reexamine the root mass for long taproots that can be shortened. Remember that the decisive factor is not the extent of rootage that was or is to be removed but the amount of fibrous roots that can be retained.

Training Pots. The collected tree may be replanted in the ground or potted in a roomy training pot. Depending on the size of the tree, this can be a wooden box nailed together at home or a tub, pail, or flowerpot of any material. Make sure there are holes for drainage.

Potting Mix. Examine the texture of the soil remaining on the roots and use a comparable potting mix. If the soil around the root ball is loose and grainy, match it with a mix containing a large proportion of coarse aggregates. If the soil contains a noticeable amount of humus, incorporate extra peat moss in the mix. But if the roots are in clay or tightly compacted soil, remove the original soil completely; it is not suitable for a container.

Potting. Use regular potting methods for collected trees. Take special care to protect the fragile, often sparse roots.

If the root mass is severely limited, mist the tree with water several times a day for a week or so after potting. Discontinue the misting gradually. Place a collected tree in the ground or in a container where it will receive filtered sun and protection from drying winds until it becomes well established in its new environment.

Care. After a month or so, when growth has resumed, begin a program of regular light fertilizing once a month during the growing season. Do not trim new growth the first year unless it is excessively abundant. Rather, let the tree gain strength; resume bonsai training the following year.

Wilderness Collecting

Natural wilderness sites for collecting abound in North America. Bonsai material is found in an incredible variety of environments—coastal areas, lowland swamps or pockets of wet areas at higher elevations, dry sandy terrains, rocky cliffs and mountains. On rocky sites it is often difficult to obtain sufficient roots for the tree's survival. The tree may be wedged in a steep stone crevice, or its taproot may extend a long distance before it reaches a pocket of soil where fibrous roots can grow. Consequently, some of the most desirable bonsai material may have roots that are difficult or impossible to dig.

Inducing Root Growth. Dan Robinson, a nationally known expert and innovative bonsai grower in the Pacific Northwest, collects bonsai material in the Cascade Mountains and other areas at high elevations. He has devised an ingenious method of stimulating a mass of new fibrous roots at the base of a tree before removing it from its rocky site. With this technique of root enhancement, he obtains magnificent rock-bound trees that otherwise could not be moved.

After selecting a tree, Robinson searches for a small root near the bottom of the trunk. Size is not important; it may be a thin wisp of a root, as long as it contains living root cells. He carefully raises the root from the soil and packs it in moist sphagnum peat moss, which he wraps and seals in black plastic. He places the package next to the tree in a sunny spot on the ground or on a stone or sheetrock where the heat of the sun will stimulate the rapid growth of fibrous roots in the moist medium. Successful root activation may occur within three weeks under favorable conditions in midsummer. Robinson checks the package from time to time to see if the moisture in the package has been depleted by new root growth. As soon as adequate roots are formed, he severs the tree from its taproot and carries it down the mountain.

Robinson obtains remarkable results with pines including *Pinus ponderosa*; *P. contorta* var. *latifolia*, lodgepole pine; and *P. flexilis*, limber pine. His method of utilizing solar energy may be effective in other sunny collecting areas, such as the New Jersey Pine Barrens, and mountainous areas.

Collecting by Region

In the north, tamarack or larch, *Larix laricina*, is a handsome species for bonsai. It spans the North American continent from Alaska through Canada and Nova Scotia to the northeastern United States.

Along the Keys and the southernmost part of Florida, buttonwoods, *Conocarpus erectus*, with their naturally weathered old trunks and compact branching provide outstanding bonsai material for warm climates.

As collected material, the California juniper, *Juniperus californica*, from the Sierra Nevada and other high elevations, rivals the famous shimpaku juniper of Japan. Two examples may be seen in Figs. 2-5 and 12-3.

Farther west, in Hawaii, one of the loveliest collected species is ohio-lehua, *Metrosideros collinus*, with beautiful crimson flowers (Fig. 2-9). It is found on desolate lava formations on the island of Hawaii.

The Rocky Mountains are an excellent collecting area for many conifers, including such species as limber pine (Fig. 17-14), ponderosa pine (Fig. 17-12),

Fig. 17-14 Limber pine, *Pinus flexilis,* approximately 350 years old. Courtesy of Kai Kawahara.

Fig. 17–15 Top and bottom right, minibonsai of dwarf sagebrush, *Artemisia arbuscula,* collected in Utah. Courtesy of Allan Hills.

and Rocky Mountain juniper (Fig. 17–13). While most collected bonsai are medium to large in size, it is possible occasionally to find specimens as tiny as the sagebrush in Fig. 17–15, collected in Utah to train as a minibonsai.

For other species of trees and shrubs that may be found growing in the wild, consult the lists of native American bonsai material by geographical regions in Chapter 2.

ADDITIONAL READING

KATAGAMA, TEI'ICHI, *The Mini-Bonsai Hobby.* Tokyo: Japan Publications, Inc., 1974. Distributed in the United States and Canada by Japan Publications Trading Co. (U.S.A.), Inc. Describes Japanese growing methods, grafting, air layering, and potting mixes, with an excellent section on training azaleas for minibonsai.

LITTLE, ELBERT L., *Atlas of United States Trees (Vol. 1): Conifers and Important Hardwoods*, Miscellaneous Publication No. 1146. Washington, D.C.: U.S. Department of Agriculture, Forest Service, 1971. This large-format atlas, with 12-by-11-inch maps showing the distribution of native tree species in the continental United States and Alaska, clearly indicates the range of native trees. Some two hundred conifers and approximately one hundred hardwood or deciduous trees are covered.

NAKAMURA, ZEKO, *Bonsai Miniatures, Quick and Easy.* Tokyo: Shufunotomo Co., Ltd., 1973. Distributed in the United States and Canada by Japan Publications Trading Co. (U.S.A.), Inc. In this little book (not quite 4½ by 6 inches) a series of full-page color photographs of the author's minibonsai alternate with pages of illustrated instructions. This minivolume contains a wealth of information in an attractive format.

18

Displaying and Exhibiting Bonsai

Bonsai growers often enjoy bringing their hardy bonsai into the home on festive occasions for decorative effects. A bonsai placed on a table or in an arranged setting may easily become the center of interest in a room. Effective staging makes a bonsai more beautiful and enhances its appearance, regardless of its degree of training.

The Japanese devised an unmatched setting for home display. It is called the *tokonoma*, or alcove, and is found in the traditional Japanese house with its walls of paper panels and straw-matted floors. The display of objects in the tokonoma is described in detail because the principles employed may be adapted for bonsai displayed in Western dwellings.

THE JAPANESE TOKONOMA

The tokonoma is a rectangular recessed area raised slightly above the floor and extending to the ceiling, as shown in Fig. 18–1. It is usually located in the principal room of the house, the entrance hall, or the guest room. It provides a built-in display area for works of art, articles of religious or cultural significance, family heirlooms, flower arrangements, bonsai, and other valued objects. The average tokonoma is 2 or 3 feet deep and 4 to 8 feet wide. In a large home, the tokonoma is deeper and may occupy the entire wall of a room.

Fig. 18–1 Japanese tokonoma. Courtesy of Dover Publications.

A Meaningful Theme

The display in the tokonoma is often staged to express a theme. A bonsai, for example, may be selected to reflect the season of the year. During the spring months, bonsai of flowering cherry, quince, and azalea are on display. Persimmon bonsai in fruit, red-berried holly, and maples in orange and crimson foliage are chosen for fall. In summer, a willow tree may suggest a scene by a cool, flowing stream, or an ancient juniper may evoke a lofty mountain. In winter, deciduous trees such as zelkova, with their beautiful, intricate network of bare twigs and branches, are enjoyed in Japanese interiors without central heating.

The Components

As the major object, the bonsai is usually placed on a small stand or table on one side of the tokonoma. Unless the tokonoma is large, only one sizable bonsai is displayed at a time. An accessory is often added on the opposite side of the tokonoma. It may be a vase with a few flowers, a small bonsai, an herbaceous planting, or an interestingly shaped stone. These stones, called "viewing stones," may resemble a natural formation such as an island or a mountain, or they may suggest a chrysanthemum flower, as shown in Fig. 18–2. A drawing of the tokonoma with a scroll painting hung on the wall completes the rather formal display shown in Fig. 18–3.

Fig. 18–2 Japanese chrysanthemum viewing stone, 5 inches long.

Fig. 18–3 Display of bonsai with bonsai stand, accessory planting, and scroll painting.

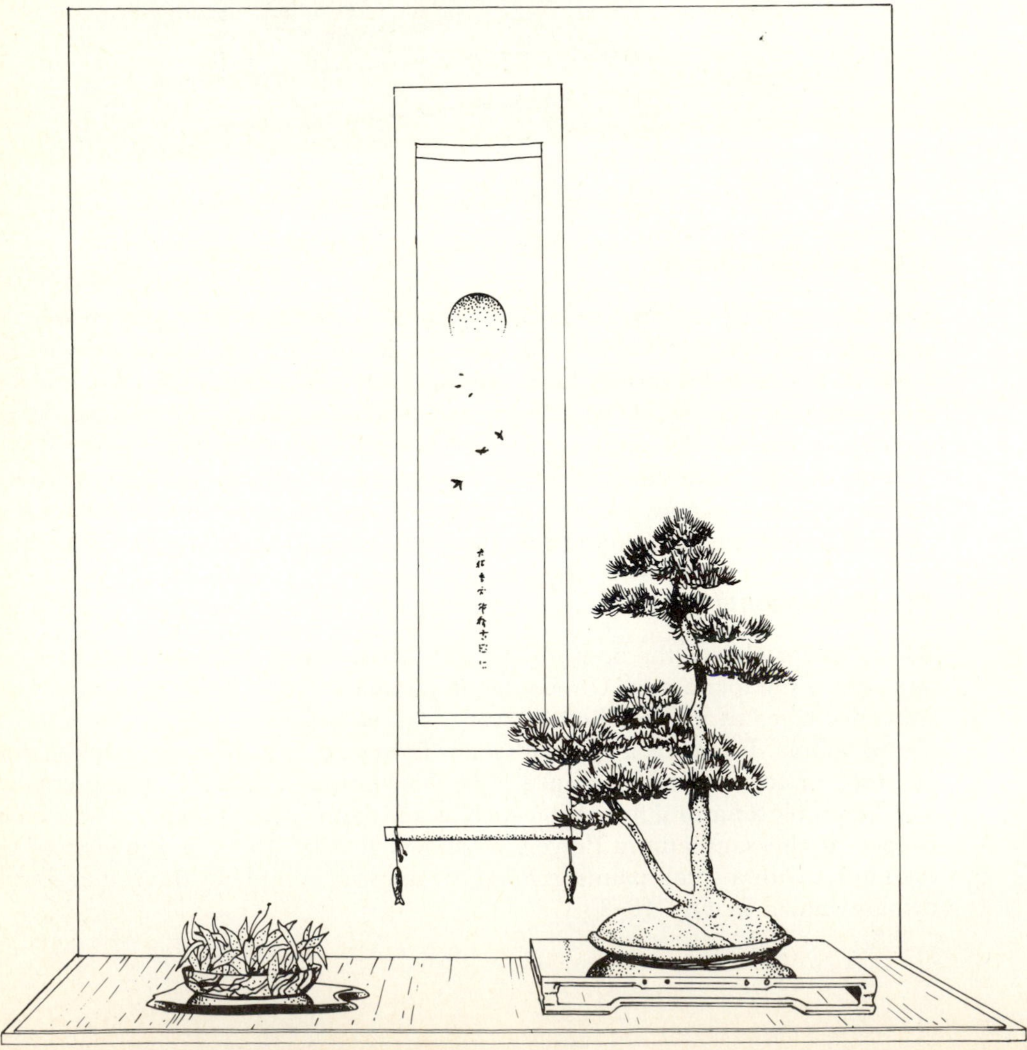

The Triangular Arrangement

The articles in the tokonoma are arranged in a triangular composition. The bonsai forms one of the lower angles of a scalene triangle, the accessory on the other side constitutes the second bottom angle, and the scroll painting serves as the apex. Each object may be viewed individually, yet the three are closely related by their position in the defined recessed space of the tokonoma.

WESTERN ADAPTATIONS FOR BONSAI DISPLAYS

It is not necessary to have a tokonoma to display bonsai to their best advantage. The effect can be duplicated in Western homes by a clearly defined area with a plain background set apart from distracting objects, preferably at eye level—in other words, a stage for bonsai. The staging is strengthened by placing a low stand under the bonsai and arranging the objects in a triangular composition.

Considerations

A Defined Area. The defined area may be any space that sets apart the bonsai from other furnishings in the room. It may be a small table against a plain wall, a shelf, or part of a counter separated from other uses by a strip of wood or bamboo at either end.

The Plain Background. To conceal patterned wallpaper or other distracting material on the wall, use a flat, removable panel. It is easily improvised from a section of plywood or heavy cardboard covered with cloth or painted a neutral color. It may be framed or unframed and as simple or as elaborate as desired. If the panel needs to be secured, it may be hung on the wall or placed on simple footed supports. Another attractive background is a small folding screen with plain panels, sometimes in gold or silver.

Size and Dimensions. The location and size of the display area is dependent on the available space in the home. Whenever possible, select an area that is more than twice the length of the tallest bonsai and deep enough for the bonsai to be positioned without the foliage touching the rear wall or extending beyond the front edge of the shelf or table. A high wall behind the bonsai will provide space for an Oriental scroll painting or other art.

Elimination of Distractions. Remove unrelated vases, bowls, and other miscellaneous objects no matter how lovely or exquisite they may be. The only objects included in the display are those that complement the bonsai.

Eye-level Height. Place the bonsai so that it can be seen at eye level. In Japan this can be as little as 2 feet where the bonsai will be viewed by people seated on the tatami floor. A 4-foot height is suitable for public displays where visitors are standing or walking. Eye level is approximately 3 feet for viewers seated in chairs. The top of a table or sideboard in Occidental homes provides an excellent height.

The Interior Environment. All outdoor bonsai, at some time during the year, can safely be brought indoors for brief periods of time. This is usually no longer than several days. In cold winter climates, when bonsai are completely dormant, they must not be moved into heated interiors. In mild climates, however, bonsai can experience indoor environments whenever there is no pronounced difference between the indoor and outdoor temperatures. During their brief visit indoors, keep bonsai away from bright sun and direct sources of heated or cooled air.

While indoors, bonsai may require watering. Check the container each day; if the soil is dry, water promptly.

Selection and Preparation for Display. Plan to display bonsai when they are at their best. This varies with each species. For some, it may be seasonal—featuring lovely flowers in the spring or attractive fruit in the fall. A tree with excessively large leaves, for example, is almost always displayed in winter (when the leaves are absent) or in early spring, as the tender new growth begins to unfurl.

At any time of the year, exhibit only bonsai that are healthy, clean, well groomed, and in an appropriate container. The question is sometimes asked, "Are bonsai exhibited with wire on their trunk or branches?" The answer is a qualified yes. Yes, if the wiring is minor and inconspicuous. A heavily wired bonsai is considered to be in training. Generally, such a tree is not exhibited until the wire has served its purpose and has been removed.

It is important that a displayed bonsai be carefully groomed and in a clean container. Exhibitors often polish the outside of the container with a soft cloth or fine steel wool containing a few drops of household oil. Tidy the surface of the soil in the container by removing old leaves, weeds, or other miscellaneous objects that have accumulated out of doors.

STANDS

The beauty of a bonsai is tremendously heightened when it is displayed on a handsome stand. There is an old Oriental saying that a bonsai without a stand is like a person without shoes. The stand gives the bonsai a finished appearance, elevates it physically and in importance, and sets it apart from the surroundings. Shown on a stand, the little tree more than ever becomes the focus of attention.

Stands may be made of wood, porcelain, bamboo or reed mats, stone, metal, or plastic. Most are made of wood. Illustrations of bonsai on a stand may be seen in this and other chapters. On a fine stand, hard seasoned wood is smoothed and polished to a soft sheen. The wood is usually stained a dark brown or black. Occasionally it may be given a natural or light brown finish or painted black or vermilion. While stands are customarily imported from the Orient, beautiful handcrafted bonsai stands are also produced in many Occidental countries.

A well-made stand is a valued piece of furniture, and with proper care it will last for generations. When using a stand, handle it carefully to avoid scratching and do not let water collect on the surface of the wood. Always remove the bonsai when it requires watering and let it drain well before returning it to the stand. Wax the stand from time to time, and, when not in use, cover it with a cloth and store it in a box for protection from accidental damage.

Placing the Container on the Stand

Because of the many variables involved, there is no single rule that dictates the precise placement of a bonsai on a stand. In Japan, most often, the stand is larger than the container, providing open space on all sides. In Chinese practice, the stand and container tend to be the same size. With the close synergism between a bonsai and its display stand, the stand is carefully selected to complement the aesthetic impact of the tree and its container. A few considerations are listed for using stands of different shapes.

Rectangular and Oval Stands. Where the length is longer than the width, as with a rectangular or oval stand, the bonsai may be placed near the center of the stand, or it may be positioned more to the right or left of center in the same manner that a tree is planted in a container. A bonsai with a slanting trunk may be placed toward the side of the stand opposite to the direction of the slant, while a tree with a vertical trunk is often placed closer to the center of the stand.

A rectangular stand is an excellent choice for a beginner's first stand. It is a multipurpose stand suitable for vertical, slanting, and semicascade trunks including single, multitrunk, and group plantings, of young or old bonsai and small or large specimens. Both oval and rectangular containers look good on a rectangular stand, but a rectangular container rarely looks good on an oval stand. Rectangular stands are available with or without feet; of the two, the footed stand is more useful. Flat ovals and rectangles without feet are generally associated with informal displays, accessory plantings, and literati bonsai. An oval stand is used for round or irregularly shaped containers, stone slabs, or oval pots that are similar in shape to the stand.

Square and Round Stands. Round stands and stands with angled equidistant sides, such as squares and hexagonals, are often raised on long feet for use with cascading or semicascading bonsai. They are usually matched with pots that are round or have equidistant sides. Square and angled stands evoke a feeling of great strength appropriate for an imposing or active bonsai. Round stands, on the other hand, are used with graceful bonsai. Round and irregularly shaped flat stands are suitable for accessory plantings and literati bonsai.

Other Considerations. A slightly raised stand with sturdy feet is well matched with a strong bonsai in a massive container; stands with fine moldings and feet are more suited to trees with a light airy structure. A stand with an exquisite inlaid design (Fig. 18–4) is lovely for bonsai with delicate foliage or flowers. Elaborate stands with crosspieces between the legs or stands with flaring feet make a strong impact. Such stands are appropriate for antique pots

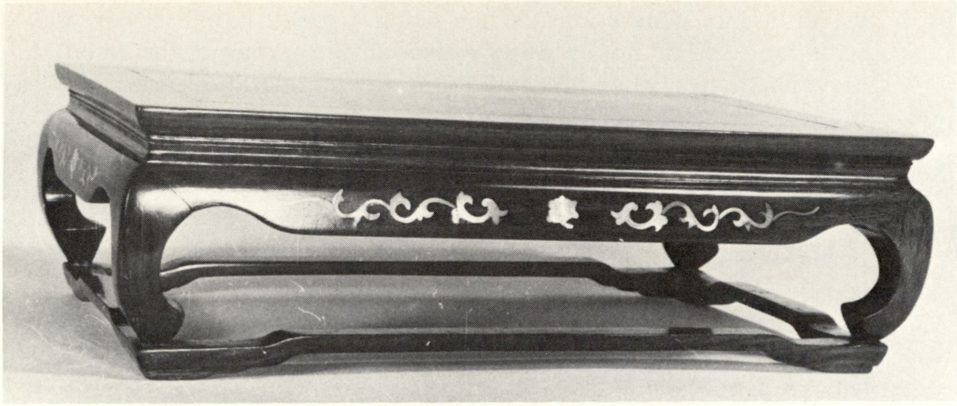

Fig. 18–4 Chinese bonsai stand inlaid with mother-of-pearl.

and specimen bonsai. Stands of this type ask for a tree with an impressive trunk and a clearly defined structure. Ovals, rectangulars, and other stands without feet are generally associated with informal displays, accessory plantings, and literati bonsai.

Homemade Stands

Attractive stands can be made from readily available material ranging from simple informal stands of flat boards to copies of elaborate Oriental models.

Boards. Stands cut from boards are pleasing and easy to make. Select straight boards of any width desired from ¼ inch to several inches thick. Cut three or four sections of the same length. They may be arranged in various ways—as a rectangle or staggered.

For all stands, use cured wood to avoid warping. Long-lasting redwood, cypress, and cedar are preferred for outdoor stands. Treat all wood for outdoor stands with a wood preservative, such as clear zinc naphthenate.

Look for old boards washed by rain, wind, or water or weathered boards from old barns; these make excellent slabs. Use a wood preservative to protect their silvery sheen.

Wood slabs may be finished in a number of other ways. Repeated light applications of tung oil produces a handsome water-resistant surface. It is used on new wood or old wood sanded to a hard, smooth surface. Or wood may be treated with a waterproof varnish over a natural finish or stained and then varnished. Polyurethane finishes are tough, durable, and highly resistant to water. Lacquer, paint, or enamel also produces an attractive finish. With regard to colors, black is most often used, but Chinese red or vermilion adds a bright note to a display.

Reed and Split Bamboo. Reed and split bamboo window curtains may be cut into mats for displaying bonsai. Make the pieces slightly larger than needed to allow either end to be unraveled. Then knot the strings in the fringe to fasten the woven slats securely. To make a raised stand suitable for a cascade bonsai, cover the top and sides of a sturdy box with woven reeds or burlap. Burlap may also be fastened over plywood or boards to make various sizes of low, flat stands.

Cross Sections of Trunks. Cut cross sections of a trunk or burl to make beautifully shaped natural-wood slabs. To increase their length, cut the wood on the diagonal. If possible, keep the bark intact along the edge of each slat. The finest slabs are made from close-grained wood such as maple, cypress, and chamaecyparis. They may be sanded and rubbed with tung or linseed oil to bring out the subtle shades of color in the wood. Slabs less than ½ inch thick are popular for bonsai with thin trunks, such as young trees in group plantings, literati bonsai, and bamboo or herbaceous plantings. Thick, heavy slabs are suitable for bonsai with large trunks that require strong support.

Used Furniture. A reservoir of potential bonsai stands may be discovered in attics, basements, flea markets, and secondhand shops. Shelves and small tabletops are salvageable. Legs on small tables may be shortened to a length suitable for a low stand. Old plant racks may offer possibilities for cascade bonsai. Chipped or slightly damaged marble furniture tops may be recut into attractive stone bases and undamaged ones used as they are. An adventuresome spirit and sharp eyes will uncover other possibilities.

Copies of Oriental Stands. A copy of a beautiful Japanese or Chinese stand is second only to the original. Many such stands are made by persons skilled in woodworking. Some hobbyists have turned their woodworking skills into a profession in response to the demand for well-made bonsai stands and are producing stands of walnut and other native American woods.

Root Stands. Beautiful stands of naturally intertwining roots are collectors' items that can be made from throwaways. The exquisite two-tiered stand in Fig. 18–5 was fashioned from the roots of a discarded Japanese holly, *Ilex crenata*, by Doris W. Froning, a nationally known grower of miniature bonsai. The instructions in the next three paragraphs are condensed from Froning's article on making a root stand, which appeared in the *Mame Bonsai Growers of America* newsletter.

The material consists of roots and a section of the lower trunk. Start by washing the roots to remove all soil. Take care not to break or damage the roots and retain them all for a variety of shapes and thickness. Study the root mass and lower trunk to determine exactly where the trunk can be cut and at what angle to make a level base for the bonsai. After the trunk is cut, remove the outer bark on the trunk and roots. On freshly dug roots, squeeze the roots with pliers; the covering is easily pulled off in the same way as bark is stripped from a thin branch or trunk. If the roots have dried, scrape off the covering with a sharp knife. Starting with medium grade sandpaper and progressing to the fine grades, sand each root and the top of the stand to a smooth finish.

To level the stand, turn it upside down and secure it firmly in a level position. Run a disk sander over the root ends to reduce them to an even height,

Fig. 18–5 A minibonsai of *Chamaecyparis pisifera* cv. Nana on a stand made from holly roots. Courtesy of Doris W. Froning.

parallel to the base. Return the stand to its upright position for the final adjustment of the roots. Do this by trial and error. Use a level and shorten an overly long root as required. It is not necessary to have all the root ends supporting the stand; only enough to provide a stable base are needed.

Stain the stand to a color desired (use spare pieces for a trial test). Traditionally, darker colors are preferred, but stands are finished in varying shades from light to dark. Apply spar varnish as a finish and wax afterwards. Shoe polish is effective for darkening the stain to give variation to the color, and is easier to use than regular wax.[1]

Shrubs and small trees or vines likely to have multiple strands of roots suitable for stands include species of *Ilex, Buxus, Rhododendron, Juniperus*, and wild honeysuckle, *Lonicera*. By close observation, other usable roots can be found. To reduce the time spent on scraping and sanding, it may be possible to have the roots cleaned and polished by sandblasting.

ACCESSORIES

An accessory in a bonsai display is optional. When used, it is always smaller than and subsidiary to the bonsai. It serves two purposes: Its relatively small size makes the bonsai appear larger and it forms the third angle in the triangular

[1]Doris W. Froning, "A Winter Project," *Mame Bonsai Growers of America*, 4, no. 5 (January 1980), published by the Mame Bonsai Growers of America, 639 Rosedale Road, Kennett Square, Pa. 19348.

Fig. 18–6 An accessory planting of variegated lilyturf, *Liriope Muscari* cv. Variegata, by Jerald P. Stowell. Courtesy of Associates at Shoppons' Run.

composition of the display. When an accessory is not used, the far edge of the display area becomes the third point of the triangulation.

The following brief listing includes examples and sources of accessories for bonsai:

1. Herbaceous plants grown as a thick clump in a shallow container. Use low-growing dwarf species such as small sedges, dwarf iris, sedums, dwarf horsetail, and other small, compact ground covers, as in Fig. 18–6. Other suggested plant material for accessory plantings is listed in Chapter 14. Interesting material may be found in yards, gardens, vacant lots, or fields. Rock-garden plants are promising candidates, and even weeds may be attractive. The only requirements are that the plant be small and amenable to confinement in a container. Perennials are longer lasting, but annuals should not be ruled out.
2. Small landscape plantings of low-growing plants and rocks in shallow trays, or moss plantings.
3. Small bonsai contrasting in texture and shape to the major bonsai.
4. Viewing stones (Fig. 18–7) as used in Japan are placed on a wooden stand or in a shallow tray. Hut stones, natural rock formations resembling thatched houses, are sometimes placed on or next to a bonsai planting. Several such stones are shown in Fig. 18–8.
5. Bronze or ceramic figurines and artifacts are especially popular in Chinese bonsai (Fig. 18–9).
6. American introductions to bonsai accessories include driftwood, geodes and unusual geological rock formations and petrified wood, and small bowls of goldfish to add a touch of color and suggest a nearby pond.

Fig. 18-7 Japanese viewing stone, 4¼ inches long, in an old bronze suiban.

Fig. 18-8 Japanese stones resembling rustic huts. Height, left to right, 1¼ inches, 1 inch, 1¾ inches.

Fig. 18-9 Small Chinese ceramic figures used in bonsai and miniature gardens.

Accessories have an emotional appeal. They brighten a display by introducing new colors, shapes, and textures. For example, a little clump of plants with flowers or rounded leaves provides a pleasing contrast to the sharp-pointed foliage of a needle evergreen. With a large specimen juniper, a small flowering cherry or a tiny clump of bamboo adds a gentle touch.

More and more bonsai growers are choosing accessory plantings that are compatible environmentally with the bonsai. This could be woodland violets, for example, with bonsai of forest trees, or peperomia and other indigenous southern plants with native warm-climate bonsai. Carried to extremes, environmental associations may be restrictive; used freely and imaginatively, they add an extra meaning to the display.

SCROLL PAINTINGS

A scroll painting or wall hanging at the back of the display provides the apex for the triangular staging and completes the arrangement. This may be a painting, an etching, a woodblock print, or other graphic art appropriate for bonsai. Many bonsai growers hang an Oriental scroll painting at the back of the bonsai display. The following guidelines on the choice and use of scroll paintings are adapted to Western usage.

Guidelines

Size. The scroll may be less than a foot or several feet wide. The long band of paper or silk on which the painting is mounted is hung from the top. A narrow shaft at each end allows the scroll to be rolled into a small cylinder and stored in a minimum amount of space when not in use. When hanging a scroll, select a size that fits comfortably in the available space, neither crowding the display nor lost in the background. Use a narrow scroll where space is limited and a wide one with a large bonsai and display area.

The traditional Oriental scroll is designed to be unrolled for its entire length, which may be 6 feet or more. If the top and bottom borders are too long for the space available in the display area, unroll the portion containing the painting and as much of the top and bottom borders as needed. Carefully secure the still-wound sections with soft twine or other fasteners to prevent them from unrolling.

The painting. Choose a painting with a scene or subject that harmonizes and is in scale with the bonsai. Distant landscapes are highly favored. The bonsai placed in front of the painting becomes a large tree framing the view of small distant trees in the landscape. Other popular subjects are a rising or setting sun, a sprig of bamboo or wild orchid, flowers, rocks and mountains, abstract forms, or, in the Orient, calligraphy. This last is admired for its form and composition as well as its meaning. When selecting paintings as a backdrop for bonsai, look for ones in subdued colors or black ink (*sumi-e*) and avoid bright colors that distract from the bonsai. Whatever subject the painting portrays should be clearly discernible by the viewer at a distance of 4 to 6 feet.

ARRANGING A BONSAI DISPLAY

A Single Bonsai

The most simple display is a single bonsai without a stand or other supportive accessories (Fig. 18–10). It is often used when a bonsai is temporarily brought indoors. For the most pleasing effect, place the bonsai off center, toward the

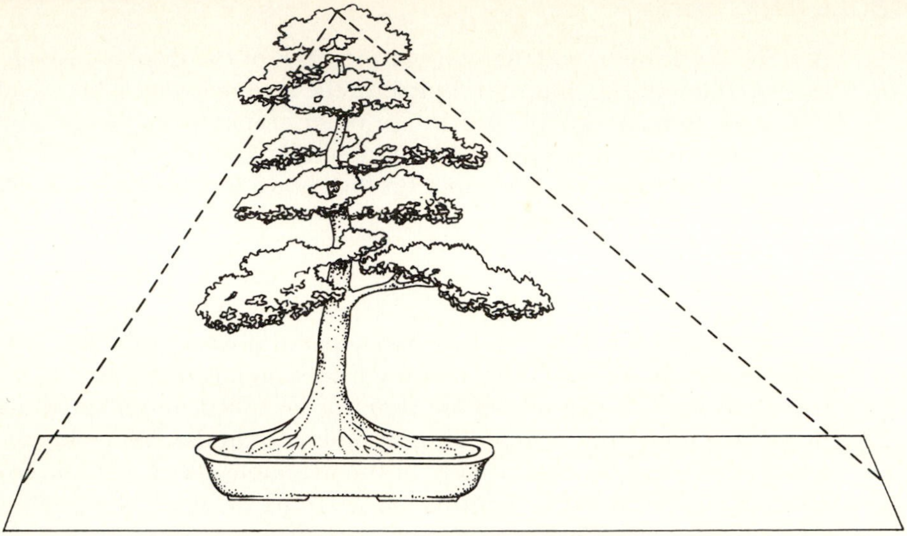

Fig. 18–10 A bonsai display without props.

right or left side of the display area, with the visual weight of the tree extending into the open space of the display area. A triangular pattern is established from the top of the bonsai to either edge of the display area.

Bonsai and Stand

To give the bonsai more emphasis, place it on a stand (Fig. 18–11). Not only is it more clearly defined, but its visual height and weight are increased. To accommodate the larger dimensions of the bonsai and stand, a wider display area may be needed.

Bonsai, Stand, and Accessory

When adding an accessory planting or object, place it at a location where the eye of the viewer moves easily from the bonsai to the accessory. A visual connection can be established by projecting a line from the periphery of the bonsai to the accessory. Such a line is often formed along the top of several branches or a lower branch as in Fig. 18–12.

The Complete Display

Where space is available, a complete display will include a bonsai, a stand, an accessory, and a scroll or other graphics that unite all the components into a triangular pattern. The painting serves as the apex of a triangle with unequal sides. To emphasize the bonsai, the painting is placed closer to the bonsai than

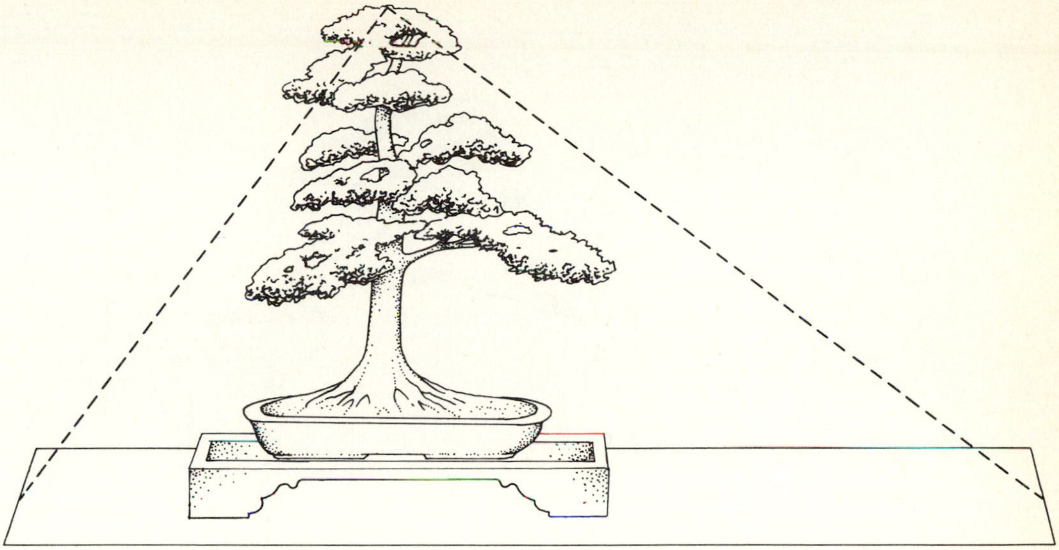

Fig. 18–11 A bonsai and stand.

Fig. 18–12 A display with bonsai, stand, and an accessory planting.

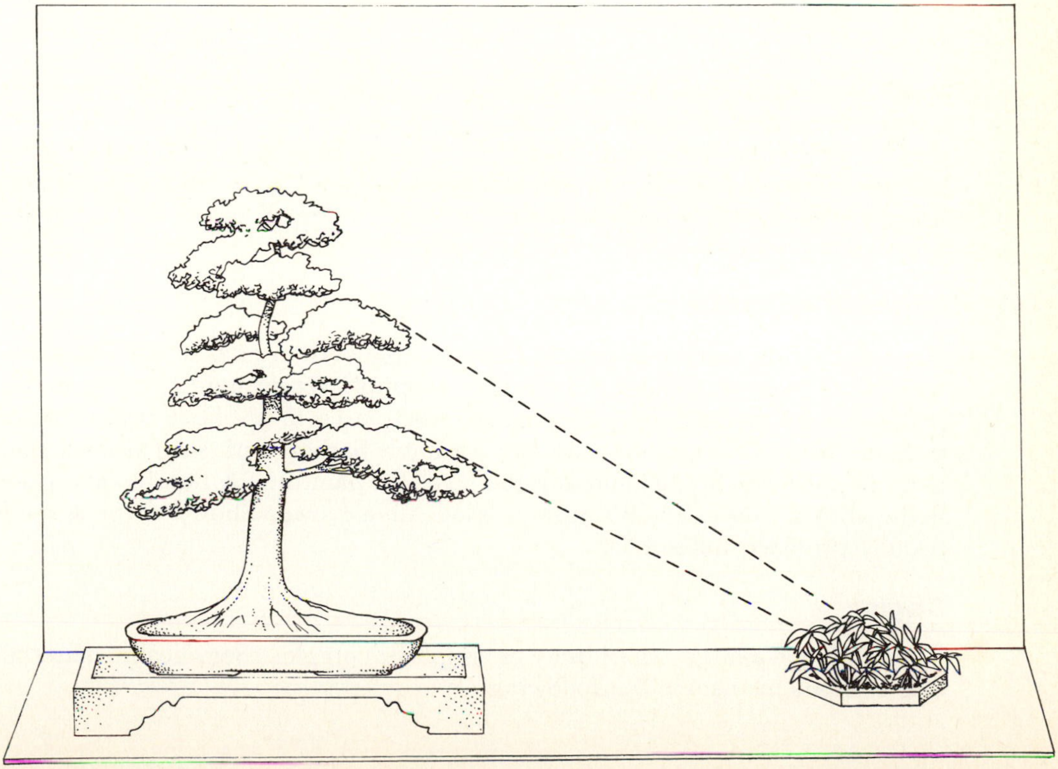

Fig. 18–13 The relationship of an accessory planting to a semicascade bonsai is strengthened by its careful placement under the bonsai.

to the accessory, as shown in Fig. 18–3. It is not necessary to place it in the center of the display area.

Note: With a semicascade bonsai, the accessory is frequently placed at the bottom of a downward line formed along the periphery of the major trunks and branches, as shown in Fig. 18–13.

PUBLIC BONSAI EXHIBITS

A public bonsai exhibit is a small display expanded on a large scale in an informal or elaborate setting. An example of simple yet dramatic staging is seen in Fig. 18–14. Scrolls and paintings are rarely used in public bonsai exhibits, even in Japan. This is mainly because a suitable background, such as a tall plain wall, is not available for hanging the scroll or painting. A notable exception is the annual bonsai exhibit at the Philadelphia Flower Show, where space is usually provided for scrolls.

Staging

The staging at a large exhibit may be simple or complex. Serviceable materials and equipment include the following:

Fig. 18-14 Portion of the Puget Sound Bonsai Association's 1981 exhibition at the Seattle Center. Photo by Charles M. Gordon, Photojournalist.

1. A table or counter about 40 inches high and 30 inches or more deep, often divided into separate areas for each bonsai. Cover the surface with paper, burlap, or other materials in a solid off-white or neutral color. Or fasten a strip of wood or metal a few inches high to each edge and add a layer of pebbles, cork nuggets, or other material to the top of the table.
2. Provide a plain background, slightly higher than the tallest bonsai, whenever possible. Paint or cover it to harmonize with the counter.
3. Set up a protective barrier to separate the bonsai from the viewers. This is usually placed on the floor several feet in front of the display shelves. To make it decorative as well as functional, use posts connected with an attractive rope, a mulch or ground cover, or, as seen in China, rows of potted flowers several feet deep in front of the bonsai.
4. At indoor displays, spotlights and theater lighting add drama. A lighting technician is able to highlight the beauty of each bonsai by skillful manipulation of light. At a minimum, keep the area adequately illuminated for the bonsai to be clearly seen.

5. Identify each bonsai by genus and species. Place unobtrusive labels by each entry, or key the bonsai by numbers on an information sheet. The use of botanical names is strongly recommended; local custom varies on the inclusion of the name of the owner and the tree's common name.

Bonsai in Assigned Spaces. A bonsai show may offer special settings or allotted space of different sizes to be filled by one or several persons. Sometimes space is assigned with specifications, such as the inclusion of stands, accessories, and wall hangings.

Special Focus. An outstanding bonsai may be singled out and given a special setting, such as a free-standing pedestal or a specially designed alcove, perhaps resembling a tokonoma.

PRACTICE AND REVIEW

A Paper Bonsai Display

Materials: Tracing or carbon paper, stiff black or colored paper for cutouts, white background paper, scissors, and glue.

Make a mock-up bonsai exhibit. Take tracings of bonsai trees and stands from the text for the cutouts. Outline a display area and arrange the bonsai for a display. Include scrolls or paintings and accessory plantings, if you wish.

Staging a Bonsai Exhibit

Materials: Bonsai started by members of a group; stands, purchased or homemade; and wall hangings, if available.

With the information given in the chapter, stage an informal bonsai exhibit. Often a table placed against a plain painted wall will serve as a counter and background for the display. If necessary, cover the table with plain paper or other material. Designate areas for each person to use. Label each bonsai with its botanical name and any additional information the group wants to include.

Visiting Public Bonsai Exhibits

Attend bonsai exhibits. Dates and locations of area shows may be obtained from the major bonsai organizations listed in Appendix A. Observe how the bonsai are displayed, especially their placement in relation to other objects such as accessories. Also examine the stands and the choice of the stand for a particular bonsai. Analyze the features of the show you especially like and include them in future bonsai displays.

Accessory Plantings

Materials: Potting tools and potting mix, containers, and plants for a small planting.

Accessory plantings are treated with a great amount of freedom in the selection of both the plant material and the container. Their use can be innovative. Consult the list of suggested species for accessory plantings in Chapter 14. Visit nurseries and garden centers for cultivated plants or plan a trip to collect wildings from meadows, woodlands, or marshes as accessories for bonsai in your collection. Look for plants such as maples, pines, bald cypresses, figs, and spruces in their natural environment. For planters, use old tiles, weathered wood, bark, slabs of fired clay, rocks, and other objects as well as ceramic containers.

ADDITIONAL READING

MORSE, EDWARD S., *Japanese Homes and Their Surroundings*. New York: Dover, 1961. This is an unaltered republication of Morse's copiously illustrated and detailed description of Japanese homes originally published in 1886.

Note: Contemporary photographic albums of Japanese bonsai are highly recommended for study and pleasure. For examples of displaying bonsai, observe the choice of a stand, the placement of the bonsai, and the nature and location of accessory plantings.

Part Two
Bonsai by Species

INTRODUCTION

Part Two provides information on training methods and growing needs of warm- and cold-climate species frequently used for bonsai.

Information on each species includes the geographic origin as an indication of the extent of the species' range and its native environment. Growth habit, height, leaf size, flowers or fruit, bonsai forms, training, and care are described. For most listed species, cold-temperature tolerance is keyed to the USDA Plant Hardiness Zone Map (Appendix D); this is a broad indicator that may be modified by colder, warmer, drier, or more humid microenvironments within each zone.

Light requirements are the levels needed for normal, healthy growth. Interior light and temperature ranges are given for indoor bonsai.

Pruning or wiring is mentioned for special or unusual circumstances. As used here, a basic potting mix is a mix containing equal parts of soil, sphagnum peat moss, and coarse sand, or any mix that is suitable for most bonsai.

Watering refers to the normal watering schedules for bonsai described in Chapter 10. Fertilizing is mentioned when a species needs more or less than the amount of fertilizer generally provided. Likewise, regular intervals of repotting young bonsai every two years are implied unless stated otherwise.

Species easily propagated by seed are noted.

Hortus Third, as revised and expanded by the staff of the Liberty Hyde Bailey Hortorium,* is the source of much of the information regarding tree height,

*Liberty Hyde Bailey Hortorium Staff, *Hortus Third* (New York: Macmillan, 1976).

leaf size, and descriptions of flowers and fruit. It is recommended as a reference for further information.

The descriptive material is arranged alphabetically by genus and by species within each genus. The following list is a cross-reference by common name and genus.

Common and Botanical Names of Trees, Shrubs, and Vines for Bonsai

Common Name	Genus
Andromeda	*Pieris*
Apple, crab apple	*Malus*
Apricot	*Prunus*
Aralia	*Polyscias*
Australian pine	*Casuarina*
Arborvitae	*Thuja*
Azalea	*Rhododendron*
Bald cypress	*Taxodium*
Barbados cherry	*Malpighia*
Beech	*Fagus*
Black olive	*Bucida*
Bottlebrush	*Callistemon*
Bougainvillea	*Bougainvillea*
Boxwood	*Buxus*
Brazilian pepper tree	*Schinus*
Brush cherry	*Syzygium*
Buddhist pine	*Podocarpus*
Buttonwood	*Conocarpus*
Camellia	*Camellia*
Cape myrtle	*Myrsine*
Carob tree	*Ceretonia*
Cedar	*Cedrus*
Cherry	*Prunus*
Chinese box orange	*Severinia*
Citrus	*Citrus*
Coontie	*Zamia*
Cotoneaster	*Cotoneaster*
Crape myrtle	*Lagerstroemia*
Cycad	*Cycas*
Cypress	*Cupressus*
Elephant bush	*Portulacaria*
Elfin herb	*Cuphea*
Elm	*Ulmus*

Enkianthus	*Enkianthus*
Eugenia	*Syzygium*
False cypress	*Chamaecyparis*
Fig	*Ficus*
Fir	*Abies*
Fire thorn	*Pyracantha*
Forsythia	*Forsythia*
Fukien tea	*Ehretia*
Gardenia	*Gardenia*
Golden larch	*Pseudolarix*
Hackberry	*Celtis*
Hawthorn	*Crataegus*
Heavenly bamboo	*Nandina*
Hemlock	*Tsuga*
Holly	*Ilex*
Holly olive	*Osmanthus*
Honeysuckle	*Lonicera*
Hornbeam	*Carpinus*
Horsetail tree	*Casuarina*
Ivy	*Hedera*
Jaboticaba	*Myrciaria*
Jade plant	*Crassula*
Japanese cedar	*Cryptomeria*
Jasmine	*Jasminum*
Juniper	*Juniperus*
Kumquat	*Fortunella*
Lantana	*Lantana*
Larch	*Larix*
Maidenhair tree	*Ginkgo*
Miniature holly	*Malpighia*
Maple	*Acer*
Myrtle	*Myrtus*
Natal plum	*Carissa*
Nandina	*Nandina*
Norfolk Island pine	*Araucaria*
Olive	*Olea*
Orange jasmine	*Murraya*
Pepper tree	*Schinus*
Pine	*Pinus*
Pittosporum	*Pittosporum*
Plum	*Prunus*

Podocarpus	*Podocarpus*
Pomegranate	*Punica*
Powder puff	*Calliandra*
Privet	*Ligustrum*
Quince, Chinese	*Cydonia*
Quince, flowering	*Chaenomeles*
Rhododendron	*Rhododendron*
Rosemary	*Rosmarinus*
Sageretia	*Sageretia*
Schefflera	*Brassaia*
Sea grape	*Coccoloba*
Serissa	*Serissa*
Silk oak	*Grevillea*
Snow in June	*Serissa*
Spruce	*Picea*
Star jasmine	*Trachelospermum*
Texas ebony	*Pithecellobium*
Water elm	*Planera*
Willow	*Salix*
Wisteria	*Wisteria*
Witch hazel	*Hamamelis*
Yew	*Taxus*
Zelkova	*Zelkova*

ADDITIONAL READING

BAILEY, LIBERTY HYDE, AND ETHEL ZOE BAILEY, comps., revised and expanded by the staff of the Liberty Hyde Hortorium, Cornell University, *Hortus Third*. New York: Macmillan, and London: Collier Macmillan, 1976. An unsurpassed botanical reference on thousands of woody and herbaceous plants cultivated in the North Temperate Zone, including most species popular for bonsai.

CARE AND CULTURE BY SPECIES

ABIES FIR

These tall evergreen conifers, native to high mountainous regions in the North Temperate Zone, are usually shaped into bonsai with upright, slanting, or cascading trunks. Firs require a cool, humid growing area protected from hot midday sun. They do not survive where the summers are hot or the air is heavily polluted.

Fig. A1–1 Alpine fir, *Abies lasiocarpa.* Courtesy of R. Kataoka.

To slow down the lengthening of a branch, remove the terminal bud; shoots from the secondary buds will be smaller and shorter. Enrich the potting mix with an extra amount of sphagnum peat moss or other moisture-holding materials except clay. Do not let the mix become dry between watering.

A. lasiocarpa Nutt. ALPINE FIR 60–100 ft.
Alaska to New Mexico. Zone 3.

Alpine fir, also known as Rocky Mountain fir, is one of the smallest of the Pacific firs. A group planting of firs collected in the Rockies is shown in Fig. A1–1. This species has pale bluish-green needles to 1½ inch long and 4-inch cones. The cultivar Compacta is a dwarf form.

A.l. var. *arizonica*, Arizona fir, is distinguished by its creamy white corky bark, Zone 5.

ACER MAPLE

The maples described here respond favorably to bonsai techniques and are among the most valued species for bonsai. Within the genus, species may be found for nearly all styles of bonsai, from a straight vertical trunk to a cascade. These are graceful trees with curved trunks or branches and soft foliage.

Maples are shallow-rooted, a desirable feature for bonsai. Leaves, arranged in pairs and usually lobed, are reduced with bonsai training. Small flowers appear from late winter to early summer. The winged seeds are called samaras. Maple bonsai are outstanding for their colorful fall foliage. Species used for bonsai are found in areas spanning thousands of miles from Zone 3 southward to the northern limits of Zone 10.

The thin tissue of their leaves frequently make maples vulnerable to "sunburn." In all climates, protect maple bonsai from strong winds and the drying, scorching hot summer sun.

During the growing season, provide a location with partial shade and, if possible, early morning sun. Several hours of sun daily shortens the length of the internodes and heightens the color of the fall foliage.

Pruning presents no problems. Unlike most trees, after maples are pruned drastically, they send out new shoots from buds beneath the bark, as well as from buds already formed on the shoots and branches.

Maples exude an alarming flow of sap if pruned early in the spring. There is some question as to whether this is harmful to a bonsai. Moderate pruning is not damaging, but the loss of sap from repeated and excessive pruning over several years may weaken the tree. "Bleeding" can be avoided by pruning later in the season.

Bud formation in pairs on opposite sides of a shoot establishes an unwanted branching pattern. This is easily remedied by removing one of the two buds in early spring. Tools are not necessary. Simply rub or snap off the bud with the fingers. From time to time, maples sprout new shoots from buds at unexpected, and often unwanted, locations on the trunk and branches. Remove these buds selectively to eliminate future nonconforming branches.

When maples are only a few years old, their wood becomes stiff, hard, and brittle. Withhold water for a day or two prior to wiring, and wire with caution. Use either aluminum wire, or copper wire wrapped with strips of paper or other material to soften contact with the thin bark. If extensive repositioning is necessary, bend the wired trunk or branch gradually at intervals of several weeks or a month.

Give maples plenty of water to compensate for the large amount of moisture their thin leaves lose through evaporation. Water regularly and protect them from drying conditions.

Use a basic mix; only *A. barbatum* seems to prefer a mix that is slightly alkaline.

A. barbatum Michx. FLORIDA MAPLE 50 ft.
Florida to Texas, Virginia, and Missouri. Zone 7.

The gray bark, smooth on young trees, becomes shallowly ridged and furrowed on older trunks. Leaves are 1½ to 3¾ inches long and 1½ to 3 inches wide. Because this Florida species grows naturally in clay or sandy limestone soil, use a neutral or slightly alkaline potting mix.

A. Buergeranum Miq. TRIDENT MAPLE 50 ft.
China. Zone 6.

This is a tree (Figs. 7–10 and 12–6) with gray bark which tends to shed on older trees. Leaves are 2¼ to 4 inches long, with three lobes. The foliage turns red and orange in fall. The tree is susceptible to winter damage from below-freezing temperatures.

As it ages, this maple develops a distinctive bark (Fig. 12–5) and makes a spectacular bonsai by surrounding the base of its trunk with thick, molten roots. It is superb for planting on a rock, as seen in Fig. A2–1. In time, the roots spread over the rock like lava. To achieve this effect, follow the techniques for planting roots over a rock described in Chapter 15. Use a tree with many fibrous roots. First shorten the trunk or trunks drastically to direct the tree's energy into root growth. Fasten the roots tightly to the rock and secure them with twine or rubber bands. Be sure that the base of the trunk is placed squarely on the stone. To encourage roots to thicken, the entire stone is often buried in the ground or in a large container, or the roots above the soil are covered with a heavy layer of potting mix and moss. According to Andrew N. Lenz, writing in the *Bonsai Journal*, a thick covering of soil tends to produce unnatural, bulbous roots, while with a light covering of potting mix, the roots reflect the contour of the rock as they slowly spread over its surface.*

A. campestre L. HEDGE MAPLE 35–80 ft.
Europe, Turkey, Caucasus, and Iran. Zone 5.

This is a tall shrub or roundheaded tree. The trunk develops a fissured corky bark with age. The leaves, 2 to 4 inches across with three to five lobes, are thicker than those on most maples. Autumn foliage is a clear yellow.

A. Ginnala Maxim. AMUR MAPLE 20 ft.
China, Mongolia, Manchuria, Korea, and Japan. Zone 5.

On this fast-growing tree or shrub, the leaves are 3½ inches long and 2½ inches wide, with three (or sometimes five) lobes, the central of which is largest. Amur maple is short-lived and susceptible to blight but is grown for its brilliant scarlet fall color and interesting bark.

A. japonicum Thunb. FULL-MOON MAPLE 20–30 ft.
Japan. Zone 5.

The unusual leaves on this shrub or tree are 3 to 5½ inches long with seven to thirteen lobes, and turn gold or crimson in the fall. This is an attractive bonsai subject with many forms and varieties. The cultivar Aureum is shown in Fig. A2–2.

*Andrew N. Lenz, "Root Formation in Trident Maples," *Journal of the American Bonsai Society*, 15, no. 2 (Summer 1981), 40–43.

Fig. A2–1 Trident maples planted over a rock in Japan.

Fig. A2–2 Golden full-moon maple, *Acer japonicum* cv. Aureum, by William N. Valavanis.

A. palmatum Thunb. JAPANESE MAPLE 20–50 ft.
Korea, China, and Japan. Zone 5.

When relatively young, this species is a large shrub or small, spreading tree. With age it becomes a tall, striking tree with one or many trunks, usually well branched. The green leaves are 2 to 4 inches long. Examples are shown in winter (Fig. 2–1), spring (Fig. 14–1), and summer (Fig. 7–4).

A. palmatum produces many varieties and numerous cultivars, which range in color from green to many shades of red, red-purple, yellow, and gold, with lobes that may become finely incised and featherly. Generally, the species of a genus is stronger than its varieties and cultivars. For the inexperienced novice, *A. palmatum* will prove to be sturdier for bonsai than most of the exotic or rare forms. A notable exception is cv. Kiyo-Hime (Fig. A2–3), a vigorous grower with small green leaves and dense horizontal branching. Among many other attractive cultivars are Dissectum, with weeping branches and finely dissected green leaves. Atropurpureum, Crimson Queen, and Burgundy Lace have weeping branches and red dissected leaves. Each lobe is subdivided, creating a threadlike or lacy effect. (These and similar red-leaf cultivars are popularly known as *A.p. dissectum atropurpureum*.) Give extra protection to bonsai with finely dissected thin leaves. Keep them out of direct sun, except early in the morning, and away from drying winds to prevent browning and shriveling of the delicate tissue. And, of course, do not defoliate such trees.

Fig. A2–3 A yatsubusa form of *Acer palmatum,* cv. Kiyo-Hime, among the Japanese bonsai at the U.S. National Arboretum. Photo courtesy of USDA.

A. rubrum L. AMERICAN RED MAPLE 100 ft.
Newfoundland to Florida, Minnesota, Iowa, and Texas. Zone 3.

This is one of the most widely distributed species in America. Leaves are divided into three or five lobes, varying from 3 to 6 inches across. They readily reduce in size when grown as bonsai. In early spring, before the leaves appear, many small, inconspicuous flowers cover the tree with a reddish haze. In the fall, the foliage turns a brilliant red and orange. The gray bark, smooth on young trees, forms shallow ridges with age. Planted on a rock, the roots show a slight tendency to spread over a rock somewhat in the manner of *A. Buergeranum*. American red maple is not demanding in its soil requirements. It withstands periods of dryness and tolerates wet conditions better than most trees. In a container (Figs. 14–5.1 and 14–5.4) it develops thin roots, is tolerant of pruning and wiring, and does not readily attract pests and pathogens. With all these highly desirable traits, it would seem uncharitable to mention shortcomings. However, this species does not send out new shoots as readily as *A. palmatum*, and its relatively long petioles foster open rather than compact foliage.

A.r. var. *trilobum* (C. Koch) has smaller leaves with three lobes. This shorter, more compact tree is found from Florida west to Texas and north to Illinois, Quebec, and Nova Scotia.

A. saccharum subsp. **leucoderme** Desmarais *(A. leucoderme)* CHALK-MAPLE 30 ft.
North Carolina to Georgia and Louisiana.

The bark is a chalky gray-brown; the leaves, with three to five pointed lobes, are 2 to 3 inches across and yellowish green beneath. Fruits are brick red and tan. An example of this beautiful little tree is shown in Fig. A2–4.

Fig. A2–4 Chalk maple, *Acer saccharum,* subsp. *leucoderme,* at the Monastery of the Holy Spirit, Conyers, Georgia.

ADDITIONAL READING

VERTREES, J. D., *Japanese Maples, Momyi and Kaede* (Forest Grove, Ore: Timber Press, 1978). A definitive work listing and describing the many varieties and forms of *Acer palmatum*.

YOUNG, DOROTHY S. "Acer Rubrum: A Native Maple for Bonsai," *Journal of the American Bonsai Society*, 7, no. 3 (Summer 1973), 30–31.

VALAVANIS, WILLIAM N., "Plant Profile: Kiyo-Hime Yatsubusa Japanese Maple," *International Bonsai*, 1, no. 3 (Autumn 1979), 16–18. This issue contains extensive information on growing maples as bonsai.

ARAUCARIA ARAUCARIA

The araucaria most often used for bonsai is the juvenile form of Norfolk Island pine, *A. heterophylla*, in single or multitrunk plantings. Its thin trunk is slow to thicken and shows little taper, but the soft foliage is unusually attractive, even on young plants. Small plants may be grouped together effectively into attractive forest plantings.

Provide warm year-round temperatures and keep from freezing. In summer, give the bonsai partial shade, out of hot sun. In winter, choose a cool indoor location with temperatures from 50° to 60°F. and medium to strong light, but little direct sun. When trees in healthy condition are pruned, the branches send out new growth readily. Avoid removing the top of the trunk; this bonsai does not produce a new apex except on young seedlings. Pinch new shoots on branches while they are still soft.

Use a basic potting mix that drains well. Keep the soil partially moist, but not wet, between waterings. The slow-growing roots will require repotting about every third year.

Norfolk Island pine has few problems caused by pests. It may be propagated by seed as a conditioned tree for lower than usual light levels as described in Chapter 16.

A. heterophylla Franco *(A. excelsa)* NORFOLK ISLAND PINE
50–200 ft.
South Pacific. Zone 10.

This coniferous evergreen (not a true pine) has horizontal branches in symmetrical whorls. The needles are awl-shaped and up to ½ inch long on young trees; on mature trees, the needles become flat and 2 inches long. This subtropical species is enjoyed as indoor bonsai in cold climates.

BOUGAINVILLEA BOUGAINVILLEA

Bougainvillea are popular for bonsai in warm and subtropical climates. These vines are easily trained into treelike forms. As indoor bonsai, they should be moved outdoors in summer.

Bougainvillea bonsai are seen as single or double trunks (Fig. 15-1) in many styles from upright to semicascade. Select a specimen with a strong trunk that can support the flowers. Arrange the branches to provide space for the flowers, which are often borne continuously during the growing season.

Bougainvillea grow best with bright light and sun. If indoors, place them at a sunny south window or under high levels of artificial light.

Cut back each branch immediately after it has flowered. In warm climates with a long growing season, bougainvillea respond well to training by the grow-and-clip method described in Chapter 15. These plants do not have demanding soil requirements, but good drainage is vital. Use a basic potting mix and allow it to become moderately dry between waterings. Water lightly after a period of profuse bloom to encourage a rest period. Repot the sparse, slow-growing roots as needed, generally at three-year intervals. Late spring or early summer is preferred. Remove or shorten large roots but do not prune the root mass severely.

B. glabra Choisy PAPER FLOWER, BOUGAINVILLEA
Brazil. Zone 10.

This warm-climate woody vine has small spines, smooth, slender, 1-inch leaves, and profuse purple and magenta flowers. It flowers almost continuously and is easy to grow. Many dwarf forms are available with flowers in a variety of colors.

B. spectabilis Willd. BOUGAINVILLEA
Brazil. Zone 10.

This species has larger spines, up to 2 inches long, with brick red flowers, fading to orange. There are many forms and cultivars with clear-colored flowers.

BRASSAIA SCHEFFLERA

While schefflera lack a traditional treelike appearance, their large leaves at the end of long, upright petioles have an exotic tropical look, as in Fig. 16-2. As bonsai, they are unsurpassed for home interiors with little or no direct sunlight.

They grow outdoors in warm climates. As indoor bonsai, maintain temperatures between 60° and 70°F. or higher for maximum growth. They like bright light outdoors but adjust to low interior light levels.

New shoots soon develop where a trunk or branch is pruned. Pruning is preferred to wiring the soft trunk and branches.

A basic potting mix is satisfactory. Do not let the soil become dry between waterings. Schefflera may also be planted on a rock without soil, placed in a tray of water, and fertilized lightly. This has a pronounced dwarfing effect and allows the bonsai to be enjoyed in a office or other location where daily watering is not possible.

Drastic root pruning and frequent repotting are not necessary. This plant, which is not adversely affected by bonsai techniques, is highly recommended for the novice or for areas of low light where other species are difficult to grow.

B. actinophylla Endl. *(Schefflera actinophylla)* SCHEFFLERA, UMBRELLA TREE 40 ft.
Australia. Zone 9.

In warm climates, this is a fast growing tree, with a soft, fleshy trunk on young plants. The large compound leaves in whorls suggest a group of parasols. Schefleras are resistant to insects and disease and are one of the few plants that can be kept indoors the year round under low levels of light.

A dwarf form, Arboricola, no taller than 4 feet, with small compound leaves, is also tolerant of low levels of indoor light. Its requirements are similar to those of *B. actinophylla*.

BUCIDA Black Olive

Black olive, a subtropical tree with alternate leathery leaves, requires high temperatures and high light levels. As a bonsai, it is a relatively slow grower that does not respond quickly to pruning. Watch for thorns when wiring the dense branches.

Use a basic container mix with good drainage that is neutral or slightly alkaline to duplicate the calcareous soil of the Florida Keys, where the tree grows naturally. Keep the mix moist between waterings.

B. buceras L. BLACK OLIVE 50 ft.
Florida, West Indies, and Mexico to Panama. Zone 10.

This is an evergreen tree with dense foliage and rounded crown, seen as a handsome landscape and street tree in southern Florida. Its branches are armed with short, sharp spines. The leathery leaves, green above and yellowish green beneath, are 1 inch long. Inconspicuous ⅛-inch greenish-yellow flowers on long stalks are followed by small black fruit that resemble olives.

BUXUS Box or Boxwood

With their small leaves, dense growth, and shallow roots, boxwoods are excellent bonsai material. Most often they are shaped to upright or slanting styles; the stiffness of the wood limits its manipulation by wiring. Boxwoods grow in partial shade or partial sun. Shelter them from hot midday sun. In cold climates, provide winter protection.

Boxwoods can withstand repeated pruning and trimming. They are easily wired and bent when young; exercise caution when wiring the hard, stiff older wood.

Use a basic potting mix and do not let it become dry between waterings.

When repotting every few years, trim the root ball sufficiently to create space for new potting mix. On old bonsai, prune the roots using the wedge method (described in Chapter 10).

Boxwoods are easily rooted from cuttings. Young specimens, four or five years old, are popular for rock plantings, saikei, and minibonsai. Boxwoods are also attractive as indoor bonsai in cool areas of the home or in an indoor light garden.

B. microphylla Siebold & Zucc. 3 ft.
Japan. Zone 6.

This is a slow-growing compact evergreen shrub with glossy dark green leaves ½ to 1 inch long. The rounded leaves are broadest at or above the midrib. The cultivar Compacta, known as Kingsville boxwood (Fig. 17–10), is a dwarf form popular for bonsai.

B.m. var. **japonica** Rehd. & E. H. Wils. Japanese box 6 ft.
This variety, native to Japan, is larger and hardier than the species. It is a vigorous grower with spreading branches.

B.m. var. **koreana** Nakai Korean boxwood 2 ft.
Korea. Zone 4.

This small upright shrub native to Korea has dark green leaves less than ½ inch long. It is hardier than the species and grows very slowly.

B. sempervirens L. COMMON BOXWOOD 3–15 ft.
Europe, North Africa, and western Asia. Zone 6.

This is the Old World box used in the South, sometimes called English boxwood because it was brought to Virginia by the English colonists in the seventeenth century. The leaves are slightly larger than *B. microphylla* and broader at or below the midrib.

CALLIANDRA POWDER PUFF

These tropical shrubs and trees, grown primarily for their showy flowers, are usually styled with graceful upright trunks as bonsai. They are accustomed to bright light and subtropical climates. Indoors, keep this bonsai at a sunny south window or under high levels of artificial light, with temperatures of 65° to 75°F. or higher.

Immediately after flowering, cut each shoot back enough to retain a compact shape. Wire when the wood is young; old wood is brittle.

Use a basic potting mix and keep the soil moist, but not wet, between waterings. Fertilize regularly to strengthen the plant and induce frequent flowering.

This species may be propagated from seed.

Fig. C1–1 Flowers of dwarf powder puff, *Calliandra emarginata.*

C. emarginata Benth. DWARF POWDER PUFF 15 ft.
Southern Mexico to Honduras.

This is a warm-climate shrub or small tree with dense foliage, alternate leaves, and 1-inch pink or red powder puff–like flowers (Fig. C1–1), which bloom profusely. The flower buds resemble small red raspberries.

CALLISTEMON BOTTLEBRUSH

These are small trees or shrubs with alternate leaves and showy red or yellow flowers resembling a bottlebrush. As bonsai, shape this species to an upright, curved, or slanting trunk and open crown.

This is a sun-loving plant for warm climates; when grown indoors, give it a south sunny window and a warm 65° to 75°F. temperature.

Prune regularly after flowering and heavily every two or three years to maintain a compact bonsai shape.

Use a basic potting mix and let the soil become moderately dry between waterings. Fertilize regularly as for other flowering bonsai.

Bottlebrush is easily propagated by seed. Gather seed in the summer and allow the capsules to open in boxes or paper bags prior to sowing.

C. phoeniceus Lindl. BOTTLEBRUSH 8 ft.
New South Wales and Western Australia.

This is a one of several callistemons native to Australia. It is a shrub with spines and narrow leaves to 4 inches and red flowers. It grows well outdoors in California and other warm regions.

CAMELLIA CAMELLIA

These evergreen shrubs or small trees have alternate leathery leaves, dense foliage, and beautiful flowers. Arrange the trunk and branches in an essentially upright structure with a slanting, curved, or semicascade trunk. Camellias thrive in partial shade and a slightly humid atmosphere. Full sun is harmful, and full shade will retard bloom.

As with other flowering bonsai, prune each shoot or branch immediately after it has flowered. Postpone more extensive pruning until spring, but avoid severe pruning at any one time.

Start with a basic potting mix that drains well and is neutral or slightly acid, and enrich it with organic matter such as oak leaf-mold. Repot in the spring. Keep the soil moist, especially during the flowering season, but not wet. Water thoroughly so that water will reach all the roots. Fertilize regularly to promote flowering.

Remove a number of the flower buds, especially those crowded in one area, to distribute the flowers throughout the bonsai and conserve the plant's vigor. Do this after the buds are clearly formed and before they are mature.

C. japonica L. COMMON CAMELLIA 45 ft.
Coastal Japan, South Korea, and Taiwan. Zone 8.

This plant has dark green shiny evergreen leaves up to 4 in. long. Roots form near the surface. Flowers have five petals, single or double, are red to pink to white or variegated, and measure 5 inches across. It has many cultivars.

C. Sasanqua Thunb. SASANQUA CAMELLIA 15 ft.
South Japan. Zone 7.

This camellia has slender twigs and profuse single or double flowers with a delicate fragrance and a range of colors similar to *C. japonica*. However, this species flowers in the autumn, from September to December. It is smaller and hardier to cold than *C. japonica*, and preferred for bonsai by many growers.

CARISSA CARISSA

This is an evergreen, often spiny, shrub or a small tree with opposite leaves, native to the Old World tropics. Milky sap is visible when it is pruned. The natural forms of this species vary widely from upright to cascade. Pruning produces the dense, compact foliage wanted for bonsai. It is popular for indoor bonsai in northern climates.

It is grown outdoors in warm, sunny climates the year-round; indoors, temperatures should be 65° to 75°F. For flowers, provide a sunny south window or high levels of artificial light.

Prune carissa throughout the growing season as needed; cut back branches that have flowered except where fruit is wanted. Wire when the plant is young. Older wood becomes stiff and hard to bend.

Use a porous, medium-rich mix. Repot in warm weather when the roots are in active growth. This will be during the spring in the South and during the summer months in colder climates. Remove or shorten overly large roots, but do not reduce the root mass severely. Keep soil slightly moist between waterings, and fertilize regularly to encourage flowering.

Carissa can be easily propagated by seed or cuttings.

C. grandiflora A. DC. NATAL PLUM, AMATUNGULU 18 ft.
South Africa. Zone 9.

This much-branched woody shrub has dark green leaves, spines, and fragrant 2-inch white flowers followed by red plumlike fruit. Cultivars include Bonsai, Boxwood Beauty, and Nana Compacta.

CARPINUS HORNBEAM, IRONWOOD

These small, bushy deciduous trees may be shaped to an upright, curved, or slanting trunk style. They are also excellent for multitrunk and group plantings as well as specimen bonsai.

They need partial sun or light shade. As a bonsai, hornbeam does not respond to pruning as readily as the maples; allow more time to develop dense branching.

Use a basic potting mix and keep the soil moist, but not wet, between waterings. For less frequent watering, add extra moisture-retention ingredients such as sphagnum peat moss to the mix. Repot every year or two in the spring and trim roots regularly, especially the taproot, if present. Do not let roots become so large that drastic pruning will be required. If large roots are present, remove them over a period of time.

C. Betulus L. EUROPEAN HORNBEAM 60 ft.
Europe to Iran. Zone 5.

Larger and with thicker leaves than the American hornbeam, the leaves on this species are 4 inches long, turn yellow in the fall, and remain on the tree during the winter. The flowers, which appear as catkins, are 5 inches long. Large, smooth buds of ¼ to ⅓ inch, distinguish this species from American hornbeam, whose buds measure ⅙ inch or less and are often fringed with hair. The European hornbeam is slow-growing and less demanding in care than the American species.

C. caroliniana T. Walt. AMERICAN HORNBEAM, IRONWOOD 40 ft.
Maryland to Florida, west to Texas and southern Illinois. Zone 7.

This is a handsome, small, bushy deciduous tree. Trunks are fluted on old trees. The bark is blue-gray. The 4-inch leaves turn scarlet and orange in the fall. Its catkins are 4 inches long. This species is commonly found growing in wetlands and along streams.

C.c. var. **virginiana** Fern. NORTHERN AMERICAN HORNBEAM 40 ft.
From New England to South Carolina, west to Minnesota and Arkansas. Zone 2.

This is the northern form of American hornbeam. It has ash-gray bark and smaller and narrower leaves. Its bonsai training is similar to that of *C. caroliniana.*

C. cordata Blume CHINESE HORNBEAM 50 ft.
Northern Asia, China, and Japan. Zone 5.

A hornbeam with scaly bark, 5-inch-long leaves, and catkins 3 to 4 inches long.

C. laxiflora Blume JAPANESE HORNBEAM 50 ft.
Japan. Zone 6.

This hornbeam, popular for bonsai in Japan, has the smallest leaves of all: 2¾ inches. The catkins are of the same length.

CASUARINA AUSTRALIAN PINE

These are strange-looking trees or shrubs. Their twigs are slender, jointed shoots somewhat resembling horsetails (*Equisetum*), and the leaves are minute and scale-like. In subtropical climates, collected specimens of casuarinas are popular with bonsai growers as a substitute for pine. According to Ted T. Tsukiyama, an accomplished bonsai grower in Honolulu, casuarinas can be shaped to nearly all bonsai styles.*

Casuarinas grow best where they receive plenty of sun, but they are tolerant of partial shade. In cold climates, protect them from freezing. Use a basic mix, or increase the proportion of sand if the bonsai can be watered frequently.

These trees can be trimmed continuously by plucking the jointed shoots to develop compact branches.

C. Cunninghamiana Miq. AUSTRALIAN PIN, IRONWOOD 50 ft.
Eastern Australia. Zone 10.

Cultivated in Hawaii and southern portions of California and Florida, the Australian pine produces a symmetrical, pyramidal crown and many root suck-

*Ted T. Tsukiyama, "Hawaii Matsu," *Journal of the American Bonsai Society*, 8, no. 3 (Fall 1974), 51–53.

ers. It is hardier than *C. equisetifolia* and can survive occasional below-freezing temperatures. It is not tolerant of salt spray.

C. equisetifolia J. R. Forst. & G. Forst. HORSETAIL TREE 70 ft.
Southeastern Australia to Pacific Islands. Zone 10.

This species is used extensively in Hawaii and southern Florida. It has widely spaced horizontal branches and forms an open, straggly crown. It does not produce suckers at the roots and will withstand salt spray without injury.

CEDRUS CEDAR

Although many evergreens are called cedars, members of the *Cedrus* genus are the true cedars. They have wide-spreading branches, gray bark, and upright, oval cones. The pointed, angled needles are clustered in tufts on short spurs. Cedars usually grow in mild climates. They are long-lived and develop open crowns with age.

Young species of *Cedrus* can be shaped to nearly any style of bonsai. They are available as container-grown nursery stock 1 to 4 feet tall.

Provide a growing area with partial sun and open shade. Avoid exposure to hot sun or drying conditions. Cedars are accustomed to cool mountain air and grow best where the soil is warm and the air comfortably cool and moist.

Cedrus species may readily be pruned and wired when young. Trim or pinch new shoots while they are soft and tender. For potting, use a basic mix that drains well; extensive stands of these trees are found growing on mountain sites that are unusually well drained. Instead of the usual practice of early spring repotting, postpone potting and repotting cedars until June or later in the summer. By then the soil will be warm and the roots will be growing actively. At each repotting, trim the taproot if it has elongated. Do this regularly to avoid more drastic root pruning at a later date.

C. atlantica G. Manetti ex Carrière ATLAS CEDAR 100 ft.
North Africa. Zone 7.

This is a large pyramidal tree with ascending branches when young and 3-inch cones. Its bluish-green needles are less than 1 in. long. Cultivars Argentea and Glauca (Fig. 7-2) are attractive forms with silvery needles.

C. Deodara G. Don DEODAR CEDAR 150 ft.
Himalayas. Zone 7.

This is a symmetrical pyramidal tree with drooping branches and blue-green needles less than 1 inch long. Its cones are 5 inches long.

C. libani A. Rich. CEDAR OF LEBANON 100 ft.
Asia Minor. Zone 6.

C.l. var. *brevifolia*, known for its many dwarf and slow-growing forms, is a tree with spreading or ascending branches. It has 1-in. needles, bright or dark green, and 4-inch cones.

CELTIS HACKBERRY

Hackberries are deciduous trees with alternate leaves that are lopsided at the base and turn yellow in the fall.

As bonsai, they are often seen as well-branched upright trunks with corky warts that add interest.

These trees are vigorous growers. Place them in partial sun and open shade. They are tolerant of both pruning and wiring. Use a basic potting mix, but keep it slightly moist between waterings. Because their roots grow actively in a container, repot in the spring of each or every other year, whenever the roots fill the container. During each repotting, prune any large taplike roots to encourage the growth of fibrous roots. Apply fertilizer regularly.

C. laevigata Willd. MISSISSIPPI SUGAR HACKBERRY 90 ft.
Florida west to Indiana, Texas, and New Mexico. Zone 6.

This tree is frequently seen along streets in southern cities. It has light gray bark covered with prominent corky warts and slightly loose and pendulous branches. Its pointed leaves are 1½ to 4 inches long and have smooth edges.

C. occidentalis L. HACKBERRY to 120 ft.
Quebec to North Carolina and Alaska. Zone 4.

The straight, rigid trunk has light brown to gray bark with corky warts or ridges. The branches are somewhat zigzag-shaped. Leaves are bright green and smooth, 2 to 4½ inches long, with deeply toothed edges. This species often produces witches'-brooms, which become visible after the leaves have fallen.

C. sinensis Pers. CHINESE HACKBERRY 60 ft.
China, Korea, and Japan. Warmer parts of Zone 7.

This tree has a smooth gray trunk and 4-inch-long leaves (Fig. C2-1) that reduce quickly with bonsai training. Winter views of two Chinese bonsai are shown in Figs. 7-6 and 15-3. This species is a trouble-free bonsai, relatively immune to pests and disease.

Fig. C2-1 Chinese hackberry, *Celtis sinensis,* trained as a bonsai in China.

CERATONIA CAROB TREE

The carob tree, from the eastern Mediterrean region, is a vigorous grower, but it responds slowly to bonsai training. It is of interest primarily as a legendary tree of ancient civilizations. Its natural style is a curved or slanting upright trunk.

This tree is adapted to the same climatic range as the orange. When grown in the ground, it may survive an occasional frost, but as a bonsai, protect it from cold. Give it a sunny growing area outdoors in a mild climate or a sunny south window and a 60° to 75°F. indoor temperature in cold regions.

Use a basic container mix with good drainage. Let the soil become moderately dry between waterings. Prune, wire, and repot as needed.

Carob trees are easily propagated from seeds, which are sometimes found at natural food shops selling edible nuts and seeds.

C. Siliqua L. CAROB TREE, ST. JOHN'S BREAD 50 ft.

This is a warm-climate evergreen tree with compound leaves up to 4 inches long. Small red flowers are followed by 1-foot long fruit pods (rarely seen on bonsai), which are the source of carob flour and gum.

CHAENOMELES FLOWERING QUINCE

These are deciduous or semievergreen shrubs with alternate leaves and showy flowers that appear in early spring before the leaves.

Young nursery-grown plants make attractive clump-style bonsai and multitrunk plantings with curved or slanting trunks. They also make colorful minibonsai.

Provide partial sun outdoors and a sunny window or high levels of artificial light indoors. Winter protection is required in cold climates.

Prune severely immediately after flowering to allow flower buds to form during the summer for the following year. With plantings of more than one trunk, remove new shoots that emerge near the edge of the container and keep those that are well positioned in relation to the other trunks. In early spring, before flowers appear, remove dead wood and unwanted branches.

Pinch back new growth through the end of June to maintain a compact form. After June, as new growth continues, remove the terminal bud on each shoot to strengthen the lateral flowering buds. Use a basic mix and repot, when potbound, early in the spring or after flowering. Remove large old roots to encourage new fibrous ones. Fertilize regularly in the early spring when new growth has begun and again during the summer after flowering.

Quince are self-sterile. If fruits are wanted on *C. speciosa*, place the bonsai in the vicinity of other flowering quince when it is in flower.

C. japonica Lindl. ex Spach JAPANESE FLOWERING QUINCE 3–4 ft.
Japan. Zone 5.

A spreading dwarf with short slender spines (or spineless) and 1- to 2-inch leaves, this shrub has salmon to orange flowers about 1 inch across. Cultivars include Alba; Maulei, with single flowers of salmon pink to orange; and Sargentii, a dwarf form with salmon pink to orange flowers.

C. speciosa Nakai *(C. lagenaria)* FLOWERING QUINCE to 10 ft.
China. Zone 5.

This is a spiny shrub with many irregular branches developing close to the ground. Its leaves are 1½ to 3½ inches long. Flowers are 1½ to 2 inches across and usually red, but they may be white or pink. The Japanese bonsai in Fig. C3–1 is a Toyo Nishiki, one of many cultivars. It has multicolored flowers from dark red to white.

The small pear-shaped fruit, hard and inedible when raw, is used in preserves.

Fig. C3–1 Flowering quince, *Chaenomeles speciosa* cv. Toyo Nishiki. Courtesy of *International BONSAI.*

CHAMAECYPARIS FALSE CYPRESS

These are 100-foot or larger evergreen conifers with flattened branchlets and scalelike leaves (juvenile leaves are awl-shaped or needlelike). Thin white lines on the underside of the leaves distinguish *Chamaecyparis* from *Thuga*, arborvitae, which is similar in appearance.

As bonsai, chamaecyparis are most often seen with upright trunks. They range in size from medium or large bonsai to miniatures, as shown in Fig. C4–1.1.

They grow best in partial sun and shade; protect them from hot midday sun. *Chamaecyparis*, like *Cedrus*, are moisture-loving trees. Give them growing areas free of drying winds. They are difficult to grow as bonsai in hot arid climates.

These species respond favorably to wiring and moderate pruning. Use a basic potting mix that is completely free of lime. Spring is the preferred time for repotting, but chamaecyparis can be repotted with care during the growing season.

Fig. C4–1.1 *Chamaecyparis obtusa* cv. Gracilis in a 2¾-inch-wide container.

Fig. C4–1.2 *Chamaecyparis obtusa.*

C. obtusa Endl. HINOKI CYPRESS 120 ft.
Japan. Zone 5.

This cypress has reddish-brown bark and fanlike, flattened branchlets with glossy, green scalelike leaves. It is shown as bonsai in Fig. C4–1.2. The many cultivars include Compacta, a dwarf form; Gracilis, and pyramidal form with dark green leaves; and two very slow-growing dwarf forms, Juniperoides, and Minima.

C. pisifera Endl. SAWARA CYPRESS 120 ft.
Japan. Zone 5.

The flattened branches, with fernlike leaves, are slightly drooping. Among the many popular cultivars are Aurea, with golden yellow leaves; Filifera, with threadlike, drooping branches; and Squarrosa, with dense growth, feathery branches, and silvery leaves.

C. thyoides BSP. WHITE CEDAR, SWAMP CEDAR 90 ft.
Maine to Florida and Mississippi. Zone 5.

This is a tree of lowlands and bogs along the Atlantic and Gulf coasts from Maine to Mississippi. Its delicate foliage is thinner and not as compact as *C. obtusa*, yet it is attractive with its light brown bark and silvery sheen on the underside of the leaves. Ericoides is a slow-growing dense cultivar with juvenile foliage.

CITRUS CITRUS TREES

These evergreen trees are usually spiny with shiny leathery leaves. They are cultivated for their fruit in the southern United States and other warm climates (Zone 10).

Upright, curved, straight, or slanting trunks are preferred, with open branching to provide space for fruit. Medium to large bonsai are more proportional to the size of the fruit than smaller specimens.

Species with small fruit are preferred for bonsai. If grown outdoors, provide bright light and filtered sun; indoors, a sunny south window and temperatures between 60° and 75°F. are required.

Citrus trees respond well to pruning and, when young, to wiring. Wire branches before they harden; mature wood tends to revert to its old position after the wire is removed. Use a basic mix and allow the soil to become moderately dry between waterings. For flowers and fruit, fertilize regularly.

Citrus plants grown for foliage are easily propagated from seed.

C. Limon Burm.f. LEMON 20 ft.

A small tree cultivated in Italy and California for its fruit, Meyer is a dwarf cultivar with 3-inch fruit. It is the hardiest of the lemons. The cultivar Ponderosa, or Wonder Lemon, grows to 10 feet in height and has 4-inch fruit.

C. x limonia Osbeck *(C. taitensis)* OTAHEITE ORANGE

This is a small, thornless bush with 2-inch fruit, often grown as an ornamental pot plant by florists, and is an attractive indoor bonsai.

COCCOLOBA SEA GRAPE

Specimens of sea grape are easily shaped by pruning and wiring and thrive in warm areas of bright light, sun, and high humidity. Leaf size is reduced by pruning the leaves—do this by cutting the petiole or leaf stalk.

Use a basic potting mix with good drainage. The mix should be neutral or slightly alkaline. Water frequently.

Sea grapes suitable for bonsai may be grown from seeds obtained from nursery stock or found growing in the wild.

C. Uvifera L. SEA GRAPE 20 ft.
Southern Florida to South America. Zone 9.

Sea grape grows on beaches, sand dunes, and coastal hammocks in southern Florida and the Caribbean. It is an evergreen tree with stout branches and 8-inch glossy, leathery leaves that are nearly circular in shape. Small yellowish-white flowers are followed by bunched grapelike fruit used to make jelly. Its striking circular leaves make this plant a dramatic and unusual species for warm-climate bonsai.

CONOCARPUS BUTTON MANGROVE, BUTTONWOOD

Beautiful bonsai are created from buttonwoods found in mangrove swamps along the coast of southern Florida and the same coastal, subtropical environment as the preceding *Coccoloba*. They are old, stunted trees. Their thick, twisted trunks resemble the trunks of ancient junipers collected for bonsai in the mountains of Japan.

Place newly collected buttonwood in a container of water for a period of time if additional root growth is wanted. When planting, use a porous, slightly alkaline mix. Water frequently to prevent the roots from drying. Healthy, vigorous buttonwoods respond favorably to pruning and wiring and are tolerant of confinement to a container. They require growing conditions of intense light and sun and high temperatures and humidity.

C. erectus L. BUTTONWOOD 60 ft.
Tropical America and West Africa. Zone 10.

Buttonwoods are found in diverse forms, from a prostrate shrub to an erect tree. They are native to the coastal areas of Florida and the Keys. The tree has stout branches, a narrow crown, and 2- to 4-inch leathery leaves. Greenish ½-inch flowers are followed by reddish-brown buttonlike fruit.

C.e. var. **sericeus** Fors ex DC. SILVER BUTTONWOOD 40 ft.
Florida Keys. Zone 10.

The leaves of this choice variety are covered with silky hair, like velvet, giving the foliage a silver sheen.

COTONEASTER COTONEASTER

These are evergreen and deciduous shrubs with alternate leaves, tiny pink or white flowers, and red fruit that resembles miniature apples. They are found mostly in warm regions; few are hardy in the north.

The spreading horizontal growth habit of cotoneasters is naturally suited to semicascade, cascade, weeping, or over-a-rock styles, as seen in Fig. C5–1.

Give these species winter protection in cold climates, and temperatures of 60° to 65°F. indoors. Provide an outdoor growing area with sun and partial shade or an indoor location at a window or on a cool sunporch.

The growth of some cotoneasters tends to be angular. Modify unwanted branch patterns by pruning or wiring. Use a basic potting mix and allow the soil to become moderately dry between waterings. Repot in the spring. When pruning roots, retain a large portion of fibrous roots.

Cotoneasters are easily propagated by seeds sown when ripe.

C. horizontalis Decne. ROCK COTONEASTER 3 ft.
Western China. Zone 6.

A low, spreading semievergreen shrub, this cotoneaster has herringbone-like branching and glossy green leaves ¼ to ½ inch long. It produces a profusion of pinkish flowers and bright tiny red fruit.

Fig. C5–1 *Cotoneaster* sp. Courtesy of J. Nakahara.

C. microphyllus Wallich ex Lindl. CHINESE COTONEASTER 3 ft.
Himalayas and western China. Zone 7.

This wide-spreading, low evergreen shrub is densely branched. It has ¼-inch leaves that are gray underneath. The small flowers are white and the fruit is bright red. The cultivar Cochleatus is a low-growing dwarf form.

C.m. var. *thymifolius* is a compact variety with pink flowers.

CRASSULA SUCCULENT HERBS AND SHRUBS

Two warm-climate species of jade plants listed below are used for bonsai. These are accommodating plants willing to grow indoors or outdoors under less than optimum conditions. Protect from freezing.

To suggest a treelike form, strip the succulent leaves from the lower trunk and at the fork of the branches. Choose a straight or nearly straight trunk to support the weight of the heavy, plump foliage. If the bonsai tends to be top-heavy, select a deeper than usual container to counterbalance the weight.

In warm climates, place crassula where they will receive direct sun and bright light. They are able to adjust to lower light levels indoors.

Prune crassulas to shape them to bonsai. It is difficult if not impossible to wire their soft trunks and branches without causing injury.

Repot at any time except when the plant is dormant. Use a basic potting mix, and water only after the soil begins to dry.

Jade trees are self-rooting from leaves placed flat on the surface of the potting mix, and shoots or branches root easily from cuttings.

C. arborescens Willd. SILVER JADE PLANT 10 ft.
South Africa.

The succulent 1½- to 2½-inch gray leaves are usually marked with red margins. In cold climates, this plant is slow-growing and rarely flowers in a container. A variegated form, Variegata, is available.

C. argentea Thunb. JADE TREE 10 ft.
South Africa.

This succulent shrub has 1- to 2-inch thick, plump leaves, often marked with red margins. Its pink or white flowers are abundant in warm climates but are slow to blossom as house plants or indoor bonsai in the north.

CRATAEGUS HAWTHORN

These small deciduous trees are horizontally branched, often with thorns. Leaves are alternate, flowers are white or, occasionally, red. The small fruit ripens in the fall. This naturalized genus has many hybrids and more than 800 species in North America. The long, sharp thorns are a handicap for bonsai. A few species with small thorns are listed here.

Fig. C6–1 Hawthorn, *Crataegus* sp. Courtesy of Puget Sound Bonsai Association. Photo by Charles M. Gordon, Photojournalist.

These slow-growing, long-lived trees are usually shaped with an upright trunk (Fig. C6–1) to display their flowers and fruit to best advantage. Their care and training are similar to those for crab apples, *Malus* spp. Hawthorns like a basic mix slightly on the alkaline side.

Bonsai may be created from old, stunted trees found in lowlands, in fields, or on hillsides.

C. cuneata Siebold JAPANESE HAWTHORN 5 ft.
Japan and China. Zone 6.

This small, shrubby hawthorn has ¼-inch thorns and profuse white flowers ½ inch across and red fruit in the fall.

C. laevigata DC. ENGLISH HAWTHORN 25 ft.
Europe, North Africa, and Western Asia. Zone 5.

A compact tree with 1-inch thorns, it has leaves 1 to 2 inches long, white flowers, and ½-inch dark red fruit.

C. mollis Scheele DOWNY HAWTHORN 30 ft.
Ontario to Minnesota, south to Alabama, Arkansas, and Mississippi. Zone 5.

Thorns are sparse, to 1 inch, and leaves are 2½ to 4 inches long. The small white flowers are followed by bright red fruit used for jellies.

CRYPTOMERIA Cryptomeria

As bonsai, these natives of eastern Asia are seen with upright single or multiple trunks and excurrent branches. Young plants are leggy and develop slowly. Select larger plants from nursery stock for specimen bonsai. Keep the interior of the tree free of dead brown twigs and foliage. Dwarf forms are popular for minibonsai.

In cold climates, provide winter protection. Indoor bonsai need temperatures of about 60° to 65°F. Place cryptomeria in partial sun outdoors or at a well-lighted window or under artificial light indoors.

Pinch new growth while it is still soft, between ¼ and ½ inch. Prune mature and new growth as needed to open the interior to air and light. Use a basic potting mix, which may be enriched one-sixth by volume with decayed leaf mold or peat moss. Repot in late spring or early summer when the soil is warm. Keep the mix slightly moist, but not wet, between waterings.

Cryptomeria are propagated by seed or cuttings.

C. japonica D. Don Japanese cedar 150 ft.
Zones 7 and 8.

This tall, straight-trunked evergreen tree of mild temperate climates is frequently planted on Japanese temple grounds. Its awl-shaped leaves are ½ inch long. In cold regions, the foliage turns brown in winter. Dwarf forms, cvs. Compacta, Nana, Vilmoriniana, and small Japanese yatsubusa, are preferred for indoor bonsai, especially when grown under artificial light.

CUPHEA Elfin herb

This is mostly a warm-climate shrub or herb. In northern climates it can be grown indoors, in a greenhouse, or as a tender annual. The versatile elfin herb is seen in many single- and multitrunk styles as well as in group plantings and minibonsai. It requires warm year-round temperatures outdoors and between 60° and 75°F. indoors. Place it in bright light or sun or under high levels of artificial light.

Prune vigorously and frequently. Flowers form on the tips of small shoots and branches. For continual flowering, cut back each shoot after it has flowered. Use a basic potting mix. In a warm environment this species grows rapidly and requires frequent watering. Fertilize as for a flowering plant.

C. hyssopifolia HBK. Elfin herb 2 ft.
Mexico and Guatemala.

Elfin herb is a dense, woody shrub with small, narrow leaves and tiny, profuse pink or white flowers.

CUPRESSUS CYPRESS

This is the true cypress, a coniferous evergreen of mild climates. Among the following species, only *C. arizonica* can be grown in colder regions.

An upright trunk is a natural style for three species discussed here.

Young trees are excellent for group plantings, saikei, indoor bonsai, and minibonsai. Older specimens of Arizona cypress are collected in the mountains.

For Monterey and Italian cypress provide year-round warm temperatures accompanied by bright light and sun. Indoors, keep at 60° to 70°F. or higher at a sunny window or under high levels of artificial light.

For compact foliage, pinch new growth when it is ¼ to ½ inch long. These species respond favorably to regular pruning and wiring. Use a basic potting mix and let the soil become slightly dry between waterings.

Most cypresses are easily propagated from seed.

C. arizonica Greene ARIZONA CYPRESS 40 ft.
Southern Arizona and Mexico. Zone 6.

Arizona cypress is an attractive rough-barked tree with small scalelike grayish needles.

C. macrocarpa Hartweg MONTEREY CYPRESS 40 ft.
Monterey County, California. Zone 8.

This is the picturesque cypress of the Monterey Peninsula. It has small, scale-like leaves.

C. sempervirens L. ITALIAN CYPRESS 80 ft.
Southern Europe to western Asia. Zone 8.

This cypress is a narrow, tall, symmetrical tree, widely grown in Italy. The cultivar Horizontalis is a spreading form.

CYCAS CYCAD

Cycas, with palmlike leaves or fronds, are among the most primitive of the seed-bearing plants. Cycas are easy to grow and practically free of insects and disease. Their exotic appearance makes them popular for bonsai in Japan, Hawaii, and other warm climates, as well as indoors in cold-winter regions. They grow as a single trunk or in clumps, as shown in Fig. C7-1.1. Because of their size, only young seedlings are suitable for the average indoor light garden. Older cycads can be grown indoors near a sunny south or east window.

Two methods are used to reposition young fronds from their normally upright growth to a more pleasing horizontal position. Both techniques are applied to newly emerging leaves. Although old leaves are stiff and rigid, new leaves are soft and tender. One method uses twine to tie the new fronds to the desired position. When a frond has emerged and is fully opened but not yet rigid, tie

Fig. C7–1.1 Cycad, *Cycas revoluta,* growing by the ocean in Hawaii.

strands of twine at three or four locations along the midrib. Move the frond to its new position and tie the strand of twine nearest the trunk to the container or to wire fastened to the pot. Continue outward and tie each strand along the midrib taut with the container. Take care to form a smooth, graceful arch with a natural appearance. Do not let too short a length of twine cause a dip along the midrib—it will be there permanently. As the frond hardens, it will become fixed in the tied horizontal position.

Edward Nishida, an expert Hawaiian bonsai grower, demonstrated for stateside visitors a more precise method of repositioning the fronds. He uses the following techniques on soft fronds only a few days old.

Hold the tip of the small frond with one hand and carefully bend it into an arched horizontal position. Then rub the index finger of the other hand back and forth along the underside of the midrib. Repeat the strokes gently several times. Continue the treatments for several days. The position will become permanent as the frond hardens. All the fronds on the cycad in Fig. C7–1.2 were treated in this manner by a beginner practicing the technique for the first time.

Fig. C7–1.2 Fronds on a young cycad trained in Pennsylvania using Nishida's methods.

Nishida explains that in warm climates, smaller fronds can be obtained by removing all the old fronds before the cycad is repotted. Water lightly until new growth appears, then withhold water as the new fronds emerge. The new fronds will be noticeably smaller. However, in cold climates, prune cycads only to remove dead fronds.

Use a basic potting mix that contains organic material and provides good drainage. Allow the soil to become partially dry between waterings. In warm climates, repot cycads in the fall. In cold regions, repot in late spring or early summer after the soil is warm.

Cycads are able to adjust to varying levels of light intensity, according to Severn C. Doughty, horticulturist with the Louisiana Cooperative Extension Service in Metaire. He described his observations as follows:

> The leaf color is often a helpful guide to growing various cycads. Those with blue leaves require a lot of light—up to full sunlight—and little water. In their native habitat they probably receive between 15 and 20 inches of rain per year.
>
> Cycads with blue-green leaves need less light—perhaps 25 to 40 percent shade—and more water. In their native habitat they require about 30 to 40 inches of rain per year.
>
> Finally, dark green leaves suggest a cycad tolerant of up to 65% shade. In their native habitat, these cycads require between 40 and 50 inches of rain per year.
>
> Many cycads can be grown in deeper shade than they would tolerate in their natural environment. However, their leaves usually become much longer. The grower can regulate the size of the leaves and the ultimate size of the plant by placing it in full sun or shade.
>
> A cycad grown in shade is more open and possibly more graceful, provided the symmetry is maintained. One grown in the sun is more compact and often more symmetric. Cycads grown in the shade usually produce greener, less leathery and thinner or wider leaves than those grown in full sun.*

Cycads are easily propagated by seed, which suggest their use as conditioned plants indoors, but the seedlings are exceedingly slow-growing.

C. revoluta Thunb. SAGO PALM, CYCAD to 10 ft.
Southern Japan, Ryukyu Islands. Zone 9.

On this small cycad, the stout trunk with its rough surface resembles a pineapple. The thick, leathery fronds are in whorls (Fig. C7-1.3). Their color varies from a bluish cast to blue-green and green. In warm climates, new leaves appear once or twice a year.

*Severn C. Doughty, "What Are Cycads?" *American Nurseryman*, December 1, 1981, pp. 62–63. Doughty's article is one of the few available sources of detailed information on botanical characteristics and care and culture of cycads.

Fig. C7–1.3 A five-trunk clump bonsai of cycads. Courtesy of Edward Nishida.

CYDONIA QUINCE

In China and Japan, quince trees are esteemed as bonsai; with age, they become spectacular. To support the heavy fruit, the large trunk is usually upright, and the leaves are shiny and display beautiful fall color.

Allow only a few fruit to mature to avoid overtaxing the bonsai. Follow the pruning directions for flowering and fruiting trees in Chapter 10.

This bonsai grows best in sun and partial shade. Use a basic, neutral potting mix. Prune, wire, and fertilize as for other flowering and fruiting bonsai.

C. sinensis Thouin CHINESE QUINCE 20 ft.
China. Zone 6.

With age, this small tree develops a beautiful mottled bark of brown and tan. Leaves are 3 to 4 inches long. The pink spring flowers are about ½ inch across. The fruit (Fig. C8–1) is dark yellow. In fall, the foliage turns deep red and crimson.

EHRETIA EHRETIA

Fukien tea, the species used for bonsai, is a handsome evergreen that thrives in Florida, southern China, and Hong Kong. It is not easily grown indoors in cold northern regions. It may be trained in many styles: as a specimen bonsai, from upright to cascade trunks, and on or over a rock. It is also used for group plantings and saikei.

Place this bonsai where it will receive bright light and sun. Prune only during the growing season; pinch new growth while it is soft. Wire with care to avoid damaging the closely clustered leaves.

Fig. C8–1 Chinese quince, *Cydonia sinensis,* in fruit. Courtesy of *International BONSAI.*

Use a basic mix that is slightly enriched with humus and drains well. Roots grow slowly. Repot every two or three years during hot weather in early summer. Fertilize regularly.

E. microphylla Lam. *(Carmona microphylla)* FUKIEN TEA 6 ft. India, southern China, Malay Peninsula, and the Philippine Islands.

This evergreen shrub has glossy 1- to 2-inch leaves, tiny starlike flowers, and red fruit that turns black. Fukien tea, (Fig. 3–11) is known as the Star of Canton in China and Hong Kong, and as Philippine Tea in the Philippine Islands.

ENKIANTHUS ENKIANTHUS

These deciduous Asiatic shrubs have leaves crowded toward the ends of the branch, with racemes of flowers and brilliant fall foliage.

Enkianthus is a lovely spring-flowering bonsai, most suitable for an upright, slanting, or semicascade trunk. Provide sun and partial shade. To obtain short stems, pinch the new shoots while they are soft. To modify the whorl effect, eliminate a portion of new shoots in each cluster.

Use a slightly acidic mix that contains peat moss or humus and is completely free of lime or slag.

E. perulatus C. K. Schneid. JAPANESE ENKIANTHUS 6 ft. Japan. Zone 5.

Fig. E1–1 *Enkianthus perulatus* flowering at the Morris Arboretum. Photo by Paul W. Meyer.

This is a slow-growing shrub whose branches emerge in whorls. Profuse flowers cluster at the tips of slender shoots (Fig. E1–1). The white flowers appear before the 2-inch leaves, which reduce in size with bonsai training. Enkianthus has beautiful scarlet foliage in the fall.

ADDITIONAL READING

KOLLER, GARY L., "Japanese Enkianthus," *Journal of the American Bonsai Society*, 15, no. 3 (Fall 1981), 47–48.

FAGUS BEECH

These distinctive deciduous trees have long, pointed buds, alternate leaves, and upright trunks with smooth gray bark. Surface roots are extensive at the base of older specimens. The fruit, which is a nut, is enclosed in a bur. Beeches prefer partial shade. Prune old trees sparingly because replacement growth develops slowly. Trim new growth only once each year.

Prepare a basic mix, neutral or slightly alkaline—beeches grow well in alkaline soil. Make sure that it drains well. Water generously but do not keep the soil wet. Repot established bonsai about every third year in the spring. Because root growth is sparse, do not prune the root mass severely; selectively shorten or remove overly large roots.

F. crenata Blume *(F. Sieboldii)* JAPANESE BEECH 90 ft. Japan. Zone 6.

This stately tree has a rounded crown and 3-inch leaves, which are broadest below the middle and persistent through the winter.

Fig. F1–1 Collected American beech, *Fagus grandifolia.* Courtesy of Allan Hills.

F. grandifolia J. F. Ehrh. *(F. americana)* AMERICAN BEECH 60 ft.
New Brunswick to Ontario, south to Florida and Texas. Zone 4.

This large tree has branches close to the ground and thin, smooth, light gray bark (Fig. F1–1). Its 5-inch leaves persist through the winter. This species is a tree of the wild and takes less kindly to cultivation and bonsai training than the Japanese and European beeches.

F. sylvatica L. EUROPEAN BEECH 80 ft.
Europe. Zone 5.

Leaves measure 2 to 4 inches on this beech, which has been cultivated for centuries in Europe. It has many forms and cultivars.

FICUS FIG

This worldwide genus contains a diversity of trees, shrubs, and vines for bonsai. Leaf size varies from a fraction of an inch to more than a foot. On most species, flowers and fruits are small or hardly visible. A notable exception is *F. carica*, the common fig, which has been cultivated for its edible fruit since ancient times.

Figs are vigorous growers. In the ground they produce strong aggressive roots. Many species form extensive surface roots, while others develop buttressed trunks similar to those of bald cypress. In a warm climate, banyan figs drop aerial roots from their trunks and branches; these gradually thicken into columns to support wide canopies of green foliage. Banyans often start as epiphytes from seeds lodged in a fork or crevice of another tree. The young seedling then sprouts roots that enlarge and eventually may strangle the host tree.

Among figs, all bonsai styles and sizes are possible, including single- and multitrunk, upright and cascade, and on and over a rock. An upright style is preferred for banyan figs in climates where they send out long aerial roots. As a genus, figs are unsurpased for indoor bonsai and are free of many pests and pathogens that may invade other genera.

Species listed here show a reduction in leaf size early in their bonsai training, are easily wired, and are tolerant of pruning and repotting. They are able to adjust to less than optimum conditions.

Provide warm year-round temperatures and protection from freezing. Outdoors, figs prefer an area of bright light and partial shade. Indoors, place figs by an east window or a lightly screened south window with indoor temperatures of 60° to 70°F. or more.

Prune at any time during the growing season. Most species are tolerant of repeated pruning. Wire at any season. Use a basic potting mix and keep the soil slightly moist between waterings. Repot annually during warm weather; late spring or early summer is preferred.

Figs, which are native to warm and tropical regions of every continent, are among the most versatile and trouble-free plants for bonsai. All are evergreens and have a milky sap containing latex.

F. aurea Nutt. STRANGLER FIG, FLORIDA FIG 60 ft.
Southern Florida and the Caribbean. Zone 10.

This banyan fig (Fig. 16–5) has aerial roots, leaves 2 to 4 inches long, and small fruit. Considered a weed tree in southern Florida, it is not generally available from commercial sources. However, it may often be found growing as an unwanted seedling in cultivated areas and greenhouses.

F. benjamina L. BENJAMIN FIG, WEEPING FIG 40 ft.
India, Malay Archipelago, Australia. Zone 10.

This fig usually has strong surface roots, drooping branches, 5-inch leaves, and a well-developed crown. In favorable environments, aerial roots, as seen in Fig. F2–1, may appear. Benjamin figs can withstand short periods of dryness and are able to adjust to less than optimum light levels.

F. carica L. COMMON FIG 35 ft.
Mediterranean region. Zone 8.

This is the fig grown for its edible fruit. It is deciduous in the northern limit of its range. Branching is sparse, with 3- to 5-inch-long leaves. It rarely fruits as bonsai.

F. citrifolia Mill. *(F. brevifolia)* SHORTLEAF FIG 60 ft.
Florida south to Paraguay. Zone 10.

Native to the hammocks of southern Florida and the Keys, this fig has a broad

Fig. F2–1 *Ficus benjamina* with aerial roots, grown in Hawaii in an Ole Orchard Hills plastic container. Courtesy of Fuku-Bonsai.

crown. Within the species, some trees produce many aerial roots, others produce few. Leaves measure 4 to 8 inches. It can be grown easily in warm areas.

F. deltoidea Jack *(F. diversifolia)* MISTLETOE FIG 6 ft.
Malay Peninsula.

This is a small shrub with a slender trunk and branches. A specimen planted over a rock is shown in Fig. 16–3. Leaves measure 1 to 3 inches, and the attractive, small yellow fruit turns red or orange when ripe. Mistletoe fig may be identified by a few small black dots on the underside of the leaf. The thin trunk thickens slowly. This species needs high levels of light for best growth but is able to adjust to reduced light.

F. microcarpa L.f. *(F. retusa)* CHINESE BANYAN 28 ft.
Malay Peninsula to Borneo.

This can be a tree or shrub with a buttressed trunk, erect branches, leaves to 3 inches, and a few aerial roots. It is widely used for bonsai. A popular cultivar, Retusa, is shown in Figs. 13–3.1 and 13–3.2.

F. neriifolia Sm. *(F.n. regularia* and *F. celebensis)* NARROW-LEAF BANYAN, WILLOW-LEAF FIG
Florida south to Paraguay. Zone 10.

This is a small, graceful tree with dense foliage and broad-spreading branches. It has willowlike leaves 3 to 6 inches long, aerial roots, and thick surface roots.

F. pumila L. *(F. repens)* CREEPING FIG
East Asia and Japan. Zone 9.

The roots of this small woody vine cling to supporting surfaces. Its leaves are 1 inch long or less. This species also branches freely, allowing it to be trained

Fig. F2-2 Port Jackson fig, *Ficus rubiginosa.* Courtesy of Fuku-Bonsai.

as a small tree. The cultivar Minima, which has tiny leaves resembling little hearts, is growing as a ground cover in Fig. 16-3.

F. rubiginosa Desf. ex Venten. *(F. australis)* PORT JACKSON FIG, RUSTY FIG 20 ft.
New South Wales.

These small trees have leaves 4 to 6 inches long with a rusty covering on new growth and leaf undersides. It is a rapid grower with many forms and varieties. A clump with five trunks is seen in Fig. F2-2.

ADDITIONAL READING

CONDIT, IRA J., *Ficus: The Exotic Species.* Riverside, Calif.: University of California, Division of Agricultural Sciences, 1969. The author of this definitive work is an authority on *Ficus.* His usage is followed here for the nomenclature of *Ficus* species.

FUKUMOKO, DAVID W. "Ficus: Part I. An Introduction to the Ficus Family," *Journal of the American Bonsai Society,* 12, no. 2 (Summer 1978), 75-80. This is part of a continuing study of the *Ficus* genus conducted by the author at the Harold L. Lyon Arboretum, University of Hawaii.

FORSYTHIA GOLDEN BELLS

This undemanding, beautiful flowering shrub grows well in sun and partial shade. Its showy yellow flowers appear in the early spring before the leaves. Immediately after flowering, cut back the shoots and branches drastically to obtain new growth with flower buds for next spring. Wire carefully with aluminum wire (or wrapped copper wire) to avoid scarring the soft woody tissue. Use a basic potting mix and let the soil become partially dry between waterings. Fertilize regularly for spring flowers. When purchasing a forsythia for bonsai, ask for a plant that flowers profusely from among the many available hybrids and varieties.

F. suspensa Vahl. FORSYTHIA 10 ft.
China. Zone 5.

The branches of this species are hollow, but solid at the nodes. The leaves are 4 inches long, and the flowers are a golden yellow. This popular forsythia flowers abundantly.

F. viridissima Lindl. FORSYTHIA 10 ft.
China. Zone 6.

Branches are erect, and leaves are 6 inches long. This species differs from *F. suspensa* in not having a solid pith at the nodes. Cv. Bronxensis is a popular dwarf form for bonsai. Its yellow flowers are easily forced in late winter or early spring to brighten the home or a spring bonsai exhibit.

FORTUNELLA KUMQUAT

These evergreen shrubs and small trees have alternate, thick, dark green leaves, white flowers, and small fruit. They are grown in warm climates as a novelty citrus fruit.

Kumquats are used as flowering and fruiting bonsai. Their care and bonsai training are similar to those for *Citrus* spp. They are tolerant of a variety of soils, but not ones that are poorly drained. Use a basic mix and let it become partially dry between waterings.

F. japonica Swingle ROUND KUMQUAT
South China. Zone 9.

A spiny, much-branched shrub, round kumquat has 3-inch leaves and edible orange fruit 1¼ inches in diameter.

F. margarita Swingle NAGAMI KUMQUAT 15 ft.
South China. Zone 9.

This shrub or small tree is nearly thornless. Its leaves measure up to 4 inches long, and it has orange-yellow fruit 1 inch in diameter.

Fig. G1–1 *Gardenia jasminoides* trained as a cascade bonsai. Courtesy of Lynn R. Perry.

GARDENIA GARDENIA

These shrubs and small trees of mild climates are valued for their fragrant white flowers and shiny green leaves. In cold climates they are enjoyed as indoor bonsai. Outdoors, provide sun except during the heat of the summer. Indoors, place gardenias by a sunny window.

Use a slightly acidic mix containing organic matter and do not let the soil become dry between waterings. Repot established bonsai every two or three years.

Prune gardenias in early spring; flowers form on new growth. To obtain small flowers in scale with a bonsai, Lynn R. Perry, author of *Bonsai: Trees and Shrubs*, recommends removing the large terminal bud to allow the smaller buds to produce flowers.*

G. jasminoides Ellis *(G. radicans)* COMMON GARDENIA, CAPE GARDENIA 6 ft.
China. Zone 8.

This beautiful shrub has glossy green leaves and fragrant white flowers. Provide warm daytime temperatures both outdoors and indoors. A bonsai trained in the cascade style is shown in Fig. G1–1.

*Lynn R. Perry, *Bonsai: Trees and Shrubs, A Guide to the Methods of Kyuzo Murata*, p. 133. (New York: The Ronald Press Company, 1964.) The author provides detailed information on culture and training for many species used as bonsai.

Fig. G2–1.1 *Ginkgo biloba* in early spring, showing wartlike *chi-chi* on the central trunk.

GINKGO GINKGO
Southeast China. Zone 5.

This tree is extinct in the wild and has survived only as a cultivated tree. It is now widely distributed and grown as an ornamental tree in temperate climates.

The ginkgo's naturally upright trunk and ascending branches are duplicated in bonsai forms, as seen in early spring in Fig. G2–1.1. Provide daily sun and partial shade and, of course, winter protection in cold climates.

Although this tree does not produce twiggy branches, it is tolerant of pruning and roots easily. The trunk, branches, and roots of older specimens may be cut back drastically. New roots and shoots will form when the trunk is replanted in the ground or in a large training pot and given proper care. In early spring, prune overly long shoots from the previous summer. Later, trim the new growth and retain only a few nodes on each shoot.

Use a basic mix with good drainage. Water well and allow the soil to become partially dry between waterings. Fertilize regularly to obtain dense foliage and healthy growth.

Ginkgoes, unlike most trees, are tolerant of polluted urban air and are free of pests. As bonsai they are valued for these traits as well as their attractive silvery fruit, the golden fall color of their foliage, and their long, hanging knoblike growths called *chi-chi* in Japan. Studies by the noted botanist, Hui-Lin Li,* indi-

*Hui-Lin Li, *The Origin and Cultivation of Shade and Ornamental Trees* (Philadelphia: University of Pennsylvania Press, 1963). Paperback edition, 1974, p. 96.

cate that these unusual protuberances, which appear mostly on older trees, are caused by the abnormal development of dormant buds beneath the bark; if they reach the ground, they take root and bear leaves.

Chi-chi formations may be seen on the Japanese bonsai in Fig. G2–1.1. In Japan, these strange growths are valued on bonsai, and such trees are propagated by cuttings to obtain bonsai with *chi-chi* in a relatively short period of time.

The fruit, called "silver apricot" (Fig. G2–1.2), appears on female trees more than twenty years old. Although both female and male trees are required for fruit, there is no certain way to identify the gender of a ginkgo that is not of fruit-bearing age.

As bonsai, ginkgoes do not show a marked reduction in leaf size, nor do they respond favorably to defoliation. In fall, a ginkgo is a blaze of brilliant yellow that persists for several weeks before the leaves drop, after which the bonsai is enjoyed for the structure of its trunk and branches and, if present, the *chi-chi* formations and fruit.

G. biloba L. MAIDENHAIR TREE 120 ft.

This deciduous tree of temperate climates has a straight trunk, erect branches, and curiously shaped fanlike leaves 2 to 3 inches long. The nut—inside the round, 1-inch-long, fleshy fruit—is eaten in the Orient.

This species grows well as bonsai; care is not demanding. Ginkgoes are easily propagated by seed.

Fig. G2–1.2 Ginkgo with its "silver apricot" fruit. Courtesy of Lynn R. Perry.

GREVILLEA GREVILLEA

As bonsai, silk oak is used as a single upright trunk or for group plantings and, in cold climates, is grown indoors. The trunk elongates rapidly, and taper is not pronounced. Silk oak needs a warm year-round climate with indoor temperatures of 65° to 75°F. Provide sun and partial shade outdoors, a sunny south window indoors. Trim new growth repeatedly to keep this tree small and compact. The large leaves become smaller with bonsai training.

Use a basic mix. Allow the soil to become slightly dry between waterings. Repot when the weather is warm in late spring or early summer.

Grevillea is highly recommended, especially for novice bonsai growers. It is easily propagated from seed and responds favorably to bonsai training.

G. robusta A. Cunn. SILK OAK 40–150 ft.
Queensland and New South Wales. Zone 9.

This is a tall tree with large, compound fernlike leaves, alternately arranged, and orange flowers, which are seldom seen on silk oak grown as bonsai. It is planted as a street and garden tree in California, Florida, and Hawaii.

HAMAMELIS WITCH HAZEL

Witch hazels are deciduous shrubs or small trees grown for their distinctive flowers, which appear in autumn, late winter, or early spring. The trunk is naturally upright, with fairly open branching. A detail of the beautiful Japanese witch hazel (Fig. 3–3) at the National Arboretum in Washington, D.C., is shown in Fig. H1–1.1.

Fig. H1–1.1 Detail of leaves and flower buds on Japanese witch hazel, *Hamamelis japonica,* at the U.S. National Arboretum.

Place witch hazels in open shade and provide protection in winter. Although these species respond slowly to severe pruning, they react favorably to annual trimming of their new growth. Use a basic mix enriched with organic matter, and keep the soil slightly moist between waterings.

H. japonica Siebold & Zucc. JAPANESE WITCH HAZEL 30 ft.
Japan. Zone 5.

This witch hazel may be shaped as single- or multitrunk bonsai. It has spreading branches and 5-inch leaves and is beautiful in flower (Fig. H1–1.2) during the late winter months. Flowers have ¾-inch slender, long yellow petals with a red center. The cultivar Flavo-purpurascens, with reddish petals at the base, is a popular form.

H. mollis D. Oliver CHINESE WITCH HAZEL 30 ft.
China. Zone 5.

The Chinese witch hazel is a tree or shrub with leaves to 6 inches. It has ½ inch dark yellow flowers with a purplish red center that appear in winter and early spring. Foliage turns a beautiful yellow in autumn.

H. x intermedia, a cross between *H. mollis* and *H. japonica*, is highly variable as to leaves and the size and color of the flowers; a dark red flower is frequently seen.

H. vernalis Sarg. OZARK WITCH HAZEL 6 ft.
Missouri to Louisiana and Oklahoma. Zone 5.

A shrub that spreads by means of short stolons, the Ozark witch hazel has 4-inch leaves and ¾-inch yellow flowers with a dark red center. The flowers, appear-

Fig. H1–1.2 Japanese witch hazel flowering at the Morris Arboretum. Photo by Paul W. Meyer.

ing in early spring, are more fragrant but less showy than those of most other species.

H. virginiana L. WITCH HAZEL 15 ft.
Eastern North America. Zone 4.

This shrub has 6-inch leaves and golden yellow flowers with ¾-inch-long ribbonlike petals in autumn. The fruit, enclosed in a hard case, matures the second year along with flowers of the current year. This interesting witch hazel has medicinal attributes and is used in water witching.

HEDERA IVY

Ivy is an evergreen woody vine. The leaves are lobed on the juvenile form, which is most often used for bonsai. Many cultivars with small or variegated leaves are popular for indoor bonsai. Ivy is easily shaped to numerous styles, from upright to cascade, with one or more trunks.

When the vine can no longer grow upward, it alters its growth at the very top and produces a small treelike form with a trunk and branches. This unusual growth can be cut from the vine, rooted in a moist medium, and grown as a separate plant for bonsai and other uses.

To obtain a bonsai with a large trunk from the juvenile form, dig an old vine and shorten its thick trunk by pruning. If branches are present, wire the trunk and branches to a treelike form. Plant it in a training pot to establish fibrous roots and prune the new growth to a bonsai design. After several years of training, the ivy will be ready for a bonsai container.

Outdoors, provide partial sun and shade; indoors, place the bonsai on a windowsill or in the interior of a room with bright light or under artificial light.

Use a basic potting mix containing organic matter. Keep the mix slightly moist, but not wet, between waterings.

Ivy is propagated by cuttings, which can be rooted in water.

H. Helix L. ENGLISH IVY
Europe, North Africa, and western Asia.

This vine, with glossy green leaves, is naturalized in the United States. Among the many cultivars that have arisen, the self-branching dwarf forms are especially adaptable for indoor and minibonsai. They include cvs. Jubilee, with variegated leaves, Pittsburgh, and Needlepoint.

ILEX HOLLY

These are small trees, or shrubs, evergreen and deciduous, with alternate leaves (often thick and leathery) and tiny flowers followed by small round red or black fruit. For fruit, both male and female trees are required.

Evergreen hollies are cultivated in moderate climates, mostly through Zone 7. Deciduous hollies are hardier and are found through Zone 5.

Ilex are excellent material for bonsai. They adjust easily to a container and are responsive to bonsai training. Most often they are shaped to an upright trunk—straight, curved or slanting—and used as minibonsai, in saikei, and in group plantings. In cold climates, hollies need winter protection.

For optimum outdoor growth, place them in bright, but not hot, sun and partial shade; indoors, provide a sunny south window when temperatures are 70°F. or higher, or a north or east window at lower temperatures.

Hollies respond favorably to pruning. For a compact bonsai, trim the new growth without fail, especially on deciduous species. Wiring is effective on young wood; old wood is brittle and hard to reposition.

Use a basic potting mix containing organic materials. Keep the soil slightly moist between waterings. Fertilize regularly for good growth and fall fruit.

Repot in midspring when the days are warm. Roots on evergreen hollies are not as fibrous as those of deciduous species and may require more care in pruning. Remove long, thick roots gradually during a number of repottings.

I. cornuta Lindl. & Paxt. CHINESE HOLLY 15 ft.
East China. Zone 7.

This densely branched evergreen shrub has lustrous dark green leaves, about 2 inches long. The spring flowers appear on last year's growth and are followed by showy bright red berries. Three small spines are clustered at the apex of the leaves.

I. crenata Thunb. JAPANESE HOLLY 15 ft.
Japan. Zone 6.

The compact evergreen Japanese holly resembles boxwood. It has 1¼-inch leaves, small white flowers, and black fruit about ¼ inch in diameter. This species has numerous cultivars. Dwarf forms include cvs. Globosa and Helleri; cvs. Microphylla and Nana have unusually small leaves.

I. decidua Walt. POSSUM HAW 30 ft.
Illinois to Florida and Texas. Zone 5.

A deciduous shrub or small tree, the possum haw has thin brown bark with warty projections. It readily develops surface roots around the bottom of the trunk. Leaves are dull green, up to 3 inches. Small flowers form on the new spring growth. The glossy red, sometimes yellow, fruit is ⅛ to ¼ inch in dimater.

I. serrata Thunb. JAPANESE SAWTOOTH HOLLY 10 ft.
Japan and China. Zone 5.

The leaves of this Japanese deciduous holly (Fig. 6-9) are 3 inches long and

Fig. I1–1 Japanese deciduous holly, *Ilex serrata,* with fruit. Photographed in October in Japan.

have serrated margins. They reduce readily with bonsai training. Small white flowers are formed on new shoots in the spring. The tiny, red, round berries (Fig. I1–1) are the most persistent of the fruit produced on the three deciduous hollies listed here. They remain on this species well into the winter.

I. verticillata A. Gray WINTERBERRY, BLACK ALDER 15 ft.
Newfoundland to Minnesota, south to Texas and Georgia. Zone 4.

This is a deciduous shrub, sometimes a small tree, with 4-inch leaves. It has $\frac{3}{16}$-inch red fruit, which is not as persistent as the berries of the two preceding deciduous hollies.

I. vomitoria Ait. YAUPON 24 ft.
Virginia to Florida and Texas. Zone 7.

Its compact growth, leathery evergreen leaves to 1½ inches long, and shiny red or yellow fruit make yaupon excellent material for bonsai. (A bitter tea, cassine, is produced from the dried leaves.) In areas where it grows, natural specimens may be found and used as bonsai. In cold climates, yaupon is popular as an indoor bonsai. Dwarf forms include cvs. Schellings Dwarf and Nana.

JASMINUM JASMINE OR JESSAMINE

These tropical and subtropical shrubs, often climbers, are deciduous and evergreen, with attractive flowers. A number of species are hardy to Zone 7.

Jasmines are grown as bonsai for their bright display of flowers. The branches and stems of this vinelike shrub tend to be slender and long. For bonsai, look for an old specimen with a large trunk and branches that can be shaped to a basic bonsai framework, then fill in the top with new growth. Trim all the new shoots to make them compact. Use a basic potting mix and fertilize regularly. Jasmines may be trained to any style that the trunk suggests. Their arching branches fit naturally into cascade and weeping styles. They are responsive to pruning and wiring. Outdoors, provide both sun and shade. As indoor bonsai, place them at a sunny south window where they will receive five hours of sun daily. Use dwarf forms for minibonsai or growing under lights.

J. nudiflorum Lindl. WINTER JASMINE 15 ft.
China. Zone 6.

This is a deciduous shrub with small, showy yellow flowers that appear before the leaves, arching branches, and four-angled shoots. The compound leaves have 1-inch leaflets.

J. Parkeri S. T. Dunn YELLOW-STARRED JASMINE 1 ft.
Himalayas. Zone 7.

This slow-growing prostrate shrub has tiny yellow flowers in June and July. It is similar to *J. nudiflorum* but not as hardy, and it may be grown indoors.

JUNIPERUS JUNIPER

These coniferous evergreen trees and shrubs have a thin or shreddy bark. Mature leaves are scalelike and pressed closely on the branchlets. Juvenile leaves are needlelike, sharp and pointed. The fruit is a cone that resembles a berry. Junipers, many of which reach an old age, are among the most important species used for bonsai.

Any style or size bonsai can be made from the many species and forms of junipers available. Shrubs with trailing branches, for example, lend themselves to a cascade style, while junipers with large trunks collected from the mountains are trained as driftwood or informal upright bonsai. The hard, durable wood of junipers plus their vigor and endurance make them especially suitable for windswept and driftwood bonsai.

If at all possible, place junipers in direct sun for part of the day and open shade for the balance. If junipers are grown indoors at temperatures of 70 °F. or above, provide plenty of sun at a south window or high levels of artificial light. Junipers wintered indoors on an unheated sunporch or a cool windowsill at temperatures of 60 °F. or lower do not require direct sun.

Junipers respond vigorously with new growth when pruned. Latent buds under the bark of many junipers will sprout when the tree is severely pruned. (Keep the bark moist at this time by frequent misting to encourage sprouting.)

Trim new annual growth by plucking or pinching while it is soft, as described in Chapter 4.

When wiring junipers, use copper or aluminum wire. If the wood is stiff or old, withhold water for several days before wiring and bending the tree.

Prepare a grainy basic mix with good aeration and drainage, one that is neutral or slightly alkaline. If a large proportion of ingredients have a low pH reading, neutralize their acidity with powdered limestone or dolomite. Several times a year, many growers routinely scatter a tablespoon of powdered limestone on the surface of soil in containers where junipers are growing. Junipers do not like wet or constantly moist soil. Let the soil become partially dry between waterings. Fertilize lightly and regularly.

Although spring is the safest time for repotting, junipers can be repotted at any time immediately before or during their growing season.

Sometimes a juniper bonsai will show both juvenile and mature foliage. To obtain the preferred adult foliage throughout the bonsai, remove the juvenile foliage when pruning. In time, the tree will produce only the mature scalelike leaves.

J. californica Carrière CALIFORNIA JUNIPER 25 ft.
California. Zone 8.

A shrub or tree with deeply infolded or fluted trunks, the California juniper (Fig. 2-5) has yellow-green overlapping scalelike leaves and light reddish-brown berries. It is a native of mountainous areas of California.

J. chinensis L. CHINESE JUNIPER 60 ft.
Eastern Asia. Zone 4.

This species, which may be a shrub or a tree, is frequently used for bonsai. The adult leaves are scalelike and the juvenile ones are sharply pointed needles; the small berries are brown or brownish purple. *J. chinensis* has numerous varieties and many cultivars, such as Torulosa in Figs. 9-1.1 and 9-6.

J.c. var. **Sargentii** A. Henry SHIMPAKU JUNIPER
Japan.

This shrub or small tree with dense, compact foliage is the famous shimpaku juniper of China and Japan, shown in Figs. 1-1 and 7-1. Its compact growth habit and small scalelike foliage make it a choice variety for bonsai.

J.c. var. **procumbens** Miq. PROCUMBENT JUNIPER
Japan. Zone 4.

The foliage of this low shrub permanently retains the juvenile form with ⅜- to ½-inch sharply pointed needles. Its compact growth, tolerance to pruning, and ease of wiring make it a popular species for bonsai.

J. communis L. COMMON JUNIPER 35 ft.
North America and Eurasia. Zone 3.

An erect or prostrate shrub or a small tree, the common juniper has 1-inch awl-shaped linear needles and dark blue berries. Unlike most junipers, this juniper prefers an acidic soil. It is a species with variable growth found in colder regions of North America, Europe, and Asia. Many cultivars are available.

J.c. var. **depressa** Pursh GROUND JUNIPER 3 ft.
British Columbia to New York and Montana. Zone 2.

The ground juniper is a wide-spreading plant with horizontal branches and erect branchlets. Its ⅜-inch needles are sharply pointed and marked above with a narrow white band.

J. horizontalis Moench *(J. prostrata)* CREEPING JUNIPER
Nova Scotia, Alaska, south to New Jersey and Montana. Zone 3.

This is a procumbent shrub. Its long, trailing branches form a mat about 1 foot high. It has scalelike leaves and blue-black berries. Cultivars of this variable species include Bar Harbor, a low, compact form with steel-blue foliage, and Wiltonii, a dwarf form.

J. occidentalis Hook. SIERRA JUNIPER 40 ft.
Washington to central California. Zone 6.

Sierra juniper can be a tree or shrub with light cinnamon-brown bark, cordlike twigs, scalelike overlapping leaves, and bluish-black berries.

J. rigida Siebold & Zucc. NEEDLE JUNIPER 30 ft.
Eastern Asia. Zone 6.

A pyramidal tree or shrub with drooping branchlets, the needle juniper has long, spreading, pointed needles marked with white bands above. Berries are brownish black.

J.r. subsp. **nipponica** Franco JAPANESE NEEDLE JUNIPER
Japan. Zone 6.

This low dwarf Japanese shrub or tree with closely placed ⅜-inch needles is the needle juniper often used for bonsai in Japan.

J. scopulorum Sarg. ROCKY MOUNTAIN JUNIPER 30 ft.
British Columbia south to Arizona and Texas. Zone 4.

The Rocky Mountain juniper (Fig. 17–13) has scalelike green leaves. Its small ¼-inch bright blue berries mature in two years. Many cultivars are available, and collected species are shaped into splendid bonsai.

J. virginiana L. RED CEDAR 75 ft.
Northeastern North America. Zone 3.

This tree, with tan to reddish-brown shreddy bark and slender twigs, has sharply pointed juvenile needles and scalelike adult foliage. It grows well in a moderately alkaline soil. The fruit is a bluish berry about the size of a pea with a whitish bloom. This is an extremely hardy and variable species. As bonsai, it tends to be more open than compact. As practice material (Figs. 5-7.1 through 5-7.7), it is superior and readily available in the eastern part of the United States. The cultivar Canaertii is a handsome, compact, conical tree with cordlike branching.

LAGERSTROEMIA CRAPE MYRTLE

Select any trunk line from upright to cascade for these small flowering trees. For sustained and profuse flowers, provide sun and bright light. Indoors, choose a sunny south window. Trim new growth early in the season and prune each shoot or branch again immediately after flowering.

Use a basic mix and keep the soil moderately moist, but not wet, between waterings. Fertilize as for other flowering bonsai. In warm climates, this fast-growing plant may need repotting twice a year, in the early spring and again in the late summer. In colder climates, repot once in the late spring once the days are warm.

L. indica L. CRAPE MYRTLE 20 ft.
China. Zone 7.

Crape myrtle is a deciduous upright tree or shrub with reddish-brown bark, 2-inch leaves, and showy panicles of white, pink, or purple flowers. This species is one of the few crape myrtles that grows in both warm and moderately cold climates. Small compact forms, developed commercially, are also promising material for bonsai.

LANTANA LANTANA

Lantanas make stunning bonsai. These perennial herbs respond favorably to bonsai training. They are naturalized in Florida and Texas and are considered a weed in parts of Hawaii.

Lantanas are generally trained as upright trunks. Their branching tends to be slightly stiff and open. Trim the new growth regularly to induce compact shoots. Provide direct sun and bright light for a maximum of flowers.

Use a basic mix containing organic matter. After repotting, water more than usual until the plant is established. Fertilize as for other flowering plants.

L. Camara L. LANTANA, YELLOW SAGE 4 ft.
Tropical America. Zone 9.

This shrub is sometimes prickly. It has 5-inch leaves and flowers, which form at the tip of the branches. The flowers, 2 inches across, open in colors of orange-yellow and orange, then change to white or red. The small fruit is black. Dwarf cultivars are available.

LARIX LARCH

These deciduous conifers, native to the colder part of the Northern Hemisphere, have soft, green needlelike leaves approximately 1 inch long. The leaves are arranged in dense clusters on short spurs. They turn an attractive yellow in autumn. The small cones are ¾ to 1½ inches long. Larches grow rapidly, especially when young.

With their soft, delicate foliage and splendid fall color, larches make handsome bonsai material for single, multitrunk, group plantings, and saikei in upright or slanting styles.

Larches prefer cool climates and are difficult to grow as bonsai in warm or dry climates. Give them full early morning sun in spring and fall and bright light and open shade during the summer. Do not water the leaves when they are in the sun.

In late winter or early spring, shorten overly long shoots from the previous summer to the desired bonsai shape. Later, trim new growth as it elongates.

For the following larches, except *L. decidua*, increase the basic mix by one-fourth with sphagnum peat moss or rich compost. Keep the mix slightly moist but not wet between waterings.

Root growth is variable. Repot larches when the roots have filled the container, in early spring before new growth appears or during the latter part of the summer.

Larches in some areas are susceptible to insect infestations. Watch for the woolly larch aphid; the larvae hibernate over the winter in small cases attached to the trunk and branches. Remove them before new growth starts in the spring.

L. decidua Mill. EUROPEAN LARCH 75 ft.
Europe. Zone 3.

Leaves measure up to 1½ inches and cones are 1½ inches long on the European larch. Because this larch prefers a sandy soil, use a basic mix to which extra sand has been added. Let the soil become slightly dry between waterings.

L. Kaempferi Carrière *(L. leptolepis)* JAPANESE LARCH 50 ft.
Japan. Zone 5.

A Japanese larch trained as a formal upright is shown in Fig. L1–1. This species is smaller than most larches. The bluish-green leaves, 1½ inches long, are flattened and broader than those of the European larch. The leaves may be identified by two conspicuous bands underneath. The cultivar Minor is a dwarf form.

Fig. L1–1 Japanese larch, *Larix Kaempferi (L. leptolepis),* with cones. Courtesy of J. Nakahara.

L. laricina C. Koch AMERICAN LARCH, TAMARACK 60 ft.
Alaska and Canada, south to Minnesota, Illinois, and Pennsylvania. Zone 2.

This cold-climate tree extends as far north as the limit of tree growth. The southern portions of its range are confined mostly to cold swamps and sphagnum bogs. The narrow, soft leaves, 1½ inches long, are densely crowded in rosette-like clusters. The small, shiny cones are ¾ inch long. The foliage turns a lovely yellow before dropping in autumn.

L. occidentalis Nutt. AMERICAN WESTERN LARCH 180 ft.
Rocky Mountains and British Columbia to Montana and Oregon. Zone 5.

This tall tree, which has brown bark and slightly stiff leaves up to 1¾ inches long, makes beautiful bonsai in the Pacific Northwest.

LIGUSTRUM PRIVET

Privets are deciduous or evergreen shrubs with opposite, often thick leaves, white flowers, and black berrylike fruit. The privets listed here share the following characteristics, which make them highly suitable for bonsai use:

Vigorous growth habits.
High tolerance to pruning.
New shoots from latent buds beneath the bark.
Readily available as large-size plants (from hedges).
Small leaves.

Fig. L2–1 Privet, *Ligustrum vulgare*. Courtesy of Tom Scott.

An example of the common privet is shown in Fig. L2–1. Privets are frequently trained as bonsai with a single upright trunk but also in groups and as minibonsai. Large trunks on privets found in hedges or other plantings may be cut back drastically and made into bonsai by shaping the new growth. Material of this nature lends itself to the Lingnan method.

Provide partial sun and bright light during the hot summer season and full sun in spring and fall. Trim the new growth repeatedly to induce dense branching. Repot in the spring whenever the roots are becoming potbound.

Pierre Kaufke, of Pensacola, Florida, one of the few bonsai growers who has worked with privets, reports that privet responds favorably to bonsai techniques and that it is a good starting plant for beginners.*

L. japonicum Thunb. JAPANESE PRIVET 10 ft.
Japan and Korea. Zone 7.

A semievergreen bushy shrub and rapid grower, the Japanese privet has 3-inch leaves, small white flowers in 2- to 4-inch panicles, and black berries. It is grown extensively in the southern United States, where it is evergreen.

L. sinense Lour. CHINESE PRIVET 12 ft.
This is a deciduous shrub with leaves 3 inches long and flower panicles to 4 inches.

*Pierre Kaufke, "Consider Privet: For Bonsai," *Journal of the American Bonsai Society*, 15, no. 1 (Spring 1981), 8–10.

L. vulgare L. COMMON PRIVET, EUROPEAN PRIVET 15 ft.
Mediterranean region. Zone 5.

The leaves of this deciduous shrub are 2½ inches long, and the flowers are in dense 1½ inch panicles. It is naturalized in the eastern United States.

LONICERA HONEYSUCKLE

These rampant growers adjust readily to bonsai training. Start with large trunks on old vines found growing as weeds in woods and meadows and along roadways. Prune drastically. Honeysuckle can be wired and shaped into any style the trunk suggests. Be sure to trim new shoots to prevent long internodes and open growth. Flowers are produced on the tip of small auxiliary shoots. These species do not demand exacting care. For compact growth, provide bright light and open shade, or direct sun in early spring and fall. Use a basic mix, keep it slightly moist but not wet between waterings, and fertilize regularly. Root growth is variable. Check the root mass every two years to see if repotting is indicated.

For growing indoors under light, honeysuckle can easily be propagated from seed after it has ripened.

L. japonica Thunb. JAPANESE HONEYSUCKLE
Eastern Asia. Zone 5.

This climbing shrub is wholly or partially evergreen, with 3-inch leaves, fragrant white and cream flowers 1½ inches long, and small black fruit. This vigorous grower, now naturalized in the United States, is a serious pest in some areas.

L. nitida E. H. Wils. BOX HONEYSUCKLE 6 ft.
China. Zone 7.

The leaves of this evergreen shrub in the southern states are a mere ½ inch long, accompanied by small white flowers and amethyst fruit. It is a vigorous grower.

MALPIGHIA MALPIGHIA

Malpighias make attractive warm-climate bonsai. They are grown in large or small sizes with a curved or slanting upright trunk or used for saikei and group plantings. The species described here grow best under strong outdoor light and direct sun during part of the day. Indoors, provide a sunny south window or high levels of artificial light.

Prune and trim during the growing season. After pruning, *M. glabra* branches out more readily than *M. coccigera*. Use a potting mix that drains well. It can be slightly acidic and rich in organic matter. Water when the soil becomes moderately dry. Repot, as needed, during warm weather in early summer.

Malpighias are easily propagated by seed for conditioned indoor bonsai, as described in Chapter 16.

M. coccigera L. MINIATURE HOLLY 3 ft.
West Indies. Zone 9.

This is a small evergreen shrub of coastal tropical America, with compact foliage, tiny pink flowers, and red fruit. Under conditions of bright light, it produces the dense growth wanted for bonsai. Its spiny, glossy, hollylike leaves are ¾ inch long. The shrub is naturalized in southern Florida.

M. glabra L. BARBADOS CHERRY 15 ft.
Texas, Central and South America, and the West Indies. Zone 9.

This is a small evergreen tree or shrub larger than *M. coccigera*. It has 3-inch leaves, pink flowers, and red fruit, and it grows well in southern Florida.

MALUS APPLES AND CRAB APPLES

Apples and crab apples provide beautiful flowering bonsai for cold climates. These small, well-branched trees, or sometimes shrubs, have showy spring flowers and attractive autumn fruit. Because of the small size of their fruit, seen in Fig. 2-3, crab apples, rather than apple trees, are usually preferred for bonsai. However, old collected apple trees, miniaturized by adverse environments and grazing animals, are also prime material.

Because their fruit is green, the American species are grown primarily for their pink and white flowers. Oriental species with both colorful fruit and flowers are more desirable as bonsai. The flowers, which appear in midspring, range in color from white to pink to purplish red. They last for a week or ten days unless the weather is unusually warm.

The *Malus* genus is beset by scab disease, juniper rust, and insects. In an excellent article on crab apples, Donald Wyman, horticulturalist emeritus of the Arnold Arboretum, Jamaica Plains, Massachusetts, notes that at the arboretum, crab apples with small fruit, about the size of a pea, are the least troubled by insects and require a minimum of spraying.* This is an advantageous combination for bonsai, where a small-sized fruit is preferred. Choose a disease-resistant species that flowers each year (some blossom every other year), has small fruit, and grows well. Consult nurseries or pomologists for recommended disease-resistant crab apples in your area.

When selecting a specimen, look for a plant with branches low on the trunk so that the height of the tree can be reduced. On a grafted plant, examine the union where the separate trees are joined for a smooth, close fit that will not form an unsightly bulge.

Forsaken, stunted apple and crab apple trees in old fields make handsome bonsai with thick trunks and strong major branches. After they are dug, prune them severely to a stout trunk and a few branches. While establishing a basic

*Donald Wyman "Crab Apples," *American Horticulturist*, 54 no. 5 (October 1975) 9–11.

shape, prune the bonsai every year in the early spring before new growth begins. Remove dead, damaged, and nonconforming interior branches. Shorten last year's shoots to conform to the shape of the tree, and wire as needed. For more information on collected *Malus* spp., consult Jerald P. Stowell's *The Beginner's Guide to American Bonsai* listed at the end of this section.

Each summer, flower buds for the following year will form on short spurs along the branches. Retain as many as possible when pruning. As soon as fruit appears after flowering, selectively thin and distribute the fruit evenly around the tree. This will improve the appearance and preserve the vigor of the tree.

Provide direct sun and open shade. Use a basic potting mix and allow the soil to become slightly dry between waterings. Fertilize regularly with a balanced fertilizer; do not omit nitrogen, needed for healthy growth.

M. baccata Borkh. SIBERIAN CRAB APPLE 16 ft.
Eastern Asia. Zone 2.

This hardy crab apple for cold climates regularly produces white flowers 1 to 1½ inches across in the spring and yellow and red autumn fruit about ⅜ inch in diameter. The shining leaves are 1 to 3 inches long.

M.b. var. *Jackii* is a Korean crab apple with white flowers and bright red persistent fruit measuring about ⅜ inch.

M. floribunda Siebold ex Van Houtte SHOWY CRAB APPLE 25 ft.
Japan. Zone 5.

The sharply serrated leaves on the arching branch of this crab apple are 2 to 3 inches long. Rose flowers about 1 inch across appear regularly each year and are followed by 5/16-inch yellow fruit.

M. Halliana Koehne HALL'S CRAB APPLE to 18 ft.
Japan and China. Zone 6.

This is a shrub or small tree with 1½- to 3-inch leaves, bright rose flowers 1 to 1½ inches across, and 5/16-inch purplish fruit. The cultivar Parkmanii has double flowers. An example of Hall's crab apple from Japan is shown in Fig. M1-1.

M. Sargentii Rehd. SARGENT'S CRAB APPLE 6 ft.
Japan. Zone 5.

This horizontally branched shrub has fragrant pure white flowers about 1 inch across and ⅜-inch round dark red fruit. The serrated leaves are 2 to 3 inches long.

M. spectabilis Borkh. CHINESE FLOWERING CRAB APPLE 25 ft.
China. Zone 5.

This rather tall crab apple has bright pink flowers 2 inches across and yellow fruit 1 inch in diameter. The leaves are 2 to 3 inches long. The cultivar Van Eseltine has double bright rose flowers and yellow and red fruit.

Fig. M1–1 Hall's crab apple, *Malus Halliana,* in the Japanese bonsai collection at the U.S. National Arboretum. Photo courtesy of USDA.

Note: Every spring, Red Jade, a cultivar developed at the Brooklyn Botanic Garden, is covered with profuse white flowers ⅝ inch across, followed by small bright red fruit. The branches have a weeping form. This beautiful patented crab apple is about 15 feet tall.

Among the species listed, those that are not hybrids may be raised from stratified seed, including *M. baccata, M. floribunda, M. Halliana, M. Sargentii*, and *M. spectabilis.*

ADDITIONAL READING

STOWELL, JERALD P., *The Beginner's Guide to American Bonsai.* Tokyo, New York, San Francisco: Kodansha International Ltd., 1978. Contains a detailed section on developing collected *Malus* spp. as bonsai.

MURRAYA MOCK ORANGE

Orange jasmine is seen most frequently with a curved or slanting upright trunk. It may also be shaped as a semicascade or cascade bonsai. The lower trunk develops a woody appearance within a few years.

Outdoors, orange jasmine needs warm year-round temperatures and diffused bright light or open shade. Indoors, provide temperatures of 60° to 70°F. or higher and an east or a lightly screened south window. Prune after flowering and as needed during the growing season. Use a basic mix and let the soil remain slightly moist between waterings. It is important to fertilize regularly. If the leaves turn yellowish green, apply chelated iron or other iron supplements.

Orange jasmine is easily propagated by seed.

M. paniculata Jack ORANGE JASMINE OR JESSAMINE 10–12 ft.
Southeast Asia and Malay Peninsula. Zone 10.

This is an evergreen shrub with glossy pinnately compound leaves and ¾-inch fragrant white flowers that blossom several times a year. It is a popular, trouble-free bonsai in Hong Kong, southern China, and other warm climates. It is grown as indoor bonsai in colder climates.

MYRCIARIA JABOTICABA

Outstanding in this genus is jaboticaba, an unusual tree of the American subtropics that forms flowers and fruit directly on its trunks and branches. The molted bark on old trunks resembles that of sycamores or plane trees.

As bonsai, jaboticaba is trained with an upright trunk and open growth to display its flowers and fruit. Provide bright light and a year-round warm, frost-free climate. Use a mix containing humus or decomposed compost. Keep the soil slightly moist between waterings. Fertilizer as for a flowering bonsai.

Jaboticaba is easily propagated by seed.

M. cauliflora O. Berg JABOTICABA 40 ft.

This fascinating evergreen tree is found in Florida. The leaves are 4 inches long. The white flowers and 1-inch round purple edible fruit grow on the trunk. This bonsai prefers a deep, rich soil and a moist climate without frost or excessive heat.

MYRSINE AFRICAN BOXWOOD

African boxwood is a dwarf tree or shrub of warm climates trainable to any style that is appropriate to its trunk. Provide warm temperatures and sun or bright light year round. Use a basic mix and keep it slightly moist between waterings. Prune and shape as boxwood.

M. africana L. AFRICAN BOXWOOD, CAPE MYRTLE 6 ft.
The Azores to China.

This shrubby evergreen bush resembles boxwood with its dense growth and shining ½- to 1-inch leaves. Small flowers are followed by purple-red berries.

MYRTUS MYRTLE

Myrtle has white to pink flowers and berrylike fruit. It is grown outdoors in the south and as an indoor plant in colder regions.

Myrtle is used in upright styles, group plantings, saikei, and minibonsai. In frost-free climates, grow myrtle outdoors in bright light and partial shade. Indoors, place it on a sunny windowsill or under high levels of artificial light at temperatures between 60° and 70°F. During the winter, myrtle may be maintained in a "resting" state at a cool north window or on an unheated sunporch.

Prune and trim new growth as for holly or boxwood. Use a basic potting mix and allow the soil to become moderately dry between waterings.

This species is easily propagated by cuttings.

M. communis L. GREEK MYRTLE 15 ft.
Mediterranean region. Zone 9.

This evergreen shrub with dark green dense foliage is the classic myrtle of ancient Greece. It has been cultivated for centuries. Dwarf forms include cvs. Compacta, Minima, and Nana.

NANDINA HEAVENLY BAMBOO

This is an evergreen shrub native to India and eastern Asia and rich in folklore. In China it was traditionally planted at the door of newly married couples to ensure their health and happiness.

As bonsai, nandina is grown as a clump of straight trunks. It thrives in partial sun and open shade. Use a basic mix containing organic matter and keep the soil slightly damp between waterings. Nandina is not demanding, but it requires protection from cold.

N. domestica Thunb. HEAVENLY BAMBOO, NANDINA 10 ft.
India and eastern Asia. Root-hardy to Zone 6 but grows best in Zone 7 or warmer.

Lacy double compound leaves emerge on the nonbranching, stiff trunks. White flowers are borne in panicles up to 1 foot long, followed by bright red berries about ¼ inch in diameter. The leaves turn a beautiful red in fall and are persistent in warm climates; in cold climates, nandina are not reliably evergreen. A few dwarf forms are available.

OLEA OLIVE

The species used for bonsai, *O. europaea*, is grown in warm regions of the world for its fruit, which is the source of olive oil. Olive trees, with their gray bark and dark green leaves, are seen as bonsai with upright trunks. These can be straight, slanting, or curved, single or double. Young plants are suitable for group plantings, saikei, and minibonsai. In warm climates, older, collected trees are pruned back severely and reconstructed as bonsai.

Place this species outdoors in year-round warm climates where it will receive bright light and sun; indoors, provide a sunny south or east window or high levels of artificial light. A specimen grown as an indoor bonsai is shown in Fig. O1-1.

The tree is tolerant of pruning and wiring. For a compact bonsai, trim new growth whenever it occurs.

Fig. O1-1 Common olive, *Olea europaea,* grown as an indoor bonsai in Philadelphia.

Use a basic potting mix and make sure that the drainage is good. Allow the mix to become moderately dry between waterings.

Olives are easily propagated by cuttings.

O. europaea L. COMMON OLIVE 25 ft.
Mediterranean region. Zone 9.

The olive, an evergreen tree, has leaves 1½ inches long and small white flowers and fruits. It is cultivated and naturalized in Italy, Spain, California, and other warm climates.

OSMANTHUS DEVILWEED

This is a genus of mainly Asiatic evergreen trees and shrubs. Established plants normally will have an upright trunk, but young material can be trained into any style that seems appropriate. Provide open shade or sun except during the heat of midday. Use a well-drained mix containing organic matter and allow the soil to become slightly dry between waterings. Fertilize regularly during the growing season.

For indoor bonsai, place at a sunny window or under fluorescent light. To obtain optimum growth, keep indoor temperatures between 65° and 75°F. during the day and 50° to 60°F. at night.

O. heterophyllus P. S. Green HOLLY OLIVE 20 ft.
Japan and Taiwan. Zone 7.

On this small evergreen tree, the glossy, toothed leaves, up to 2½ inches long, are opposite. White flowers bloom in the fall. Variegatus, a native of Japan, up to 5 feet tall, is a cultivar hardy to Zone 7. It is attractive as indoor bonsai material in cooler regions. Small, fragrant green-yellow flowers appear in late summer. The fruit is a tiny blue-black berry.

PICEA SPRUCE

Spruces are attractive conical evergreen trees with an excurrent trunk and horizontal branches in whorls. They are native to the cooler regions of the Northern Hemisphere. The needle on a spruce is four-angled and grows from a raised base. The little knobs holding the needles remain on the stem after the needles fall. This is one way of distinguishing spruces from firs, which they closely resemble. Spruces may also be identified by their cones, which hang down from the branches.

As bonsai, spruces are generally trained to an upright trunk style—straight, curved, or slanting.

To make spruce growth more compact, remove the large terminal bud on each shoot in late winter or early spring before growth begins. Then, as buds open and start to elongate, pinch or pluck out the tip of each bud.

Spruces like a cool climate. They are not trees for warm regions. Give them partial sun in spring and fall and bright light with open shade during the summer. Protect them from drying winds. Use a basic mix that drains well, and water thoroughly. Unlike pines, spruces cannot survive long periods with little water. Their thin, threadlike roots fill the container very slowly. Frequent repotting and root pruning is not needed.

P. glauca Voss *(P. alba)* WHITE SPRUCE 70 ft.
Canada and northern United States. Zone 3.

The thin grayish-brown bark is scaly on this spruce, whose needles are ¾ inch long. Cones are 2 inches long. The many forms and cultivars include Conica, a dense narrow conical dwarf form, and Nana, also a dwarf form with dense growth.

P.g. var. **albertiana** Sarg. ALBERTA SPRUCE
British Columbia to Montana. Zone 3.

The needles are close together on this spruce. Cones are 1½ inches long. Alberta spruce are shown in Fig. 2-6 and 13-12.

P. Glehnii M. T. Mast. SAKHALIN SPRUCE 100 ft.
Japan and Sakhalin Island. Zone 4.

Also known as Yezo spruce, this is the spruce frequently seen in Japanese bonsai. Its deep green needles are only ½ inch long, and the cones measure 3 inches. An old specimen of the species from Japan is now at the U.S. National Arboretum (Fig. P1-1).

Fig. P1–1 Sakhalin spruce, *Picea Glehnii,* among the Japanese bonsai at the U.S. National Arboretum. Photo courtesy of USDA.

P. pungens Engelm. COLORADO SPRUCE 100 ft.
Wyoming, Utah, Colorado, and New Mexico. Zone 3.

Colorado spruce is also known as Colorado blue spruce. The bark is dark grayish-brown with loose scales. The bluish-green needles are stiff, sharply pointed, and 1¼ inches long. Many cultivars are available. The cultivar Glauca, blue spruce, has bluish needles.

P. rubens Sarg. *(P. rubra)* RED SPRUCE 90 ft.
Nova Scotia to the mountains of North Carolina. Zone 3.

Red spruce has ½-inch-long needles and 2-inch cones. A clump collected from the mountains of West Virginia is shown in Fig. P1–2. This tall, narrow tree grows best in a cool, moist environment.

Fig. P1–2 Nine collected red spruces, *Picea rubens,* planted on a rock. Courtesy of Richard Meszler.

Fig. P2–1 *Pieris japonica* at the Morris Arboretum of the University of Pennsylvania. Photo by Paul W. Meyer.

PIERIS ANDROMEDA

These evergreen shrubs or small trees have alternate or whorled leaves, which are rarely opposite. The white flowers in racemes resemble lily-of-the-valley. They require a rich, moist, well-drained container mix without lime.

Styles include mainly upright trunks, single or multiple, which are often curved to reflect the graceful natural appearance of this genus, as seen in Fig. P2–1.

This is a hardy outdoor cold-climate bonsai. It needs protection during the winter and partial sun and shade during the growing season.

Prune immediately after flowering; trim the flower stems to two or three leaves to encourage compact new growth. Usually several shoots will emerge where the old shoot was cut. Keep only one or two to continue growth in the desired direction and remove the others. Flower buds form at the tip of the shoots. Where flowers are wanted, plan to trim new shoots shortly after flowering in the spring. Wire the trunk and branches at any time except when flower buds have opened or are about to open.

If repotting is needed, do it immediately after flowering. Use a peaty-sandy mix such as two parts sphagnum peat moss and two parts coarse sand with one part soil.

Andromedas are not aggressive growers and are usually repotted at intervals of two or three years. Water them more frequently than other bonsai to keep the soil moist (not wet) at all times. A dry surface on the potting mix is not a problem so long as moisture is present below the surface. It is essential not to allow the soil around the roots to dry. Promote healthy growth and abundant flowers by regular fertilizing from spring until late summer.

P. floribunda Benth. & Hook. MOUNTAIN ANDROMEDA 6 ft.
Virginia and Georgia. Zone 5.

This attractive native evergreen shrub, in cultivation since 1800, has deep green 3-inch leaves and showy small white bell-shaped flowers on erect panicles in spring. It is easily distinguished from the Japanese andromeda, *P. japonica*, whose flower panicles are drooping.

P. japonica D. Don & ex G. Don LILY-OF-THE-VALLEY BUSH to 30 ft.
Japan. Zone 6.

Leaves on this species are 3 inches long. It has drooping 6-inch panicles of flowers, which appear in the spring. This species may also flower a second time in late summer or fall. Cultivars of bonsai interest include Bonsai, a very small dwarf form; Compacta, also dwarf; Pygmaea, minute and bushy; and Variegata, with white margins on the leaves. The cultivar Christmas Cheer is a small, compact grower with a red tinge on its new shoots.

PINUS Pine

These evergreen conifers are native to the Northern Hemisphere. Needles are generally arranged in bundles of two to five. Each bundle, or cluster, is surrounded by a small sheath at its base. For example, white pine, named for the color of its wood, has needles in bundles of five, while the needles on ponderosa pine are in bundles of three. Among the ninety or so species of pine, a high proportion, about 20 percent, are grown as bonsai.

A number of characteristics are shared by all pines: The needles remain on the tree for two to six years or longer; branches emerge from the trunk in whorls; the bark on old trees develops handsome furrows and plates. Nearly all pines prefer a deep, well-drained, sandy loam and do not thrive in clayey soils. They suffer if waterlogged but can withstand dryness.

In bonsai, pines of all sizes and styles, from single- to multitrunk, are found in climates as diverse as cold northern mountains and warm sunny plains.

Pines are sun-loving trees. An area too sunny for maples will be quite suitable for pines. Pines are rugged outdoor trees that need fresh air and sunshine; they do not survive in buildings or enclosed structures.

When pines are pruned, a resinous sap collects at the cut and forms a lump as it hardens. To avoid this, make the initial cut about ½ inch above the callus collar. This leaves a stub, which in a year or two can be cut flush with the collar. No sap forms at the second cut. However, pines are not tolerant of drastic pruning. When pruning a pine extensively, retain sufficient foliage for photosynthesis to support the tree until new green growth develops.

Five-needle pines rarely produce lateral buds on their stems. The buds form at the tip of each shoot. If last year's shoot is cut below the terminal buds, no further growth occurs from that shoot. To shorten or remove an old shoot, prune it at the fork of the nearest shoot or branch. Two- and three-needle pines, however, tend to sprout from latent buds on their trunk and branches.

A well-shaped pine with short needles is a great achievement in bonsai. Fortunately, pine needles shorten with bonsai training. The reduction is increased further by withholding water and providing sun. A clear relationship exists in bonsai between the amount of water a pine receives and the length of its needles. Apply the following methods to produce compact growth and short needles:

1. Prevent the retention of excessive moisture between waterings either by increasing the aggregates in the mix or reducing the moisture-holding ingredients. Or use a basic mix and water less often. Give only the minimum water required. This is learned by experience. Instead of discarding unpromising young pines, grow them as learning material. Experiment in withholding water on expendible material rather than on a pine pruned and wired to a beautiful shape.
2. Provide the maximum available sun that your time and schedule allows. Do not place pines in the heat of the sun when no one will be present to water them. Give them only as much sun as they can safely take without the soil becoming parched between intervals of watering.
3. Fertilize lightly. Apply a diluted fertilizer once a month after the new needles are no longer lengthening. Cease fertilizing well before the end of the summer. Two or three applications during the growing season are ample.
4. To prevent the accumulation of water around the roots of valuable pines, use a simple Japanese method to facilitate drainage. Tilt an oval or rectangular container by placing a strip of wood an inch or so thick under one end. This will cause the water to drain rapidly through the holes rather than accumulating around the roots at the bottom of the container. This is especially helpful during periods of heavy rain.

No species responds to wiring better than a pine. Properly applied wire will not damage the thick layer of bark that covers the cambium. The limber wood of the trunk and branches is easily repositioned. Unless a pine has become stiff with age, it is possible to shift the position of a major branch sideways on the outside of the trunk. Do this by twisting the trunk along with the branch in the wanted direction. First anchor the wire securely—for example, by inserting it well into the mix at the bottom of the trunk. The next step is critical: Spiral the wire upward in the same direction—clockwise or counter-clockwise—in which you wish to rotate the branch. Continue the wiring well beyond the branch. Then grasp the trunk with both hands, one above and the other below the branch, and twist the trunk slowly and carefully until the branch is eased into the desired position. Let the wire remain on the trunk until the branch is set in its new location.

Pines do not require frequent repotting. Repot only when they become slightly potbound. They are sensitive to root pruning. Remove overly thick roots and shorten long ones while retaining as much of the root mass as possible. Avoid severe root pruning.

P. aristata Engelm. BRISTLECONE PINE to 40 ft.
Mountains from British Columbia to California. Zone 4.

Old specimens of this famous tree are found growing on dolomitic mountain sities in the West. Many are more than 4,000 years old, which places bristlecone pines among the oldest living entities in the world. Their dark green needles in bundles of five are 1 to 1½ inches long. For bonsai, this species is not difficult to confine in a container. The tree will feel at home with dolomitic limestone in the mix. Unfortunately, growth is slow and trunk taper is imperceptible. Although it adapts to a container, this fascinating pine does not respond readily to bonsai training.

P. Banksiana Lamb. JACK PINE 75 ft.
Nova Scotia to Wisconsin and northwest into Canada. Zone 2.

This species, which thrives in poor soil, is found in the farthermost northern range of pines. It is usually small and shrubby. The stiff, twisted needles, widely spaced in bundles of two, are ¾ to 1½ inches long. Cones are 2 inches long. While tolerant of confinement to a container, this species lacks the compactness usually seen in bonsai.

P. Cembra L. SWISS STONE PINE 75 ft.
Europe and northern Asia. Zone 3.

Slow-growing, long-lived, and usually small, this pine has straight dark green needles in bundles of five, up to 5 inches long, but they will shorten in bonsai training. Cones are 3½ inches long. *P. Cembra* has dense twigs and short branches. It is tolerant of transplanting and container growth.

P. clausa Vasey SAND PINE 70 ft.
Florida. Zone 9.

Generally, sand pine is a small to medium-size tree with smooth bark and flexible needles 2 to 4½ inches long in bundles of two. Cones measure 2 to 3½ inches. It can produce new growth from latent buds. The most southern of North American pines, the sand pine has an open pattern of growth in poor soil. When moved to better soil, it changes to a more compact form.

P. contorta Dougl. ex Loud. SHORE PINE 20–30 ft.
Alaska to northern California. Zone 7.

This is a shrub or small tree. Its needles, in bundles of two and up to 2 inches long, are stiff, twisted, and dark green. Cones are 2 inches long. On the coast, this pine is a small tree with a short, thick, corky trunk and dense growth. It responds poorly to pruning and does not sprout from latent buds.

P.c. var. **latifolia** Engelm. ex S. Wats. LODGEPOLE PINE 100 ft.
Alaska to California, Nebraska, and Colorado. Zone 4.

The variety *latifolia* is preferred for bonsai. This inland pine is a tall tree and the most common conifer in the Rocky Mountains. Its needles, bundled in pairs, are 1 to 3 inches long and of an attractive yellowish-green color. This long-lived tree responds favorably to bonsai training. Its latent buds break easily. Many dwarfed forms are found in the wild.

P. densiflora Siebold & Zucc. JAPANESE RED PINE 100 ft.
Japan. Zone 5.

Japanese red pine has bright bluish-green needles, 5 inches long, in bundles of two. Its cones are 2 inches long. It is a tree of irregular growth and dense, spreading branches with reddish-brown bark. It is subject to winter damage in cold climates. The cultivar Umbraculifera, Tanyosho Japanese umbrella pine, is a dwarf form with an umbrellalike head.

P. flexilis James LIMBER PINE 60 ft.
Alberta to Montana, south to California and Texas. Zone 4.

Limber pine (Fig. 17–14) has needles in bundles of five of a yellow-green color. They are stiff and about 3 inches long. Its cones are 3 to 10 inches long. Young trees have a narrow pyramidal form that becomes broader with age. This species has not become widely popular as bonsai, but it is well worth using where it is available.

P. leucodermis Ant. BALKAN PINE 90 ft.
Italy and the Balkan Peninsula. Zone 6.

This pine has rigid, sharply pointed 3½-inch needles in bundles of two and 3-inch cones. The bark is dark gray, with angular plates on old trees. Although its growth is less compact, the needles and general appearance of this species resemble *P. Thunbergiana*, Japanese black pine. Balkan pine is tolerant of container growth and bonsai techniques. The trunk, however, is slow to form a taper.

P. Mugo Turra MUGO PINE, SWISS MOUNTAIN PINE 30 ft.
Mountains of central and southern Europe. Zone 3.

The bright 2-inch-long needles in bundles of two are crowded on the branches to produce dense foliage. The cones are 2 inches long on this small pine.

P.M. var.**Mugo** is a small shrub with prostrate growth and small cones.

P. parviflora Siebold & Zucc. JAPANESE WHITE PINE 50 ft.
Japan. Zone 6.

This graceful pine (Figs. 5-1, 7-8, and 12-6), with its soft foliage and small needles, is one of the most popular species for bonsai in Japan. It has needles in bundles of five, up to 1½ inches long, and 3-inch cones. New growth emerges only from terminal buds. There are numerous forms and cultivars, including cvs. Glauca and Nana with short needles. This species and its variants are most amendable to bonsai training. For further information on this species, consult *Japanese Five-Needle Pine* by William N. Valavanis, listed at the end of this section.

P. Peuce Griseb. MACEDONIAN PINE 60 ft.
The Balkans. Zone 5.

This species is similar to *P. parviflora* but has longer needles and is more winter-hardy. The needles, in bundles of five, are 4 inches long. They soon reduce with bonsai training.

P. ponderosa Dougl. ex P. Laws & C. Laws. PONDEROSA PINE to 200 ft.
British Columbia to Nebraska, Texas, and Mexico. Zone 5.

Ponderosa pine is the most widely distributed pine in North America. It is found at elevations up to 9,000 feet. Usually it attains less than its maximum height. The coarse, stiff needles are in bundles of three, from 5 to 11 inches long, and remain on the tree for three years. Cones are 6 inches long. New growth can occur from latent buds. On old trees, bark is fissured in ridges or in large flat plates. Ponderosa pine grows in all types of soil, but it does best in dry, well-drained sites with a high water table. The most popular specimens for bonsai are naturally dwarfed trees collected from the wild, as in Fig. P3-1.

P.p. var. **scopulorum** Engelm. ROCKY MOUNTAIN PINE
South Dakota to Mexico and Texas. Zone 4.

This species is similar to ponderosa pine, although it is smaller. The 3- to 6-inch-long needles are in bundles of three. Its cones are 3 inches long. The furrowed bark is nearly black. Specimens collected from the wild are highly appreciated as bonsai.

Fig. P3–1 Ponderosa pine, *Pinus ponderosa,* collected in Colorado. Courtesy of Harold Sasaki.

P. rigida Mill. PITCH PINE 60 ft.
New Brunswick to Kentucky and Georgia. Zone 5.

The pitch pine has fairly stiff needles in bundles of three, 3 to 4 inches long. Its cones are 1½ to 4 inches long. It thrives in poor soil. Trees collected in the wild respond well to bonsai training. Pitch pine sprouts frequently from adventitious buds beneath the bark. As with other species that are essentially forest trees, starting with larger stock gives results far sooner than starting with seed.

P. Strobus L. EASTERN WHITE PINE 120 ft.
Eastern North America. Zone 3.

This pine has slender greenish-blue needles in bundles of five, up to 5 inches long. Its cones are 4 to 6 inches long. Eastern white pine, so beautiful growing in the ground, is slow to produce dense growth as a bonsai. Better results are obtained in the same length of time from larger material than from seedlings. A number of dwarf forms with compact growth are available.

P. sylvestris L. SCOTS PINE 120 ft.
Eurasia. Zone 3.

A very hardy pine, Scots pine (Fig. P3–2) has bluish-green, stiff, often twisted needles in bundles of two. The needles are 3 inches long and the cones 2½ inches long. Scots pine is another species that sends out shoots from buds beneath the bark. Dwarf cultivars suitable for bonsai include Beauvronensis, Compressa, and Nana.

Fig. P3–2 Scots pine, *Pinus sylvestris,* trained as a bonsai from nursery stock in the Middle Atlantic states. Courtesy of Thomas G. Wright.

P. Thunbergiana Franco *(P. Thunbergii)* JAPANESE BLACK PINE 130 ft.
Japan. Zone 5.

Despite its long needles (3 to 4½ inches, in bundles of two), Japanese black pine is one of the best pines for bonsai. The sharp, well-defined needles quickly shorten with bonsai training. Terminal buds form readily and send out strong shoots. Shoots also sprout from lateral buds beneath the bark. If dense foliage blocks light to the interior of the tree, shorten the needles to open the bonsai to light. It spans a range of climates and grows in both southern California and eastern Pennsylvania.

Use the following method to obtain shorter needles and more compact growth on Japanese black pine: In climates where bonsai do not experience below-freezing winter temperatures, completely remove each candle longer than an inch or two. Do this in midspring. Make the cut where the candle originated. A second set of shoots will develop. In early fall, shorten these shoots by removing one-half or two-thirds of each shoot. (Remember to cut all pine shoots only where needles are present.) Another set of buds will form during the fall and winter. In cold-winter climates, modify this procedure. Remove the first candles completely in late June or early July. The second candles will be smaller. Allow them to develop without further pruning.

Another attractive feature is the thick corky bark on some specimens, designated as *P. Thunbergiana* cv. Corticosta, or cork-bark black pine, as seen in Fig. 3–2.

P. virginiana Mill. SCRUB PINE 50 ft.
New York to Georgia and Alabama. Zone 5.

Scrub pine has stiff, twisted needles in bundles of two, up to 3 inches long, and 2½-inch cones. It grows on barren soil, and its bonsai use is similar to that of *P. rigida*.

ADDITIONAL READING

VALAVANIS, WILLIAM N., *Japanese Five-Needle Pine*, Atlanta, Ga.: Symmes Systems, 1976. A thorough study of *Pinus parviflora* in Japan that describes the tree in nature, as landscape material, and as bonsai. Documented and profusely illustrated.

PITHECELLOBIUM

Texas ebony, *P. flexicaule*, a shrub or tree in the American Southwest, is the species used for bonsai. Edith Sorge, a professional bonsai grower in Adkins, Texas, who works extensively with this species, has provided the following information:

Texas ebony is excellent for outdoor bonsai in frost-free climates as well as for indoor bonsai and growing under light. It prefers full sun but also thrives in nearly full shade. Use a basic mix with good drainage. Water thoroughly and do not let the soil become dry between waterings. During the summer, fertilize once a week for faster growth.

For dense foliage, trim or pinch new growth. Leaves reduce with bonsai training, and this species responds well to defoliation in summer. Spines may be cut off before wiring.

Texas ebony is easily propagated from seed and can be used as a conditioned plant for indoor bonsai. Prior to planting, pour boiling water over the seeds and let them soak for 24 hours. Plant very shallowly in a basic mix and keep the seedbed warm and damp. Germination usually takes place within ten days.

P. flexicaule J. Coult. TEXAS EBONY 50 ft.

This tree has zigzag branching, small spines, and featherlike leaves about 2 inches long with ¼- to ½-inch-long leaflets that close at night. Fragrant light yellow or cream-colored flowers appear on dense 1½-inch-long spikes from June to August. The fruit is a 2- to 6-inch-long pod that ripens in the fall and remains on the tree until the following year. This species is suitable for many styles. An example of an upright trunk style grown in Texas is seen in Fig. P4–1.

Fig. P4–1 Texas ebony, *Pithecellobium flexicaule.* Courtesy of the Bonsai Farm.

PITTOSPORUM PITTOSPORUM

Pittosporums are evergreen shrubs and trees native to the warm subtropical and tropical climates of the world.

The species used for bonsai, *P. Tobira*, has relatively large leaves. It is most effective as a medium to large bonsai. Nearly any style of a slanting or curved, single or double trunk is suitable.

Grow outside year-round in warm zones with bright light and some sun. Indoors, place pittosporums at a sunny south or east window with temperatures between 65° and 75°F.

Prune immediately before or during the active growing season. Use a basic mix and allow the soil to become moderately dry between waterings.

P. Tobira Ait. MOCK ORANGE 18 ft.
China and Japan. Zone 8.

Mock orange is a shrub or small tree with leathery leaves 4 inches long. It forms terminal clusters of ½-inch white or yellow flowers. This species is planted extensively in warm climates and is used as a pot plant for the home or greenhouse in the north. The leaves of cv. Variegata are edged with white.

PLANERA WATER ELM

A short trunk and spreading crown make this North American species attractive for bonsai. Shape, prune, and wire it as an elm (*Ulmus*). Use a basic mix, but because this is a tree of wet lowlands, do not let the soil become overly dry.

P. aquatica J. F. Gmel. WATER ELM 35 ft.
Kentucky to Florida and west to Illinois and Texas. Zone 7.

This elmlike tree ranges in size from a shrub to an occasional tall specimen more than 60 feet high. It has scaly grayish-brown bark on a short trunk topped by a low-spreading crown. The leaves are alternate and about 1 to 3 inches long. The small flowers appear with the leaves, and the fruit is a nutlike drupe with short spurs.

PODOCARPUS PODOCARPUS

This genus is native to temperate regions of the Southern Hemisphere and higher elevations of the tropics from the West Indies to Japan.

Indoors or outdoors, *P. macrophyllus* and varieties make handsome bonsai with well-developed trunks, from upright to cascade. Young plants are used for saikei, minibonsai, and indoor light gardens.

Provide year-round warm temperatures and bright light or partial shade outdoors. Indoors, keep daytime temperatures around 60° to 70°F. Place podocarpus at a window, in other well-lighted areas, or under medium- to high-intensity artificial light.

These plants are tolerant of wiring and repeated pruning. Use a basic mix and keep the soil slightly moist but not wet between waterings.

P. macrophyllus D. Don JAPANESE YEW, BUDDHIST PINE 45 ft.
Central and southwest Japan. Zone 8.

This is a coniferous evergreen with horizontal branching and dense foliage. The glossy dark green leaves are 2 to 4½ inches long and ¾ inch wide. Podocarpus is popular as bonsai in Hong Kong, China, Japan, the southern United States, and other warm areas; it is an indoor bonsai in colder areas.

P.m. var. **Maki** Endl. CHINESE PODOCARPUS
China.

For bonsai use, this variety is similar to *P. macrophyllus*. The straight needles are 1½ to 3 inches long, ¼ inch wide, and abruptly narrowed at the tip, and the branching is more upright than horizontal.

POLYSCIAS ARALIA

These tropical shrubs and trees are used in gardens and hedges in warm climates and grown as pot plants in colder regions.

Aralias make exotic bonsai with a single or multiple trunks in any upright style. Their graceful appearance and attractive foliage are highly decorative.

Outdoors, provide year-round warm temperatures and bright light or partial sun. Keep indoor temperatures around 65° to 75°F. Choose a location with bright light, such as a sunny south window.

Shape aralias by pruning; their soft trunks are easily damaged by wire. If wiring is necessary, wrap the wire first with soft paper. Use a basic mix and keep it moderately moist between waterings.

Exotic plants of this nature, especially when grown as indoor bonsai, are often planted in decorative glazed containers.

P. fruticosa Harms MING ARALIA 8 ft.
India to Polynesia. Zone 10.

The finely divided leaves are a distinctive feature of this evergreen shrub. Among the cultivars, Elegans is compact with dense leathery foliage, and Deleauana is a dwarf form with variegated foliage.

PORTULACARIA ELEPHANT BUSH

Elephant bush is a deciduous shrub or small tree. Although it has a woodier trunk and smaller leaves than a jade plant, when seen at a distance it resembles a crassula. Both are warm-climate succulents.

Elephant bush is grown outdoors as bonsai in southern coastal California and southern Florida. In colder climates, it is used as indoor bonsai. It is usually trained with a upright or slanting trunk, in single- or multitrunk styles, as group plantings, saikei, and on-a-rock plantings.

Give this bonsai plenty of strong light outdoors but protect it from direct hot sun at midday. Indoors, place it at a sunny south window or other sunny exposure or under fluorescent lamps.

As bonsai, it is tolerant of pruning and confinement to a container. As with other succulents, the soft trunk and branches are more easily shaped by pruning than wiring.

Use a basic potting mix and allow the soil to become slightly dry before watering. Repot in the late spring or early summer. Elephant bush is easily propagated by cuttings.

P. afra Jacq. ELEPHANT BUSH 12 ft.
Arid parts of South Africa. Zone 10.

P. afra (Fig. 7–5) has nearly horizontal branches and small leaves up to ¾ inch long. The tiny pale pink flowers appear in clusters. Cultivars include Tricolor and Variegata.

PRUNUS

Apricots, almonds, peaches, nectarines, cherries, and cherry laurel are all included in this genus of more than 400 species. Only a few, mainly cherries and apricots, are used for bonsai. Most species of *Prunus* are not demanding as to soil, but many are intolerant of heavily polluted air. Their abundant spring flowers and colorful fall fruit are highly desirable for bonsai.

The use of this genus is limited. *Prunus* spp. do not like areas of extreme cold, heat, or humidity. They grow best in moderate climates.

Choose material with upright trunks to form an open branch structure that will display effectively the flowers and/or fruit. Provide early morning sun and bright light. Prune as for other flowering bonsai; remember that its spring flowers are produced during the preceding summer. Cut back branches immediately after flowering unless fruit is wanted.

Use a basic mix containing some organic matter, but make sure that it drains well. Let the soil become partially dry between waterings. Fertilize regularly as for other flowering bonsai. Repot young, fast-growing material every year, if needed. Repot well-established trees when their roots fill the container.

P. Mume Siebold & Zucc. FLOWERING APRICOT OR PLUM 30 ft.
China and southwestern Japan. Zone 7.

This is a rounded deciduous tree with slender green twigs and pointed leaves 1½ to 4 inches long. The profuse white to pink to dark red flowers are about 1 inch across. The yellow or green fruit is 1 inch in diameter. This Oriental species is called *mei* in China and *mume* in Japan. The flowers appear so early that often snow is still on the ground. They signal the end of winter and the coming of spring.

The cultivar Halley Jolivette, a flowering cherry hardy through Zone 6, is a hybrid propagated at the Arnold Arboretum at Harvard University. It was obtained by crossing *P. subhirtella* with *P. yedoensis*, then crossing the hybrid with *subhirtella*. The profuse pink flowers (Fig. P5-1) turn to white on this hybrid.

Fig. P5-1 Flowers of *Prunus* cv. Halley Jolivette.

They are 1 inch across and appear over a period of several weeks. Leaves are 1½ to 3 inches long. This vigorous rapid growth requires repeated pruning while it is young to establish and maintain its bonsai shape.

PSEUDOLARIX GOLDEN LARCH

Golden larch (which differs from larch in a few botanical characteristics) makes a beautiful formal or informal upright bonsai. Bonsai training methods and growing requirements are the same as for larch, *Larix*. *Pseudolarix* is intolerant of lime.

P. Kaempferi Gord. *(P. amabilis)* GOLDEN LARCH 130 ft.
Eastern China. Zone 6.

The bright, pliant green needles, clustered on short shoots, are 3 inches long and turn yellow in autumn. Cones are 3 inches long. This deciduous conifer has dense, soft foliage that gives it a graceful appearance.

PUNICA POMEGRANATE

Pomegranates grow best where there is heat and abundant water for their roots. When grown indoors, plan to provide warm temperatures, a sunny south window or high levels of artificial light, and a period of rest or partial dormancy during the winter months. Outdoors, place a pomegranate where it will receive bright light and sun.

Flowers bloom on the tips of the shoots. Cut back shoots severely immediately after flowering unless fruit is wanted. Select fruiting branches from diverse locations on the tree to distribute the fruit evenly on the bonsai. When wiring, use aluminum or wrapped copper wire.

Use a basic mix containing organic materials such as rich compost with sufficient aggregates for good drainage. Keep the mix moist but not wet between waterings.

Pomegranates are easily propagated from seed.

P. Granatum L. POMEGRANATE 20 ft.
Southeastern Europe and southern Asia. Zone 9.

Pomegranates are shrubs or small trees with 3-inch leaves, red flowers 1½ inches long, and red-orange fruit 2½ to 5 inches in diameter. Since ancient times, they have been cultivated for their fruit, shown in Fig. P6–1. A dwarf form, cv. Nana, is also used for bonsai; it reaches a height of up to 6 feet and has small leaves ¾ to 1½ inches long, 1-inch red flowers, and red-orange 2-inch fruit.

PYRACANTHA FIRE THORN

These handsome evergreen shrubs have small white flowers, red berries, and usually thorns; they are found mostly in mild climates.

Fig. P6–1 A pomegranate, *Punica Granatum,* in fruit.

Fire thorns can be wired and pruned to any bonsai style, including cascade. They are usually seen as single- or occasionally double-trunk bonsai in all sizes.

Outdoors, provide protection from freezing, and partial sun or bright light. Indoors, keep fire thorns at a sunny south or east window or under high-intensity artificial light. Move them, if possible, outdoors in the summer where they will receive fresh air and natural light.

Use a basic potting mix containing organic matter. Keep it slightly moist but not wet between waterings. Fertilize regularly. Repot in the late spring or early summer when the plants are in active growth. Fire thorns do not transplant easily. Root-prune mature bonsai with caution; where extensive root pruning is needed, shorten the roots over a period of several years. Preserve as many fibrous roots as possible.

P. coccinea M. J. Roem. EVERLASTING THORN 15 ft.
Italy to western Asia. Zone 7.

The dark green leaves on this shrub are 1 to 1½ inches long. Flower clusters are 5/16 inch across, and the scarlet berries are ¼ inch in diameter. This is among the most winter-hardy of the fire thorns used for bonsai.

P. Fortuneana H. L. Li CHINESE FIRE THORN 15 ft.
China. Zone 7.

This fire thorn has 1- to 2-inch leaves with flowers in groups 1½ inches wide. It produces 5/16-inch scarlet berries in the fall.

P. Koidzumii Rehd. FORMOSA FIRE THORN 12 ft.
Taiwan.

This is a much-branched shrub with 1- to 2-inch leaves, small flowers in groups, and flattened ¼-inch orange-scarlet berries. Protect this species from freezing.

RHODODENDRON AZALEA AND RHODODENDRON

The 800 or so species of evergreen, semievergreen, and deciduous shrubs in this genus (the botanical classification *Rhododendron* includes both rhododendrons and azaleas) thrive in climates where moisture is in the air and the temperatures are moderate. The alternate leaves are often crowded at the ends of shoots and branches. The flowers form at the terminal of the shoots.

Azaleas and rhododendrons have many assets for bonsai including:

Long life, reaching ages well over a hundred years.

Beautiful flowers in a wide range of colors and sizes, produced in profusion.

Many species with twiggy growth, small flowers and leaves, and short internodes.

A favorable response to pruning and wiring.

Compact fibrous roots that adjust to growing in a small container.

Best results are obtained by selecting azaleas and rhododendrons that grow well locally. In areas where they do not thrive, they may require a special environment.

As bonsai, azaleas are usually seen with upright trunks, but they may assume any style that their trunk and branch structure dictate. Give close attention to the roots. Whenever possible, choose a plant with surface roots at the base of the trunk to give a shrubby azalea a treelike appearance. Prune and wire as required to establish the initial bonsai size and shape. Use aluminum wire, or copper wire wrapped with soft paper or cloth to protect the thin bark. Azaleas are most flexible for wiring immediately after flowering.

After a period of training, when a pleasing form is attained, repot the azalea in a bonsai container. Do this in the spring, before new growth commences, or immediately after flowering. Use a basic potting mix containing organic materials with a low pH, such as sphagnum peat moss. The addition of five percent cotton meal by volume will increase the acidity of the mix and contribute a little nitrogen to the roots. Or prepare a special mix for azaleas with equal parts of sphagnum peat moss and sand. Regardless of the formula, make sure that the mix drains well. Keep the mix slightly moist between waterings. In the spring, start a regular fertilizing schedule, such as once every two weeks. Use a balanced fertilizer and continue fertilizing (except when the azalea is in flower) until a month or so before the end of summer. During this time, if the leaves are yellow or lack a healthy green color, apply chelated iron or a supplemental fertilizer prepared for plants that prefer an acid soil.

Provide a growing area with bright light and open shade. In warm climates, protect azaleas from the hot summer sun. To grow warm-climate azaleas indoors in cold climates, choose a location that receives winter sun and in summer move the azaleas outdoors where they will be in open shade. During cold winter months, protect all potted azaleas from freezing.

In early spring, before growth starts, groom bonsai azaleas for their coming display of flowers. Remove dead or broken branches, unwanted shoots in the interior from last summer's growth, and overly long shoots that break the periphery of the bonsai shape. After flowering, pluck the wilted flowers and their short stems from the tip of each twig or branchlet. Five or so new shoots will sprout in this area. Selectively pinch or trim all but one or two. Eliminate the long, strong shoots and keep the small ones. As the shoots grow and begin to harden, shorten them to two or three leaves. Let subsequent shoots develop and set flower buds for the coming year. Meanwhile, prune all unwanted shoots that emerge on the trunk or branches during the summer.

Satsuki Azaleas

These azaleas, which are cultivars of *R. indicum*, grow especially well in mild climates. They are prized for their beautiful flowers. Many satsuki azaleas have bicolored flowers or flowers of different colors on one plant. Flowers appear in late May or in June, when most other azaleas have finished flowering.

Their normal growth habit, consisting of many low-spreading horizontal branches, is not compatible with a treelike form and must be modified for bonsai. This can be done with a special pruning program. When shaping a young satsuki azalea, remove the strong side branches and keep the thin ones; they will thicken and be in proportion to the future trunk and the overall bonsai shape.

Select a strong shoot at the top for the continuation of the trunk. Wire it, if necessary, to the shape wanted for bonsai and let it thicken without pruning. Each year, remove all flower buds on the shoots along the upper trunk. Shorten upward-growing shoots on the horizontal branches to develop a cloudlike periphery. When a bonsai form is established, shorten the trunk to the desired height.

ADDITIONAL READING

NAKA, JOHN Y., RICHARD OTA, AND KENKO ROKKAKU, *Bonsai Techniques for Satsuki*. Orange, Calif.: Ota Bonsai Nursery, 1979. Describes styles and training methods for satsuki azaleas with forty-two color photographs of identified flowers.

Only a few of the many *Rhododendron* species used for bonsai are listed here.

R. indicum Sweet *(R. lateritium)* MACRANTHUM AZELEA 6 ft.
Southern Japan. Zone 6.

This evergreen azalea has 1½-inch-long leaves. Its rose and scarlet flowers, 2 inches across, appear in early summer. It is the parent species of the prized Satsuki cultivars in Japan. An example trained in an upright style is shown in Fig. R1–1.

Fig. R1–1 Satsuki azalea, *Rhododendron indicum* cv. Wakebeisu. Courtesy of David E. Cook.

Fig. R1–2 Kyushu azalea, *Rhododendron kiusianum,* by William N. Valavanis. American container by J. Godwin. Courtesy of *International BONSAI.*

R. Kaempferi Planch. (*R. obtusum* var. *Kaempferi*) TORCH AZALEA 8 ft.
Japan. Zone 6.

This loosely branched deciduous or semievergreen shrub has 2½-inch leaves and 2-inch flowers in many colors of red.

R. kiusianum Mak. (*R. obtusum* var. *japonicum*) KYUSHU AZALEA 3 ft.
Japan. Zone 7.

This is a twiggy, semievergreen azalea with 1-inch bright green leaves. In spring it is covered with light purple (or sometimes white or crimson) flowers 1 inch across. One trained as a cascade is shown in Fig. R1-2.

ROSMARINUS ROSEMARY

Rosemary is a shrub, or in northern gardens an herb, with narrow, leathery leaves ½ to 1½ inches long and small light blue flowers. It is a species of warm, sunny climates. In cooler climates, it is grown as a greenhouse or pot plant.

Rosemary can be shaped to any trunk line, from an upright to cascade, and in all sizes from large to minibonsai. Handle old plants with care, especially those moved to cold climates with reduced levels of temperature and light.

Place rosemary where it will receive sun and bright light and protect it from cold temperatures. If indoors, keep it on a sunny south or east window or under high levels of artificial light. Young plants respond favorably to pruning and wiring. Old wood is brittle and may be difficult to bend.

Use a basic mix with good drainage. Let the soil become dry between waterings. This bonsai does not grow in moist soil. Repot when the temperature is warm, but prune the roots cautiously and retain as many feeder roots as possible. Fertilize lightly.

R. officinalis L. ROSEMARY 4 ft.
The Mediterranean region, Portugal, and northwestern Spain.

The narrow leaves are a soft gray-green, and the tiny flowers are blue. It is a delightful bonsai indoors on a sunny kitchen windowsill or, in a warm climate, outdoors as a shrub with a thick, woody trunk.

SAGERETIA SAGERETIA

The all-purpose species for bonsai, *Sageretia Thea*, is from China. This tree lends itself to nearly all styles, from upright to cascade, on or over a rock, large to minibonsai. Sageretia is a vigorous grower. It is remarkably free of insects and disease, although borers are sometimes a problem on older trees. In China, specimens with thick trunks are grown or collected, to be severely pruned and shaped to bonsai. This species sprouts readily from buds beneath the bark and responds favorably to pruning. It is excellent material for the Lingnan grow-and-clip method as seen in Fig. S1-1.

Outdoors, provide sun and bright light and protect from freezing. Indoors, place sageretia at a sunny south or east window for growth at 60° to 70°F. Or it may be wintered in a "resting" state at a cool north window.

S. Thea M. C. Johnst. *(S. theezans)* SAGERETIA 25 ft.
Central and eastern China. Zone 7.

Fig. S1-1 *Sageretia Thea* trained as a bonsai in China.

This tree with thin short spines has dense foliage. The 1-inch-long leaves are quick to reduce with bonsai training. Tiny pink flowers are followed by reddish-purple fruit. Sageretia grows abundantly in the Chinese countryside, where it is often seen in hedgerows and along roadways.

This is an outstanding deciduous bonsai. It thrives in a regular potting mix. The growth is twiggy and compact.

SALIX WILLOW

These trees and shrubs are well adapted to moist locations. They are native mainly to cold-temperature regions of the Northern Hemisphere.

Willows are especially attractive as weeping bonsai with graceful drooping branches. Such bonsai can be made in a short time from cuttings. However, willows are short-lived species that do not approach the longevity of pines, maples, and azaleas.

Start in spring: When the buds are beginning to open, select a strong branch up to 2 inches wide with several branchlets. Consider the trunk line when choosing the branch. A curved trunk will allow space below for future drooping branches. If a straight branch is used, plan to plant it at a slant for the same effect. Remove the branch from the tree with a sharp cut and shorten it to a bonsai trunk and branch structure about a foot high.

Remove ½ inch of bark around the bottom of the "trunk" to bring the thin, green cambium layer in contact with the rooting medium. Insert the branch in a flowerpot containing a mix of equal parts sand and peat moss. Keep the mix moist at all times and out of direct sun. Provide bright indirect light. Misting the branch with water from time to time will aid root growth.

In about a month, after leaves have appeared, begin to fertilize regularly and provide partial sun. Let the new growth develop without pruning. In late summer or early fall, repot the cutting in a basic mix containing organic matter and a heavy aggregate to stabilize the weight of the weeping branches. Keep the soil slightly moist between waterings. Be careful not to damage the fragile new roots. Do not root-prune during this initial repotting. Protect from freezing during cold weather.

Early the following spring, remove nonconforming shoots and cut back the remaining shoots to the first few buds. Select buds in locations where a weeping branch is desired and prune slightly beyond these buds. As the new shoots emerge, let them grow during the spring and summer into long, weeping branches. Meanwhile, resume fertilizing shortly after leaves appear.

The next year, repeat the pattern of severe early spring pruning and repotting and regular fertilizing. From then on, when the new shoots harden in late spring, cut them back to one or two buds. Let the second round of growth develop fully (except to thin crowded branches). The following spring, start the cycle again by drastically cutting back the long shoots from the previous summer to one or two buds. A few of the willows that have proved adaptable to bonsai are listed here.

S. babylonica L. WEEPING WILLOW 30 ft.
China. Zone 5.

This willow, with its graceful weeping habit, has narrow, finely toothed leaves. They are 6 inches long, ⅜ to ⅝ inch wide, and grayish underneath. The dark brown trunk becomes ridged and furrowed with age.

S. nigra Marsh. BLACK WILLOW 35 ft.
Central and eastern United States and northern New Mexico. Zone 4.

The trunk is dark brown or blackish, and the branches are yellow. The narrow leaves are 5 inches long and pale green beneath. This is the largest and most widely distributed of the native willows. It grows along streams, low-lying lake shores, and other moist areas.

SCHINUS PEPPER TREE

For bonsai, this warm-climate species is grown with upright, straight, or curved trunks. It has fairly open branching to accommodate the compound leaves and to display the red fruit.

Outdoors, keep the plant in sun and bright light; indoors, place it on a sunny east or south window. Prune and wire as needed.

Use a basic potting mix and allow it to become slightly dry between waterings. This tree has strong bonsai potential, especially in warm climates.

Pepper trees may be propagated by seed or cuttings.

S. terebinthifolius Raddi BRAZILIAN PEPPER TREE, CHRISTMAS BERRY 20 ft.
South America.

This is a bonsai with stiff upright branches and compound leaves 4 to 8 inches long, subdivided into five to nine leaflets. On female trees, bright red flowers are followed by 3/16-inch round fruit in late fall or winter. The pepper tree is naturalized in Hawaii and parts of Florida, where it is used for wreaths at Christmas.

SERISSA SERISSA

Serissa is a shrub with small white flowers and berrylike fruit. The leaves are opposite and become fetid when bruised.

It is used in all upright styles, as a single- or multitrunk planting and as a minibonsai. In warm climates, keep it outdoors year round; indoors, maintain it between 65° and 75°F. Provide bright filtered light outdoors and light from an east or slightly screened south window indoors.

Serissa responds favorably to pruning and wiring. An example is shown in Fig. 16-4. Older wood, however, is stiff. Use a basic potting mix. Keep the soil moderately moist, but not wet, between waterings.

Repot when the weather is warm. Take great care to avoid letting the roots become dry during repotting. Prune lightly to retain as many fibrous roots as possible.

S. foetida Lam. SNOW IN JUNE 2 ft.
Southeast Asia, China, and Japan.

The small leaves on this dwarf shrub are ½ inch long, and the tiny flowers are about ½ inch across. On a variegated form, the leaves are marked with a white margin. Serissa is widely cultivated in warm climates, where it has become naturalized in some areas.

SEVERINIA BOX ORANGE

An upright style is suitable for box orange. It develops a woody trunk and dense foliage with bonsai training. Provide bright sunlight and open shade outdoors and a sunny window or high levels of artificial light indoors.

Wire while the growth is young and before the trunk and branches stiffen with age. Use a basic mix containing organic materials and keep it moderately moist but not wet between waterings.

Severinia is easily propagated from seed.

S. buxifolia Ten. CHINESE BOX ORANGE
Southeastern China. Zone 10.

This box orange is a small evergreen tree of dense growth, short thin spines, and dark green leathery leaves 1½ inches long. It has tiny, fragrant white flowers and shining black fruit. It is hardy along the coast of the Gulf of Mexico and similar climates.

SYZYGIUM BRUSH CHERRY

Brush cherry, *S. puniculatum*, is a tropical plant grown as bonsai with an upright, straight, or curved trunk. It may be planted over a rock, made into a minibonsai, or used as indoor bonsai. Young plants are popular for group plantings and saikei.

Provide warm temperatures year round. Choose an outdoor location with bright light and sun. Indoors, a sunny south window or high levels of artificial light are required, as are daytime temperatures between 60° and 70°F. Brush cherry responds favorably to pruning and wiring. Use a basic potting mix and keep it moderately moist between waterings.

Brush cherry is easily propagated by seed and cuttings.

S. paniculatum Gaertn. *(Eugenia australis)* BRUSH CHERRY, EUGENIA 40 ft.
Australia. Zone 9.

This tropical evergreen shrub, which is used for outdoor and indoor bonsai, has shining dark green leaves up to 3 inches long and fragrant white flowers measuring ½ to 1 inch. It is seen as a hedge plant in California, in Hawaii, and along the Gulf Coast.

TAXODIUM CYPRESS

Bald cypress, one of the most unusual trees found in the United States, is in this genus.

These trees naturally have the straight trunk but not the pointed conical shape of evergreen conifers; bald cypresses develop a flat, slightly rounded crown, as described in Chapter 13. Information on shaping, pruning techniques, and trimming new growth is found in that chapter.

Cypresses are highly tolerant of pruning and wiring. They grow most vigorously as bonsai in their southern range. It is important to remember that their growth rate is reduced in the north. For this reason, northern bonsai enthusiasts often begin with a specimen that has been collected in the south and is already started on its bonsai training.

Place cypresses in bright light and open shade. Provide direct sun only in early summer or late fall. Protect from freezing temperatures.

Use a basic mix containing organic matter. Keep the soil in the container moist at all times. During hot summer weather, set bald cypresses in a shallow tray of water to give the roots ready access to moisture. Repot in late spring or early summer when the soil is warm. Prune the roots as needed. Cypress trees adapt to, and are pleasing in, relatively shallow containers. They are attractive as specimen trees and group plantings.

T. distichum L. Rich. BALD CYPRESS 150 ft.
Delaware to Florida, west to Arkansas and Texas. Zone 5.

The extensive range of bald cypress indicates that this deciduous conifer can adjust to diverse climatic conditions. It reaches its maximum development in the wet lowlands and swamps of the southeastern United States. This species is able to grow in wet soils of muck, clay, or fine sand, varying from acidic to alkaline, but it cannot survive in dry sandy soil.

Bald cypresses have peculiar structures called knees that protrude above the water level of their wet habitat. Their exact purpose is not known, but they may have aerating functions. The tall, straight trunks with dark brown bark are buttressed at their base. The short needles are a soft green color.

T.d. var, **nutans** Sweet *(T. ascendens)* POND CYPRESS
Virginia to Florida and Alabama.

This variety is smaller but similar to bald cypress. Its leaves, also smaller, are awl-shaped and usually appressed. Its range is limited to shallow ponds and poorly drained areas in the southeastern United States. For bonsai purposes, it is treated much like bald cypress.

TAXUS YEW

The needlelike foliage of these slow-growing trees and shrubs is dark green above and pale green or yellowish underneath. The soft red fruit resembles a berry.

The naturally spreading, horizontal branching of many yews has limited their use as bonsai. However, they are tolerant of pruning and wiring and are long-lived. When considering yews for bonsai, examine each plant for the presence of a potential trunk line.

Provide a basic, well-drained potting mix and allow the soil in the container to become slightly dry between waterings. Yews will thrive in sun and partial shade and are relatively free of insects and pests.

Many cultivars and forms of the two species listed here can be sought out as potential bonsai material. The easy-to-grow yews have been passed by as bonsai material.

T. baccata L. ENGLISH YEW 60 ft.
Europe, North Africa, and western Asia. Zone 7.

The dark green needles, glossy above and pale underneath, are ¾ to 1¼ inches long. This densely branched tree has been cultivated since ancient times.

T. cuspidata Siebold & Zucc. JAPANESE YEW 50 ft.
Japan, Korea, and Manchuria. Zone 5.

This spreading tree with upright branches is hardier than the English yew. The ¾- to 1-inch needles are abruptly pointed and form a V-shaped trough along the stem. The mature twigs are reddish brown.

THUJA ARBORVITAE

Arborvitae are slow-growing evergreen trees with erect branches and scalelike leaves. Old collected specimens of American arborvitae make handsome bonsai. The many compact dwarf forms available offer material for small bonsai and minibonsai.

Thuja are tolerant of pruning, wiring, and confinement to a container. However, they do not grow well in shade. Provide plenty of sun and bright light. Morning sun is ideal. Avoid keeping *Thuja* spp. in direct sun for long periods during the hot summer.

Use a basic container mix that drains well; do not let it become completely dry between waterings.

T. occidentalis L. AMERICAN ARBORVITAE 60 ft.
Nova Scotia to North Carolina and Illinois. Zone 3.

The scalelike leaves are dark green above and yellowish green beneath on this species of pyramidal growth. The female cones are ½ inch long. Nursery plants of this species are generally seen with upright trunks, but arborvitae are also found in the wild with all possible shapes and trunk lines.

TRACHELOSPERMUM STAR JASMINE

These tropical and subtropical shrubby vines are grown in mild climates for the fragrance of their flowers. They contain a milky sap that is visible when they are pruned.

Star jasmine, the species frequently used for bonsai, is often seen as a cascade bonsai that flowers in the spring and throughout the year. As nursery stock it is shipped north, where it may be used as indoor bonsai.

Star jasmine needs warm year-round temperatures and bright diffused light. Indoors, a minimum of 60° to 70°F. is required with light from an east or lightly screened south window, or high to medium light intensity under fluorescent lamps.

Prune during the growing season; severe pruning may be necessary to establish a trunk line and a treelike form. Trim the shoots and branches after flowering. Wire at any time to maintain the desired form.

Use a basic mix and allow the soil to become moderately dry between waterings. Repot in late spring or early summer. Fertilize regularly as for other flowering bonsai.

T. jasminoides Lem. STAR JASMINE, CONFEDERATE JASMINE 30 ft.
China. Zone 9.

The branches of this lovely and popular climbing evergreen vine are equipped with holdfast roots. The dark green glossy leaves are up to 4 inches long; the white flowers are highly fragrant.

TSUGA HEMLOCK

These graceful evergreen conifers have slender, usually flat, needles. Two white bands visible on the underside of the needles distinguish hemlocks from yews. Older specimens are difficult to transplant. These trees of mountain forests like plenty of moisture and well-drained soil.

Upright or slanting trunks, from a single tree to group plantings, are favored. A windswept style is shown in Fig. 13-8.

Provide a cool growing area with partial shade under direct overhead light. Protect hemlocks from hot sun and drying winds.

Avoid drastic pruning that would remove a significant portion of the trunk or branches; otherwise, prune and wire as needed. Hemlocks withstand repeated shearing and light pruning and respond with a noticeable reduction in needle length.

Use a container mix that drains well yet retains a slight amount of moisture, such as a basic mix of equal parts of soil, sphagnum peat moss (or other peat), and coarse aggregate to which more peat moss is added. If three measures of sphagnum peat moss, for example, were used, add one more measure. Do not let the mix in the container become dry between waterings.

Root growth is slow, so frequent repotting is not needed. Repot in early spring every third or fourth year; root-prune lightly and take extra care to prevent the roots from drying.

T. heterophylla Sarg. WESTERN HEMLOCK to 200 ft.
Alaska to California. Zone 7.

Needles measure up to ¾ inch, and cones are 1 inch long. This is a beautiful tree for bonsai in its native range. A dwarf form (Fig. 2-7) found in Iron Springs, Washington, has all the appearance of *T. heterophylla* except that the needles are only ⅜ inch long and the internodes are closely spaced, ½ to ¾ inch apart.

T. Mertensiana Carrière MOUNTAIN HEMLOCK 150 ft.
Alaska to California. Zone 6.

This hemlock, which has slightly rounded 1-inch needles and 3-inch cones, is a fine species for bonsai in the Pacific Northwest. Mountain hemlock is easily distinguished by its needles, which are arranged radically around the stem rather than in the flat pattern seen in other hemlocks.

T. canadensis Carrière CANADA HEMLOCK 80 ft.
Nova Scotia to Alaska. Zone 3.

Both needles and cones are about ¾ inch long on this hemlock. Many dwarf forms are available, including cvs. Compacta and Gracilis, with small needles and branches that droop at the tips.

T. caroliniana Engelm. CAROLINA HEMLOCK 70 ft.
Mountains from Virginia to Georgia. Zone 5.

Needles measure ¾ inch and cones up to 1½ inches.

Both Canada and Carolina hemlocks do not respond favorably to bonsai training over a period of time. For this reason, they cannot be recommended for lasting specimen bonsai. Young seedlings, however, are popular for saikei and group plantings. Dwarf cultivars of *T. canadensis* are sometimes grown and shaped to bonsai and planted in rather deep containers.

ULMUS ELM

Elms are outstanding material for bonsai. However, the beautiful American elm, *U. americana*, does not willingly acquiesce to confinement in a bonsai container or to bonsai techniques; perhaps, in the future, a cultivar that is more adaptable to bonsai will be developed.

Elms provide excellent material for bonsai. Their upright trunks can be straight or curved, used in group plantings, on or over a rock, and as minibonsai.

Give the elms listed here protection in winter. From spring to fall, place them in bright light and open shade. Provide a sunny window or medium to high light intensity for elms such as Catlin elm that are grown indoors.

Prune in the early spring before growth begins, and trim the new growth regularly as it develops. Wire as needed.

When shaping an elm for bonsai, study the growth habit of the species. The branching may be vase-shaped, horizontal, a mix of spreading and upright forms, or drooping. Many growers like to incorporate the dominant branching of the tree into the bonsai to create a replica of its counterpart in nature.

Elm leaves reduce as a result of bonsai techniques. To accelerate the process, remove the largest leaves during the first half of the summer. Their replacements will be smaller.

Use a basic potting mix and allow the soil to become moderately dry between waterings. Repot deciduous elms in early spring and evergreen ones when the weather is warm.

U. alata Michx. WAHOO ELM, WINGED ELM 50 ft.
Virginia to Florida, west to Texas. Zone 5.

Corky wings, about ½ inch high, form on the branches. The narrow leaves are 2½ inches long. This elm is dug from the wild for bonsai in the United States

Fig. U1–1 Siberian elm, *Ulmus pumila*, by Andrew N. Lenz. Photo courtesy of Lenz.

from Mississippi delta bottomlands to the hill country of Tennessee and abandoned fields in Illinois.

U. crassifolia Nutt. CEDAR ELM 60 ft.
Mississippi to Texas and northern Mexico. Zone 7.

The rather stiff branches of this medium-size tree have corky or scaly ridges. The leaves are 1 to 2 inches long. The elm is widely collected in Texas.

U. parvifolia Jacq. CHINESE ELM 75 ft.
China and Japan. Zone 6.

This elm of compact growth is deciduous in cold climates and evergreen or partly evergreen in warm regions. It becomes a tall tree in the ground. Examples of its use as bonsai are seen in Figs. 13-15, 13-17, 15-8, and 15-11. The shining, smooth leaves are 1 to 2 inches long. Several compact forms with small leaves include cv. Catlin (Fig. 14-3) and the Japanese forms with exceedingly small leaves, cvs. Hokkaido and Seiju, both of unknown hardiness.

U. pumila L. SIBERIAN ELM, DWARF ELM to 45 ft.
Eastern Siberia and northern China to Turkestan. Zone 3.

This is a fast-growing, small, short-lived, sometimes shrublike tree with 2- to 3-inch leaves and a rough, textured bark. This species, which is often confused with the long-lived *U. parvifolia*, is a rapid grower subject to winterkill and twig dieback in cold climates. However, it is an attractive tree and useful in situations where longevity is not required. An outstanding mature specimen is shown in Fig. U1–1.

WISTERIA WISTERIA

These deciduous climbing woody vines with twining stems are grown outdoors as bonsai for their long clusters of spring flowers. In early spring, before growth commences, remove crowded shoots and branches. Examine each shoot before pruning to identify those with flower buds. Wire or prune to create space for the long-hanging flower clusters that will appear.

Provide sun and open shade. Consult Chapter 13 for pruning the top growth. Repot in a basic mix containing organic matter. Prune the roots moderately each year to avoid excessive root pruning at one time. A wisteria bonsai requires extensive roots to support its vigorous growth and large flowers.

Keep the mix slightly moist between waterings. In hot weather, place wisteria in a tray of water about 1 inch deep for the roots to absorb each day. Do not let the roots remain in the water continually. It is important to fertilize regularly.

Because of the weight of its flowers and its large root mass, a wisteria bonsai is often planted in a deeper than usual container.

W. floribunda DC. JAPANESE WISTERIA
Japan. Zone 5.

The fragrant flowers are in clusters of violet, violet-blue, pink, red, or white. The fruit is a velvety 6-inch pod. The compound leaves contain seven to thirteen leaflets. Japanese wisteria, which blooms in May, is hardier than Chinese wisteria.

W. sinensis Sweet CHINESE WISTERIA
China. Zone 5.

Bluish-violet or white flowers are in clusters up to 12 inches long. They are slightly fragrant and appear before the leaves. *W. sinensis* flowers earlier than Japanese wisteria. Its long compound leaves contain thirteen to nineteen leaflets.

ZAMIA SAGO PALM, COONTIE

Zamia, also called sago palm or coontie, are dwarf herbaceous perennials in warm climates. They are similar to cycads, and their bonsai care and culture are the same.

Use a well-drained basic potting mix containing organic matter. Provide sun and partial shade and allow the soil to dry between waterings.

According to Charles Bush and Julia Morton, authors of *Native Trees and*

Plants for Florida Landscaping, coontie may be propagated from seed by covering the seeds with a thin layer of soil and transferring them to pots shortly after sprouting.*

Z. floridana A. DC. SAGO PALM, COONTIE 3 ft.
and **Z. integrifolia** Ait.
Florida. Zone 10.

The light grayish-brown trunks, which may be underground, are tuberlike. Shining green leaflets 6 inches long and ¼ inch wide are located on long midribs. Coontie plants grow wild throughout sandy areas of Florida. The trunks contain a poisonous starch, that years ago Indians processed into an edible form. The sale of zamia dug from the wild is prohibited under Florida law, but nursery-grown specimens are available.

ZELKOVA ZELKOVA

These are elmlike trees and shrubs with alternate leaves. They are easy to grow and popular for bonsai.

The broom style (Fig. 13-2), consisting of upright branches fanning out from the top of a short, straight trunk, was developed especially for this species. Zelkova are also shaped to other upright styles, including group plantings, forest plantings, and minibonsai.

Provide sun and partial shade for these outdoor trees and, of course, protection in cold weather. Zelkova are highly tolerant of pruning and wiring. Repeatedly trim the new growth as it appears during the growing season.

Use a basic potting mix. Keep the mix slightly moist between periods of watering for this shallow-rooted tree. Young trees transplant readily; repot them in the spring or during the summer. Chapter 17 provides information on growing and shaping zelkova from seed for a broom-style bonsai. Chapter 13 contains directions for making a broom-style bonsai from large nursery stock.

Z. serrata Mak. JAPANESE ZELKOVA 100 ft.
Japan. Zone 5.

This is a species with smooth gray bark, a stout trunk, and many branches. The sharply toothed leaves (Fig. 12-2.1) are 2 inches long. It is a favorite bonsai subject in Japan, where trees with a reddish tinge to their new shoots are preferred for their smaller leaves.

*Charles S. Bush and Julia R. Morton, *Native Trees and Plants for Florida Landscaping*, Bulletin No. 193, p. 115. (Tallahassee, Fla.: Florida Department of Agriculture and Consumer Services, n.d.). This concise publication is an excellent handbook for growers interested in using native Florida plant material for bonsai. It contains descriptions and information on the care and culture of palms, trees, shrubs, vines, ferns, orchids, aquatics, and other warm-climate plants found in Florida.

Appendix A

Bonsai Organizations and Publications

The two following nationwide, nonprofit bonsai organizations in the United States hold annual conventions, publish bonsai periodicals, offer audiovisual programs and educational aids, and serve as bonsai information centers for individuals and local and regional organizations throughout the United States.

American Bonsai Society, Inc., P.O. Box 358, Keene, NH 03431, publishes the *Bonsai Journal* quarterly and *ABStracts* in interim months.

Bonsai Clubs International, 800 West Virginia St., #501, Tallahassee, FL 32304 publishes *Bonsai Clubs International* six times yearly.

Additional bonsai publications with national distribution include:

Bonsai Bulletin, published quarterly by the Bonsai Society of Greater New York, Inc., P.O. Box 154, Malverne, NY 11565.

Bonsai in California, a photographic bonsai album in color published annually by the California Bonsai Society, Inc., P.O. Box 78211, Los Angeles, CA 90016.

Florida Bonsai, published quarterly by the Bonsai Societies of Florida, Inc., 579 Man O War Circle, Catonment, FL 32533.

International Bonsai, published quarterly by the International Bonsai Arboretum, 412 Pinnacle Road, Rochester, NY 14623.

Potomac Bonsai Society Newsletter, published monthly by the Potomac Bonsai Association, Inc., c/o National Arboretum, 24th and R Sts., NE, Washington, DC 20002.

Note: The profusely illustrated, 355-page book on Chinese bonsai (Chapter 15) by Wu Yee-sun, *Man Lung Artistic Pot Plants* (Hong Kong: Wing Lung Bank Ltd. Artistic Publications, 1974) is not for sale but is available with a donation in U.S. dollars of $10.00 or more, plus $3.50 for overseas shipping, from Hong Kong Baptist College, 224 Waterloo Road, Kowloon, Hong Kong.

Appendix B

Oriental Bonsai Styles and Species

The beautiful bonsai of China and Japan are a precious heritage from the Orient. They are described here for those who wish to model their bonsai on Oriental styles and as prototypes for the formulation of new styles that reflect trees and environments in other parts of the world.

JAPAN

Japanese styles focus on the tree alone, without the inclusion of other elements of the landscape such as rocks, buildings, or figurines. The few exceptions to this are saikei (landscapes of trees and rocks) and plantings of a tree on or over a rock. Japanese styles are delineated by the line of the trunk and the placement of the branches.

MAJOR STYLES OF JAPANESE BONSAI

Single-Trunk Bonsai

Formal Upright. This is a straight tapered trunk perpendicular to the top of the container. Approximately two-thirds of the trunk is visible, except for the very top where growth is dense. The branches, also tapered, are arranged with the two longest at the bottom. One of the two is positioned as the lowest branch on either the right or left side of the trunk; the other is on the opposite side of the trunk and higher than the first; both extend slightly toward the viewer.

A third branch, considerably shorter than the first two, is located preferably between the first and second at the rear of the trunk, or if not there, at a higher location on the back of the trunk. This three-branch pattern forms a group that is repeated as the branches ascend the trunk. The arrangement is especially suited to excurrent trees (trees with a single trunk and lateral branches). This difficult style is not often seen because of its strict requirements. It is important because it clearly delineates a branch arrangement that is used with many other styles.

Slanting. This style is similar to the formal upright style except that the trunk is slanting beyond the container.

Informal. A curved, tapered trunk that may also be twisted is depicted in this style. The top of the trunk, called the apex, is located over the area of the container, and it may be directly above the bottom of the trunk. The very top of the trunk on excurrent trees is tilted slightly toward the viewer.

Broom. This style portrays a short, straight trunk with branches emerging in a cluster at one location and spreading out in a fanlike shape resembling a broom. The style was developed in the first quarter of the twentieth century for an elmlike species, *Zelkova serrata*, and it is now popular for many deliquescent trees.

Windswept. This involves a tapered trunk, which may be straight, slanting, or slightly curved, with the major branches growing in one direction as if from the force of the wind over a long period of time.

Driftwood. In this style, an old tree is portrayed with portions of its trunk or branches dead and bleached from adverse weather. Dead wood on the top of the trunk is called *jin* in Japan; bleached dead wood appearing on the surface along the length of a living tree is called *shari*.

Cascade. The straight or curved trunk in this style extends below the top of the container. As it descends, it reflects the struggle between the pull of gravity and the tree's upward thrust toward the light. Branches are positioned on either side of, rather than under, the trunk.

Semicascade. This style is a modification of the cascade style. The trunk, either straight or curved, extends somewhat horizontally and far beyond the container but does not drop below the container's rim.

Literati (Bunjin). This is a free-form style with a tall, thin trunk that has few branches and only sparse foliage. The trunk rarely displays a pronounced taper. It is a style without rules—an opportunity for bonsai growers to express their own feeling for composition and balance.

Bonsai with Two or More Trunks

When a bonsai has more than one trunk, one trunk is always dominant: taller, thicker, and more prominent that the others. With two or more trunks, the height and diameter of the trunks are varied; with three or more trunks, the distance between the trunks is also varied. The Japanese divide this style into two categories. In the first are two or more trees growing from the same root system, while the second category consists of individual trees, each with its own roots.

As trees arising from the same roots are fixed in their positions and difficult to arrange, these plantings are more esteemed than multitrunk arrangements from individual trees.

1. Trees from the Same Roots:

Two trunks and three trunks. When the trunks are growing from the same roots, separation close to the base is preferred.

Clump. Three or more shoots growing closely together from the same root are developed as separate trunks; unwanted shoots are removed. In time, the trunks may fuse together at their base.

Stump. Selected shoots from an old stump are trained to form a group. The unwanted shoots are eliminated. The arrangement is restricted by the location of the available shoots. However, growers with advanced horticultural skill are able to graft shoots at desired locations on the stump.

Sinuous. Numerous shoots from a root or a long, winding trunk, placed horizontally, are trained as trunks. The planting may be augmented by grafting.

Raft. Several new trunks are formed by burying the parent trunk, which is usually straight, on its side and developing selected branches into vertical trunks; alternatively, a low branch is buried and new trunks trained from its smaller branches. This style and the sinuous style are difficult, but they offer the advantage of uniform, consistent foliage or flowering since all trees are part of the same parent tree.

2. Trunks of Separate Trees:

Two-, Three, and Five-trunk Styles. These multitrunk approaches are popular in cluster arrangements. The trunks are placed close together at their base (the base is the lower portion of the trunk where it emerges from the ground). Four trunks, which are considered difficult to arrange as a single group, are rarely seen together.

Group plantings. Groups may contain three to eleven trees, usually of the same species. Prime numbers three, five, seven, and eleven are preferred; a group of nine trees is considered troublesome to arrange without resulting in a simplistic pattern of three groups of three trees or an unwanted group of four.

Forest plantings. This style is similar to group plantings but contains a greater number of trees. Because a large number of trees is not readily counted, their exact number is not considered important.

Additional Styles

Clinging to a Rock or on a Rock. No distinction is made as to the number of trees or species. The roots of each tree are planted and grow entirely on the rock. When a rock has mass, it may be placed in a shallow tray (called a *suiban*) with water or sand. When a planting is made directly on a flat stone, the stone serves as the container.

Root Over Rock. This style is similar to the preceding style except that the roots of the tree are brought along the side of the rock into the soil in the container. Trees planted by this method are easier to maintain than those with the roots planted entirely on the rock.

Miniature Landscapes. Plantings that combine trees and rocks, in an arrangement similar to group plantings of trees, are called saikei (pronounced "sigh-kay"). Saikei is the newest of the Japanese styles and has become popular in Japan and elsewhere since its appearance after World War II.

Bonsai by size. Japanese bonsai may also be classified by size according to the number of persons required to move the bonsai.[1] Moving the largest bonsai,up to approximately 3 feet, requires two persons. Medium-size bonsai, from 1 to 1½ feet, may be carried by one person. Little bonsai, up to 12 inches, are moved with one hand, while miniature (or *mame*, pronounced "ma-may") bonsai, from 3 to 6 inches, are easily carried in the palm of the hand. Fingertip bonsai, *shito*, less than 3 inches, are so tiny that they may be carried on the tip of the finger.

JAPANESE SPECIES

The display of Japanese bonsai at the U.S. National Arboretum in Washington, D.C., is a sampling of trees and shrubs that have been used for many years as bonsai in Japan. Species in the collection were selected for their suitability to the climate of Washington, D.C.; nearly all are native or indigenous to Japan.

Japanese Bonsai at the U.S. National Arboretum, Washington, D.C.[2]

Acer Buergeranum Miq. Trident maple
A. palmatum Thunb. Japanese maple
Camellia japonica L. Camellia, Higo camellia
Carpinus laxiflora Blume Red-leaved hornbeam
C. Tschonoskii Maxim. Hornbeam
Chaenomeles japonica Lindl. ex Spach. Japanese quince, lesser flowering quince
Chamaecyparis obtusa Endl. Hinoki cypress
Cornus officinalis Siebold & Zucc. Japanese Cornelian cherry
Crataegus cuneata Siebold Hawthorn
Cryptomeria japonica D. Don Japanese cedar
Cydonia sinensis Thouin *(Chaenomeles sinensis)* Chinese quince
Elaeagnus pungens Thunb. Thorny elaeagnus
Fagus crenata Blume Japanese beech

[1]Lynn Perry Alstadt and Dorothy S. Young, eds., *Bonsai Manual for Appreciating, Judging, and Buying Bonsai*, p. 5 (Erie, Pa.: American Bonsai Society, 1974).

[2]Eric Neumann and Robert Drechsler, *The National Bonsai Collection at the National Arboretum*, Program Aid 1158, rev. ed. (Washington, D.C.: Science and Education Administration, USDA, 1978). A folder with a brief descriptive text and a complete listing of the Japanese bonsai and viewing stones in the national collection.

Ginkgo biloba L. Maidenhair tree
Hamamelis japonica Siebold & Zucc. Japanese witch hazel
Ilex serrata Thunb. Japanese sawtooth holly, Japanese winterberry
Juniperus chinensis var. **Sargentii** A. Henry Shimpaku juniper
J. rigida Siebold & Zucc. Needle juniper
Loropetalum chinense D. Oliver Loropetalum
Malus Halliana Koehne Hall's crab apple
M. Sieboldii Rehd. Toringo crab apple
Picea Glehnii M.T. Mast. Sakhalin spruce, red Yezo spruce
Pinus densiflora Siebold & Zucc. Japanese red pine
P. parviflora Siebold & Zucc. Japanese white pine
P. Thunbergiana Franco Japanese black pine
Rhododendron indicum Sweet Japanese satsuki azalea including cvs. Hakata-shiro, Izayoi, Kaho, and Shi-o
R. Kaempferi Planch. Kurume azalea, torch azalea
R. kiusianum Mak. Kyushu azalea
Stewartia Pseudocamellia Maxim. Japanese stewartia, summer camellia
Taxus cuspidata Siebold & Zucc. Japanese yew
Tsuga diversifolia M. T. Mast. Japanese hemlock
Ulmus Davidiana var. **japonica** Nakai Japanese elm
Wisteria floribunda DC. Japanese wisteria
Zelkova serrata Mak. Japanese zelkova

ADDITIONAL READING

NAKA, JOHN, AND YUJI YOSHIMURA, eds., *The National Collection Guidebook.* Atlanta, Ga.: Symmes Systems, 1977. A small guidebook with a description and photograph of each bonsai and viewing stone at the National Arboretum.

CHINA

Chinese bonsai is a composite of numerous styles, ancient and contemporary, found among the provinces of China. The Chinese word for bonsai, *penjing*, is used in the People's Republic of China for both dwarfed miniature trees and landscape plantings of rocks with small trees or herbaceous plants. Chinese bonsai may be large; some are 6 feet tall or taller and planted in deep containers suitable for display in public places or large buildings.

Certain cities are famous for their distinctive methods of training or growing bonsai. Hangzhou (Hangchow) is known for bonsai with thick, hollow trunks and closely contoured foliage. In Suzhou (Soochow), bonsai are trained into graceful shapes, while Shanghai is a center for flowering bonsai, miniature bonsai, and rockeries. In the province of Guangdong (Kwangtung) and other areas of southern China, bonsai with tapered trunks and a natural appearance are trained by the Lingnan method. The following contemporary styles of bonsai that have emerged in China are based on descriptions by Wu Yee-sun, author of *Man Lung Artistic Pot Plants*.

MAJOR STYLES OF CHINESE BONSAI

Single Tree. A tree with a trunk that may be straight or slightly curved, but is essentially vertical, characterizes this style.

Two trees. Two separate trees are planted as a matched pair. Their trunks may be similar in thickness. Their height, however, is varied.

Mother with Son. Two contrasting trees, a large tree with a small one at its base, suggest a mother with her small son.

Drift-out, or Leaning. One or two trunks extend in an upward and outward direction beyond the container.

Reclining, or Lying. Either one or two trees are used in this style, with the lower portion of the trunk lying parallel to the top of the container.

Overlooking the Water. The trunk extends outward on a horizontal plane beyond the container.

Cascade. The trunk bends downward and its top extends below the rim of the container.

Dropping. The upper portion of the trunk or a large branch of an old tree grows downward, as if weakened by age or adversity.

With Roots. This style features a major tree with smaller trees sprouting from its roots.

Forest or Grove. A group of trees are arranged as a forest or a grove. One of the trees is dominant.

On a Rock. One or more trees are planted with the roots growing entirely on a rock. The rock may be tall and massive, with the roots in a crevice, or it may be flat.

Over a Rock or Clinging to a rock. The roots of the tree or trees are planted on a rock and extend into the soil of the container beneath the rock.

Rockeries. These are miniature plantings of rocky islands or mountains in large, shallow containers or trays, which are often carved from soapstone or marble. Figurines are included, and ferns or other small herbaceous plants may be added to suggest distant trees in the landscape.

As seen in its many styles, Chinese bonsai opens the concept of bonsai design: Rocks, for instance, are not relegated to a minor position but may appear as the dominant object in the bonsai composition, a role reserved for the tree in Japanese bonsai. In addition, rocks or figurines that are relevant may be placed beneath a tree to strengthen the design or enhance the meaning of the scene created by the bonsai.

CHINESE SPECIES

Species of trees and woody plants used for bonsai in Hong Kong and the People's Republic of China span wide geographical areas and diverse climatic regions, ranging from extreme cold in northern China to the subtropical climate of southern China.

The following listing is derived from the author's observations during travels to Hong Kong between 1970 and 1981 and to the People's Republic of China in 1981. In the nineteenth century, Western plant explorers in the Orient sent to their native countries numerous samples of seeds of trees and shrubs from China, Korea, and Japan. As a result, a large number of outstanding species now used as bonsai in China and Japan are also popular in Occidental garden and landscape plantings. Many are widely distributed and available throughout the Temperate Zones.

Native Species of Chinese Bonsai

Acer Buergeranum Miq. Trident maple
Bambusa glaucescens Siebold ex Holtt. *(B. multiplex)* Hedge bamboo
B. ventricosa McClure Buddha bamboo
Buxus microphylla var. **sinica** Rehd. & E. H. Wils. Dwarf boxwood
Celtis sinensis Pers. Chinese hackberry
Chaenomeles speciosa Nakai Flowering quince
Ehretia microphylla Lam. *(Carmona microphylla)* Fukien tea
Fortunella Hindsii Swingle Kumquat
Ginkgo biloba L. Maidenhair tree
Ilex cornuta Lindl. & Paxt. Chinese holly
Jasminum nudiflorum Lindl. Winter jasmine
Juniperus chinensis L. Chinese juniper
Lagerstroemia indica L. Crape myrtle
Liquidambar formosana Hance Formosan gum
Loropetalum chinense D. Oliver. Loropetalum
Malus Halliana Koehne Hall's crab apple
M. spectabilis Borkh. Chinese flowering apple
Metasequoia glyptostroboides H. H. Hu & Cheng Dawn redwood
Murraya paniculata Jack Orange jasmine
Nandina domestica Thunb. Heavenly bamboo
Osmanthus heterophyllus P. S. Green Chinese holly
Phyllostachys bambusoides Siebold & Zucc. Timber bamboo
Pinus Bungeana Zucc. ex Endl. Lace-bark pine
P. tabuliformis Carrière Chinese pine
Podocarpus macrophyllus var. **Maki** Endl. Yew podocarpus
Prunus Mume Siebold & Zucc. Mei tree, flowering apricot or plum

P. triloba Lindl. Flowering almond
Pseudolarix Kaempferi Gord. *(P. amabilis)* Golden larch
Rhododendron Simsii Planch. Sims's azalea
Sageretia Thea M. C. Johnst. *(S. theezans)* Sageretia
Tamarix chinensis Lour. Tamarisk
Trachelospermum jasminoides Lem. Star jasmine
Ulmus parvifolia Jacq. Chinese elm
Wisteria sinensis Sweet Chinese wisteria

Appendix C

Glossary

Accessory plant. A small plant in a container used as a complementary planting in a bonsai display, or included in a miniature landscape.

Acclimatization. A plant's adjustment to a new and different environment.

Adventitious bud. A bud arising at a place other than the base of a leaf petiole, such as on a root, trunk, or branch or between the nodes of a shoot.

Aeration. The presence of air from the atmosphere in open pores of the soil or a growing medium. The air in well-aerated soil is similar to the air in the atmosphere; in poorly aerated soil, it contains more carbon dioxide and less oxygen than the air in the atmosphere.

Aggregates. Mineral matter, such as particles of sand or stone, in the growing medium.

Alternate branches. The preferred branch arrangement in bonsai, with only one side branch at any specific elevation on the trunk.

Amendment. A material other than fertilizer added to the growing medium to make it more productive for plant growth.

Anneal. To soften copper wire by heating it over a moderate fire between approximately 850° and 925°F.

Arborization. The progressive division of a branch from its thickest diameter at the trunk into smaller and smaller branchlets, twigs, and shoots.

Balled and Burlapped (B&B). A B&B tree or shrub is dug with a ball of soil around its roots and wrapped in burlap.

Bonsai. Living trees miniaturized in small containers and shaped into beautiful treelike forms; a Japanese word coined from the Chinese, literally translated as "shallow pot and tree."

Bud. An embryonic flower, leaf, or shoot protected by scales and containing the undeveloped parts of a plant's future growth. (See also *adventitious bud, latent bud, terminal bud.*)

Callus collar. The ridged ring around the base of a branch where it is attached to the trunk or to another branch.

Cambium. A layer of living cells, one cell thick, between the tree's bark and sapwood.

Chlorophyll. The green pigment in plant cells required for photosynthesis.

Clay. Fine soil material less than 0.002 mm in diameter.

Cold frame. An outdoor rectangular boxlike structure (without a bottom) set into the ground and covered with a glass or plastic top; used to create a protective environment for plants.

Collected trees. Naturally stunted trees found in wilderness terrains, dug and removed for bonsai use; also, trees found retarded by adverse environmental conditions.

Components. The parts of a composition.

Composition. In the arts, an ordered relationship between significant parts or elements.

Compost. A mixture of decomposed grasses, leaves, and other vegetative and organic matter used to enrich a soil or container mix.

Conditioned plant. A plant germinated from seed and grown to maturity under lower than normal light intensity to adjust it permanently to low levels of light; applicable to indoor bonsai.

Conditioner. A mineral element, such as lime, added to the growing medium to change the pH level.

Container mix. A growing medium formulated with organic and/or inorganic materials for container-grown plants.

Crown. The top of a tree formed by branching above its trunk or trunks.

Cultivar. A horticultural variant that originated and has persisted in cultivation.

Deciduous. A tree that sheds all its leaves or needles in the fall.

Design. An arrangement of elements or parts to satisfy an intention; a composition. Often an arrangement with an obvious geometric order.

Defoliate. To remove all or part of the leaves on a bonsai to obtain smaller leaves in the replacement foliage.

Deliquescent. Describing a tree with a main trunk that divides into many upward-growing branches to form a spreading crown.

Directional pruning. Shortening a shoot to a bud from which new growth will emerge in the direction wanted.

Dormancy. A relatively inactive period during which many growth processes of a tree temporarily slow or cease.

Environment. All the external conditions that affect the life and growth of plants, animals, and other living things.

Espalier. A tree or shrub trained to grow in a flattened form, often in a pattern, on a trellis, along a fence, or on a wall.

Evergreen. Describing a tree that does not lose all its needles or leaves at one time but sheds them partially, at intervals.

Excurrent. Describing a tree with a single dominant trunk, lateral, more or less horizontal branches, and a narrow or pointed apex.

Exotic. A foreign or nonnative species introduced to a region beyond its natural range—for example, the dawn redwood, *Metasequoia glyptostroboides*, introduced to the United States from China in the twentieth century.

Fertilizer. A natural or manufactured material added to the growing medium to provide one or more plant nutrients. *Balanced fertilizer* contains the three major elements, nitrogen, phosphorus, and potassium. *Complete fertilizer* contains the three major elements and the minor elements, calcium, magnesium, and sulfur; trace elements may also be included.

Fibrous roots. The small, thin feeder rootlets that obtain nutrients from the growing medium for the tree.

Footcandle. A measure of the illumination on a flat surface at a distance of one foot from a standard candle.

Framework. The trunk and branch structure of a bonsai that forms its shape.

Fungicide. A substance used to inhibit or destroy the growth of fungus.

Generic dwarfs. Plants with dwarf characteristics transmitted from the parent stock rather than induced by environmental or growing conditions.

Genus. A group of species sharing similar botanical characteristics. Plural, genera.

Growing medium. Natural or artificial soil suitable for plant growth.

Hardiness. The ability of a plant to withstand winter cold.

Hardiness Zones. Ten regions of the United States and southern Canada numbered from 1 to 10 (coldest to warmest) by the U.S. Department of Agriculture according to their average annual minimum temperatures.

Heel in. To cover lining-out stock with soil temporarily (usually in a trench) until it can be planted.

Herb. A plant with no woody tissue above the ground.

Herbaceous. Describing plant tissue that is fleshy rather than woody.

Humus. Partially or thoroughly decomposed vegetative matter in the soil.

Hybrid. A plant obtained by crossing two or more different species.

Indoor bonsai. Bonsai that do not require a cold-winter dormancy and can be kept and grown in heated interiors during the winter, usually species from warm and subtropical climates.

Insecticide. A substance used to kill or inhibit insects.

Internode. The section of a shoot between two nodes where buds are located.

Jin. A Japanese word for driftwood.

Latent bud. A bud beneath the bark, which sprouts on old wood; common on many maples and junipers.

Leaching. The removal of minerals and other matter in solution by water passing through the soil.

Leaf mold. Decomposed leaves, often found on the forest floor.

Light intensity. The amount or quantity of light energy.

Loam. A medium-textured soil with moderate amounts of sand, silt, and clay.

Liners. Small plants, seedlings, or cuttings, usually one to three years old, suitable for planting in nursery rows or containers. Also called *lining-out stock*.

Mass. A three-dimensional solid form as distinguished from the space that surrounds it.

Medullary rays. Thin openings in the wood of a tree trunk radiating from the center outward toward the bark.

Microclimate. The climate in a specific place that differs from the prevailing climate of the area.

Micronutrients. Nutrients needed by plants in only small amounts. Also called *trace elements*.

Mineral aggregates. Sand, crushed rock, slag, and similar material used in bonsai container mixes.

Mulch. A covering on the ground or around a container to provide winter protection from freezing and drying.

Muck. Highly decomposed organic materials and peat.

Mycorrhiza. A symbiotic association in the soil of fungi and the roots of certain plants, such as pines and beeches.

Native. Growing wild in the territory where it was originally found.

Naturalized. Growing wild outside its native territory.

Negative space. The configuration of the areas or volumes between forms in a composition.

Node. A swollen area on a shoot where a bud has formed.

Peat moss. An accumulation of undecomposed or slightly decomposed mosses found in sedge or sphagnum moss bogs.

Penjing. The Chinese word applied to miniature trees and landscapes in the People's Republic of China. It developed from the older *pun-sai* and *pun-ching*, which refer to artistic potted trees and potted trees with landscapes, respectively.

Perched water table. A water table near the bottom of a container suspended between the potting mix and a dry zone consisting of shards or other hard, large aggregates.

Perennial. A plant that survives two or more years; usually refers to nonwoody plants.

Petiole. A leafstalk, the slender stalk that attaches the blade of a leaf to the shoot or twig.

pH. A numerical designation from 1 (acidic) to 14 (alkaline) of the relative acidity and alkalinity in soil, with a pH level of 7 indicating neutral.

Photosynthesis. The process in which green chlorophyll in plant cells uses light to convert water from the roots and carbon dioxide from the air into energy in the form of carbohydrates; oxygen is released to the air in the process.

Pinch. To shorten new growth by twisting or breaking it between the thumb and fingers.

Potbound. Describing a condition that occurs when the roots of a plant become so crowded in a pot that there is little or no room for additional growth.

Radiant energy. The energy in light, transferred by radiation, that is utilized for plant growth.

Repeat motif. A repeated figure or design in a composition.

Saikei. Miniature landscapes of trees and rocks.

Salt hay. Salt or marsh hay is a light, moisture-resistant, clean, pest-free hay. It does not mat and may be saved and reused.

Samaras. Winged seeds found on maples and a number of other genera.

Sand. A soil component containing 85 percent or more sand and not more than ten percent clay; sand particles are 0.5 mm to 2.0 mm in size.

Sapwood. The outer wood of trees, including living cells that conduct water upward from the roots to the leaves.

Soil. The natural medium for the growth of land plants.

Soil texture. The relative proportions of large to small particles in a soil.

Space. The measurable linear and angular relationships between forms and/or the areas or volumes defined by these measurements.

Species. Plants that share distinctive botanical characteristics, which they transmit by interbreeding.

Stand. A base for displaying a bonsai, often footed, and carefully made of wood or, occasionally, other materials.

Style. A predetermined pattern for the arrangement of a bonsai's trunk, surface roots, branches, and overall form.

Suiban. A shallow tray without holes, for displaying rocks or rock plantings.

Sun pit. An enlarged cold frame with the bottom below the frost line, usually large enough for a person to enter; usable for storing bonsai during the winter.

Taproot. A long, primary, downward-growing root that anchors a plant in the soil.

Terminal bud. A bud, usually large, located on the tip of a shoot.

Thin. To open the interior of a bonsai by selectively removing portions of overly dense growth.

Tokonoma. A recessed floor-to-ceiling alcove used for the display of valued and artistic objects in the traditional Japanese house.

Tolerance. A tree's inherent ability to withstand unfavorable conditions of sun, shade, dryness, moisture, disease, or other environmental factors.

Topiary. A tree or shrub clipped to grow in an ornamental or geometric shape.

Training pot. A work pot, larger than a bonsai pot, with ample space to promote root growth during a tree's training for bonsai.

Tree identity features. A combination of features that clearly distinguish a tree from other natural objects, include surface roots, a tapered trunk, branches, coverings such as bark, leaves, flowers, fruit, and a simple overall treelike shape.

Tufa rock. A light rock produced from calcareous deposits in fresh-water springs, ponds, marshes, or under ground. Deposits are found in Ohio and other parts of the United States.

Variety. A group of plants with similar botanical characteristics but differing too little from the species to be classified as a separate species.

Viewing stone. A natural rock with a shape, texture, or markings that suggest a mountain, island, chrysanthemum, or other object in nature, usually displayed on a stand or in a tray.

Appendix D Plant Hardiness Zone Map

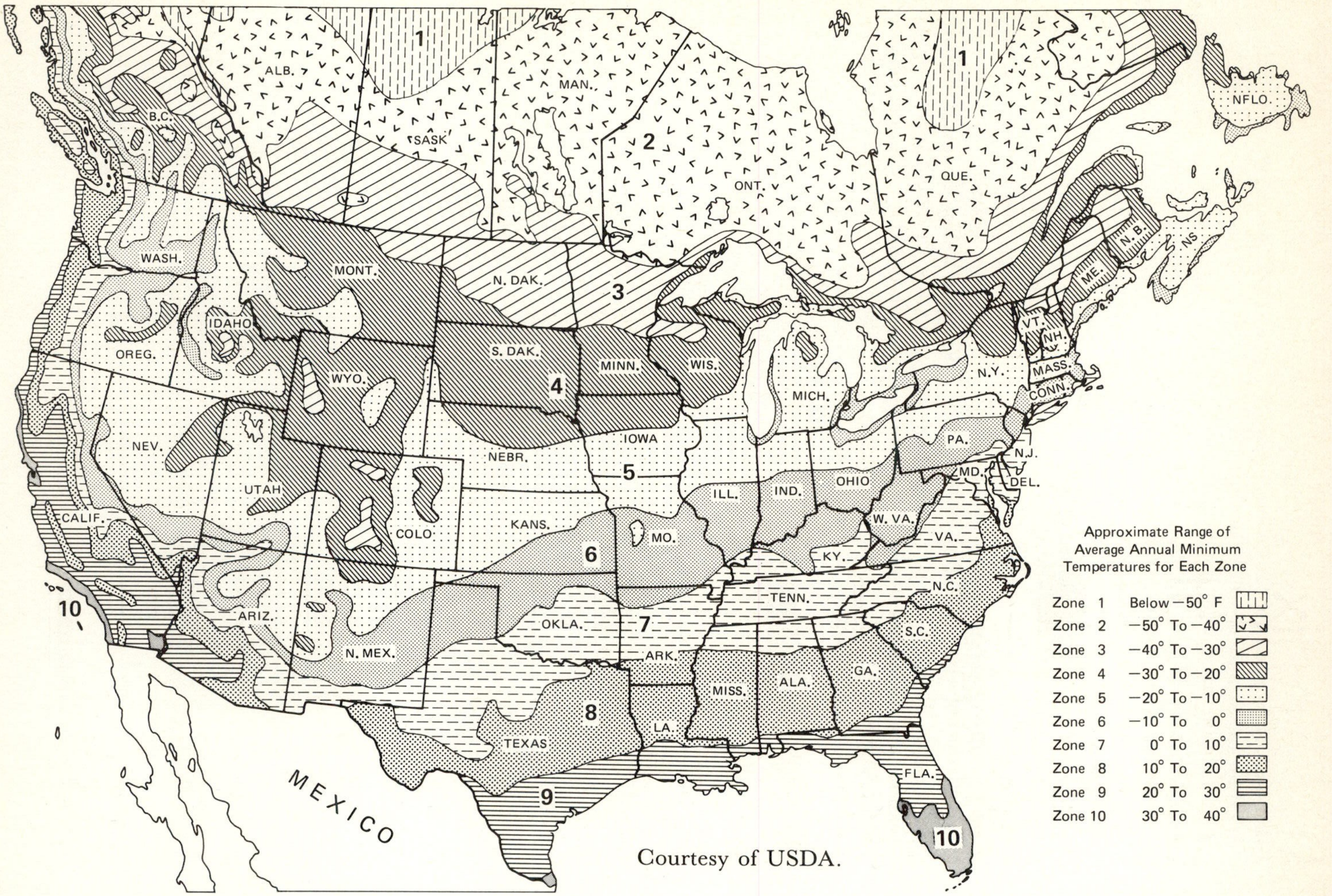

Courtesy of USDA.

Appendix E

Identification of Containers

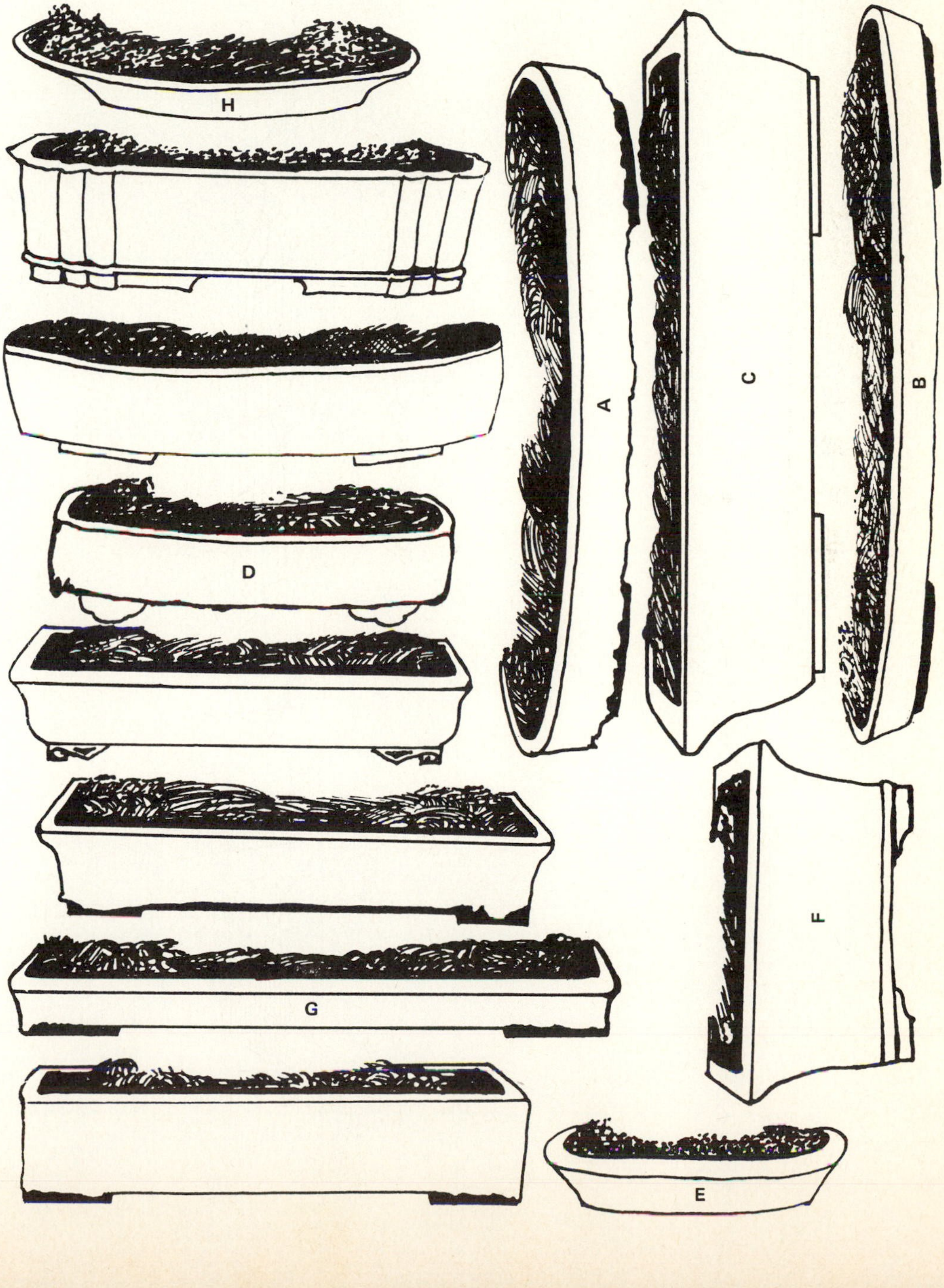

Index